# CIVIL SERVICE SYSTEMS IN COMPARATIVE PERSPECTIVE

EDITED BY
HANS A. G. M. BEKKE,
JAMES L. PERRY, AND THEO A. J. TOONEN

INDIANA UNIVERSITY PRESS
Bloomington & Indianapolis

The paper used in this publication meets the minimum requirements of American National Standard for Information Sciences —Permanence of Paper for Printed Library Materials, ANSI Z39.48-1984.

Manufactured in the United States of America

**Library of Congress Cataloging–in–Publication Data**

Civil service systems in comparative perspective / edited by Hans
   A. G. M. Bekke, James L. Perry, and Theo A. J. Toonen.
      p.    cm. -- (Public affairs)
   Includes bibliographical references and index.
   ISBN 0-253-32969-8 (cl : alk. paper). -- ISBN 0-253-21032-1 (pa :
alk. paper)
    1. Civil Service.   2. Comparative government.   I. Bekke, A. J. G.
M.  II. Perry, James L.  III. Toonen, Th. A. J.  IV. Series: Public
affairs (Bloomington, Ind.)
JF1601.C55   1996
350.6--dc20                            95-22444

1  2  3  4  5  01  00  99  98  97  96

# CONTENTS

# PREFACE

This book had its origins in a small research conference held at Leiden University in March 1990. The participants, members of public administration faculties at Erasmus, Leiden, and Indiana universities, came together to discuss common research interests and to plan a program of empirical research on civil service systems. The participants quickly realized that before they could embark on a program of empirical research, a good deal of effort needed to be devoted to developing common language, concepts, and empirical categories. This realization was the genesis of the present book.

The backdrop for our initial discussions was the ferment in eastern Europe and many other areas in the world. The global sweep of recent change is impressive, unmatched by comparable developments in the last half century. Transformation of civil service systems in Europe has spread rapidly. At least twenty-seven African countries are restructuring their systems according to prescriptions imposed by multi- and bilateral donors. The situation in the People's Republic of China provides yet another picture of the transformation of civil service systems. Even in the United States, the federal civil service has been subjected to repeated reforms during the Carter, Reagan, and Clinton administrations.

We realized that while civil service systems play critical roles throughout the world, our basic knowledge of civil service systems is woefully inadequate. Much of the theory and empirical research on civil service systems dates from the comparative administration movement of the 1960s. In spite of an obvious need and a receptive audience, there is a lack of knowledge about how civil service systems function and how they might be managed.

Participants in the March 1990 conference agreed to work together to build a knowledge base. Research was to proceed in two phases. The first would be devoted to developing theory, concepts, and indicators useful for the comparative study of civil service systems. A key element was an October 1991 international conference in Rotterdam and Leiden that was attended by leading scholars from Europe, North America, Asia, and Australia. Seventeen papers were commissioned for the conference. The presentations were lively and informative, the discussions of technical points sometimes heated, the informal exchanges always stimulating.

Fourteen of those conference papers and one newly commissioned paper are included in this volume.

The second phase of research involves applying the comparative framework in order to describe and analyze civil service systems throughout the world. The conferees agreed to create an informal Comparative Civil Service Research Consortium (CCSRC). The Consortium will eventually consist of a worldwide network of scholars interested in comparing the structures and processes of national and international civil service systems. Membership in the Consortium will grow over time to include knowledgeable scholars and practitioners who can contribute to and benefit from participation.

Although the goals of the CCSRC are ambitious, the goals for this volume are modest. We hope we have laid the foundation for the Consortium's data collection efforts. Our success will be measured by our ability to create a data collection protocol based on this volume and, ultimately, by the value of the data we have collected. More generally, we hope that this volume will serve as a foundation for building middle-range theories about civil service systems.

Following a general introduction, the book is divided into five parts. Part 1 provides a general orientation to theory and methodology. B. Guy Peters places the theory and methodology of civil service systems in the context of similar issues confronting the fields of comparative politics and administration. Eugene B. McGregor Jr. and Paul Solano take up questions of data availability for the comparative study of civil service systems. They argue that the success of comparative research depends on achieving a balance between data requirements and availability, and they offer advice on reaching that goal.

Part 2 is devoted to an examination of the history and structure of civil service systems. Jos C. N. Raadschelders and Mark R. Rutgers develop an historical perspective on civil service systems that covers the evolution of those systems from the Middle Ages to the present. Their model identifies five stages in the evolution of civil service systems. Lois Recascino Wise conceptualizes the operating rules of civil service systems as internal labor markets. She illustrates how these internal labor markets vary and how these variations influence outcomes. Frits M. van der Meer and Renk L. J. Roborgh consider the meaning and significance of representativeness in civil service systems.

Part 3 examines contextual characteristics of civil service systems. In the opening chapter, William P. Hojnacki discusses the politicization of civil service systems. Michael Hill and Desi Gillespie explore a more limited aspect of the relationship between civil service systems and their external environments. They discuss participation and grievance mechanisms as expressions of social control over civil service systems. Hal G. Rainey develops a model for investigating how public opinion influences civil service systems.

In part 4, Ferrel Heady and E. Philip Morgan examine civil service systems from a holistic perspective. Using configuration analysis, they look at how relevant dimensions of civil service systems cohere empirically. Heady identifies four configurations that are commonly found across national systems. Morgan focuses on the special problems of analyzing civil service systems in developing countries, where the state and other political and governmental factors have little historical identity and are minimally institutionalized.

Part 5 examines change and transformation in civil service systems. Patricia W. Ingraham describes four dimensions of recent civil service reforms. Christopher Hood subjects to empirical exploration the determinants of the "new public management," a series of reforms that swept through many OECD countries during the 1980s. Part 5 concludes with John Halligan's analysis of the diffusion of civil service reforms.

In the concluding chapter of the book, we examine common themes and identify an agenda for future research.

In addition to the scholars represented in this volume, a number of others participated in the conferences and facilitated the development of the ideas presented here through their formal papers and commentaries, informal discussions, and good-humored colleagueship. They include James Bjorkman (Leiden University), Mark Bovens (Leiden University), Cees Breed (Dutch Ministry of Home Affairs), Hans de Bruijn (Erasmus University), John Burns (University of Hong Kong), Harry Daemen (Erasmus University), Gerrit Dijkstra (Leiden University), Peter Hupe (Erasmus University), George Jones (London School of Economics), Walter Kickert (Erasmus University), Joop Koppenjan (Erasmus University), Athumani Liviga (University of Pittsburgh), Hanneke Mastik (Erasmus University), Johan P. Olsen (University of Bergen), Louis Picard (University of Pittsburgh), Jon Quah (National University of Singapore), Arunaselam Rasappan (National Institute of Public Administration, Malaysia), Uri Rosenthal (Leiden University), Ignace Snellen (Erasmus University), Menno Tuurenhout (Leiden University), Jouke de Vries (Leiden University), Hendrik Wagenaar (Leiden University), Charles Wise (Indiana University), Jan Wuysman (Leiden University), Jacqueline Zaaijer (Dutch Ministry of Home Affairs).

The editors would like to thank everyone who has commented on the manuscript. We are especially grateful to Richard Stillman and the late William Siffin for their comments and suggestions. We also appreciate the support of the School of Public and Environmental Affairs at Indiana University, and the Department of Public Administration at Leiden University. Finally, we thank the Netherlands Department of the Interior for their generous financial support.

# CIVIL SERVICE SYSTEMS IN COMPARATIVE PERSPECTIVE

# 1 INTRODUCTION: CONCEPTUALIZING CIVIL SERVICE SYSTEMS

Hans A. G. M. Bekke, James L. Perry, and Theo A. J. Toonen

Civil service has been part of the day-to-day vocabulary of public affairs for over a hundred years. The term "civil servant" was first used formally by the British in the late eighteenth century to distinguish the civilian from the military personnel of the East India Company (Drewry and Butcher, 1988). In the course of this century, civil service in a British context has come to mean, according to the *Blackwell Encyclopedia of Political Institutions,* "the remunerated personnel, other than those serving in the armed forces, whose functions are to administer policies formulated by or approved by national governments" (Bogdanor, 1987: 104). (Civil service is differentiated from "public service," which also includes civilian personnel working with the armed forces, armed forces personnel serving government in a civilian capacity, the judiciary, employees of local governments and public corporations, school and university teachers, police and other agencies.)

This book seeks to advance the formal study of civil service systems. Since public administration originated as an academic field over a century ago, civil service has been a staple of the discipline. Just as politics is the center of political science and social organization the core of sociology, one could argue that civil service is the center of public administration. Among the analytic units encompassed by public administration, the civil service system is the only one not largely shared with other social sciences (Morgan and Perry, 1988).

One reason for calling for formal study of civil service systems is that bureaucracy, a construct on which comparative scholars have relied for years, has failed to propel comparative administration much beyond its status in the 1960s. Bureaucracy often means different things to different investigators. The title of an article by Fred W. Riggs (as cited in Riggs, 1980), one of the intellectual leaders of the comparative administration movement, summarizes the problem: "Bureaucracy is a shifty word." Bureaucracy has been used in the literature of comparative administration to describe a particular organizational unit, an entire administrative system, or some combination of the two. Heady (1991), for instance, adopts a structural approach to comparative administration across nation states. However, he limits the definition or bureaucracy to three structural features: hierarchy, specialization, and competence; and he excludes from consideration all but higher civil servants, that is, bureaucrats in top or middle-management roles.

Given the shifting foundations of the bureaucracy construct and the excess meaning it has acquired over the years (Goodsell, 1994), there is a need to develop complementary analytic tools. Although use of the term civil service does have a history, the concept, except, perhaps, in Britain, is not linked to an identifiable theory. This has the advantage that, in principle, it allows us to use the concept in an exploratory and inductive manner so that we can map current developments in different administrative systems and mold and develop the central organizing concept accordingly.

Our interest in advancing the study of civil service systems is more than just a reflection of their historic role in public administration. It has gained impetus from recent intellectual developments in public administration, political science and, more broadly, the social sciences (March and Olsen, 1984; Peters, 1988). Two are particularly relevant. One is a renewed interest in the concept of the state (Peters, 1988; Jackson, 1988; Evans, Rueschemeyer, and Skocpol, 1985). The second is the resurgence of institutional analysis (Ferris and Tang, 1993; North, 1990; Peters, 1988; Kiser and Ostrom, 1982; March and Olsen, 1984; March and Olsen, 1989). Focusing on civil service systems, as we and the other contributors to this volume shall emphasize, positions the state and institutions at the center of analytic attention.

We define civil service systems formally as mediating institutions that mobilize human resources in the service of the affairs of the state in a given territory (Morgan and Perry, 1988). The definition suggests that civil service systems are structures, that is, a combination of rules and authority relationships that act as bridges between the polity or state and specific administrative organizations. The definition implies that the dominant concern of civil service systems involves human, rather than financial or physical, resources.

The definition is intended to "bring the state back" into the study of civil service systems in more than a superficial way. In many jurisdictions, civil service systems are authorized by constitutional rules. In others, civil service is legitimated by political or state traditions, widely accepted by members of society. With the exception of stateless or anarchic societies, formal or informal constitutional rules typically outline the functions and roles of the civil service. The connections between the state and civil service systems merit intensive study. As several contributors argue later in this volume, the character of civil service systems is highly dependent on the identity and cohesiveness of the state.

The institutional content of this volume does not adhere to a particular orthodoxy of institutional analysis (see Powell and Dimaggio, 1991, for a comparison of institutional approaches). Instead, it borrows liberally from different perspectives, including rational choice (Ostrom, 1986) and new institutionalist approaches (March and Olsen, 1989). The institutional perspective employed here does subscribe to two tenets central to most institutionalist approaches; as articulated by Krasner, these are "the derivative character of individuals and the persistence of something—behavioral patterns, roles, rules, organizational charts, ceremonies—over time" (Krasner, 1988: 73). We are particularly interested in how civil service systems shape the behavior of members and, in turn, how civil service systems are shaped by other social institutions and the perceptions of citizens.

Given our institutional emphasis, rules are important for understanding the behavior of civil servants. By rules we mean both understandings about prescribed behavior (Ostrom, 1986) and implicit or explicit principles or norms around which actors' expectations converge (Krasner, 1983). It would be premature to attempt to codify the range of rules embedded in civil service systems, but it is possible to provide some examples that demonstrate their significance. For example, in his history of the U.S. federal civil service, Van Riper (1958) describes the informal rules that surrounded patronage in the early 1800s. One informal rule that developed during Jefferson's presidency was that of equal division of offices between parties (Van Riper, 1958: 22). This rule prevailed for almost thirty years, from 1801 to 1829, until Andrew Jackson took office. Jackson sought to adapt federal service to democratic ideals and introduced the spoils rule that limited tenure and rotated offices for partisan purposes. These informal rules had a powerful impact on defining the character of the civil service through most of the nineteenth century. They were eventually supplanted by new rules governing job tenure that have had an equally dramatic effect on the character of the U.S. civil service during the twentieth century.

Aside from identifying what rules define the character of a civil service system, the institutional perspective also calls attention to the origin of rules and why they persist (Krasner, 1988; Tolbert and Zucker, 1983). For instance, on its face, an "equal division of offices" rule may appear to be highly arbitrary. How did Jefferson arrive at this limit? How was the "rule of three" (requiring personnel to be selected from among the top three scorers on civil service exams) settled upon as the certification rule in the U.S. civil service and, furthermore, how did it become so widespread? Given the many criticisms of the rule of three, how has it managed to persist for so long? A limited body of research exists about these issues (e.g., Tolbert and Zucker, 1983), and much more needs to be done.

Before we proceed further, it is important to note that our definition of civil service systems raises several boundary questions that cannot be definitively resolved but merit explicit discussion. One involves the people who are encompassed by the definition of civil service. What shall be the criteria for inclusion in civil service, that is, what defines a civil servant? Does the definition cover only career, appointed officials? Are elected or appointed political officials excluded? Following traditional conventions, we are inclined to include career, appointed officials but exclude elected, political officials. Despite general agreement about this distinction, other efforts at categorization are likely to be more controversial. For instance, although we include appointed, noncareer officials in our accounting of civil servants, others might object. In general, we do not believe that the classification problem can be resolved on purely categorical or nominal grounds; it is resolved instead through some combination of functional and institutional assessment in the context of particular systems.

Another boundary question involves whether the definition includes military service. As we noted earlier, when the term civil servant first came into use by the British in the late eighteenth century, it was used to distinguish civilian employees of the East India Company from military personnel (Drewry and Butcher, 1988). The nonmilitary connotation of the term carried over until the early nineteenth century, when it gradually came to mean holders of permanent positions in contrast to those who held posts that changed hands upon a change of government. Although we prefer to exclude military personnel from our working definition of civil service, the definition is intended to include individuals working for the military in a civilian capacity, for instance, support personnel in the defense departments of most countries. We can also conceive of circumstances in which military personnel would displace civilians and thus be viewed as civil servants.

Although our definition refers to the state and the focus of this book is on national systems, it is not our intention to exclude other levels of government. We believe the logic and the analytic approaches can be extended to other governmental levels (Goodsell, 1981; Morgan and Perry, 1988). One basic assumption of this research is that civil service systems, whether national, subnational, or local, vary across political jurisdictions and that this variation merits study in its own right and for its implications for the management and development of these systems.

Another set of issues raised by our definition is the nature and extent to which civil service in a given political jurisdiction may be referred to as a "system." System has been used, at various times, to mean both a whole or a set of interdependent parts. In fact, we use the term in both senses, depending on the analytic purposes. Aberbach and Rockman (1987) suggest that the extent to which national administrative systems may be defined holistically varies with the domain of interest. The functions of national systems invariably lead one to focus on parts of national systems rather than on wholes. Focusing on public culture and institutions has the opposite effect, calling attention to more encompassing, systemic issues. Efforts to identify the structure of the public sector in a country (Peters, 1988: 77) or configurations of attributes of civil service systems (Miller and Mintzberg, 1984) also lead one toward a holistic perspective.

Although our bias is to treat civil service holistically, this is an empirical question. Aberbach and Rockman (1987) employ a statistical analogy to address the issue. They suggest that if administrative systems exhibit more within-system than between-system variation, then it is inappropriate to consider them holistically for research purposes. On the other hand, if administrative systems can be characterized by their central tendencies rather than by their diversity, they are appropriately studied as systems.

## CIVIL SERVICE SYSTEMS: THREE WORLDS OF ACTION

An institutional perspective from which we draw explicitly is Kiser and Ostrom's (1982) metatheoretical framework for the integration of different approaches to institutional analysis. They distinguish three interrelated, but separate, "worlds of action" that they suggest give rise to distinct analytical questions and levels of theoretical analysis: constitutional choice, collective choice, and operational. These three levels capture the multiple roles civil service systems play in administrative systems. Understanding the roles and their interplay is important for a complete picture of civil service systems.

### Operational Level: Civil Service as Personnel Systems

Most scholars associate civil service systems with personnel systems or systems of employment. As personnel systems, civil service systems are typically the primary means for staffing the administrative organs of the state. McGregor (1990: 4) suggests that there are a large array of options surrounding personnel designs illustrated by the following types of issues:

Recruitment: Is it open or closed?
Selection basis: Selection for a career or program?
Job evaluation: Are rank and pay vested in positions or persons?
Training and development: Shall training and upward mobility be based on elitist or nonelitist criteria?
Performance appraisal: Shall there be merit pay or a fixed pay formula?

McGregor suggests that the critical need is for better knowledge about combinations of design attributes and the relationship of these packages to the effectiveness and performance characteristics of personnel systems.

How the personnel system is organized and operates varies across political jurisdictions. In more advanced states, the personnel function is a highly complex undertaking, replete with specialized practitioners engaged in a range of activities such as testing, training, job classification, and seeing to compliance with laws designed to promote representativeness and other desirable social goals. In developing countries, the apparatus for performing personnel activities is likely to be less specialized. In the least developed countries, the personnel function may be performed by actors who have no specialized responsibility for staffing and related functions but who perform these activities because of their investiture of authority by virtue of other roles they play.

## Collective Choice Level: Civil Service as Governance Institution

While the operational level of analysis involves the world of action, the collective choice level of analysis involves the world of collective decisions. Kiser and Ostrom (1982: 208) suggest that "collective decisions are made by officials (including citizens acting as officials) to determine, enforce, continue, or alter actions authorized within institutional arrangements." Our interest is not all collective decisions, only those central to the institutional arrangements surrounding civil service systems. These collective decisions encompass a range of issues, including how personnel rules will be changed, how sanctions for noncompliance with operating rules will be imposed, and how civil servants will be made accountable to officials for their actions.

Two classes or types of collective decisions that are particularly consequential for the institutional arrangements of civil service systems are those involving civil service reforms and those associated with the policy-making prerogatives of civil servants. The mechanisms through which civil service arrangements are altered goes to the heart of who governs. These collective decisions influence the content of reforms, their likely success, to whom civil servants are answerable, and the distance between civil service and state institutions. Collective decisions surrounding the policy prerogatives of civil servants often have a direct influence on political life. Whether and by what mechanisms the actions of civil servants in their official roles are subject to review or modification have profound implications for governance.

## Constitutional Choice Level: Civil Service as Symbol Systems

A third role of civil service systems is as symbol for interpreting actions involving the general public, system members, and third parties (March and Olsen, 1984; March and Olsen, 1989). The evolution and development of civil service systems gives rise to myths and symbols that become instruments of interpretive order. In some polities, the role of the civil service system may be primarily or purely symbolic. Even in advanced polities such as the United States, civil service systems may be important legitimating devices. The U.S. federal "merit system" conveys meaning beyond the personnel policies that define it and the rules embedded within it. It implies a normative order that emphasizes equity based upon achievement, regardless of the system's actual performance.

The present attention to pay-for-performance schemes in all types of governmental units in the United States, among them federal, state, local, and school districts, suggests that civil service laws and rules are symbolically important for maintaining institutions even where civil service is highly embedded. From a symbolic perspective, pay-for-performance schemes represent an attempt by politicians, administrators, and the public to assert control over bureaucracy (March and Olsen, 1983). It is a message from politicians and the public that the governed are in control and things are as they should be. At the same time, it is a way for administrators to communicate that they are responsive to important external constituencies and that they are doing something about perceptions of lagging performance (Tolbert and Zucker, 1983). In sum, pay for performance is one of the rituals that helps to maintain the legitimacy of the governance mechanism, but it may have little consequence for individual and organizational performance (Perry, 1988–89; Ingraham, 1993).

The study of civil service systems is thus an important avenue for understanding the "people" dimension of public administration, which Peters (1988: 14) identifies as a critical variable for comparative research. Civil service systems are important in three ways: as operating personnel systems, as governance institutions, and as constitutional symbol systems. Understanding civil service systems requires an understanding of these roles and their interactions, and comparative research can shed light on these phenomena.

## THE GOALS OF A COMPARATIVE APPROACH

One of the objectives of comparative research on civil service systems, theory development and testing, is central to social science and largely implicit in the motivations for such research. Comparative analysis is necessary for the identification of key concepts, of relations among concepts, and of the underlying logic or dynamic of the relations. Comparative research is also an antidote for the narrowness sometimes associated with studying a single system. Peters writes (1988: 4):

> Such approaches to administration are ethnocentric not just because of their origins (the genetic fallacy) but because the constructs, hypotheses, and theories are not necessarily representative of reality (valid) in other political and cultural contexts.

The comparative approach also provides the necessary range of phenomena for testing theory empirically.

Many recent developments in national civil service systems suggest remarkable parallels, but we have only a rudimentary understanding of whether the phenomena are similar and, if they are comparable, of whether they flow from similar processes or forces. For example, it appears that eastern European and African countries pay a high price for the size of their state bureaucracies. It is not obvious, however, that large-scale reduction of the number of civil servants is an equally good path for development in each of these countries. In some countries, personnel retrenchment may be necessary to achieve a productive balance between public and private employment; in others, it may simply exacerbate existing instabilities.

A second objective of the comparative study of civil service systems is to develop a better understanding of their historical evolution. If civil service systems are important institutions in most societies, then two general questions need to be answered: what are the more encompassing structures that define the character of individuals in such systems, and what accounts for the persistence of civil service systems? The answers to these questions require some historical background. It is clear from the U.S. experience that persistence of civil service systems cannot be explained fully or even primarily in terms of a utilitarian or instrumental rationale. For example, the rule of three and other civil service procedures have long been criticized as contrary to the human resource goals of the agencies upon which they have been imposed (Savas and Ginzburg, 1973), but the practices continue to survive in many jurisdictions.

In addition to understanding the historical context of civil service systems, it is also important to understand their relationship to the political, social, and economic context. Attention to ecology has been a long-standing concern within public administration (Gaus, 1947). A comparative approach assures that a variety of contextual factors will be incorporated into theory building and testing.

A final objective of comparative study is to enhance the policymaker's capacity to design civil service systems. One challenge is to design civil service systems that work at all levels—as personnel systems, governance institutions, and symbol systems. What policymakers frequently encounter are trade-offs among the various roles played by civil service systems. For example, responses to personnel problems are frequently constrained by rules and by the interpretation of alternatives held by an attentive constituency. Although it is unlikely that comparative study can quickly shed light on complex trade-offs among the roles played by civil service systems, it may help fill a far simpler need—that of increasing the efficiency of public administration as a purposive activity.

## SUMMARY

In the basic framework for the comparative investigation of civil service systems addressed in this book, civil service systems are defined as mediating institutions that mobilize human resources in the service of the affairs of the state in a given territory. This definition establishes several priorities: the centrality of human resources in the study of civil service systems, the relationship between the civil service system and the state, and the embeddedness of action within civil service systems. A complete picture of civil service systems requires that they be viewed in the context of three worlds of action: operational, collective choice, and constitutional choice. These three levels account for the multiple roles civil service systems play in administrative systems. By undertaking comparative research, we hope to advance the theory of civil service systems and, more generally, of comparative public administration.

## REFERENCES

Aberbach, J. D., and B. A. Rockman. 1987. "Comparative Administration: Methods, Muddles, and Models." *Administration and Society* 18 (February): 473–506.

Bogdanor, V., ed. 1987. *The Blackwell Encyclopedia of Political Institutions.* New York: Blackwell Reference.

Drewry, G., and T. Butcher. 1988. *The Civil Service Today.* Oxford: Basil Blackwell.

Evans, P. B., D. Rueschemeyer, and T. Skocpol, eds. 1985. *Bringing the State Back In.* Cambridge: Cambridge University Press.

Ferris, J. M., and S. Tang. 1993. "The New Institutionalism and Public Administration: An Overview." *Journal of Public Administration Research and Theory* 3, no. 1: 4–10.

Gaus, J. 1947. *Reflections on Public Administration.* Tuscaloosa: University of Alabama Press.

Goodsell, C. 1981. "The New Comparative Administration: A Proposal." *International Journal of Public Administration* 3, no. 2: 143–55.

———. 1994. *The Case for Bureaucracy: A Public Administration Polemic.* 3rd ed. Chatham, NJ: Chatham House.

Heady, F. 1991. *Public Administration: A Comparative Perspective.* 4th ed. New York: Marcel Dekker.

Ingraham, P. W. 1993. "Of Pigs in Pokes and Policy Diffusion: Another Look at Pay-for-Performance." *Public Administration Review* 53 (July/August): 348–56.

Jackson, R. 1988. "Civil Science: Comparative Jurisprudence and Third World Governance." *Governance* 1, no. 4: 380–414.

Kiser, L. L., and E. Ostrom. 1982. "The Three Worlds of Action: A Metatheoretical Synthesis of Institutional Approaches." Pages 179–222 in E. Ostrom, ed., *Strategies of Political Inquiry.* Beverly Hills, CA: Sage.

Krasner, S. D., ed. 1983. *International Regimes.* Ithaca, NY: Cornell University Press.

————. 1988. "Sovereignty: An Institutional Perspective." *Comparative Political Studies* 21, no. 1: 66–94.

McGregor, E. B., Jr. 1990. "The Comparative Civil Service Research Agenda: Getting the Questions Right." Bloomington, IN: School of Public and Environmental Affairs Working Paper.

March, J. G., and J. P. Olsen. 1983. "Organizing Political Life: What Administrative Reorganization Tells Us about Government." *American Political Science Review* 77, no. 2: 281–96.

————. 1984. "The New Institutionalism: Organizational Factors in Political Life." *American Political Science Review* 78 (September): 734–49.

————. 1989. *Rediscovering Institutions: The Organizational Basis of Politics.* New York: Free Press.

Miller, D., and H. Mintzberg. 1984. "The Case for Configuration." Pages 10–30 in D. Miller and P. H. Friesen, *Organizations: A Quantum View.* Englewood Cliffs: Prentice Hall.

Morgan, E. P., and J. L. Perry. 1988. "Re-orienting the Comparative Study of Civil Service Systems." *Review of Public Personnel Administration* 8 (Summer): 84–95.

North, D. 1990. *Institutions, Institutional Change, and Economic Performance.* Cambridge: Cambridge University Press.

Ostrom, E. 1986. "An Agenda for the Study of Institutions." *Public Choice* 48: 3–25.

Perry, J. L. 1988–89. "Making Policy By Trial and Error: Merit Pay in the Federal Service." *Policy Studies Journal* 17 (Winter): 389–405.

Peters, B. G. 1988. *Comparing Public Bureaucracies: Problems of Theory and Method.* Tuscaloosa: University of Alabama Press.

Powell, W. W., and DiMaggio, P., eds. 1991. Introduction to *The New Institutionalism in Organizational Analysis.* Chicago: University of Chicago Press.

Riggs, F. W. 1980. "Three Dubious Hypotheses: A Comment on Heper, Kim, and Pai." *Administration and Society* 12 (November): 301–26.

Savas, E. S., and S. G. Ginzburg. 1973. "The Civil Service: A Meritless System?" *The Public Interest* 32 (Summer): 70–85.

Tolbert, P. S., and L. G. Zucker. 1983. "Institutional Sources of Change in the Formal Structure of Organizations: The Diffusion of Civil Service Reform, 1880–1935." *Administrative Science Quarterly* 28: 22–39.

Van Riper, P. 1958. *A History of the United States Civil Service.* Evanston, IL: Row, Peterson.

# PART ONE

# THEORY & DATA

Every research enterprise must confront basic questions of theory and method. The contributions in part 1 suggest that comparative civil service research faces more than the normal impediments. In chapter 2, B. Guy Peters discusses the broad questions of theory and methodology confronting scholars engaged in comparative research. He draws upon the experiences of comparative politics and comparative public administration in charting the challenges faced by scholars interested in comparing civil service systems. Peters draws attention to a range of theoretical problems in comparative public administration, among them levels of analysis, cross-level inference, the equivalence of phenomena in different societies, and relational issues.

Although Peters develops a realistic map of theoretical problems, he also offers useful advice about methodologies for building knowledge. Peters is not optimistic about taking comparative research to the same methodological levels as other fields in the social sciences. He does not, for instance, envision as much attention to quantification and statistical analysis. Instead, he envisions broader use of ideal types, classification schemes, and theoretical case studies. The goal should be development of new knowledge, not a premature attempt at quantification.

Concern about a premature quest to quantify is reinforced in chapter 3. Eugene B. McGregor Jr. and Paul Solano assess the requirements and availability of data for comparative civil service research. Their organizing thesis is simple: the development of comparative civil service data depends upon a successful matching of data requirements to available data. They define data requirements using design variables associated with the three civil service roles introduced in chapter 1: personnel system, governance, and symbol system. Among the design variables identified in McGregor and Solano's classification are internal and external labor markets, accountability mechanisms, and service ethics.

McGregor and Solano observe that the list of data requirements is long while the availability of comparable data is limited. They illustrate their argument about the difficulty of acquiring comparable data across systems in an appendix that focuses on the measurement of government employment in eighteen countries for three time periods. They conclude that given the substantial obstacles, data sets will inevitably be partial and based on opportunity. A panoramic view of civil service systems will require a variety of information sources—surveys, operational program information, anecdotes, and institutional and ecological histories.

# 2 THEORY AND METHODOLOGY

B. Guy Peters

This chapter addresses methodological and theoretical problems in the study of comparative civil service systems. This is a difficult task, given the varied meanings of such key words as "comparative" and "civil service." To some degree, this must then be a discussion of general questions and problems in comparative research, because only the particular subject matter distinguishes the concerns of this volume from other research in comparative government. The difference in subject matter is, however, sufficiently important to warrant exploration of the intellectual roots of our concerns in order to better understand this project. Further, as I and others (Heady, 1991; Lundquist, 1985) have often argued, theoretical and methodological issues appear central to the failure of the field of comparative administration to live up to the expectations many scholars had for it during the 1960s and 1970s. That is to some extent true for comparative politics as a whole, but it is particularly true for comparative administration. Riggs's optimistic forecast (1976) that comparative public administration would become "the master science" in public administration is not yet close to realization.

## INTELLECTUAL ROOTS AND THEIR IMPACT ON THE STUDY OF COMPARATIVE ADMINISTRATION

The study of comparative public administration involves elements of at least two broader strands of social inquiry. On the one hand, the principal substantive focus of comparative administration is on the structure and activities of public administration and public administrators. Administrative studies raise a number of related questions about the efficiency and effectiveness of administrative systems. In administrative studies, the major variables and subjects of investigation are either at a microlevel (human behavior within organizations or between clients and administrators), or are premised on the shared and largely unquestioned knowledge of a single political system. Although always occurring within a socioeconomic and cultural setting, those external factors are largely irrelevant for most studies of public administration.

On the other hand, most comparative public administration involves examining organizational structures and the administrative behaviors within more than one cultural and  political setting. At a minimum comparative public administration involves comparison of the administrative system in a country different from that of the researcher, and it involves at the least an implicit comparison with the researcher's own national system. This second intellectual root of comparative administration—comparative analysis—requires explicit attention to questions of comparative research of all types, but with particular emphasis on the comparison of institutions and the behavior of actors within those institutions. Coming as it does from these two backgrounds, comparative public administration brings with it some of the elements of comparative analysis and administrative studies, and some of the intellectual problems of each. Further, blending the two traditions also presents some difficult and unique intellectual problems.

### Public Administration

First, from the perspective of public administration there are important questions about the definition of administration and of bureaucracy, as well as about the point at which the researcher can draw the boundaries of his or her concern. For example, should we include political appointees in the United States as a part of "administration" because they occupy roles at the head of administrative organizations, or should we consider them as a part of the political executive? (Heclo, 1977; Aberbach and Rockman, 1987). More broadly, should we include government ministers with the political responsibility for managing large public organizations as a part of comparative administration, or are they better dealt with as a part of the "political" government? At the other end of the spectrum, do we include clients specifically within the system and assess the impact of their characteristics on the performance of public organizations? To what extent should private organizations performing public functions be included as a part of the bureaucracy; to what extent should the administrative apparatus be taken more broadly? (Hood and Schuppert, 1988; Milward, 1991). This question becomes all the more acute as numerous scholars advocate ideas about "networks" and "polycentrism" as the best approaches to the study of public administration (Laumann and Knoke, 1987; Klijn and Teisman, 1991). These are all definitional questions that have a substantial impact on what we will uncover with an inquiry into comparative administration.

In addition to the empirical, definitional questions, there is a question of where the boundary between normative and empirical analysis exists in public administration. Indeed, the fundamental question is whether there is, or should be, such a boundary. To what extent should the study of public administration be concerned primarily with the analysis and description of existing structures? Conversely, what role should the study of public administration play in designing new institutions of government (Olsen, 1990; Pollitt, 1984; Leemans, 1976; Lane, 1990), and in changing managerial behavior within existing bureaucracies? These questions exist whether administration is being studied in the United States or any other single country, but they become especially acute when there is to be a comparative analysis. Public administration does have a practical and reformist side that comparative political science research rarely has, at least overtly, and the important role for comparative research in policy prescription must be addressed (Rose, 1990). This is true even after the untimely demise of much of our interest in development administration (Esman, 1980). Adopting such a reformist and involved stance, however, quickly puts us crosswise with our more "purely" scientific colleagues doing comparative politics and comparative sociology.[1]

I should say at the outset that although this volume is devoted primarily to the "civil service," I will be taking a somewhat broader approach to the question. Thus, the following discussion will necessarily range well beyond personnel questions to cover some of the problems arising in the more general study of comparative public administration. Indeed, my own concerns are likely to be more with the structural transformation of the administrative system than with understanding or altering the details of public personnel systems.

## Comparative Politics

The research questions commonly arising in comparative politics are even more vexing for the scholar. First, much of the tradition of comparative politics has been that, in practice at least, the term "comparative" usually means politics in a country other than that of the author rather than an emphasis on genuine comparison; I have characterized this tendency elsewhere (1988) as the "stamps, flags and coins" approach to comparative politics. The field has been predominantly descriptive rather than analytic. The tendency toward description persisted even after the "revolution" in the 1950s and 1960s and the increased emphasis on theory construction in comparative politics. There are, of course, numerous important exceptions to that unkind generalization about the state of the field (Almond and Verba, 1963; Collier and Collier, 1991). In addition, many of the single country and more descriptive efforts that populate comparative politics are extremely useful, have potential theoretical importance, and are able to address theoretical issues from extremely interesting perspectives (Power, 1990). However, there remains a pronounced need to emphasize the direct comparison of political systems.

This continuing need is especially damning given that comparison is the only laboratory open to most social scientists, and the generation of comparative statements does appear to be the principal route to theory construction

(Lijphart, 1971; Dogan and Pelassy, 1990). Despite its crucial importance in the advancement of the social sciences, including public administration, the comparative method (like the principles of any religion) is more often bowed to than followed. This is in part because of our limitations as individual scholars who lack the ability to make the types of comparisons that might be meaningful, for example, between the contemporary Soviet Union and the Hapsburg Empire, or between democratization in Taiwan and Argentina. In addition, training and funding tends to come in rather tightly constrained geographical packages rather than on the basis of functional equivalencies. Also, we often lack the theoretical guidance that would direct us toward the crucial comparisons, especially if those comparisons lie outside a particular geographical or historical setting. Finally, comparative research is just plain hard work. If anything (in large part because of the problems already mentioned above), the comparison of administrative systems is even more primitive than the comparison of whole political systems, or of some other components of political systems such as elections and legislative behavior (Dalton, 1988; Laundy, 1989). We simply have not had either the theoretical approaches available for deductive analysis (other than the ideal types mentioned below), or the comparable data for inductive analysis, that might make directly comparative work in public administration readily "doable." While the existence of usable deductive models, for example, public choice, may be questioned (Bendor, 1990), it is to me very clear that we have not had the data bases nor the agreed upon conceptualizations necessary for more empirical work. Further, the relative state of ignorance of even many country and area specialists about the nature of administrative systems (sometimes including their own) implies that our descriptive analyses of public administration in individual countries can be of greater value than, say, similar descriptions of parliaments or party systems.

Associated with the descriptive character of much of comparative politics is a static quality in much of the work. The existing literature is much better at describing the status quo than it is at explaining the dynamics of the political system(s) in question. While the literature on third world countries often has a prescriptive element concerning change and "development," little of the literature on the first world is very good at understanding changes, and particularly not for advising governments engaged in reform efforts. This is true despite (for our particular concerns) the importance of continuing efforts at change and reform in most political, and especially administrative, systems (Peters, 1991; Olsen, 1990; Caiden, 1991). We as scholars of comparative politics are faced with massive political changes, but often appear to lack the tools or the inclination to do very much to shape those changes. To be of greater utility, the study of comparative politics and therefore of comparative public administration will need to be able to speak more effectively—descriptively and prescriptively—to the problems of change.

A final important question about the study of comparative politics that is relevant here (there are doubtless many others) is the relationship between the systemic level of analysis and the individual level of analysis. Scholars engaged in comparative analysis are often skating between ecological fallacies and individualistic fallacies, and often falling into one or both. Researchers often characterize whole systems and then assume that individuals occupying roles within those systems will behave in a corresponding manner. For example, we can attribute a particular political culture to a system and then assume that an individual within the system will behave that way. On the other hand, we can characterize empirically the behavior of individuals in political roles and then assume that the encompassing systems will behave accordingly. Therefore, a major challenge to comparative politics continues to be to develop an ability to link the micro- and the macrolevels of analysis, and to be able to make meaningful statements about both levels. Those statements should also be able to show how the two levels interact as governments operate to make and administer public policies.

## Mixing Comparative Politics and Public Administration

It should not be surprising, given the descriptions of the two fields offered above, that melding them is also difficult. On the one hand is a field (public administration) that tends to be rather ethnocentric, microlevel for much of its work, somewhat descriptive, but at the same time normative and ameliorative. On the other hand, comparative politics is a field that is also often descriptive but is pressing vigorously and self-consciously toward nomothetic statements. It strives (often with limited success) not to be based solely on the experiences of the industrialized democracies, and to be "scientific" rather than practical or reformist in its orientation. Further, comparative politics tends to focus its attention on the macrolevel and countries constitute a major unit of analysis, and the major (presumed) source of variance in its studies even if the data themselves are micro level. The flowering of comparative public administration during the heyday of development administration meant that it acquired more of a practical and reformist bent, but the roots of the field in comparative politics might make it less practical.

The variety of intellectual problems that comparative public administration faces have generated a number of doubts among scholars concerning the viability of the field (Aberbach and Rockman, 1987; Sigelman, 1976). This current skepticism follows several decades of great optimism and enthusiasm about the contributions of and prospects for comparative administration. I have argued elsewhere (Peters, 1988) that much of the current malaise is a function of the apparent absence of widely accepted and easily operationalizable dependent variables. The published work in comparative public administration rarely looks as "scientific" as that published in other areas of comparative inquiry. The observation of the "unscientific" nature of comparative administration has been made most particularly in relation to the apparent successes of comparative public policy studies. Interestingly, there is now substantially more skepticism about the progress of comparative policy studies, especially work based on easily identified and utilized quantitative data such as public expenditures. The world of public policy may actually be more complex and may require substantially greater contextual and institutional knowledge (Ostrom, 1990) than has been assumed by some analysts. As pointed out by Bekke, Perry, and Toonen in this volume, politics is occurring on several levels simultaneously and must be understood through the linkages of those levels. Rather than being peculiar to comparative public administration, the malaise of comparative studies may be a very widespread phenomenon.

Although it may have more company than often thought, still comparative public administration appears to remain somewhat in the doldrums (Aberbach and Rockman, 1987). This apparent malaise is not a function of an absence of interest, as the recent success of some journals[2] and other scholarship in the field clearly indicates. Further, the connections of comparative administration to several broader strands of inquiry are not entirely disadvantageous. Although some problems are shared across these fields, there are also some shared strengths. There is no lack of interest and research opportunity, but a number of important theoretical, methodological, and substantive questions remain unanswered about comparative administration (and indeed they impact this particular project). These questions must be addressed if this area of inquiry is to progress. After this perhaps excessively long preamble, I would now like to discuss some of those questions. In addition to detailing the problems, I will try to provide at least some inkling of answers that may be beneficial for the continuing work of this project as well as for the field more broadly.

## THEORETICAL PROBLEMS FOR COMPARATIVE PUBLIC ADMINISTRATION

The first questions we will raise about comparative public administration are primarily theoretical. To some extent they go back to questions already discussed (Peters, 1988), questions about the appropriate focus of inquiry for this field of study. What are we trying to explain? What is the appropriate boundary of our study, and how does it relate to other concerns within public administration and comparative politics? We will be discussing these questions from a theoretical perspective here, but any choices made about the focus of the inquiry will have ramifications for the methodological stances that are required. There may be some very basic questions about methodology implied in the selection of theoretical foci, because some of the methodologies usually associated with the "scientific" thrust of the social sciences may be inappropriate for approaches that are more holistic and humanistic. In the complex world of administration, identifying independent and dependent variables may require as much faith as science, so that somewhat less precise methods and language may be useful.

## What Do We Want to Know?

The most basic question we must ask here is what do we want to know about comparative public administration. As Richard Rose once wrote, "First, catch your dependent variable." As noted above, most of the history of this field, as indeed in comparative politics more generally, has been descriptive. There are any number of excellent descriptions of the structure of administrative systems (Timsit, 1986), and even of the behavior of individuals within those systems (Suleiman, 1974), though often they are not systematic. If that is to be the focus of our work, then we might terminate the paper here, for there would be little need for an extensive discussion of theory and methodology. Even if the focus were to be descriptive, however, we might have some implicit theoretical questions and associated with them some implicit methodological questions. Single country studies, even if descriptive, can have substantial theoretical importance if they are selected properly and are motivated by the appropriate questions (Lijphart, 1975; George, 1979). On the other hand, if what we want to know is more theoretical and analytic, then the theoretical and methodological problems become paramount. If we assume for the time being that what we are after is indeed more nomothetic statements about administrative life, then we must confront the substance of that desired knowledge. On the one hand, we may not want real comparative knowledge but may instead be seeking universals about the behavior of individuals working within public organizations. The very fact of this book and its structuring indicates that is not the case, although at the end of the research that level of theoretical knowledge (improbably) might still be the outcome if we were able to remove the nominal country titles from variables (or actually packages of variables) and assign to them other, more conceptual, names. In the short run, however, the question remains: what can we learn within particular national or subnational contexts that can be used to build broader theoretical statements about administration and its relationship to the rest of policymaking and politics? A universal theory of public management will have to wait. I once offered a set of four possible dependent variables (Peters, 1988)—people, structures, behavior and power—that captured some of what we would want to know. First, we need to know who is in public administration—their skills, values, and their socioeconomic backgrounds. This is important not only for reasons of sociological voyeurism but also because who is there will influence what can and does happen. Also we need to know something about the structures of public organizations. Despite some heroic efforts, we still lack readily usable and comparable means of classifying the structures of government departments and the entire constellation of public organizations (and quasi-public organizations) in a country. We also need to know what the members of the public service do, in the everyday administration of programs and in their roles as organizational if not partisan politicians. Finally, we need to know something about the powers that the public service has relative to other policymaking institutions and how that power is exercised in the policy process.

These are all important topics, but it is not clear that, taken together, they really capture the essence of the administrative system of a country. Further, if we move away from these rather simple categories, we need to ask more basic questions about administrative systems and the knowledge we need of them. Many of those questions are relational. As a number of the studies in this volume point out, we need to understand better how administration fits with the remainder of the political system and how it "interfaces" with the social system. The fit with the remainder of the political system may go beyond simple questions of power to the match of the bureaucratic elements in administration with the remainder of the system; this is in essence a large contingency theory question. This may be especially important in less developed political systems, but it is also crucial for understanding the politics of the industrialized democracies. Likewise, the issues of meshing with the social system will extend beyond administrative recruitment to how societal demands are processed and how decrees issued from government are processed in the social and economic system.

## Level of Analysis

One of the fundamental questions we need to ask about research in comparative public administration concerns the level of analysis at which we want to proceed: where will we find our dependent variable? The existing literature on public administration, or "bureaucracy," or civil service systems, is replete with examples of research that is conducted by macrolevel analysis. At bottom, there is an assumption that the nominal categories of countries are meaningful and useful in explaining observed variations in administrative behavior. The concept of bureaucracy is also situated at the macrolevel and is an attempt to describe a set of structural properties of administrative systems found in, as Weber presumed, developed societies, or perhaps even in all societies (Crozier, 1964; Page, 1985; Berger, 1957; Etzioni-Halevy, 1983; Wilson, 1989). All of this macrolevel research is important and useful, provided that our purpose is to make comparative statements about countries, or statements about the impacts of the structural properties of regimes.

Likewise, public administration literature is filled with microlevel concepts and analyses that focus attention on the individual working within the public service, and on his or her behavior in office. The (by now vast) work on "images" and role perceptions in public administration (Aberbach, Putnam, and Rockman, 1981; Aberbach and Rockman, 1987; Campbell and Peters, 1988;

Muramatsu and Krauss, 1984; Mayntz and Derlien, 1989) is all concerned with the attitudes and behaviors of individuals as they function within government. The managerial literature is also largely oriented toward the microlevel and is concerned with how best to motivate workers and gain their participation and compliance (Perry and Wise, 1990). Finally, the literature on representative bureaucracy is largely oriented toward the collection of microlevel information. There is no right or wrong answer about what level of analysis at which to work, but the selection of one does imply something about the types of findings the research on comparative administration can produce.

Concentrating on macrolevel analysis, for example, tends to direct attention to the connectedness of administrative institutions to other important social and political institutions in society. Thus, when we focus on macrolevel analysis, we are concerned with questions of accountability or responsibility (Day and Klein, 1987) and the way in which administrative organizations are involved in the governance of their societies (Peters, 1981; Lieberthal and Oksenberg, 1988). Further, we are concerned with the extent to which administrative organizations are embedded in the social system and reflect the characteristics of that system. For example, although the data used to study representative bureaucracy are from the individual level, they are useful for characterizing whole systems and saying something about how reflective the entire system is of the social structure from which it is drawn. These research questions are important for understanding civil service institutions, or the bureaucracy, and for understanding the place of those institutions in the governing system, but they are not the only important questions about the civil service.

## Problems of Linkage and Cross-Level Inference

There are two elements of special importance in this discussion of the issue of levels of analysis in comparative political analysis. The first is that civil service systems and the individuals who work within them are linked to different elements of the social system in a number of ways. The notion here is that the civil service system, as a system, shares some of the properties of the government as a whole, and that the government in turn shares some attributes of the surrounding society, economy, and culture. The behavior of individuals within the civil service is partly determined, or at least influenced, by the fact that they are members of the civil service; but their behavior is also impacted by society and by their personal and professional links with other social institutions. This portrayal of the location and connections of the civil service and its members should help forestall any attempts toward quick overgeneralization and determinism based primarily upon its structural or even personnel characteristics.

The embeddedness of public administration in broader social and political systems presents difficult methodological problems. Those surrounding systems are composed of a number of properties, some of which would be measured in our analysis and many of which would not. Therefore, when we find that there is a relationship between some $x$ and some $y$ in our analysis, we assume this is the "real" existing relationship. It may be, however, that the relationship is spurious and the product of some $z$ as yet unmeasured. So many $z$'s are tied up in any social system that, particularly when we use countries as an implicit variable in an analysis, there is a very high probability of making false inferences about relationships. This is, of course, a problem in any comparative research (Ragin, 1987), but is perhaps greater for comparative administration because of the multiple connections with society—politics and management—and the difficulties in measuring our dependent variables. Further, the civil service, like all other social institutions, has a symbolic significance within the culture that may be difficult to understand outside the culture (see Bekke, Perry, and Toonen in this volume).

Embeddedness has an additional, troublesome ramification that some philosophers of social science (Kaplan, 1964) have referred to as *act meaning* and *action meaning*. That is, actions taken within a particular social setting have meanings that are not the same as those that would be attributed to them by observers not fully familiar with that social system. Thus, similar behaviors engaged in by an American and a Dutch civil servant would signal different things to other members of their organizations. The research methods needed for effective research on the civil service might arguably be more those of the "squat anthropologist" than the more conventional social science researcher. That is, we may need to do what Kaufman (1981) did and virtually live the lives of our subjects to gain some greater insight into their administrative behavior.

In addition to the general problem of action meaning in a political setting such as that inhabited by civil servants, there may be multiple meanings for any set of actions since the individual is engaged in a number of "games" (Tseblis, 1990) that are a function of his or her multiple roles in a public bureaucracy. Even without the rationalistic logic embodied in much of this literature, these multiple and often conflicting links across levels and across segments of roles (Peters, 1991) can be crucial for interpreting behavior within institutions. Thus, the need to contextualize administrative behavior not only within society but even within the multiple roles and games of the civil servant makes understanding the outcomes of the process more difficult for outsiders. This again requires close observation of behavior within context rather than more conventional survey and descriptive analysis.

Although we would want to ensure that we keep our analysis at the appropriate level, it is also important to remember the importance of interactions among levels. This is especially true in light of the fact that citizens and their organizations (firms or whatever) are an important component of the administrative system as well. Most systems models of social and political life include a feedback loop that links actions back to inputs, and for public administration the loop is usually closed through citizens. The outputs and consequences of administrative action may be individual (benefits denied, regulations not enforced, or whatever), but the cumulation of those actions may be systemic. Thus, when we attempt to measure the individual behaviors of civil servants vis-à-vis their clients, which is certainly an important aspect of administrative behavior and administrative output, we may also be measuring some items that are of great consequence for the entire political system.

Another error we must guard against is making improper inferences across levels of analysis. There is a tendency in social research, and not just research about public administration, to make unjustified inferential leaps (Robinson, 1950; Retzlaff, 1965). It is easy to assume that if the majority of individuals, or perhaps even all individuals, who occupy roles in an administrative system think and behave in certain ways, then the system will behave in the same manner. Bureaucrats may think in certain ways, but it is not always certain that the bureaucracy itself will function that way. Given the fact that comparative politics likes to characterize entire systems, the ecological fallacy is common, and researchers assume that because they can characterize the system, the individuals within it will behave as they should. This is often true, but it is by no means always so, and deviance from prescribed roles in the system may be extremely important for some aspects of system behavior, especially the ability to change.

The growth, or now even dominance, of public choice approaches to political phenomena has made the question of cross-level inferences even more important. The question of "methodological individualism" is especially evident in the work of scholars such as Niskanen (1971), who posit that "budget maximizing bureaucrats" dominate bureaucracies and determine the outcomes of administrative decision-making. There are any number of critiques and elaborations of this basic model (Blais and Dion, 1991; Jackson, 1982) and it holds sway over a good deal of thinking in the field. The reason for mentioning it here is that it illustrates some of the problems of cross-level inferences. The model assumes that microlevel motivation (budget maximization), even if it exists among top-level bureaucrats, can define systemic properties. It appears, however, that the structural characteristics of the regimes and civil service systems within which these purported maximizers operate have as much or more impact on the actual performance of the system (Peters, 1991).

## EQUIVALENCE: THE TRAVELING PROBLEM

One of the most familiar problems in comparative analysis, but still one of the most important, is that of equivalence. It is part of the more general validity problem in social research: how can we have any confidence that we are measuring what we think we are measuring? Even if we are able to validate concepts and their indicators within a single society, can we be sure that the concepts have the same meaning, or indeed any meaning at all, in different societies. To some degree this problem might be more manageable for comparative administration than for other social phenomena. The tasks assigned to public administration are more readily comparable than the expectations of, say, legislatures in different settings. Even then, however, the nature of administrative organizations and the social meaning attached to those institutions may be widely divergent in societies, even those that appear very similar in terms of socioeconomic and political characteristics. Further, if we are interested in comparison across time as a means of expanding our number (N) of cases, then the tasks assigned bureaucracies appear to have changed substantially.

One of the most obvious examples of the equivalence problem in the study of civil service systems relates to the issue of "corruption" in the public service. One observer's corruption is often another person's conception of acceptable behavior, or perhaps even of proper and obligatory behavior. There are any number of examples of scholars studying administration in the third world and assuming that corrupt behavior is rampant and detrimental to "development." For the participants, however, it is expected that they take care of their relations when there are administrative problems, and various extracurricular payments are factored into decisions about the official rate of pay by the government (Abueva, 1966; Braibanti, 1962). We may argue that, after a period of transition, these systems would function better if they had a more Weberian system of administration, but the common charges of corruption and immorality are probably not justified in terms of society. We should also point out that it is not just in the extreme cases of third world countries that differing moral conceptions arise. Public servants and scholars socialized in the Anglo-American tradition of "neutrality" in the civil service often look askance at the manifest political involvement of civil servants in countries such as France and Germany (Mayntz and Derlien, 1989).

While bureaucratic corruption is an interesting and important example of the difficulties of generating equivalent measures across cultures, it is by no means the only example, and a good deal of our investigation into civil service systems must be influenced by this fundamental problem. Even terms with which we are very familiar and which we use without much cogitation have rather different interpretations in different countries and therefore require specification if used comparatively. If we are interested in the senior civil service as a component of the total civil service, for example, it may make a substantial difference if there is a unified concept of the service, or if senior officials enter as "high flyers" with little connection to the remainder of the personnel system.

The idea of mid-range theory is applicable here. It may be that concepts are stretchable within a particular geographical setting, or within a range of functional concerns, but lose their meaning when forced to travel any farther. However, we may want to develop theories and measures that can span a greater intellectual distance. That goal may require first doing the work necessary to generate the broader theories about public administration that are applicable and meaningful in a variety of cultural settings. We must inquire, however, whether such a goal, worthy though it may be, is really attainable within the bounds of existing resource availability and human capacity. Indeed, we must inquire if focusing on more middle range concerns—whether defined by geography or particular aspects of administrative behavior such as the civil service—is not a more fruitful avenue even without consideration of resource and intellectual constraints. We may need to begin with a better understanding of smaller parts of the intellectual puzzle before we are capable of understanding the larger entity. As Wildavsky argued about planning, if a theory can encompass everything, then it may be worth nothing.

## Impact on Application of Public Administration Research

In addition to its impact on the "scientific" aspects of our work, the equivalence problem also has an important impact on the more applied aspects of comparative administration  and on the penchant of some scholars of administration for "reform-mongering" (Hirschman, 1968). A great deal of administrative reform follows intellectual fashions (Astley, 1985), or simply political fads, with little attention to the difficult problems of matching the reform to the particular problem and to the sociopolitical system within which it must be administered. This absence of concern for cross-national learning with regard to reform points to two glaring weaknesses in the study of comparative administration and policy. One is the tendency to give insufficient attention to ideational aspects of policy and administration. Governments differ in large part because the mental pictures that people (elites and ordinary citizens alike) carry around in their heads are different. The social constructionists have gained a strong foothold in the study of substantive policy issues (Best, 1989; Nelson, 1984), but have been less successful in persuading people that administrative reality is as much socially constructed as, for example, are questions of drugs or child abuse. Thus, an attempt that is perfectly reasonable and effective in one setting is likely to be ineffective or counterproductive if implemented in another, simply because the change is not conceptualized in the same manner.

The other glaring weakness in the literature is that the desire to transplant reforms points clearly to the failure to adequately investigate conditions of policy learning, here using administrative reform as a type of policy. Some efforts have been undertaken (Rose, 1990; Wolman, 1992) to rectify this latter problem, specifically for social and economic policies; but there is as yet little attention to the implications for administrative reforms. This is true despite the widespread occurrence of reform and the impact of administrative change on governance. Even for the more developed aspects of "policy learning" there is as yet little development of a method for analyzing the crucial attributes of social and economic systems that may make them amenable to transplantation (Dommel, 1990). This is in part because there is as yet little development of ideas about the social and economic factors that lead to the success of policies, or of the attributes of policies themselves. We believe, for example, that administrative reform may be different than other policy reforms, yet we have little idea of the relevant variables which define that difference. Further, we are not sure if the variables that define the differences are manipulable. If they are not, then attempts at reform may not be worth the effort. We are probably correct in thinking that there are significant differences between administrative reforms and other policy changes, but if this insight is to be useful we need to understand why that is true.

Leaving aside problems of purposive transplantation of administrative innovations and returning to problems of understanding, we face another difficulty when we try to understand which social and economic conditions are related to particular administrative systems. The question is referred to in the anthropological literature as "Galton's problem," and it derives from the observation of similar social patterns in different cultures (Naroll, 1970; Eyestone, 1977; Klingman, 1980). Did the observed patterns arise autonomously, or was there diffusion of social innovations across cultures? This problem is increasingly evident in the contemporary political and administrative world in which communications and the existence of organizations such as the OECD and the World Bank serve to diffuse administrative innovations rapidly. While establishing the intellectual pedigree of an organizational pattern or of a reform proposal is interesting, it is not so important intellectually as understanding the conditions that generate and support those patterns. Even if an administrative innovation is found to be transplanted, it has been at least minimally successful if it still remains in place. What can that success tell us about planned transplantation of organizational patterns? We should consider the work of administrative reformers and organizational designers around the world as a natural laboratory for further planned reform efforts. The problem is to derive lessons from the experiments and to understand what can be transplanted successfully and what can not. Further, we also need somewhat clearer criteria of success if this indeed is to be an effective laboratory for change.

## Generic Administration

We commonly think of comparative administration as being cross-national comparison, but if we think somewhat more broadly, some of the same theoretical and methodological issues arise if we seek to compare across policy areas or levels of government. One issue that frequently arises when studying public administration is whether all administration is the same, or so similar that differences in policy areas do not need to be considered. This question often arises for administration in the public and private sectors (Bozeman, 1987; Allison, 1986), but it is relevant for administering different types of policies within government. The generic view that all policies are the same can be constrasted with the view that the policy problems, and associated administrative problems, of each policy area are unique and must therefore be considered differently. The latter differentiated view has great appeal, given the diversity of public functions that even the most casual observer can identify. For example, Page and Goldsmith (1987) found that particular policies administered in different countries were more similar than different policies administered in the same country; policy rather than country was the better predictor (see also Rose, 1990). The difficulty is that we do not as yet possess an adequate conceptual scheme for identifying the relevant differences among policy areas, for either policymaking or administrative purposes (Peters, 1991; Kellow, 1988).

The most common means of classifying policy areas or policy problems is functional, that is, using names that we usually see displayed on government buildings—defense, education, environment, etc. For analytic purposes, however, variation within each of these categories may be as great as the variation among them. In most countries (even the United States), health policy includes a mixture of direct service provision, regulation, subsidies, loans, etc. Health policies also deal with a range of target populations including the medically indigent, the aged, hospital administrators, and medical students. It is by no means clear that an administrative pattern effective for one policy intervention or one target population will be equally effective for others within that one (presumed) policy area. What we need is a more conceptual means of classifying policies and their targets.

Lowi's classificatory scheme for policies is one major attempt at developing such a conceptual device for public policies. His work has spawned a huge corpus of literature in political science (Peters, Doughtie, and McCulloch, 1977; Kjellberg, 1977), but it appears to be severely flawed. First, as with the nominal classification of policies, there may be as much variance within as among the cells of the typology (Spitzer, 1987; Kellow, 1988). Further, it is not clear whether the variables used to classify policies, especially the proximity to coercion, are the most effective variables for this purpose. Coercion has been used to classify the instruments at the disposal of government (Phidd and Doern, 1978; Woodside, 1986), but even there the concept appears to miss some of the subtle differences existing among policies and the many alternative means of achieving policy goals. Thus, policy studies, and the associated administrative science, should look further for analytic schemes to classify policy.

Based upon the above description and earlier work (see Linder and Peters, 1989; 1991), I would argue that using the nominal titles of policy problems, or Lowi's (or Wilson's) classifications as labeling devices is unlikely to be productive in comparative administration. Rather, it might be better to look at the instruments that government uses to reach policy goals as the basis for a more useful classificatory scheme for administrative needs. I would argue that for policy studies per se, alternative and more problem-focused schemes are necessary to provide the link with instrument choices, but for *administrative* purposes instruments constitute an acceptable basis for classification. If we consider that governments attempt to influence their economies and societies by means of one or the other instrument, then these become the central content of administration.

In addition to capturing much of the content of policy, there is substantial variance in how instruments must be administered. At one end of the spectrum, some programs of government, albeit a declining number, are provided directly to clients, and government is responsible for staffing and implementation. At the other end of the spectrum, a number of public programs are provided very indirectly and rely upon private organizations or citizens themselves to take up the benefit offered. Tax expenditures are an obvious example of the latter type of program. Whereas the first category of programs is administratively intensive and requires complex hierarchies of service providers, the latter type of program requires relatively little direct administration but significant monitoring and review. In between the two extremes are public programs provided in whole or part by the private sector. These require some direct administrative actions, as well as means of specifying and monitoring private compliance with government policy intentions. Thus, the selection of one or another instrument tells us a great deal about the policy preferences of governments as well as something about the administrative needs of those governments. This may be a place to start when looking for classificatory schemes that can be helpful in understanding administrative differences.

### Relational Issues

The role of instruments may be especially important since many of the truly significant issues in comparative public administration involve boundary and relational questions. That is, what are the boundaries of the administrative system, especially the public administrative system, and what are its relationships with other significant actors? As the state increasingly becomes "hollow" and dependent upon the private sector or other governments to implement its policies and programs, the absence of clear definitions of the state become all the more evident. Further, within governments themselves issues of accountability and the role of "political" institutions in controlling the more privatized and decentralized state abound. This is especially evident in the United Kingdom, where "Next Steps" appears to have altered long standing traditions of ministerial responsibility for policy and administration.[3] Similar reforms in New Zealand (Scott, Bushnell, and Sallee, 1990) have even more greatly changed relationships between the political masters and the instrumentalities of policy implementation. A focus on the instruments of governing provides a common focus for analysis, regardless of what type of organization is actually wielding the tools.

One danger of any volume concentrating on the comparison of civil service systems alone is that these components of governance do become isolated from other important components of the process, and the relational aspects are not sufficiently attended to. We risk doing a disservice to our own understanding of the civil service and of other components of comparative politics if we disaggregate too much the institutions of government. Concern with linkage needs to extend even beyond the formal institutions of government, as the experience of corporatist states and corporatist political theory has demonstrated. Clearly, there is something to be gained by a particular focus on administration, but we also need something of the big picture of the total system of politics and government.

As with so many of the questions we must deal with in comparative research, for example, grand theory versus mid-range theory, there is a problem of balance. How wide does our theoretical and empirical net need to spread to capture enough of the nature of the total systems within which administration is embedded, and how specifically do we need to be able to focus sufficient expertise on the topic? These are difficult sets of questions to answer in any definitive way.

## APPROACHES TO METHODOLOGY

I have already discussed a number of methodological issues, but there remains a need to raise some final points about how to build knowledge in this area of inquiry. In discussing the field, I have been contrasting it implicitly with some of the more "scientific" areas of the social sciences and their emphasis on indicator construction, measurement, and statistical relationships. I have raised a number of doubts about our ability to reach that level of scientific development in this particular area. Therefore, this section discusses briefly some alternative methods that may provide useful information but that need not conform to all the requirements our colleagues in voting behavior or even judicial behavior might impose on themselves. Further, it will examine the argument that such levels of "development" might in fact be counterproductive.

### Ideal Types

If we move away from the idea of building classificatory schemes inductively, we can go back to the roots of administrative science and use the method of ideal types as a means to understand differences among actual administrative systems. Moving back to our "roots" naturally refers to Weber's ideal type model and its importance for bureaucratic theory. The method of using ideal types has the virtue of providing a standard against which real world systems can be compared. Even if the "model" itself is rather ethnocentric (as Weber's certainly is), the comparison is meaningful. We can clearly tell that country X has an administrative system that does not conform to Weber's ideas about rationality. The question then becomes why, and what difference does it make. The danger, of course, is that the ideal type analysis is converted into a different type of ideal, on the assumption that western conceptions of "good" administration provide normative standards rather than empirical referents.

The study of public administration has been advanced through the careful analysis of Weber's work and the comparison of real world experiences with the ideal model that he created. Page (1985), for example, used the method of the ideal type to explicate a number of important comparative differences among European political systems. Likewise, Torstendahl (1991) utilized Weber's ideas somewhat less precisely to examine administrative change in Scandinavia. Earlier, Berger (1957) used the Weberian ideal to understand the emergent bureaucracy of Egypt. Neither author went into the exercise expecting to find a perfect Weberian system, and indeed no one should have, but recognizing the deviations in different countries and in different time periods does explain a good deal about administrative development. This is especially true given the development logic that undergirded much of Weber's model (Mommsen and Osterhammer, 1987).

Weber's model has been the intellectual gold standard against which real-world bureaucracies have most often been compared, but there are other options that may be more meaningful for scholars seeking to understand the role of public administration in governance. For example, the model of the *administrative state* offers one view of the tasks that bureaucracy must perform in government; it can also be used as a means of identifying the manner in which those task are performed (Waldo, 1948; Redford, 1969). As with Weber, there may be a developmental perspective embedded within this framework, the assumption being that not only will "modern" administrations perform these tasks, they will perform them in certain ways. Even if this is regarded as excessively ethnocentric, the "model" does provide a basis for comparison. Much the same would be true of my own ideas about "bureaucratic government" as a means of more directly examining the role of public administration in governance (Peters, 1981; 1991). The model is derived from the experience of western democracies but has, perhaps, fewer factors peculiar to those systems. In fact, since many third world countries have bureaucracies that are strong relative to the political institutions of their governments, a notion of bureaucratic government may be particularly useful in those settings. Also applicable would be the growing body of work on steering, whether viewed from a more centralist position (Linder and Peters, 1984) or a more decentralized position (Kickert, 1991).

## The Theoretical Case Study

This discussion has pointed to the dangers of concentrating on the single case and assuming that one country is either so particular that no others need be compared, or is so general that all others are like it. American researchers, for example, tend to make the former assumption for other countries and the latter for the United States. The need to advocate case study methodology suggests that "comparative" research is not considered desirable in many settings, and indeed opponents tend to outnumber advocates. The difficulties encountered with case studies can, however, be ameliorated by using more theoretically driven case studies (George, 1979; Agranoff and Radin, 1991; Walton, 1973). The idea of such studies is to use the same methodology and the same research questions in a number of settings in order to induce generalities from the findings at a later stage (George, 1979). As pointed out above for indicator construction, this research design cannot be applied unless there is already some theoretical and conceptual guidance; the researcher must know what questions to ask (Yin, 1984). On the other hand, this approach can be useful for either theory "testing" or theory elaboration after an initial stage of deduction or simply cogitation has been completed.

A variant of the theoretical case study is the "comparable" case study (Lijphart, 1975). The idea is very similar to that of the theoretical case, though less specifically informed by theory. Rather, it is concerned with the elaboration of a particular theory as a product of the exercise; the comparable case study strategy is more concerned with comparison per se. Of course, it can be argued that comparison is the principal tool for theory development in the social sciences (Smelser, 1976), but this is really a matter of emphasis. The idea is to build theory by looking at a number of comparable cases and extracting generalizations from that research.

The theoretical case study is a useful and relatively cheap way of generating more directly comparable research in comparative politics, but it also has pitfalls. One is that the "instrument" in a series of such case studies will actually be different and can therefore represent a source of error (Campbell and Stanley, 1966). That is, each researcher is an expert in his/her area of inquiry and therefore brings to the research situation vested interests and preconceptions about what the findings should be. If that is the case, as it usually will be, then there is a strong probability of introducing bias into the findings. We can surmise the direction of the bias, but attempting to counteract or adjust for it may simply add another type of bias. The alternate strategy of using nonexperts has some appeal, but it also has rather obvious disadvantages. Again, the problem for comparative research is how best to balance breadth and depth of research. How can we marshall sufficient expertise for each case without turning the research into just another set of incomparable studies of different political or administrative systems?

The "comparable case study" strategy has some special pitfalls. The most obvious is the definition of "comparable" (see Sartori, 1970; DeFelice, 1980): in how many dimensions must cases be similar before they are considered close enough? Must the researcher assume that he or she knows in advance that the cases are comparable? If not, a need arises for (expensive) sampling of cases in order to have a sufficient number that are truly comparable. This statement of the problem also returns us to the familiar territory of Przeworski and Teune (1970), and to the need to ask ourselves whether "most different" or "most similar" cases are better for comparison. Comparable in the usual sense of the term means similar, but comparable may also mean that the cases should maximize variance on some (presumed) independent variable so that we find differences on the (presumed) dependent variable. Given the relatively low level of scientific development (especially of usable indicators) in much of comparative administration, we may well want to adopt strategies that maximize observed variance.

### False Scientism?

A final point to be addressed here is whether the expectations raised in the preceding portions of the paper are not inappropriate, and whether we should aspire to less sweeping developments of theory and especially of methodology. There have been a number of arguments advanced that public administration is not amenable to the quantitative techniques of the social sciences and that it is better understood phenomenologically (Hummel, 1987; Denhardt, 1981). A less extreme position is that the emphasis given to quantitative methodologies and indicators is misplaced; we should place greater emphasis on qualitative methodologies (Miles, 1979) and on methods ("meta-analysis") that permit greater cumulation of case studies. On the other hand, it might be argued that this is too easy an admission of defeat and that we should push ahead in the search for full scientific development of this field rather than retreat so quickly.

The barriers facing attempts to build "science" in comparative public administration are formidable. We are (usually) denied access to the experimental method to establish a causal relationship between some change in the external environment and administrative behavior, though some internal changes within organizations can be treated as experiments. Even for statistical analysis, we are in the position of having more variables than cases—especially given the fact that using "country" as an implicit control variable bundles together a huge number of variables, some not identified or even imagined (Jackman, 1985; Frendreis, 1983). Some models are at best indeterminate statistically so that the usual canons of social scientific research are not easily applicable. Therefore, we are often in the position of *illustrating* theoretical arguments with comparative examples (Smelser, 1976) rather than really being able to test theoretical arguments systematically using comparative data. Illustration may well illuminate the theories being considered, but it cannot be said to "test" the theories in the usual sense of that term.

At an even more basic level, our understanding of public administration and its milieu may not be sufficiently well developed to distinguish consistently between independent and dependent variables and allow a statistical "test" to be conceived properly. I have advised that we "catch" our dependent variable first, but that may beg the question of how one knows where different factors fall in a presumed causal sequence. For example, do patterns of recruitment into the civil service replicate the social structure, or do they help to create, or at least perpetuate, social patterns? Are certain "less developed" patterns of administrative behavior a function of lower levels of economic development, or are they causes of that low level of development? We could probably make arguments both ways in the above cases, and in many others where we would want to establish causal links. It may be that rather than seeking the precision of science, we should instead be searching at this stage for thicker and more useful descriptive statements about systems with the hope of producing first some descriptive generalizations and then perhaps science.

### Do We Want Average Performance?

Further, it could be argued that the purpose of much comparative administration research is not to generate generalizations about public administration that can push back the frontiers of social science. Rather, the purposes are more ameliorative and reform oriented: we need to know what works and what is best. If that is true, then scientific generalizations are not the appropriate target for analysis. Instead, finding exceptional performance is the desired goal. Miller (1984) made this point about public policy, and much the same can be said about administration. That is, we may want to identify administrative reforms, or continuing administrative arrangements, that have been unusually successful instead of identifying modal patterns or even stable patterns of relationship among variables. If we can do this then the possibilities of offering useful advice are enhanced. This research pattern would not go down well with "scientifically" oriented scholars in many of our departments, but it is still a viable and meaningful approach to research in comparative public administration.

Just as we may want to identify patterns of exceptional performance if the goal is to improve practice, so too we must be concerned about which variables identified are manipulable. Much of the research in comparative policy studies has identified economic development as perhaps the best predictor of public spending for education, health, etc. The lesson, clearly, is to get rich, but that is not particularly useful advice for most developing countries that are trying to do that anyway. The point is that if research is to be useful for policymakers, they must be given strings to pull that will produce results, not told that some remote factor $X$ is the root cause of the problem. Again, good social science may not always be particularly good policy or administrative science.

## CONCLUSION

This paper has plowed a good deal of ground, much of which will be familiar territory to readers. Indeed, most of the issues that now confound students of comparative public administration are the same issues that have plagued us for decades, and that have plagued students of comparative politics in general for that same length of time. That continuity does not make the questions and problems any less important. Nor does it mean that the problems raised are necessarily insuperable. What it does mean is that there is no quick technological fix for most of our research questions, not any methodological medicine that will cure all our ills.

The real hope for deliverance arises not from quick fixes but from the interaction between theory and data. The social sciences have a history of denigrating "barefoot empiricism," and often that has been justified. On the other hand, there is a great deal to be said for actually having data that speak to real issues, whether or not that data is as neatly packaged for theoretical purposes as we might like. On the other hand, some more empirically minded colleagues have tended to denigrate the work of theorists as being excessively disconnected from the real world, or as being so broad as to be useless in practice. Some of those complaints have also been valid but have assigned perhaps too little value to the development of meaningful generalizations that can guide future empirical work. Clearly then the need is for the connection of the two strands of thought and work. Further, that connection may need to be made initially at a rather low level of generalization and at the level of mid-range theory. We have noted above the possibilities of developing theories at that range, organized around both geography, instruments, and substantive policy issues. There is no shortage of things to be done, and this book and the associated collaborative research represent one way to start the enterprise.

*NOTES*

1. These scholars may fail to realize, however, that a good deal of the intellectual development of public administration, especially comparative public administration, arose from the practical need to advise governments about the development and reform of their administrative systems.

2. I refer, with an absence of modesty, to the success of *Governance* in its first four years of publication, as well as to the welcome revival of the *International Review of Administrative Sciences*. Further, some of the "mainline" journals in public administration are now showing increasing interest in comparative topics.

3. Although this appears to be true, government documents supporting the program continue to argue as if there had been no real change in the relationship between administration and Parliament.

*REFERENCES*

Aberbach, J. D., and B. A. Rockman. 1987. "Comparative Administration: Methods, Muddles, and Models." *Administration and Society* 18: 473–506.

Aberbach, J. D., R. D. Putnam, and B. A. Rockman. 1981. *Bureaucrats and Politicians in Western Democracies*. Cambridge: Harvard University Press.

Abueva, J. V. 1966. "The Contribution of Nepotism, Spoils and Graft to Political Development." *East-West Center Review* 3: 45–54.

Agranoff, R., and B. A. Radin. 1991. "The Comparative Case Study Approach in Public Administration." In J. L. Perry, ed., *Research in Public Administration*, vol. 1. Greenwich, CT: JAI Press.

Allison, G. T. 1986. "Public and Private Management: Are They Fundamentally Alike in All Unimportant Respects?" In F. S. Lane, ed., *Current Issues in Public Administration*. New York: St. Martin's Press.

Almond, G. A., and S. Verba. 1963. *The Civic Culture*. Princeton: Princeton University Press.

Astley, W. G. 1985. "Administrative Science as Socially Constructed Truth." *Administrative Science Quarterly* 30: 497–513.

Bendor, J. 1990. "Formal Models of Bureaucracy: A Review." In N. B. Lynn and A. Wildavsky, eds., *Public Administration: The State of the Discipline*. Chatham, NJ: Chatham House.

Berger, M. 1957. *Bureaucracy and Society in Modern Egypt*. Princeton: Princeton University Press.

Best, J. 1989. *Images of Issues*. New York: Walter De Gruyter.

Blais, A., and S. Dion. 1991. *The Budget Maximizing Bureaucrat*. Pittsburgh: University of Pittsburgh Press.

Bozeman, B. 1987. *All Organizations Are Public: Bridging Public and Private Organization Theories*. San Francisco: Jossey-Bass.

Braibanti, R. 1962. *Asian Administrative Systems Derivative from the British Imperial Tradition*. Durham, NC: Duke University Press.

Caiden, G. E. 1991. *Administrative Reform Comes of Age*. Hawthorne, NY: Walter de Gruyter.

Campbell, C., and B. G. Peters. 1988. "Images of the Administrative Process: Politics, Administration and Image IV." *Governance* 1: 80–101.

Campbell, D. T., and J. C. Stanley. 1966. *Experimental and Quasi-Experimental Designs for Research*. Chicago: Rand McNally.

Collier, R. B., and D. Collier. 1991. *Shaping the Political Arena*. Princeton: Princeton University Press.

Crozier, M. 1964. *The Bureaucratic Phenomenon*. Chicago: University of Chicago Press.

Dalton, R. J. 1988. *Citizen Politics in Western Democracies*. Chatham, NJ: Chatham House.

Day, P., and R. Klein. 1987. *Accountabilities*. London: Tavistock.

DeFelice, E. G. 1980. "Comparison Misconceived: Common Nonsense in Comparative Politics." *Comparative Politics* 13: 119–26.

Denhardt, R. B. 1981. *In the Shadow of Organization*. Lawrence: University of Kansas Press.

Dogan, M., and D. Pelassy. 1990. *How to Compare Nations*. 2nd ed. Chatham, NJ: Chatham House.

Dommel, P. 1990. "Neighborhood Rehabilitation and Policy Transfer." *Government and Policy* 8: 241–50.

Esman, M. J. 1980. "Development Assistance in Public Administration: Requiem or Renewal." *Public Administration Review* 27: 271–78.

Etzioni-Halevy, E. 1983. *Bureaucracy and Democracy*. Boston: Routledge and Kegan Paul.

Eyestone, R. 1977. "Confusion, Diffusion and Innovation." *American Political Science Review* 71: 441–47.

Frendreis, J. P. 1983. "Explanation of Variation and Detection of Covariation: The Purpose and Logic of Comparative Analysis." *Comparative Political Studies* 16: 225–72.

Fried, R. 1990. "Comparative Public Administration: The Search for Theories." In N. B. Lynn and A. Wildavsky, *Public Administration: The State of the Discipline*. Chatham, NJ: Chatham House.

George, A. 1979. "Case Studies and Theory Development: The Method of Structured, Focused Comparison." In G. P. Lauren, ed., *Diplomacy: New Approaches in History, Theory and Policy*. New York: Free Press.

Heady, F. 1991. *Public Administration: A Comparative Perspective*. 4th ed. New York: Marcel Dekker.

Heclo, H. 1977. *A Government of Strangers*. Washington, DC: Brookings Institution.

Hirschman, A. O. 1968. "Models of Reform-Mongering." *Quarterly Journal of Economics* 38: 236–57.

Hood, C., and G. F. Schuppert. 1988. *Delivering Public Services in Western Europe*. London: Sage.

Hummel, R. P. 1987. *The Bureaucratic Experience*. 3rd ed. New York: St. Martin's Press.

Jackman, R. W. 1985. "Cross-National Statistical Research and the Study of Comparative Politics." *American Journal of Political Science* 29: 161–82.

Jackson, P. M. 1982. *The Political Economy of Bureaucracy*, Oxford: Philip Allan.

Kaplan, A. 1964. *The Conduct of Inquiry*. San Francisco: Chandler.

Kasfir, N. 1969. "Prismatic Theory and African Administration." *World Politics* 21: 295–314.

Kaufman, H. 1981. *The Administrative Behavior of Federal Bureau Chiefs*. Washington, DC: Brookings Institution.

Kellow, A. 1988. "Promoting Elegance in Policy Theory: Simplifying Lowi's Arenas of Power." *Policy Studies Journal* 16: 713–24.

Kickert, W. J. M. 1991. *Complexiteit, Zelfsturing en Dynamiek*. Alphen aan den Rijn: Willink.

Kjellberg, F. 1977. "Do Policies (Really) Determine Politics? and Eventually How?" *Policy Studies Journal* (special issue): 554–70.

Klijn, E. H., and G. R. Teisman. 1991. "Effective Policymaking in Multi-actor Settings: Networks and Steering." In L. Schaep, M. V. Twist, C. Temer, and R. J. in'tVeld, eds., *Autopoiesis and Configuration Theory: New Approaches to Societal Steering*. Dordrecht: Kluwer.

Klingman, C. D. 1980. "Temporal and Spatial Diffusion in the Analysis of Social Change." *American Political Science Review* 74: 123–37.

Lane, J.-E. 1990. *Institutional Reform*. Aldershot: Dartmouth.

LaPalombara, J. 1968. "Macrotheories and Microapplications: The Widening Chasm." *Comparative Politics* 1: 52–78.

Laumann, E. O., and D. Knoke. 1987. *The Organizational State*. Madison: University of Wisconsin Press.

Laundy, P. 1989. *Parliaments in the Modern World*. Aldershot: Dartmouth.

Leemans, A. F. 1976. *The Management of Change in Government*. The Hague: Martinus Nijhoff.

Lieberthal, K., and M. Oksenberg. 1988. *Policymaking in China: Leaders, Structures and Process*. Princeton: Princeton University Press.

Lijphart, A. 1971. "Comparative Politics and the Comparative Method." *American Political Science Review* 65: 682–93.

————. 1975. "The Comparable Cases Strategy in Comparative Research." *Comparative Political Studies* 8: 158–71.

Linder, S. H., and B. G. Peters. 1984. "From Social Theory to Policy Design." *Journal of Public Policy* 4: 237–59.

————. 1989. "Instruments of Government: Perceptions and Contexts." *Journal of Public Policy* 9: 35–58.

Lundquist, L. 1985. "From Order to Chaos: Recent Trends in the Study of Public Administration." In J.-E. Lane, ed., *State and Market: The Politics of Public and Private.* London: Sage.

Lundqvist, L. J. 1988. "Privatization: Towards a Concept for Comparative Policy Analysis." *Journal of Public Policy* 8: 1–19.

————. 1989. "The Literature on Privatization." *Scandinavian Political Studies* 12: 271–77.

March, J. G., and J. P. Olsen. 1989. *Rediscovering Institutions: The Organizational Basis of Politics.* New York: Free Press.

Mayntz, R., and H.-U. Derlien. 1989. "Party Patronage and Politicization of the West German Administrative Elite 1970–87: Toward Hybridization?" *Governance* 2: 384–404.

Meyers, F. 1985. *La politisation de l'administration.* Brussels: Institut International de Science Administrative.

Miles, M. 1979. "Qualitative Data as an Attractive Nuisance." *Administrative Science Quarterly* 24: 590–601.

Miller, T. C. 1984. "Conclusion: A Design Science Perspective." In T. C. Miller, ed., *Public Sector Performance: A Conceptual Turning Point.* Baltimore, MD: Johns Hopkins University Press.

Milward, B. 1991. "Managing the Hollow State." Paper presented at the annual meeting of the American Political Science Association, Washington, DC.

Mommsen, W. J., and J. Osterhammer. 1987. *Max Weber and His Contemporaries.* Boston: Allen & Unwin.

Muramatsu, M., and E. S. Krauss. 1984. "Bureaucrats and Politicians in Policymaking: The Case of Japan." *American Political Science Review* 78: 126–46.

Naroll, R. 1970. "Galton's Problem." In R. Naroll and R. Cohen, eds., *Handbook of Method in Cultural Anthropology.* Garden City, NJ: Natural History Press.

Nelson, B. 1984. *Making an Issue of Child Abuse.* Chicago: University of Chicago Press.

Niskanen, W. 1971. *Bureaucracy and Representative Government.* Chicago: Aldine/Atherton.

Olsen, J. P. 1990. "Modernization Programs in Perspective: Institutional Analysis of Organizational Change." *Governance* 4: 125–49.

Ostrom, E. 1990. *Governing the Commons.* Cambridge: Cambridge University Press.

O'Toole, L. J. 1986. "Policy Recommendations for Multi-Actor Implementation: An Assessment of the Field." *Journal of Public Policy* 6: 181–210.

Page, E. C. 1985. *Political Authority and Bureaucratic Power.* Brighton: Wheatsheaf.

Page, E. C., and M. J. Goldsmith. 1987. *Central and Local Government: A Comparative Analysis of West European States.* London: Sage.

Perry, J. L., and L. R. Wise. 1990. "The Motivational Bases of Public Service." *Public Administration Review* 50: 367–73.

Peters, B. G. 1981. "The Problem of Bureaucratic Government." *The Journal of Politics* 43: 56–82.

―――. 1988. *Comparing Public Bureaucracies: Problems of Theory and Method.* Tuscaloosa: University of Alabama Press.

―――. 1991. "Public Bureaucracy and Public Policy." In D. E. Ashford, ed., *Context and Meaning in Public Policy.* Pittsburgh: University of Pittsburgh Press.

Peters, B. G., J. C. Doughtie, and M. K. McCulloch. 1977. "Types of Democratic Systems and Types of Public Policies." *Comparative Politics* 9: 327–55.

Phidd, R., and G. B. Doern. 1978. *The Politics and Management of Canadian Economic Policy.* Toronto: Macmillan.

Pollitt, C. 1984. *Manipulating the Machine.* London: Allen & Unwin.

Power, J. 1990. *Public Administration in Australia.* Sydney: Hale & Iremonger.

Przeworski, A. 1987. "Methods of Cross-National Research, 1970–83: An Overview." In M. Dierkes, H. N. Weiler, and A. B. Antal, eds., *Comparative Policy Research.* New York: St. Martin's Press.

Przeworski, A., and H. Teune. 1970. *The Logic of Comparative Social Inquiry.* New York: Wiley-Interscience.

Ragin, C. C. 1987. *The Comparative Method: Moving Beyond Qualitative and Quantitative Strategies.* Berkeley: University of California Press.

Redford, E. 1969. *The Administrative State.* Oxford: Oxford University Press.

Retzlaff, R. H. 1965. "The Use of Aggregate Data in Comparative Political Analysis." *Journal of Politics* 27: 797–817.

Riggs, F. W. 1964. *Administration in Developing Countries: The Theory of the Prismatic Society*. Boston: Houghton Mifflin.

——. 1976. "The Group and the Movement: Notes on Comparative Development Administration." *Public Administration Review* 36: 641–45.

Robinson, W. S. 1950. "Ecological Correlations and the Behavior of Individuals." *American Sociological Review* 15: 351–57.

Rose, R. 1990. "Prospective Evaluation through Comparative Policy Studies." *Studies in Public Policy* 182. Glasgow: University of Strathclyde, Centre for the Study of Public Policy.

——. 1993. *Lesson-Drawing in Public Policy*. Chatham, NJ: Chatham House.

Sartori, G. 1970. "Concept Misinformation in Comparative Politics." *American Political Science Review* 64: 1033–53.

Scott, G., P. Bushnell, and N. Sallee. 1990. "Reforms of the Core Sector: The New Zealand Experience." *Governance* 3: 138–65.

Sigelman, L. 1976. "In Search of Comparative Administration." *Public Administration Review* 36: 621–25.

Smelser, N. 1976. *Comparative Methods in the Social Sciences*. Englewood Cliffs, NJ: Prentice Hall.

Spitzer, R. J. 1987. "Promoting Policy Theory: Revising the Arenas of Power." *Policy Studies Journal* 15: 675–89.

Suleiman, E. N. 1974. *Politics, Power and Bureaucracy in France: The Administrative Elite*. Princeton: Princeton University Press.

Timsit, G. 1987. *Administrations et états: étude comparée*. Paris: PUF.

Torstendahl, R. 1991. *Bureaucratisation in Northwestern Europe, 1880–1985*. London: Routledge.

Tseblis, G. 1990. *Nested Games*. Berkeley: University of California Press.

Waldo, D. 1948. *The Administrative State*. New York: Ronald Press.

Walton, J. 1973. "Standardized Case Comparison: Observations on Method in Comparative Sociology." In M. Armer and A. Grimshaw, eds., *Comparative Social Research*. New York: John Wiley & Sons.

Wilson, J. Q. 1989. *Bureaucracy: What Government Agencies Do and Why They Do It.* New York: Basic Books.

Wolman, H. 1992. "Understanding Cross-national Policy Transfers." *Governance* 5: 27–45.

Woodside, K. 1986. "Policy Instruments and the Study of Public Policy." *Canadian Journal of Political Science* 19: 775–93.

Yin, R. K., 1984. *Case Study Research.* Beverly Hills, CA: Sage.

# 3 DATA REQUIREMENTS AND AVAILABILITY

Eugene B. McGregor Jr. and Paul Solano

The basic thesis of this chapter on the problem of data collection in cross-national civil service research can be stated as a paradox. This is the best of times to compare civil service systems; enormous ferment about government design, and substantial dissatisfaction with government performance, has spawned a global conversation about what works and does not work in public management. Yet the empirical basis for cross-national comparison remains weak; data are not available in anywhere near the quantity and quality comparative analysis would now require. Indeed, a number of factors conspire to curtail the availability of inherently comparable data. How to make progress in bringing together the two sides of the "data puzzle" is the subject of the following discussion.

At the beginning, we must acknowledge two data problems peculiar to civil service systems. One is that data are limited because the civil service institution is by nature undemonstrative and sometimes uninformative about its own affairs. While the civil service does oversee government information systems development and manages massive systems of data and statistics about the programs and policies it administers, it is not consistently in the business of producing reliable and comparative data about its own persona. By definition, civil service "serves" political principals other than itself—crown, country, state, and fellow citizens—all of which are to some extent active, visible, measurable, and knowable. By contrast, civil service employs agents who operate behind the scenes and are theoretically controlled by political principals (Ross, 1973; Pratt and Zeckhauser, 1985). While the terms of agentry permit cultural and stylistic variety, the general civil service posture is one of relative invisibility—placid, undramatic, and only partly measured. The invisibility obtains not because of a conspiracy by agents, but because the nature of public work demands some degree of agent anonymity.

The second problem is that most available data are naturally occurring artifacts created by the object of analysis. Whereas researched data are invented and collected by an investigator in response to specific research questions, naturally occurring data arise as a byproduct of activity unrelated to pure research. With few exceptions (Aberbach, Putnam, and Rockman, 1981), civil service data are artifacts of civil service operations and administrative manipulation. In short, the data are dirty. The result is that the answers to even the simplest questions about the aggregate size of a civil service system are affected by the politics of whether one government defines "civil service" broadly or narrowly, includes public corporations and government sponsored employment or not, excludes or includes contract and manual labor, and includes in the civil service domain the full range of social service and insurance programs operating at the periphery as well as at the center of the executive branch function. Thus, even the simplest of data collections, such as the measurement of public sector size, can represent a major challenge, as shown in the appendix, which lists the sources that would have to be consulted and the manipulations that would have to be performed before truly comparable data could be derived.

The argument here is that the development of comparative civil service data depends upon achieving a successful mapping of data requirements, that is, defining the data needed to answer important questions, and upon data availability, that is, the availability of information that would have to be supplied at some cost in order to provide answers. The argument begins with a survey of design variables associated with three roles (Bekke, Perry, and Toonen, this volume) played by civil service systems, namely as personnel system, as institutionalized rules of governance, and as a symbolic instrument of the constitutional order. The design variables represent dimensions of choice confronting decision-makers. The second part of the argument notes that the existence of a civil service system depends on the *configuration* of design choices (Mintzberg, 1983: 122), whereby the many design choices that are made comprise the internal employment features of an entire civil service. Finally, a brief review of some external strategic and tactical variables suggests that civil service systems also face a *congruence* problem (Mintzberg, 1983: 122) that results from environmental turbulence and the consequent pressure to achieve a fit between external situational factors and the design parameters forming the operational core. Not surprisingly, the list of data requirements—the essential civil service dimensions one would like to know—is long, while the availability of comparable data is limited. By exposing some of the gap between what is currently known and catalogued and what analysts would like to know, we hope to suggest targets for future research.

## THREE ROLES OF CIVIL SERVICE SYSTEMS

Comparative analysis of operating civil service systems involves many questions. At least three critical dimensions capture the roles played by all civil service systems and thus serve as the basis for institutional civil service comparison: first, civil service represents, by definition, a personnel system; second, institutional civil service embodies a set of rules governing joint action in complex administrative systems; third, the idea of "civil service" invokes symbols representing the value sets surrounding public service. Within each area, the list of design variables is long and involves multiple continua. Table 3.1 presents the design variables classified by the three roles.

TABLE 3.1

**Civil Service Design Variables Classified by Role**

| | CIVIL SERVICE ROLES | | |
|---|---|---|---|
| | **Personnel System** | **Rules of Governance** | **Symbol System** |
| | Labor Markets<br>  Internal<br>  External | Authority Structures<br>  Unitary<br>  Multiple | Internal Service Ethics<br>  Anonymity<br>  Departmental<br>    responsibility<br>  Sense of calling<br>  Isolation from<br>    private sector |
| DESIGN VARIABLES | Employment System<br>  Collective<br>  Merit<br>  Patronage | Agentry<br>  Agent of state<br>  Servant of crown<br>  Servant of people | |
| | Human Resources Management Design<br>  Job design<br>  Recruitment<br>  Selection<br>  Job evaluation<br>  Career<br>    management<br>System layering | Accountability Mechanisms<br>  Constitutional<br>  Structural<br>  Self-control<br><br>Policy Role<br>  Proaction/Reaction<br>  Formulation<br>  Partisan advocacy | External Service Ethics<br>  Sense of service<br>  Public confidence<br>  Prestige<br>  Partisanship<br>  Visibility<br>  Conflicts of interest |

## Civil Service as Operating Personnel System

At the heart of all civil service systems is the idea of personnel operations characterized by patterned day-to-day interactions, activities, and exchanges that define the employment relationship between employer and employee. All such systems can be characterized by an "operating ideology" (Sharpe, 1985: 371–72) consisting of elements that define the rationale, actions, structures, and modes of civil service operation used to view problems and take action. In short, the operating ideology represents the civil service manner of doing business as characterized by institutional patterns persisting over time.

By definition, all civil service systems are invariant in the sense that civil service employment and tenure are bound by rules of appointment other than direct election. Thus, civil servants tend to remain at their posts while electoral and other partisan changes occur. This is not to deny that some civil service employment may be contingent on electoral outcomes—for example, in patronage systems—but the effect of partisanship is indirect rather than direct. In general, however, the employment relationship is defined by three strategic choices (McGregor, 1991: chap. 4) associated with selection of labor market, employment systems rules, and human resource management designs. Taken together, these three sets of choices characterize civil service as an operating personnel system; they are summarized in the first column of table 3.1.

*Labor markets.*

External and internal markets (Doeringer and Piore, 1971), where external markets denote the use of a contractual workforce and internal markets denote the use of personnel employed under an "administered" system.

*Employment system.*

Collective, merit, and patronage (Mosher, 1968) rules, where employment system design principles govern the design of "internal" labor markets (McGregor, 1991). Collective rules rely on across-the-board determination of matters of interest and arbitration common to whole classes of employment covered by union agreement. Patronage ties employment rules directly to electoral or partisan political outcomes. Merit rules, by contrast, use judgments of *individual* capacities and performance as the standard for employment practices and decisions and deliberately seek to filter out partisan politics and even to reduce the scope of collective bargaining.

*Human resources management design.*

The basis for internal labor market operations, where a series of strategic design choices (McGregor, 1991: 86) define the internal characteristics of civil service operating systems:

Job Design: Basic work system structure, such as specialist and generalist work designs, which establishes the packages of work civil servants are to perform. Virtually all civil service systems embrace a complex array of both generalist and specialist positions. At the apex of the higher civil service, many forms are evident. For example, British and German designs empha-size the importance of the generalist administrator and place the higher civil servant in a central controlling position in the policy process despite clear differences in background and training (Plowden, 1984; Mayntz, 1984). The French and U.S. designs are much more complex and contain strong traditions of both generalist and specialist employment (Gournay, 1984).

Recruitment: The basic strategy for establishing pools of available employees. Strategies include drawing upon either external or internal labor markets, and thus recruitment can be said to be open or closed to lateral entry, respec-tively. European systems, for instance, are notable for maintaining closed sys-tems where only entry-level access to career systems severely limits lateral mid-career access to administrative class ranks. The United States, by con-trast, carries the reputation for being an open system of recruitment that theo-retically permits lateral access to all civil service ranks, although in practice there is much less career mobility in the white collar General Schedule than might otherwise be thought (McGregor, 1974); moreover, within the broad definition of U.S. civil service employment there are, in fact, many bureaus and agencies that operate distinctly closed career systems.

Immediately related to the concept of recruitment system design is the issue of representativeness. Representativeness refers to a host of design vari-ables associated with the extent to which public bureaucracy is comprised of the populations served by government. In crudest terms, representativeness measures the congruence of general populations and civil service recruitment and selection as expressed by Gini coefficients and Lorenz curves (Meier, 1975b), indicating the cumulative shares held by civil servants compared to the shares held by the general population characterized by class, sex, ethnic, and racial makeup. Interestingly, a paradoxical conclusion emerges (Meier, 1975a; Aberbach, Putman, and Rockman, 1981; Krislov and Rosenbloom, 1981; Peters, 1989: 93–108): in the aggregate, civil service systems are very broadly representative of their respective general populations and may be becoming more so over time, yet higher civil servants can be distinctly unrep-resentative of the general public. In addition, there are enormous differences among countries (Smith, 1984), as seen in the juxtaposed attempts of the U.S. personnel administration to deal with equal employment opportunity doc-trine; the British preference for intellectual, but not necessarily social elites;

the French preference for social as well as intellectual elites; and the German and Dutch seeming egalitarianism in recruitment, selection, and management of administrative assignments.

What is debated, however, is whether representativeness is essential to civil service design (Krislov and Rosenbloom, 1981: 66–71). Theoretical claims run in two directions. One set of claims pertains to the effects of representativeness on bureaucratic action and involves a much disputed presumption (Krislov and Rosenbloom, 1981: chap. 2) that such representational factors as social eliteness skew the responsiveness and compassion of administrative policy and mediate the implementation of public policy.

A second set of claims has been lightly researched; it views representativeness as a dependent variable, with manipulation of bureaucratic recruitment serving direct policy ends by manipulating social structure and mobility. Thus, there are reports of civil service recruitment being used as an instrument of social policy (Wise and Jonzon, 1991), where the aim is to provide upward mobility opportunities for social groups in the interest of achieving greater equity. While the question of representativeness remains one of the most interesting and hotly debated issues of civil service design, very little empirical research is available to establish the effects of a greater or lesser degree of representativeness. The issue remains one of the great puzzles in civil service research.

Selection: Choosing from the recruitment pool a person who fits civil service needs forms the heart of selection system designs. Selection designs focus on the location and duration of employment, where either program-specific skills and abilities are sought or selection criteria are based on career employment, in which case specific skills and abilities are much less important than evidence of long-term potential for trainability. In addition, each design is, in turn, subject to a strategy of risk management in which selection criteria are based on the assumption that two types of errors can be made. In type 1 error (i.e., false positive) cases, some candidates offering impressive credentials will in fact be poor performers, for which the remedy will be well-developed systems of outplacement. In type 2 (i.e., false negative) cases, selection criteria are set to reject persons whose credentials incorrectly lead to the prediction of failure on the job. Clearly, elite civil service selection systems do not worry about committing type 2 errors but do seek to prevent the type 1 mistake. Less elitist selection systems are perfectly comfortable with a competitive sorting of personnel within the work system as a small price to pay for balancing type 1 and type 2 errors.

Job Evaluation: Job evaluation fixes the basic value of the compensation package and determines the process by which rank, pay, and benefits are vested in people. Several strategic choices are available. One choice vests rank, pay and benefits in positions. Another choice vests rank, pay and benefits in persons. In the rank-in-position case, occupancy, tenure, and duties are governed by the rules and entitlements that antedate any incumbent (in which case recruitment and selection procedures are designed to achieve a "fit" between person and position). In the rank-in-person case, control of access, tenure, and duties resides in the control of the service, *corps,* or cadre to which the official is admitted and holds rank. Thus, mobility in position-based systems is governed by a sequence of position changes, whereas mobility is greatly facilitated by changes in assignment that do not necessitate reclassification.

Career Management: Control of career mobility and the conditions under which training and development investments are made constitute the heart of career management. There are several patterns. One is characterized by a lack of career mobility, confining career management to single "career cones" in one operating bureau or agency; such a career structure is typical in the United States. An alternative is to have substantial career mobility that is relatively unmanaged and limited to the civil service, as appears to be the dominant case in Britain (Plowden, 1984: 34–38). Still a third pattern exists in France, where there are wide zones of career mobility covering nearly all of the state apparatus, political institutions, and private and public enterprise as well (Gournay, 1984: 76–79).

In addition, career management consists of training and development designs. Here, decisions are also highly varied. One of the design questions is whether to invest in substantial formal training and development, as is typical of continental Europe, or whether to use on-the-job apprenticeships to achieve full performance level as is the case in Britain. The issue of training and development, however, goes far beyond fixing the nature of human capital investment. Career management also consists of managing promotion patterns. Thus, a second great design choice revolves around whether elitist or nonelitist systems of career management are used. In elitist models, decisions are made early about future prospects, and training and development investments—including career mobility patterns—reflect early designation of those who have been tapped for higher level service and those who have not. Such models are particularly notable in the British and French cases, although selection criteria are not the same in the two systems. In nonelitist models, decisions about future prospects are deferred until late in an official's career, with prospects of formal training and development maintained throughout a career; Germany and the United States appear to be examples of nonelitist investment (Smith, 1984), although once again the case of the United States contains a vast diversity of designs among operating bureaus and agencies.

System Layering: Civil service systems can differ in the extent to which it makes sense to speak of a coherent, single service with many parts, or a "civil service" that is, in reality, made up of many services. The German and British designs appear to have adopted the former pattern, notwithstanding the many operational differences separating state or *laender*-dominated forms of federalism from the unitary state. The American and French cases clearly preserve civil service plurality by retaining many services, although the American dependence on bureau-based designs and the French use of *corps* represent contrasting methods of differentiation, where the former case focuses on final missions and products and the latter case emphasizes functions, such as engineering, finance, law, inspections, and so forth.

In addition to the layering of multiple systems, the holding of multiple jobs by civil servants is an important, but little investigated subject. The simultaneous occupancy of more than one job is a major coordinative mechanism. Among elected politicians, for example, the French pattern of *cumul des mandats* is worth noting. Here, nationally elected legislators or ministers also hold other offices, typically either the position of mayor or some other local authority (Sharpe, 1985: 366). In civil service circles, however, the prospects for multiple and sequential job holding suggest many possibilities, including moonlighting and multiple full-time responsibilities. Under the Hatch Acts of 1939 and 1940, partisan political activity by U.S. civil servants was proscribed, but the possibility of additional employment, including nonpartisan political employment, was not eliminated. Continental European civil servants, by contrast, can compete for elective public office without damage to civil service reentry, pay, seniority, and pension rights. Moreover, the prospects for holding multiple civil service offices, directorships, and positions in international, transnational, and nongovernmental organizations suggest many creative possibilities for civil service design not traditionally discussed.

## Civil Service as Governance

The concept of civil service goes far beyond issues of employment, however. "Civil service" also refers to a political institution that promotes joint action among the many actors and stakeholders whose efforts must be bent toward the goals of public policy. In essence, civil service is an institution of governance programmed by rules which are, by definition, reasonably stable over time and take on the character of roles, rules, norms, and expectations about civil service attitudes, behaviors, and functions in discharging state business. The connection between strategic institutional design and the operational exercise of bureaucratic authority has long been noted (Hyneman, 1950). In the United States, for example, a pattern of institutional political separation combined with the shared powers of checks and balances often results in the provisions of more bureaucratic guidance from legislators than from "chief executives." The result is a vast array of differences among public bureaucracies in the relationships between principals and agents, the extent of political fragmentation, dominant accountability patterns, and the role expectations of civil servants.

*Authority structures.*

Define the shape of governance and whether authority and power are designed to converge at a disciplined and unified center or whether control is fractured, thus producing multiple and even competing centers of civil service authority. Notable examples of the former include the unitary states of Britain and France, while a complex federalism such as that of the United States and what was formerly West Germany suggest elements of the latter. The structure of authority, however, is not necessarily dependent on the form of government, since there are examples of unitary states, such as the Netherlands, which in practice are operationally decentralized (Toonen, 1990) while other states have designed and created unifying order in circumstances that might appear to require decentralized control (Sharpe, 1985).

*Agentry.*

Definitions of principals and agents establishes the nature of the source of power and authority for which the civil servant acts as agent. Part of the complexity of defining this dimension involves the size and power of the shadow bureaucracy, including private ministerial cabinets, which can overshadow the "official" service. The basic issue, however, is the concept of agentry, which establishes the principal on behalf of which the civil servant is empowered to serve as agent. For example, civil servants may be regarded as agents of the state, as in the case of France and Germany, or as servants of the crown, as in the case of Britain, or as servants of the people, as in the United States. Clearly, the power of civil service varies with each case. For example, control of the civil service through "prerogative powers" of the crown in Britain necessarily dilutes formal parliamentary control (Plowden, 1984).

*Accountability mechanisms.*

Establish the rationale and the machinery by which civil service behavior can be reviewed and altered. Accountability issues arise most obviously when government attempts to enhance accountability to law in order to ensure social equity, worker health and safety, fair compensation, and ethical conduct. Among the most delicate accountability issues are those involving the question: How best can we inquire fairly and quickly into asserted official impropriety or insensitivity? (Gellhorn, 1966: 1). Further complexity arises when the attempt is made to achieve accountability by installing and maintaining micromanagement process controls and audits designed to control civil service behavior. Numerous mechanisms are available to civil service systems, including the following: constitutional arrangements (e.g., checks and balances); structural arrangements within the bureaucracy (e.g., inspectors general, quality assurance divisions, and management practices and systems such as responsibility systems, total quality management [TQM] programs and the like); structural arrangements outside bureaucracy but within government, for instance, the use of ombudsmans and parliamentary commissioners (Gellhorn, 1966); self-policing and reporting through the use of whistle-blowing mechanisms and status reviews.

*Policy role.*

Finally, the policy role of civil servants in the larger polity (Aberbach, Putnam, and Rockman, 1981: 239; Williams, 1988; Campbell and Naulls, 1992: 70–72) defines the role expectations of civil servants. Particular dimensions pertain to the nonoperational functions performed by civil servants and whether, for instance, they are involved in public policy-making either in policy formulation or policy implementation and whether they play an overtly political role associated with the brokering of interests and the articulation of visions and ideals in the various media through which public opinion is influenced. Once again, the perturbations and combinations are enormous, ranging from systems where civil servants nurture secrecy and back-office involvement in policy formulation and implementation, to systems where civil servants are much more visible even to the point of public advocacy in the mass media.

## Civil Service as Symbol System

Finally, civil service systems embody public values, representing the fundamental ethical codes—the goals, aspirations, and criteria—by which civil service activity can be judged. Ethical codes are established by the constitutional foundation of a society and embodied in the "myths and symbols" surrounding the civil service institution. The symbolic dimension of civil service cannot be overemphasized, for it defines the values that dominate when especially difficult decisions must be made. In the most grand formulations, civil service ethics represent what is best about the society and its manner of conducting public business. But even in minimalist interpretations, according to Rose and Peters (1978: 234), the control of large-scale administration required by the modern democratic state rests upon "the internalized sense of their proper role on the part of civil servants." Thus, while the sense of "civic responsibility, duty, or even honor may vary across cultures. . . . the basic ideas of responsiveness to demands, responsibility to political leaders, and accountability for actions are found in virtually all systems." Rose and Peters continue: ". . . most civil servants appear to accept these values and generally try to put them into operation. If it were not for this widespread acceptance of those values, all the institutional mechanisms of control we have outlined would be buried in the sheer volume of maladministration" (Rose and Peters, ibid.).

Public service ethical codes exist both within and without civil service. Internally, civil service as symbol system consists of the service ethic by which the institutional attitudes, roles, and behaviors of civil servants can be defined and judged in the following areas: anonymity vs. visibility; ministerial or departmental responsibility; sense of calling; and feelings of isolation from private sector institutions.

Externally, the idea of civil service embodies the values attached to being French, Dutch, American, British, German, Chinese, and so forth. Thus, the concept of civil service is embedded in constitutional understandings and institutional arrangements, and in the expectations of civil servants symbolically defined in the public mind. Some of the external symbolic dimensions include the following: civil service humility vis-à-vis citizens; sense of service to citizens; public confidence in civil servants (Lipset and Schneider, 1987); partisanship vs. neutrality; civil service prestige; visibility of personal finances and aspects of one's personal life; and public-private "revolving door" prohibitions and conflicts of interest (Kelman, 1993). The last two variables—visibility and conflict of interest—are of particular interest in an era during which transactions between public and private sectors are increasingly complex, effective public management may require increased mobility, and interaction between the two sectors becomes an operational requirement of modern government (Kelman, 1993). Comparative analysis of a limited stock of comparative survey questions regarding conflicts of interest, public-private interaction, resource requirements, and disclosure of personal finances can reveal interesting patterns.[1]

## CIVIL SERVICE SYSTEMS AS INSTITUTIONAL CONFIGURATION

Operating civil service systems are created by a packaging of internally consistent employment, governance, and symbolic variables. The package might be loosely thought of as a "configuration," although the rules of civil service configuration are less well understood than the rules of organizational design (Mintzberg, 1983: 122). However, a number of classic configurations can be found. For example, among employment variables there is a logical association between specialist job designs, open recruitment systems, and program-based staffing systems. Not surprisingly, these choices are accompanied by rank-in-job compensation systems and nonelitist training and development designs. The pattern is consistent with functionally specialized, position-based, hierarchically arranged, industrial bureaucracies of the sort that mushroomed in the United States during the second half of the nineteenth and the first half of the twentieth centuries. A contrasting configuration consists of generalist job designs, closed recruitment, and career-based staffing arrangements more commonly found in Europe. Moreover, there are many combinations of design parameters that affect job design, recruitment, selection criteria, job evaluation, compensation, career management, and staffing structure. Thus, civil service systems are vastly more flexible instruments than conventional discussions of public bureaucracy would imply.

Finally, the heart of a civil service system can include the possibility that the "system" will be comprised of many configurations whose design parameters can vary, a typical pattern found in the United States and France, for example. The variables summarized in table 3.1 strongly suggest the difficulty, if not the impossibility of attempting to design, install, and manage a "one size fits all" set of personnel management principles. Recent calls for flexibility, decentralization, and deregulation of public personnel management operations are compatible with a recognition that different missions, resource constraints, and performance demands require different human resource management configurations (see Dilulio, Garvey, and Kettl, 1993: chap. 7; U.S. Office of Personnel Management, 1993). Thus, decentralized competitive experimentation with civil service configurations subject to overall governing principles is a distinct possibility.

Civil service configurations are not solely dependent on manipulations of employment variables. Parameters relating to governance and symbolic value must be taken into account as well. For example, in highly fragmented systems of governance—such as that found in the United States—where the public sector development was preceded by private institutional development, it is not surprising to find a great multiplicity of personnel systems, rather than a single coordinated "system," and a commingling of internal and external labor markets for which the revolving door spins at various speeds and at various times as public policy requires. In such systems, sheer complexity makes across-the-board generalization about the ethics of service, visibility, and eliteness very difficult, if not impossible (Wilson, 1989).

In other countries, where unitary states, disciplined parties, and common recruitment bases establish a common ethic of service, it is not surprising to find a corporate sense of civil service coexisting with, for example, highly disciplined notions of partisan political neutrality and corporate eliteness that reinforce a unitary system of governance and a closed order of civil service mandarins (Dogan, 1975). In still other cases, where "the state" looms as a significant formal presence, the civil servant as agent of the state acquires a magnified role compared to counterparts in the United States and the United Kingdom. Thus, configuration logic leads one to expect that civil servants will be politically visible, intrusive in the policy process, and will confront career prospects in which mobility among positions in civil service, partisan politics, and private business is not at all uncommon. Continental European systems, for example, stand in stark contrast to American and British systems, in part, perhaps, because of the differential development patterns in the public and private sectors, continental governments having developed before institutions of private enterprise. Thus, it is not surprising to find civil "servants" acting as political principals with a vigor and visibility thought highly unusual in systems that have carefully subordinated their "servants" through layers of governance that severely limit administrative discretion, whether in myth only or in practice.

## SYSTEM AS STRATEGIC CONGRUENCE

The packaging of design configurations finds its origin, however, not in the crafting of personnel policy, but in the designs and purposes civil servants are supposed to serve. In the end, after all, civil servants are merely agents and not principals. A reexamination of the principles of operational design is clearly under way around the world (Smith, 1984; Argyriades, 1991; Caiden, 1991; Levine and Kleeman, 1992). Countries as diverse as Australia, Brazil, Canada, China, France, Japan, the Netherlands, the United Kingdom, and the United States have, over the past two decades, placed civil service reform at the center of the administrative agenda (Caiden, 1991: 368). Virtually all civil service systems are confronted by pressures to turn away from internal to external labor markets, to streamline and simplify public bureaucracy, to reorganize the machinery of government, and to promote greater efficiency and effective management practice (Caiden, 1991; Argyriades, 1991; Savas, 1992).

Moreover, much of the analysis that has been done suggests a fundamental redesign of civil service systems that goes far beyond the idea of civil service "configuration." The most recent round of discussion stems from the sense that civil service systems around the world are approaching a watershed, as documented in such diverse characterizations of civil service change as: the post–civil service era (Ukeles, 1982: chap. 2); undergoing perestroika (Osborne and Gaebler, 1992); a postbureaucratic era (Caiden, 1991; Argyriades, 1991); the era of postmodern executives (Rose, 1991); the post–industrial era (Drucker, 1968); or taking "Next Steps" toward a progressive management model (Morley, 1993). Collectively, such diverse pronouncements arise from a fundamental conclusion that the bureaucratic systems designed for an earlier age do not match the performance requirements of the current and emerging age.

Directly implied is the existence of a problem of *congruence* rather than one of configuration. Problems of congruence occur in cases where the external situational circumstances of civil service systems do not match configuration design parameters (Mintzberg, 1983: 122). Evidence that civil service congruence problems do exist is found in mounting pressures to change the structure of public service delivery (Caiden, 1991), debureaucratize government (Argyriades, 1991), shift the structure of problem-solving and resource allocation (Sharpe, 1985), experiment with new personnel policies and procedures (Levine and Kleeman, 1992), and increase levels of entrepreneurship (Mascarenhas, 1993; Cho and Kim, 1993).

One of the great puzzles concerns the often invidious comparisons between public and private sector enterprise: on the private side, the imperative to adopt globally competitive, postindustrial forms of organization has led to large-scale corporate restructuring that includes vast reductions in overhead staff activity (Campbell, 1992: 370). A reasonable comparative expectation might be that public management institutions in western Europe, British Commonwealth countries, the United States, and many developing nations would respond to similar pressure to restructure and, in effect, to reduce their overhead staff bureaucracies. Simultaneously, eastern European countries would need to resolve, at least temporarily, the acute understaffing of their central government bureaucracies (Rice, 1992: 120–21). Certainly, some of the bureaucrat-bashing that has gone on in the United States and United Kingdom (Smith, 1984) can, in hindsight, be seen as an expression of a popular opinion that the government business appears not to have become subject to the same discipline as private business. In reality, however, the issue is much more complex. For example, it does not automatically follow that public organizations can achieve the staff economies of private enterprise inasmuch as the production of democracy itself requires the oversight of civil servants by institutions empowered to control, inspect, allocate resources, and review the performance of agents of democratic government (Diamant, 1962; Campbell, 1992: 370).

Bureaucratic representativeness will also be a continuing strategic issue for comparative civil service research. If one takes the essence of representativeness to be associated with the extent to which civil service systems represent the populations, regions, and interests contained within a community, it becomes difficult to envision effective problem-solving on complex economic and social matters in the absence of representativeness. Effective schools, policing, housing policy, health services, economic development, and so forth, appear to be alike in the sense that solutions require the application of intelligence, resources, and programmatic effort to *local* circumstances. Success would appear to derive from the ownership, empowerment, and involvement of the particular clients, producers, and decision-makers most directly affected by particular problems and their solutions (Osborne and Gaebler, 1992). Representativeness in bureaucracy would, by inference, be a requirement of success, while lack of representativeness would appear to ensure failure.

The new demand for performance, cost control, and public accountability promises to have enormous impact on civil service systems (Mascarenhas, 1993). Indeed, it is likely that future designs will have more to do with institutional reactions to external pressures—strategic demands for faster, smarter, targeted service at less cost—than with internal reforms driven by purely operational issues. The comparative catalogue of administrative reform proposals appears to be substantial and growing (Caiden and Siedentopf, 1982; Caiden, 1991; Morley, 1993; see also part 5 of this volume). In addition, enormous pressures are exerted on centralized national systems of administration as regional and local claims on public policy and management contain elements of diverse cultures, economic and ethnic interests, and social needs. The pressure to accommodate diversity within the framework of a single constitutional arrangement will test the ingenuity of civil servants. For example, the decline of national security disciplines that supported the garrison states required to prosecute hot and cold wars among nations have the effect of relaxing the grip of national civil servants on the national public life in favor of local and regional problem-solving. This finding is consistent with the observations of Joachim Jens Hesse (1991) about the confusion to be found in eastern Europe in the aftermath of the cold war. A companion comment might note, however, the inevitability of confusion due to the substantive nature of dominant problems; compared to external national security threats, economic development discussions involve intense and complicated interactions between governmental center and periphery in an attempt to match highly diverse, localized needs and information with the resources generated by a large resource base available to a whole community. Predictably, the flow of financial resources appears to be moving away from direct control by national agents and increasingly toward state and local government control (Sharpe, 1985: 363).

One implication is that the growth and decline of civil service systems parallels financial allocation patterns; it is an anomaly where it does not. Thus, systems that are cash rich and people poor (or vice versa) become analytically interesting. Assessment of the data cited in the appendix should provide important clues about the growth and decline of civil service systems over time, for there are competing experiments now under way around the world, each one of them motivated by attempts to discover the best way to align the twin problems of congruence and configuration. Design configurations will be constrained by whether or not civil service systems are growing or contracting components of the national labor force. Thus, the size and composition of the civil service workforce will mediate the boundary between configuration and congruence.

We end where the discussion began—with a data paradox. The paradox is that the times are right for conducting comparative research about civil service systems. There is extensive experimentation with civil service change and transformation. The public management atmosphere is now charged with excitement, discussion of reform prospects, and experimental innovation. Under such conditions, the need for comparative research is obvious. Yet a question remains about precisely how to augment the comparative civil service database. The most likely answer is that data sets will be partial and based on occasional collections arising from available opportunity. Thus, surveys, ecological data, operational program information, anecdotes, and institutional description and history are likely to be required to piece the mosaic together. Furthermore, civil service analysis will require a blending of operational analysis, as presented here in the discussion of configuration, with strategic assessment, as suggested in the discussion of congruence. The challenge posed by the comparative research agenda is great, but so is the potential for generating truly comparative data and empirically supported findings.

## NOTES

1. A modest amount of survey data is available for the United States' federal civil service in the "Federal Employee Attitudes Survey: 1979–1980," conducted by the U.S. Office of Personnel Management (Ann Arbor: University of Michigan, Inter-University Consortium for Political and Social Research publication #7804). Likert-scale questions solicited responses to the following questions (ICPSR, 1982, pp. 3–20):

5. How many years of full-time employment have you had in the private sector?
19. In your entire federal career, how many times have you moved geographically (outside commuting area)?
36. The employees in my organization work harder than comparable employees in private sector companies.
159. Due to the current salary ceiling, I am considering leaving federal employment.
160. There are sufficient incentives to retain highly competent executives in my organization.
220. The "revolving door" prohibitions of the Ethics in Government Act are a reasonable approach to preventing postemployment conflict of interest.
225. The federal government should not require its executive employees to discuss their personal finances.

Additional questions are provided in the 1991 U.S. Office of Personnel Management survey of federal employee attitudes (1992). Questions are related but not directly comparable to the 1979/80 survey. The 1991 survey concentrates on performance issues associated with job satisfaction, productivity barriers, customer service, career progression barriers, preferred performance rewards, training, work schedule, and dependent care responsibilities.

Limited cross-national comparison can be drawn from the Calvin G. Mackenzie and Paul Light survey of "political appointees" for the period November 1964, through December 1984; data are made available through the Inter-University Consortium for Political and Social Research (Ann Arbor: University of Michigan, ICPSR publication #8458). In addition, some comparative analysis has been done of the motivations, orientations, and attitudes of the central "agents" in Canada, the United Kingdom, and the United States during the period 1976 to 1987 (Campbell and Naulls, 1992).

## APPENDIX

### CIVIL SERVICE DATA SOURCES

The most fundamental questions about civil service appear in the most deceptively simple form: How many civil servants of what type are there? Clarification requires precise answers to many questions. For example, do we mean permanent or temporary employment? Full-time or part-time workers? Contractual or direct government payroll? If government payroll, then which payroll? Merit systems appointments only, or all employment systems and pay plans? The list of employment-related questions is a long one.

Moreover, to the extent that civil service refers to government employment, then a series of governance issues arises. For example, is employment restricted to employment attached directly to general purpose units of government? Should civil service include government instrumentalities such as public corporations, independent authorities, and government-sponsored enterprises? Should one distinguish between employment in national government versus the employment found in constituent states, provinces, republics, laender, regions, and municipalities that make up the composite civil service?

Finally, there are questions about civil service productivity and function that can only be answered when the relationship of human resources to other resources, particularly money, is established. Thus, it is only when civil service employment data are attached to data about cost and function that significant research questions can be answered. Such data have only been gathered in the most basic manner (Rose, 1984; 1985) and even then only for a few countries and limited time periods. Furthermore, answers to the questions posed above require detailed comparative data that do not presently exist.

What is available, however, are some very basic aggregate data about the cross-national size and structure of the public and civil services of several nations. While aggregate data do not and cannot reveal the details of civil service operation implied by the questions noted above, they do frame the puzzles and questions to be put to future research. What must be remembered, however, is that gathering even simple data for a single year is not a trivial exercise; gathering comparable data over a substantial time span proves even more difficult, as the source documentation provided below indicates. In addition, no two nations define civil service and public service in exactly the same way. The use of labor markets differs. The definition of the core executive function varies both among nations and over time. The instrumental uses that public policy makes of public service vary. In short, no two nations design public administration systems in exactly the same way.

Examination of the most basic data about civil service operations can yield both insight and guidance for the development of future research. Sources of basic data about government employment for eighteen countries are presented for three time periods: 1968, 1976, and 1988 (variances from these dates are noted, where appropriate). The countries include: Australia, Canada, Finland, Japan, New Zealand, Norway, Sweden, Switzerland, and the United States; and European Community members Belgium, Denmark, France, Ireland, Italy, Luxembourg, the Netherlands, the United Kingdom, and the former West Germany.

Australia: Commonwealth Bureau of Census and Statistics, *Official Yearbook of the Commonwealth of Australia*, 1968–70 and 1976–1979, Canberra; *Overseas Telecommunications,* Annual Report for Year Ending 31 March 1976, Commonwealth Scientific and Industrial Research Organization; *Annual Report,* 1975–1976, Australian Broadcasting Commission; *Annual Report,* 1976–1977, Australian Postal Commission.

Canada: Bureau of Statistics, *Canada Yearbook,* 1969–1970, 1976–1978, and 1990 (Ottawa: Queen's Printer); J. E. Hodgetts and O. P. Dwivedi, *A Survey of Public Personnel Administration in Canada's Provinces* (Montreal: Institute of Public Administration of Canada, McGill-Queens University Press, 1974); Bureau of Statistics, Statistics Canada, *Federal Government Employment* (cat. #72-004), *Advance Statistics of Education* (cat. #81-220), *Provincial Government Employment* (cat. #72-007), *Local Government Employment* (cat. #72-009), *Compendium of Selected Health Manpower Statistics* (cat. #83-31).

Finland: Statistikcentrolen, *Statistisk Arbok for Finland,* 1970, 1978–1979, and 1987–1988, Helsinki.

Japan: Bureau of Statistics, *Japan Statistical Yearbook,* 1968–1970 and 1976–1978 (Tokyo: Office of the Prime Minister); see also *Statistical Handbook of Japan,* 1969, 1977, and 1990 (Tokyo: Office of the Prime Minister).

New Zealand: Department of Statistics, *The New Zealand Official Yearbook,* 1970 and 1978, Wellington.

Norway: Statistical Sentralbyra, *Statistisk Arbok,* 1969–1972, 1976–1979, and 1987–1990, Oslo.

Sweden: Statistiska Centralbyraan, *Statistisk Aarsbok,* 1969–1972, 1976–1979, and 1990, Stockholm.

Switzerland: No Data.

United States: Bureau of the Census, *Statistical Abstract of the United States,* 1969, 1977–1978, and 1990, Washington, DC.

European Community members:

1. Belgium: *Annuaire Statistique de la Belgique,* 1969–1970, 1978–1979, and 1989 (Brussels: Institute National de Statistique); Robert Senelle, "The Political, Economic, and Social Structure of Belgium," *Memo from Belgium,* nos. 122, 123, 124 (March, April, May, 1970).
2. Denmark: Denmarks Statistisk, *Statistisk Arbog,* 1969–1970, 1976–1980, and 1989, Copenhagen.
3. France: Institute National de la Statistique et des Etudes Economique, *Annuaire Statistique de la France,* 1964–1970, 1976–1980, and 1989–1990 (Paris: Director Général, Correspondence, 1980).
4. Greece: No data.
5. Ireland: Central Statistical Office, *Statistical Abstract of Ireland,* 1969–1970, Dublin; Central Statistical Office, *Correspondence* (Dublin: Office of Ireland, June 1980).
6. Italy: Instituto Centrale de Statistica, *Annuario Statistico Italiano,* 1968–1970, 1970–1979, and 1990 (Roma: Ministero del Tesoro, Dipendenti, Delle Amministrazioni Stateli, AL 1 GENNAIO, 1979).
7. Luxembourg: Institute National de la Statistique et des Etudes Economique, *Annuaire Statistique de Luxembourg,* 1969–1972, 1976–1979, and 1988/1989, Grande-Duché de Luxembourg.
8. Netherlands: Central Bureau voor de Statistiek, *Statistical Yearbook of the Netherlands,* 1968–1972, 1976–1980, and 1988, The Hague.
9. Portugal: No data.
10. Spain: No data.
11. United Kingdom: Central Statistical Office, *Annual Abstracts of Statistics,* 1968–1972, 1976–1979, and 1991 (London: Her Majesty's Stationery Office).
12. West Germany (Federal Republic of Germany): Statistisches Bundesamt, *Statistische Jahrbuch für die Bundesrepublik Deutschland,* 1968–1969,

1977–1978, and 1989–1990 (Stuttgart: Verlag W. Kohlhammer).
(NOTE: The above data were compiled before Austria, Finland, and Sweden joined the European Union on January 1, 1995.)

## REFERENCES

Aberbach, Joel D., and Bert A. Rockman. 1987. "Comparative Administration: Methods, Muddles, and Models." *Administration and Society* 18, no. 4 (February): 473–506.

Aberbach, J. D., R. D. Putnam, and B. A. Rockman. 1981. *Bureaucrats and Politicians in Western Democracies.* Cambridge: Harvard University Press.

Argyriades, Demetrios, 1991. "Bureaucracy and Debureaucratization." Pages 567–85 in Ali Farazmand, ed., *Handbook of Comparative and Development Public Administration.* New York: Marcel Dekker.

Bekke, Hans, A. G. M. 1987. "Public Management in Transition." Pages 17–32 in Jan Kooiman and Kjell A. Eliassen, eds., *Managing Public Organizations: Lessons from Contemporary European Experience.* London: Sage.

Caiden, Gerald E. 1991. "Administrative Reform." Pages 367–80 in Ali Farazmand, ed., *Handbook of Comparative and Development Public Administration.* New York: Marcel Dekker.

Caiden, Gerald E., and Heinrich Siedentopf, eds. 1982. *Strategies for Administrative Reform.* Lexington, MA: D. C. Heath & Company.

Campbell, Alan K. 1992. "Revisiting Metropolitanism and Fiscal Disparities." *Journal of Policy Analysis and Management* 11, no. 3: 363–72.

Campbell, Colin, S.J., and Donald Naulls. 1992. "The Consequences of a Minimalist Paradigm for Governance: A Comparative Analysis." Pages 66–93 in Patricia W. Ingraham and Donald F. Kettl, eds., *Agenda for Excellence*: *Public Service in America.* Chatham, NJ: Chatham House.

Cho, Yong Hyo, and Joung Sup Kim. 1993. "The Cultural Roots of Entrepreneurial Bureaucracy: The Case of Korea." *Public Administration Quarterly* 16, no. 4 (Winter): 509–24.

Diamant, Alfred, 1962. "The Bureaucratic Model: Max Weber Rejected, Rediscovered, Reformed." In Ferrel Heady and Sybil L. Stokes, eds., *Papers in Comparative Public Administration.* Ann Arbor: Institute of Public Administration, University of Michigan.

Dilulio, John J., Jr., Gerald Garvey, and Donald F. Kettl. 1993. *Improving Government Performance: An Owner's Manual.* Washington, DC: Brookings Institution.

Doeringer, Peter B., and Michael J. Piore, 1971. *Internal Labor Markets and Manpower Analysis.* Lexington, MA: Lexington Books.

Dogan, Mattei, ed. 1975. *The Mandarins of Western Europe: The Political Role of Top Civil Servants.* New York: John Wiley & Sons.

Drucker, Peter F. 1968. *The Age of Discontinuity.* New York: Harper and Row.

Gellhorn, Walter. 1966. *Ombudsmen and Others: Citizens' Protectors in Nine Countries.* Cambridge: Harvard University Press.

Gournay, Bernard. 1984. "The Higher Civil Service of France." Pages 69–86 in Bruce L. R. Smith, ed., *The Higher Civil Service in Europe and Canada: Lessons for the United States.* Washington, DC: Brookings Institution.

Heady, Ferrel. 1984. *Public Administration: A Comparative Perspective*, 3rd ed. New York: Marcel Dekker.

Hesse, Joachim Jens. 1991. "Administrative Modernization in Central and Eastern European Countries." Discussion Paper no. 1, Nuffield College, Oxford University, February.

Hyneman, Charles. 1950. *Bureaucracy in a Democracy.* New York: Harper and Brothers.

Kaufman, Herbert. 1985. *Time, Chance, and Organizations: Natural Selection in a Perilous Environment.* Chatham, NJ: Chatham House.

Kelman, Steven. 1993. "What is Wrong with the Revolving Door?" Pages 224–51 in Barry Bozeman, ed., *Public Management: The State of the Art.* San Francisco: Jossey-Bass.

Koh, B. C. 1985. "The Recruitment of Higher Civil Servants in Japan: A Comparative Perspective." *Asian Survey* 25 (March): 292–309.

Kooiman, Jan, and Kjell A. Eliassen, eds. 1987. Preface in *Managing Public Organizations: Lessons from Contemporary European Experience.* London: Sage.

Krislov, Samuel, and David H. Rosenbloom. 1981. *Representative Bureaucracy and the American Political System.* New York: Praeger.

Levine, Charles H., and Rosslyn S. Kleeman. 1992. "The Quiet Crisis in the American Public Service." Pages 208–73 in Patricia W. Ingraham and Donald F. Kettl, eds., *Agenda for Excellence: Public Service in America.* Chatham, NJ: Chatham House.

Lipset, Seymour Martin, and William Schneider. 1987. *The Confidence Gap: Business, Labor, and Government in the Public Mind.* Rev. ed. Baltimore: Johns Hopkins University Press.

Mascarenhas, R. C. 1993. "Building an Enterprise Culture in the Public Sector in Australia, Britain, and New Zealand." *Public Administration Review* 53, no. 4: 319–28.

Mayntz, Renate. 1984. "The Higher Civil Service of the Federal Republic of Germany." Pages 55–68 in Bruce L. R. Smith, ed., *The Higher Civil Service in Europe and Canada: Lessons for the United States.* Washington, DC: Brookings Institution.

McGregor, Eugene B., Jr., 1974. "Politics and the Career Mobility of Bureaucrats." *American Political Science Review* 68, no. 1 (March): 18–26.

———. 1991. *Strategic Management of Human Knowledge, Skills, and Abilities.* San Francisco: Jossey-Bass.

Meier, Kenneth J. 1975a. *Representative Bureaucracy and Administrative Responsiveness: An Empirical and Theoretical Analysis.* Syracuse Ph.D. diss., Syracuse University.

———. 1975b. "Representative Bureaucracy: An Empirical Analysis." *American Political Science Review* 69 (June): 526–42.

Metcalfe, Les, and Sue Richards. 1987. "Evolving Public Management Cultures." In Jan Kooiman and Kjell A. Eliassen, eds., *Managing Public Organizations: Lessons from Contemporary European Experience.* London: Sage.

Mintzberg, Henry. 1983. *Structure in Fives: Designing Effective Organizations.* Englewood Cliffs, NJ: Prentice Hall.

Morgan, E. Philip, and James L. Perry. 1988. "Re-orienting the Comparative Study of Civil Service Systems." *Review of Public Personnel Administration* 8, no. 3 (Summer): 84–95.

Morley, Don. 1993. "Strategic Direction in the British Public Service." *Long Range Planning* 26, no. 3: 77–86.

Mosher, Frederick C. 1968. *Democracy and the Public Service.* New York: Oxford University Press.

Osborne, David, and Ted Gaebler. 1992. *Reinventing Government: How the Entrepreneurial Spirit Is Transforming the Public Sector.* Reading, MA: Addison-Wesley.

Peters, B. Guy. 1989. *The Politics of Bureaucracy: A Comparative Perspective.* 3rd ed. London: Longman.

Plowden, William. 1984. "The Higher Civil Service in Britain." Pages 20–39 in Bruce L. R. Smith, ed., *The Higher Civil Service in Europe and Canada: Lessons for the United States.* Washington, DC: Brookings Institution.

Pratt, John W., and Richard J. Zeckhauser, eds. 1985. *Principals and Agents: The Structure of Business.* Boston: Harvard Business School Press.

Rice, Eric M. 1992. "Public Administration in Post-Socialist Eastern Europe." *Public Administration Review* 52, no. 2 (March/April): 116–24.

Riggs, Fred W. 1980. "Three Dubious Hypotheses: A Comment on Heper, Kim, and Pai." *Administration and Society* 12 (November): 301–26.

Rose, Richard. 1984. *Understanding Big Government: The Programme Approach.* Beverly Hills: Sage.

———. 1985. *Public Employment in Western Nations.* Cambridge: Cambridge University Press.

———. 1991. *The Postmodern President: George Bush Meets the World.* 2nd ed. Chatham, NJ: Chatham House.

Rose, Richard, and B. Guy Peters. 1978. *Can Government Go Bankrupt?* New York: Basic Books.

Ross, Stephen A. 1973. "The Economic Theory of Agency: The Principal's Problem." *American Economic Review* 63: 134–39.

Sabatier, Paul, and Daniel Mazmanian. 1979. "The Conditions of Effective Implementation." *Policy Analysis* 5 (Fall): 481–504.

Savas, E. S. 1987. *Privatization: The Key to Better Government.* Chatham, NJ: Chatham House.

———. 1992. "Privatization in Post-Socialist Countries." *Public Administration Review* 52, no. 6 (November/December): 573–81.

Sayre, Wallace S. 1964. "Bureaucracies: Some Contrasts in Systems." *The Indian Journal of Public Administration* 10 (April/June): 219–29.

Sharpe, L. J. 1985. "Central Coordination and the Policy Network." *Political Studies* 33, no. 3: 361–81.

Smith, Bruce L. R., ed. 1984. *The Higher Civil Service in Europe and Canada: Lessons for the United States.* Washington, DC: Brookings Institution.

Suleiman, Ezra N. 1974. *Politics, Power, and Bureaucracy in France: The Administrative Elite.* Princeton: Princeton University Press.

Toonen, Theo A. J. 1990. "The Unitary State as a System of Co-Governance: The Case of the Netherlands." *Public Administration* 68, no. 3 (Fall): 281–96.

Ukeles, Jacob B. 1982. *Doing More with Less: Turning Public Management Around.* New York: AMACOM.

U.S. Office of Personnel Management. 1982. *Federal Employee Attitudes Survey,*

*1979–1980* (ICPSR # 7804). Ann Arbor: University of Michigan, Inter-University Consortium for Political and Social Research.

———. 1992. *Personnel Research Highlights: Special Report on Survey of Federal Employees.* May. Washington, DC: Personnel Systems and Oversight Group, Office of Systems Innovation and Simplification.

———. 1993. *Partners for Change.* Conference Wrap-up Report. June 2–3. Washington, DC: Office of Systems Innovation and Simplification.

The Volcker Commission. 1989. *Leadership for America: Rebuilding the Public Service.* The Report of the National Commission on the Public Service (Paul A. Volcker, Chairman). Washington, DC.

Williams, Walter, 1988. *Washington, Westminster, and Whitehall.* Cambridge: Cambridge University Press.

Wilson, James Q. 1989. *Bureaucracy: What Government Agencies Do and Why They Do It.* New York: Basic Books.

Wise, Lois R., and Bjorn Jonzon. 1991. "The Swedish Civil Service: An Instrument for Achieving Social Equality." Pages 625–37 in Ali Farazmand, ed., *Handbook of Comparative and Development Public Administration.* New York: Marcel Dekker.

# PART TWO
# HISTORY & STRUCTURE

What we identify today as civil service systems did not come into being overnight. These systems evolved gradually, in many countries, over periods of hundreds of years. Indeed, civil service systems originated within western—more specifically, European—governments and date back as far as the Middle Ages when the first government departments were created. Modern civil service systems came into being in the second half of the eighteenth century. What changes took place in the transition from traditional to modern civil service systems? Is it possible to identify stages in the development of civil services? What are the historical dynamics that account for the growth, change, structure, and character of civil service systems over time?

In "The Evolution of Civil Service Systems," Jos C. N. Raadschelders and Mark R. Rutgers provide interesting answers to these questions. They trace the history of civil service systems from the time civil servants were personal servants to the monarch to their present status in professionalized service systems. Several processes were central to the long-term institutionalization of civil service. Among them were processes of nation-state development, in which the distinction between public and private became important, processes of building a distinct social group of civil servants in society, processes of building a professionalized economic group, and processes of extension of governmental tasks.

The sweep of Raadschelders and Rutgers's historical overview is complemented by Lois Recascino Wise's microlevel analysis in "Internal Labor Markets." She develops a theoretical framework for understanding the relationships among the rules for human resource management in civil service systems, the efficiency of government operations, and the organizational outcomes for incumbent and potential employees. She conceptualizes civil service systems as labor markets in which behavior and outcomes are constrained by internal rules. Using the internal labor market approach, she develops a framework for comparative analysis.

Just as civil service systems can be described as internal labor markets reflecting rules and practices associated with classification, deployment, job security, and wage structures, so too can they be described in terms of external markets. Given the social functions of civil service systems, however, the external market that is important is not economic, but rather demographic and ideological. Frits M. van der Meer and Renk L. J. Roborgh argue in "Civil Servants and Representativeness" that representativeness is an important construct for understanding and comparing civil service systems. They focus on the "forms" representativeness takes in different political and administrative systems and the explanatory variables that determine the forms. They discuss three different ways of looking at representativeness. First, they distinguish between passive and active forms of representation. A second subdivision pertains to demographic, idea or opinion, and interest representation. Finally, they distinguish between equal opportunity and mirror image representativeness.

Representativeness must be viewed against the background of basic ideas concerning the raison d'être of the state and, more specifically, the changing relationship between the people and the state. Comparative research on representativeness is rendered meaningful by its focus on the importance representativeness acquires in a certain political, governmental, and social environment. Thus, van der Meer and Roborgh contend that the starting point for comparative research should be the "environment" of representativeness. In what cultural, social, and political setting does the phenomenon of representativeness exist? This strategy of inquiry permits the investigator to identify both the descriptive and normative significance of representativeness in a particular setting.

# 4 THE EVOLUTION OF CIVIL SERVICE SYSTEMS

Jos C. N. Raadschelders and Mark R. Rutgers

Throughout the world government has become increasingly important for the provision and production of public services. Ample research is available testifying to the fact that government involvement in society in terms of public preparation and execution of communal tasks has grown in this century in particular. The extent to which government is involved in society may vary from country to country, but growth is nevertheless a world-wide phenomenon. An increasing number of tasks has to be performed by a sharply increasing number of public servants.

For a long time preparation and planning for policy was under the supervision of a relatively small group of (higher) functionaries. In the second half of this century the growth rate of their numbers was larger than that of public personnel in toto. This indicates a shift from execution to the planning and preparation of tasks. It is especially this class of higher public functionaries, referred to as "civil servants," that grew rapidly. Nowadays they find themselves subject to criticism as part of a more general criticism of the size of government. One may wonder how and why the civil service developed in this way and if, in light of its history, all recent criticism is reasonable.

With a view to the increase of personnel size in the twentieth century, it is sometimes suggested that civil service systems are a recent phenomenon: they come into being upon the wings of increased government involvement. There may have been some "important" prior developments, but the birth of modern civil service is usually placed between 1880 and 1930. This, however, overemphasizes recent trends and disregards the importance of understanding the present situation in terms of historical needs, demands, and developments in general.

In this chapter we will try to outline an answer to questions concerning the origins of the civil service and its development over time, emphasizing developments up to the early twentieth century. Which political, societal, organizational, and intellectual conditions gave rise to civil service systems? Are there certain constituent principles? Special attention will be given to contemporary criticism of civil service systems. We will attempt to provide an outline, limited though it may be, as a basis for orientation and further research.

Civil service can be regarded as an institution and as such as a more or less coherent and enduring whole made up of norms and values that have developed and persisted over time. To give a rough indication of these organizational norms and values, we can regard "civil service" as referring to a government or state body in which full-time, salaried, and systematically recruited functionaries work within a system of clear hierarchical relations, under uniform rules, and with adequate provision for pension benefits (Parris, 1969: 22). Next to Parris's internally oriented definition we can set the externally oriented definition of Perry and Morgan (see chap. 1), which sees the civil service as mediating institutions that mobilize human resources in the service of the state in a given territory. However, alternative interpretations of civil service are also available. Walker, for instance, regards almost every government employee as part of the civil service and focuses on what he calls "the deskworker" (Walker, 1961: 14). There are numerous other definitions (see, e.g., Debbasch, 1989: 486; Dimock and Dimock, 1983: 313; Gladden, 1966: 96; Henry, 1989: 230; Simon, Smithburg, and Thompson, 1970: 326; Starling, 1986: 446; Thieme, 1984: 140–47).

We will focus our attention on the development of the civil service at the central government level, since developments either originate at this level or are most prominent here. This does not imply that the subnational or local levels can be ignored. A practical argument for this choice is the availability of ample empirical research at this level of government, while studies of local developments remain relatively rare. Where relevant we shall refer to the development of the civil service at the local government level. We will discuss material concerning both actual developments in the civil service and the development of ideas about the executive and its functionaries.

We will begin with some theoretical notions in order to outline the subject of inquiry more precisely. Relevant definitions will be discussed and a framework for approach, choice of cases, and levels of generalization will be introduced. For a better understanding of the evolution of civil service systems, we will relate it to the development of bureaucracy at large. This will be followed by a brief history of civil service systems and tentative comments on some of the factors that induced change. Some generalization about local and national developments will be necessary in order to reconstruct historical traits. At the same time, developmental phases will be split into several tentative periods; each phase will indicate a specific characteristic of civil service. It should be noted that this "periodization" is merely an instrument of description, not a fact of history.

## CONCEPTUAL FRAMEWORK

In historic-comparative research, the use of analytical concepts is necessary; but a culture or country-specific notion limits scope and value if it implies a sort of conceptual and historic imperialism. It is preferable to try and construct a more neutral or broader metaconcept which allows for application in quite different settings and may provide a broader scope for comparison. If and to what extent this is possible is the subject of debate in comparative history and anthropology. We might, for instance, fall back upon Weber's notions of authority *(Herrschaft)* and use his concepts of traditional, patrimonial, and bureaucratic authority for analysis of the civil service. This would at least provide a starting point for countries within the western cultural sphere. Or we might replace civil service with the ancient notion of "scribal service" as the forerunner or basis of civil bureaucracy. For the moment we will retain "civil service," without giving a sharp delineation or definition of its contents, for it makes no sense to pinpoint the beginning of the development of civil service systems in some specific time and place, for instance, the introduction of some law or regulation.

On the other hand, we should not be too hasty in using available concepts without further reflection. The problem of translation or of transference of meaning is a well-known topic in semantic theory; so-called "functional translations" remain an unsolved issue (Pawlowski, 1980: 21). Too quickly we are inclined to treat "civil servant," "Verwaltungsbeamte," "ambtenaar," and "fonctionaire publique" as synonymous terms. In a very general, usually scientifically uninteresting way they denote similar phenomena ("public servants"). Their meanings are, however, embedded in specific conceptual and cultural, that is, legal and political backgrounds; even American and English authors may differ in their interpretations. The same applies if we project present terms into the past. Amburger provides us with a fine example of the introduction in Russia, via Sweden, of the originally German and French notions of the "state secretary" in the seventeenth century. The content and development of the Russian state secretary in later centuries is, however, not the same, which means that the same terms denote different sorts of functionaries (Amburger, 1966: 20). Another case is provided by the concepts "administration" and "government": their modern content and differences are fairly recent, and the words could be used interchangeably until about 1800 (Bödeker, 1989: 18 ff.). In fact, the Dutch *bestuur* refers to both governing and administering, causing problems when an attempt is made at consistent translation. Similar problems arise if we have to translate "politics" and "policies" into German and French, for these languages do not make a distinction between the two (and curiously enough, in the Netherlands there is no equivalent for the plural "policies," so the term always has to be circumscribed as "different kinds of policy"). The problems of transferability and comparability increase if we direct our attention to civil service development in more distant regions and languages (Findley, 1980: xxvi).

We shall limit ourselves here to higher civil servants in western nations, since it is there that modern civil service systems originated. This does not imply that there are no influences or autonomous developments in such countries as Russia, Japan, China, or Turkey (Dowdy, 1972; Findley, 1980: chap. 8; Gladden, 1972: I, chap. 5, II, chap. 6; Heper, 1976; Pintner, 1970; 1975). Within the scope of this discussion it is not even possible to describe in detail developments in western nations. The literature referred to here provides much of this detail. The history of civil service systems has been investigated primarily within a national context. Systematic cross-national comparison based on empirical research and the presentation of data is lacking. Some comparative literature is available (Barker, 1944; Braibanti, 1966; Burke, 1969; Gladden, 1972; Heady, 1978; Quah, 1978). In this paper we attempt to develop a framework for comparison of national developments. We will not attempt to establish whether "western" developments also can be identified in the nonwestern world. That would require an expertise we cannot claim. What is more, it is still open to question whether nonwestern civil service systems should or could be analyzed in a framework such as this one. Too easily a particular situation in the nonwestern world could then be characterized as premodern. Our (tentative) framework is certainly not meant to be an outline for development!

In order to understand the development of civil service systems, the social context—ideas of authority, sovereignty, public service, the nature of functionaries, public ethos, politics, and economy—has to be taken into account. In short, no less than a general sociohistorical theory is needed as an explanatory context and a means for singling out the relevant phenomena. The most elaborate and most widely used theory in this respect is undoubtedly Max Weber's theory of the rationalization of society. Notwithstanding its limitations, it is and can still be used as a general framework for global and historical comparisons (Jacoby, 1973; Heady, 1991). Within the context of the theory of rationalization, the development of civil service systems can be analyzed in terms of bureaucratization. What we regard as modern in the structure and functioning of civil service systems is closely related to Weber's concept of legal-rational authority as translated into bureaucratic administration (Weber, 1980: 124–30).

It is important, however, not to confuse divergent interpretations of the term bureaucracy (Albrow, 1970: chap. 5). In the context of a history of civil service systems, it should not be regarded as an organizational concept only, but as a societal phenomenon. Even then an important distinction has to be made, that is, between governmental and administrative or executive and bureaucratic development. Administration can be conceptualized as (i) the activity of administering, (ii) a body/college of administrating actors, and (iii) a totality of persons, institutions, activities, and procedures of administering. The last meaning is the most comprehensive. Administrative development refers to the structure and functioning of administration over time. Bureaucratization is a crucial aspect of organizational development. Bureaucracy can refer to both a totality of public and subordinate functionaries and a specific type of organization. Given the importance of bureaucratization for civil service development we can identify some extra and more detailed indicators. Weber's ideal typical definition of bureaucracy offers both characteristics of functioning as well as characteristics of functionaries. He distinguished seventeen characteristics of bureaucracy (Weber, 1980: 126–30; Gerth and Mills, 1946: 196–204) that have now been elaborated to twenty (Van Braam, 1977: 459).[1] To understand the concept of the civil service system, one needs to take the entire ideal type into consideration. Given the degree to which empirical information is available, we will limit our discussion of the evolution of civil service systems to such characteristics as formal rules and procedures, use of written documents, hierarchical structure of offices, recruitment and appointment, pre- and postentry training, career-system, expertise, salary and pension facilities, and legal protection of the position.

## PHASE 1: CIVIL SERVANTS AS PERSONAL SERVANTS

We will begin with the thirteenth century, although we realize that, in essence, government dates back even further in time. However, the high Middle Ages can be regarded as pivotal since it is then that the state appears on the stage.

Originally the "civil servant" represented one of a group of three types of servants to the monarch: court, army, and clerical or civil servants. The court servants were those strictly employed for maintaining the royal household. Together with army (including naval) personnel they formed the bulk of state functionaries. Civil servants hardly existed at all in the early Middle Ages. They were an inconspicuous minority within the household, providing strictly personal, clerical, or scribal services. In feudal society administration implied mainly the maintenance of a monarch's property. The "seignorial household" was essentially a personal unit of direction and management (Gladden, 1972: I, chap. 3). Management was based on oral instruction and agreement.

In the second half of the Middle Ages, changes were at hand. Extensive attention to the investiture struggle between pope and emperor (1075–1122) would go beyond the bounds of this discussion. Yet this is the background against which we can understand the process that has been called the "papal revolution" (Berman, 1983: 47–270). For it was within church organization that new organizational principles developed. In Waldo's words: ". . . for the development of administration the Roman Church is much more important than the Holy Roman Empire" (Waldo, 1980: 8). Since the eleventh and twelfth centuries the church had operated within a strict hierarchical structure, in which each position from central to local level was clearly defined (pope, bishop, priest). In its territorial and hierarchical organization, it built upon the practices developed during the Roman Empire (differentiation of public and private; differentiation in government departments; Roman law as the public source of legitimacy of the emperor; in the context of the church, canon law as the source of legitimacy for the pope's supremacy). The influence of the papacy expanded enormously in the period 1050–1150 and came into conflict with the territorial expansion of temporal lords. In order to successfully wield papal authority, ". . . the papacy developed a highly efficient bureaucracy of specialists in various fields" (Berman, 1983: 208). In the course of the eleventh and twelfth centuries, a papal chancery, papal exchequer (or Apostolic Chamber), and a papal court (Consistory) were created. These can be understood as the first "government" departments in a modern sense. Church organization would prove to be a great influence on the development of the state (Berman, 1983: 208; Gladden, 1972: I, 209; Hattenhauer, 1978: 12). It took some time for this to surface. In a Europe that was dominated by customary law there was no place for organizational changes in the way territories were governed. Even though developments within secular government tended to be much slower, some early examples of changes are known (such as William the Conqueror installing a chancery, 1066).

During the same period, the monk Gratian wrote his *Concordance of Discordant Canons* (also known as *Decretum Gratiani* ±1140). Several of his decrees dealt with the functioning and position of those in clerical office (Hattenhauer, 1978: 13–14). They stated that the church should be organized in territorial units administered by *clerici* as subordinates of the central authority. The principles of hierarchy of office and unity of command were thus affirmed. Furthermore, Gratian prescribed that a "clerk" could only make a career on the basis of merit *(Leistungsprinzip)*, not seniority, and that he could only be appointed after a test of capability. Venality of office was not allowed. The clerk was not to perform any other duties than the ones that were part of his office and those he was to perform according to written instructions. At the Synod of Tours (1236), it was ordained that *clerici* would be required to have legal training. A formal, legal bureaucratic structure was created by the church (Berman, 1983: 213), a major innovation in Germanic Europe.

In the two centuries that followed, some temporal lords succeeded in establishing sovereignty over a larger area than their own possessions. Servants of a territorial lord had been "court" (or "household") servants performing a wide array of duties. In order to strengthen their monarchical claims for authority over the use of force, kings established their own specialized departments. Thus King Henry II of England (1154–1189) created a chancery, an exchequer, and a judiciary. As Gladden writes, "The obvious importance of effective power-manipulation as a main ingredient of primitive government—indeed of all governments—should not be allowed to mask the fact that the leader who also had administrative talent at his disposal was better equipped to make his rulership effective, as well as acceptable to the subjects whose continuing support he needed if his period of rule was to be satisfactorily prolonged"

(Gladden, 1972: I, 235). Government departments now evolved and created a power basis for the king (Berman, 1983: 414; Gladden, 1972: I, 235; Jacoby, 1973: 14; Tilly, 1975). Indeed, with the advent of the universities, rulers recruited more and more laymen instead of clergymen. This is the period during which nation-states enter the arena of international relations. By acknowledging each other's claim to legitimate authority (either ecclesiastical or secular), the papal state and the kingdom of Sicily become the first modern states in history. Frederick II of Sicily issued a decree that showed remarkable resemblance to the *Decretum Gratianus*. His *Constitution of Melfi* (1231; also known as *Liber Augustalis*) has been called the "birth certificate of modern bureaucracy" (Jacoby, 1973: 21).

This did not mean, however, that the role and position of the "servant" was clearly defined. First and foremost he was a "household servant," working on behalf of the king (Rosenberg, 1958: 6). No distinction was made between the "public" and "private" realm. Rules regarding the role and position of servants were practical rules, indicating the duties and limitations of servants. Political theorists therefore paid attention only to the role and position of the king. Servants were nothing but the administrative arm of his sovereignty. Planning and preparation for policy took place within councils (Curia Regis, Parliament, Council of State, Chamber of Accounts), which reached consensus through debate. In the fourteenth and fifteenth centuries, the principle of collegial administration was also applied to those who had to supervise and coordinate the implementation of policy in specific fields. Higher functionaries held offices that contained both political and administrative tasks. Being accountable to the highest authority (king or council), they had a mandate to make decisions and see to their implementation. Accountability was ensured through the obligation to keep records of decisions (minutes of council meetings) and expenditures. Thus high functionaries were often kept busy with administrative tasks, writing down the information the sovereign needed. The minor position of the civil servant and the orientation toward a particular ruler resulted in a lack of attention to civil servants in the literature of the day on government, or better, on kingship. These books were written solely for the personal instruction of the monarch (for instance, Thomas Aquinas's *De Regno, Ad Regem Cypri*, ±1265).

Earlier we indicated that the high Middle Ages represents a caesura since it was then that the state came into being. This cannot be understood, however, without referring to the development of cities, trade, and universities. From the twelfth century onward, the tendency to enlarge territory (centrifugal tendencies) was backed up by a strong development of the towns in northern Italy, southern Germany, and later Flemish regions. Towns received charters from the sovereign, and were thus set apart from the countryside in exchange for financial assistance. The newly born cities expanded their trade at an enormous rate. At the same time a new type of higher education developed: the first universities were created in northern Italy. They embarked upon the study of Roman law, and this had a tremendous influence on political and theoretical thinking about government.

## PHASE 2: CIVIL SERVANTS AS STATE SERVANTS

We have seen how the church appeared as a state and intervened regularly in international relations. The political and legal institutions of secular sovereigns were built according to the principles of church organization: centralization and systematization (Berman, 1983: 553). In the course of the fifteenth and sixteenth centuries, secular lords by and large managed to establish their monopoly over the use of force and the imposition of taxes. In order to maintain their monopoly, further functional differentiation was called for (Elias, 1982: 485, 491, 535). At this time the secretariats developed into formal government departments, while the councils developed into formal political-administrative bodies. Although the public service remained very much a personal, "household," service (Gladden, 1972: II, 85), processes of further formalization are noticeable. Formal instructions and ordinances were issued in which attention was paid to tasks, competencies, means, salary, hierarchy, etc. The Black Book issued by Edward IV of England in 1471/72 is a notable example. In this book two types of household services are distinguished: "downstairs" *(Domus Providencie),* with the treasury, stewards, controllers, and kitchen as well as stable personal, etc.; and "upstairs" *(Domus Regie Magnificencie),* relating to the king's personal well-being and salaries and provisions for barons, knights, secretaries, clerks, etc.

In the sixteenth century, attention in contemporary literature is no longer directed only to political questions. Notable is Claude de Seysell's *La Monarchie de France* written for François I (printed in 1519). Not only does he describe what governmental bodies he considers necessary, but he states firmly that the monarch is but a functionary to the monarchy and is not allowed to undermine his function: "Le Roi n'est que l'administrateur temporaire du royaume" (Seysell, 1961: 43).

There was still no strict distinction between the public and the private realm. There was, however, a shift in political ideology; the monarchy was regarded increasingly as an instrument to provide public welfare. This is in line with the revival of the classical Greek conception of the polis based on the inseparability of politics and ethics (i.e., the notion of "commonwealth"). The idea of the necessity and superiority of the monarchy remains unchallenged, even in academic political thinking in the Netherlands till about one hundred years after the denunciation of the Spanish sovereignty (Hinsley, 1966: 132; Wansink, 1981). Nevertheless, the personal and state household did become more and more separated over time. The separation of public and private can be seen as a prerequisite for the creation of a civil service in the modern sense.

As we move into the seventeenth century, some interesting changes occur. First, this is the century in which public administration becomes a topic of scholarly attention. The public and private spheres are not yet separate, but theoretical developments are apparent that prepared the way for that dichotomy to become a principle of government organization. Likewise the first ideas are developed about the "ideal" higher functionary. Hitherto only the king had been the object of political theory. Now the higher functionary was to be loyal and neutral. It was Martin Luther who advocated a separation of office and official (Hattenhauer, 1978: 151), although the idea can be traced back to Pope Leo I (440–461 A.D.) (Miller, 1984: 284). In his *Politica Methodice Digesta* (1603), Althusius (1557–1639) presented a list of characteristics. The higher functionary had to be wise, experienced, trained, accurate, quick, loyal, modest, flexible, and truthful. He should not falsify decrees/decisions in response to the wishes of citizens. He should not be rash, and above all there should be no personal interest standing in the way of an adequate fulfillment of his official duties (Hattenhauer, 1978: 87). Hence we see that not only the separation of public and private was prepared for in an abstract and holistic way but was also translated into a code of conduct for the higher functionary. Von Seckendorff's *Teutscher Fürstenstat*, first published in 1656, is sometimes regarded as the first book on public administration. He explicitly rejects the value of the contemporary political literature for everyday administrative practices and devotes his attention mainly to the tasks of the household and civil servant, providing him with guidelines, practical points of view, and even formulating a number of functions or job descriptions *(Amtsbeschreibung)* (Seckendorff, 1976: 526). A second important development in the seventeenth century was further centralization of government, implying the development of more efficient taxation systems as well as the introduction of the standing army ("garrison state"). Both were organized on a territorial and hierarchical basis and served as an example for the organization of administration. Centralization may even be regarded as a key concept in administrative thinking in those days, as can be deduced from the influential work *Traité de la Police* by DelaMare (Book I was published in 1702). Under the reign of Louis XIV of France (1660–1714), government departments at the central level were subdivided into bureaus, and the number of functionaries grew significantly (Barker, 1944: 7). Also, "intendants" were appointed to every region in the country to represent the central government. A staff was formed around these intendants (later known as "prefects"), and it developed a routine method of operation (Barker, 1944: 11; Gladden 1972: II, 141, 153). At about the same time *Landräte* were appointed at the central level in Prussia who took over power from the court councillors. This was the first step in the solution of the struggle between the original rulers (royal servants) in the territorial units and the public (i.e., central) law (Fischer and Lundgreen,

1975: 513, 524). Some decades later, Frederick William II of Prussia (1713–1740) appointed *Steuerräte* to exercise control over regional and local government (Barker, 1944: 20; Gladden, 1972: II, 159–162). In Norway the seventeenth-century administration was rather independent from the Danish kingdom, but a centralization of functions took place as the eighteenth century moved toward an end (Blomstedt, 1985: 117–18).

Thus the state truly became unified. It is important to realize that this absolutism resulted in the king's loss of an absolute monopoly over affairs of state. In Elias's theory, the monopoly was transferred from one person to a group; the sovereign needed his servants as much as they needed him (Elias, 1982: 496). This development was foreshadowed by the English Magna Charta (1215). At least in Prussia dynastic absolutism was replaced by bureaucratic absolutism, in which the aristocracy (again) came to dominate (Fischer and Lundgreen, 1975: 525; Rosenberg, 1958: 18). In France a bureaucratic elite developed separately from the aristocracy, recruited from among the bourgeois (Barker, 1944: 11). England appears to present a somewhat different case. Under Thomas Cromwell, principal adviser to Henry VIII, a system of services was created that functioned no matter who was appointed in a particular service. Some division occurred between the web of personal relations and public service (Fischer and Lundgreen, 1975: 480). For the administration of local government, a rather different system was created. Central control was predominantly legislative and judicial in nature. Day-to-day affairs were left in the hands of local "justices of the peace" recruited from among the local gentry (Barker, 1944: 32–33; Gladden, 1972: I, 57). It is for this reason that the myth developed that in Prussia and France, a "professional administrator" came into existence, while in England a tradition of "amateur administrators" came into being. Fischer and Lundgreen, however, have convincingly pointed out that this is a simplification of reality. In France and Prussia, a government by coercion and subjection developed; government officials became a social class of their own, while in England a tradition of government by cooperation and consensus made such exclusion from other classes impossible (Fischer and Lundgreen, 1975: 489).

These shifts in public administration implied a change in the demands on the civil servant. In previous centuries some judicial knowledge and the ability to write were adequate prerequisites for a personal secretary. With the development of the nation-state and its stronger orientation toward the economy (mercantilism), new skills were required, especially with regard to political economy and bookkeeping (Osterloh, 1970: 16).

It had been common practice on the Continent that knowledge of the law was required for higher positions. In Norway a higher functionary would have had to complete a law degree at a university. The same was required in Prussia where, since the late eighteenth century, public servants were required to take two exams before appointment (Fischer and Lundgreen, 1975: 516). The development of preentry training was intertwined with the development of formal application and recruitment procedures. This occurred both at the central and local level (for the Netherlands, see Raadschelders, 1990: 168).

The need for new knowledge and skills is reflected in French and German interest in and literature on administration. So-called cameralistic *(cameralia)* and police sciences emerged *(Polizeiwissenschaft, science de la police)*, both dealing with the administrative organization and regulation of state and township. In Germany, chairs for cameralism were created at the universities of Halle and Frankfurt an der Oder in 1727 by Frederick William I of Prussia. Cameralist programs were aimed at training for higher office, with an emphasis on "generalists," as can be seen from the subjects taught (Lindenfeld, 1989: 156–59). Within fifty years, all of the major German and Austrio-Hungarian universities provided such special education. In France, no generalist university education was provided for, although scholarly interest in administrative, especially legal, matters grew quickly. Rather, the French concentrated on technical education (the Ecole du génie, 1748, preceding the Ecole polytechnique of 1795; Ecole des ponts et chaussées in 1747), an example followed by Prussia in 1799 with the Bauakademie (Fischer and Lundgreen, 1975: 550–52).

It would appear that during the eighteenth century, the work of higher functionaries was in some respects professionalized, most notably in the field of training and recruitment. In other respects there was much still to be organized. Patronage and cooptation were common practice (Parris, 1969: 53), and open entry into public office did not exist; despite good intentions, the competence of various government departments was not always clearly defined (Church, 1981: 34); venality of offices was not restricted; the income of higher functionaries was composed of a mixture of salary, emoluments, sinecures, and immunities; no formal pension arrangements existed; collegial decision-making was still dominant. The higher functionary had become a central servant with a more or less autonomous influence derived from the fact that bureaucracy had increased. It is in the eighteenth century that bureaucracy was identified as a separate power (Albrow, 1970: 17; Cremer, 1989: 12; Hoock, 1989: 34). This indicates that bureaucracy became subject to criticism, since in its original meaning "bureaucracy" referred to the illegitimate use of power.

In England, the increase of government expenditure as well as the increase of public personnel, and hence the increase of taxes, led to more attention to extravagance and the distribution of authority among too many more or less independent legal entities and officers. The juggling with offices met with such resistance that measures were taken to separate office and official (Chester, 1981: 67; Church, 1981: 66; Cohen, 1941: 38–42). In France and Prussia, the main problems concerned the sale of offices and income structure (Church, 1981: 24–45; Hattenhauer, 1978: 113–24). In order to reorganize the public service, the English Parliament installed a Commission to Examine the Public Accounts (1780, Act of 20 GEO.III, c.54); it was given far-reaching authority to intervene in the structure of public offices. A decade later the same type of changes were put into effect on the Continent.

An understanding of the changes that took place during this phase must take into consideration the further growth of the state. Rulers were in need of an efficient bureaucracy and paid more attention to the structure and functioning of their administrative apparatuses. The state became the most important actor in international relations. As such, it took over the role of the church, as is illustrated by the first international conference on matters of state (Westphalia, 1648). The advent of absolutism in the fifteenth century and mercantilism in the seventeenth century further contributed to the need for control.

## PHASE 3: CIVIL SERVANTS AS PUBLIC SERVANTS

The period from 1780 to 1880 was of formative importance for the birth of the modern civil service. In general one could say that it was in this period that the central servant first came to be seen not as an officeholder but as an employee of the state (Chester, 1981: 123; Church, 1981: 47, 66; Hattenhauer, 1978: 183), no longer responsible to the monarch in person, but to some sort of civil sovereign power. The cameralist von Justi (1702–1771) no longer took the monarchy as the basis of power and center of administrative organization, but described administration as a service of the state (Osterloh, 1970: 18). Another important factor in the development of civil services was the introduction of the notion of a separation of powers, based on the ideas of Locke and Montesquieu. Originally they had wanted to diminish the force of absolutism, but their ideas became the basis for the structuring of a civil society (Rechtsstaat). The civil servant became a functionary in the service of the executive power. In France and Germany, "administration" and Verwaltung were being defined for the first time in a modern sense (Cremer, 1989; Bödeker, 1989). This also resulted in the call for a separation of political, administrative, and law studies.

Changes in the public service were always politically inspired insofar as the highest political functionaries wanted to increase their control over the administrative apparatus and/or new policies demanded organizational adaptation. Indeed, it has been said that changes at the central level were driven by the need to improve administrative machinery, whereas at the local level changes in the structure and functions of personnel were a reaction to the rapidly changing social and economic environment (Chester, 1981: 322).

We can distinguish between three types of development: (i) changes in the structure and processes with which the public servant had to work; (ii) changes in the conditions of appointment (including salary and pension) of higher public servants; and (iii) changes in the legal position of public higher, civil servants. The first two will be dealt with in the following discussion; changes in legal position merit separate attention in the next part of this chapter.

The structure in which the public servant had to work changed quickly. Through reorganization of the structure of existing departments and/or the creation of new departments, governments sought to establish some order in the multitude of tasks. In England, reorganization appears to have been the most important method (Chester, 1981: 138, 222), while in France both reorganization of existing departments and the creation of new ones occurred (Church, 1981: 77, 89). In the Netherlands, government departments were created for the first time (Alkemade and Raadschelders, 1992; Raadschelders, 1989). Moreover, in France a system of deconcentrated or field services developed, especially around the army, food distribution, financial organization, and "technical services" (such as field police, postal services, archives, and land registry) (Church, 1981: 93–94). These field services required central supervisors. Thus in France the number of public officers, both high and low, increased rapidly. A huge and centralized bureaucracy was built on the basis of functionaries who were loyal to a career and not to a political faction.

Closely related to changes in the structure of the central administrative organization were changes in the workflow. Many authors mention how the use of written documents increased sharply at the end of the eighteenth and the beginning of the nineteenth centuries. Written minutes of meetings no longer contained only decisions but also the extensive deliberations that led up to them (Church, 1981: 97). Memos and reports on the preparation of a particular policy started to appear (Gosman, 1989: 42). This input from written documents increased the need to regulate the workflow. Around 1800 a registration system for official documents (minutes, letters, etc.) came into existence; dossiers were used and made accessible through the introduction of indexes and archivization (Chester, 1981: 300; Church, 1981: 59, 167).

This had important consequences. Political and political-administrative functionaries could no longer supervise the total correspondence themselves. More lower-level personnel were employed to channel the workflow. This increased the nonpolitical element in the bureaus. "Politics" and "administration" became differentiated, and that provided another basis upon which a modern civil service could develop (Chester, 1981: 315; Hattenhauer, 1978: 151; Nelson, 1982: 113; Parris, 1969: 33). The distinction split the executive, which created another problem. Former higher, more administrative functionaries (in French, *fonctionnaires*) were trapped between renewed political and effective supervision and a growing number of lower personnel who brought new expertise to public service (Church, 1981: 95). Until then higher civil servants had moved in the same circles as true political servants. A "pensionary" in the Netherlands (the highest legal advisor to the Estates General) was as much a political as an administrative actor. Now that the legislative branch had clearly become the prerogative of political officials, the execution of tasks was left to administrative personnel. At first the distinction between those who performed management and those who fulfilled merely routine tasks was not clearly defined. In the course of the nineteenth century, the distinction between higher and lower functionaries became a topic of discussion and resulted in clarification of both categories (Chester, 1981: 308; Church, 1981: 229). In this respect, it is interesting to note diverging developments in the American and the continental European tradition regarding the loyalty and neutrality of civil servants. The differences are closely related to differing interpretations of the concept of the separation of powers (Cliteur and Rutgers, 1990). Because tasks were increasing, the distinction between higher and lower functionaries became sharper. Tasks in the field of planning and preparation of policy called for better-trained personnel. It was not uncommon, however, for higher functionaries to pitch in when the amount of writing and copying work demanded it. This led to another demarcation between the more intellectual tasks, that is, policy formulation, and the more routine jobs. It is interesting to note that in intellectual discourse, this can be traced back to at least the late sixteenth century, when the Leiden professor Lipsius made a distinction between *consiliarii* and *administri* (Wansink, 1981: 73). This led to further development of the ranking system.

A system of formal ranks could be based on two considerations. Matters of status were dominant when in Prussia the ranks of military and civil personnel were standardized in 1705 (Hattenhauer, 1978: 61–62). In 1722, Peter the Great introduced the same system into Russia (Amberger, 1966: 54). The second consideration had to do directly with the improvement of administrative efficiency. The abolition of sinecures necessitated the development of rank systems (Chester, 1981: 130; Church, 1981: 123). Formal criteria for promotion developed in the wake of the rank system. Some variance can be seen among different countries. In Prussia, the Netherlands, and England, both rank system and promotion criteria (instead of patronage) became standard in the years 1800–1840 (Chester, 1981: 130; Hattenhauer, 1978: 182; De Brauw, 1864: 158; van IJsselmuiden, 1988: 48, 66). In France, a rank system developed, but it was not accompanied by formalized promotion criteria. Patronage remained too strong a criterion for career, and indeed became more important again in the post-Napoleonic era (Church, 1981: 181–82, 249, 274, 294).

As can be expected, the medieval concept of "unity of command" was finally realized in the public service. Hitherto the more important functions at the central as well as the local level were not fulfilled by individual functionaries but by boards of governors. The principle of collegial administration was thought to guarantee continuity and reliability, and it existed everywhere in the western world (Amburger, 1966: 5; Rosenberg, 1958: 96). As the distinction between "politics" and "administration" was being introduced, the choice for a collegial versus a bureau system of administration became a much-debated topic. This too had a bearing on the advent of the modern civil service (Parris, 1969: 87). At the central level the change occurred in the early nineteenth century; at the local level—at least in the Netherlands—collegial administration for higher functions would not diminish in importance until the end of that century

(Raadschelders, 1988: 269–72; Raadschelders, 1990: 134). Higher administration was thus no longer in the hands of a collegial body. A permanent civil service offered the same continuity that had hitherto been provided by collegial systems. Slowly and decisively, preference was given to so-called ministerial departments in which a politically appointed minister supervised the business of a complete department. The concept of ministerial responsibility and the anonymity of the civil servant was very much an early nineteenth-century creation, especially in England and the Netherlands (Chester, 1981: 305; Parris, 1969: 82–98).

The abolition of sinecures and sale of offices was the most important instrument legislators had for controlling administration. Much of the abuse of public office was directly related to nepotism, patronage, emoluments, placeholders in office, and the unclear distinction between private and public means. A system of formal ranks was one solution. Another was the restructuring of salary income. In addition to the sources of income already mentioned, a public functionary had the opportunity to sell services to clients. Higher functionaries sometimes used extra income to finance temporarily appointed personnel. The restriction and subsequent abolition of all these practices was compensated for by the payment of a regular and adequate salary (Church, 1981: 99, 137). The abolition of sinecures was made easier by guaranteeing the public servant a pension after retirement, or after his death for his wife and children. This was of great importance since many administrative functionaries held one or more offices into very old age or even until death. In France, a pension fund for certain groups of functionaries was created during the period 1790–1810. To stock that fund, a set amount of money was deducted from regular salaries (Church, 1981: 192). At the same time, pension facilities were created in England (Chester, 1981: 129; Cohen, 1941: 60). In Prussia, the idea of a pension had existed since the eighteenth century (Hattenhauer, 1978: 113–14), but it was not until the early nineteenth century that such a practice was formally regulated (Hattenhauer, 1978: 183–84). The same was true in the Netherlands. A pension for widows and orphans had existed since 1804; a retirement and disability pension was enacted in 1814. A General Pension Fund was created in 1844 (van IJsselmuiden, 1988: 100).

By and large the structure that was created in the years 1790–1850 exists to the present day. The rank system improved the opportunities for promotion. At the same time, hierarchy inspired written procedures. A regular salary and pension guaranteed loyal service to those who were politically responsible for public policy. Salary, rank, and promotion were very much connected. The higher functionary had become a public or civil servant.

The bulk of the material presented up to now applies to Britain and the Continent. In the United States, development was different. We must now turn our attention to these developments because of their tremendous impact.

Until the early 1830s, the federal government was small. U.S. presidents believed in short-term "program" staffing, while Europeans viewed public office as a case for "career" staffing (McClenaghan, 1985: 197). President Jackson utilized the existing spoils system and the 1820 Tenure of Office Act to full effect (Gladden, 1972: II, 309; Mosher, 1977; Van Riper, 1959). He justified the spoils system out of the conviction that it contributed to the viability of political parties; that giving office to those who supported the party would consolidate power and unity within government; that rotation in office could protect against abuses by long-term officeholders without adversely affecting performance duties; and that the opportunity and privilege of serving national government would be open to a larger group of people (Rowat, 1988: 405). Government efficiency depended more on the characteristics of the men appointing and being appointed to office than on the method of selection (Sayre, 1965: 30). The patronage system lasted for some sixty years, and because government was rather small, it did not really decrease the effectiveness of government service. However, it met with much criticism because of corruption. Just as in other countries, however, inherited rank and political favor were being abandoned for meritocratic employment and advancement systems (de Swaan, 1988: 235). Reform of the civil service would bring more competence, efficiency, and integrity to the public service (Nelson, 1982: 120). The United States moved from a party-centered to a bureaucratic authority system (Nelson, 1982: 159). Both in the United States and Canada in the second half of the nineteenth century, political neutrality became a principle of civil service, just as it had been on the European continent for some decades (Kernaghan and Siegel, 1987: 467).

An interesting example of nineteenth-century development is provided by the Norwegian civil service, which also underwent a transition. Having become independent from Denmark, Norway formed a union with the monarchy of Sweden. It was at that time that the concept of the *embetsmannsstaten* came into being: a state ruled by officials of the administration, both formulating and implementing state policy—a true civil service state, in which recruitment for office was based on cooptation. The claim to power was experienced as legitimate by the Norwegian people since civil servants "defended" national interests against the Swedish monarch. The civil service also developed an alliance with the agrarian and commercial elites. The late nineteenth-century Norwegian bureaucracy was very small: its basic duties were to maintain order, protect property, and defend the nation against aggressors. There were fewer than 400 higher functionaries (Hernes, 1985: 165). At the turn of the century, however, processes of task differentiation and departmentalization occurred. Each department came under the leadership of a cabinet minister and a permanent administrative secretary. Holding office became a full-time job, and a proper salary and pension were introduced. Since 1900 the number of departments and the number of subdivisions has increased sharply (Hernes, 1985: 168).

In the nineteenth century many other major states experienced rapid growth of the civil service. Findley describes, for instance, the tremendous changes in the Ottoman Empire. By the end of the nineteenth century, "the general outlines of a rational personnel policy were adopted for the entire civil bureaucracy and in some respects made operative" (Findley, 1980: 287–88). On the other hand, developments in imperial Russia seemed to be moving at a much slower pace. Despite major changes, old principles remained. In 1826 a minister for the imperial household was appointed and the church became an even more integral part of the government apparatus (Amburger, 1966).

We may conclude that certain innovations were introduced by France, England, and Prussia. Some countries, such as the Netherlands, followed quickly; others followed somewhat later—the United States, Canada, and Norway. The innovations could occur because of the higher demands placed on civil servants, and they can be understood against the background of economic development (industrialization) and the expansion of Europe on other continents (colonization). Furthermore, in the second half of the eighteenth century, bureaucracy was recognized as an independent "power" for the first time (Albrow, 1970), and it became clear that it needed to be embedded in a structure of legitimate government. This last aspect points to an extremely important change in thinking about the state: the period 1780–1850 saw the emergence of the concept of the "constitutional state" (American Constitution, 1787; French Constitution, 1789; Dutch Constitution, 1848). As a consequence, public administration as a separate discipline dissolved and was replaced by administrative law. Administration was no longer conceptualized as a form of socioeconomic police (see phase 2) but as the execution of law.

## PHASE 4: CIVIL SERVICE AS PROTECTED SERVICE

We have arrived at the middle of the nineteenth century, when the concept of civil service came into use in Britain and the United States (Chester, 1981: 298). The civil service had turned into a professional service. Further professionalization was to follow. There was, however, one element not clearly formalized. So far most changes had been somewhat disparate, related but not unified into one coherent body of regulations. Regulation would not only provide foundation and further standardization of practices that had developed around rank and salary systems, pensions, examinations, and training systems, it would also finalize the development toward an administration that was both public and subordinate to politics. More importantly, it would protect the civil servant from being expelled from office on political and/or religious grounds. The duties of civil servants were clearly defined in the period 1780–1850, and career systems with incentives developed; professionalization and the increased self-awareness of civil servants led to demands for legal protection of public office, to the Civil Service Act. The Kingdom of Bavaria was rather early with such an act, 1805

(Hattenhauer, 1978: 183; Heyen, 1991). Comparable acts were introduced elsewhere after the 1850s.

For a proper perspective we need to take a step back in time. As early as the late eighteenth century, the British in India had taken measures to diminish patronage and corruption: candidates for colonial office were trained at professional colleges, there was some competition for admittance to those colleges, and there were open exams for admittance to the Indian civil service. Exams at Oxford and Cambridge were changed so that merit and not influence/connections decided the completion of a degree (Cohen, 1941: 81–83). These practices were introduced into the English civil service at home as a result of a Civil Service Report by Northcote and Trevelyan (1854), the latter having spent time in India. In their report they criticized the inefficiency of the civil service, the workload, and the insufficient working conditions (e.g., overtime) (Cohen, 1941: 88–104). As could be expected, the report met with admiration and criticism (among others from John Stuart Mill). Nevertheless, a Civil Service Commission was installed (1855). A Superannuation Act passed Parliament in 1859 and brought more security. With the Order in Council of 1870, which introduced the principle of merit, the Northcote-Trevelyan report achieved its main impact. De facto, the English civil servant now enjoyed security of tenure, but it was not guaranteed until the Crown Proceeding Act of 1947 (Garrett, 1980: 150–53).

As mentioned earlier, patronage and nepotism returned in the French civil service after the Empire. Higher functionaries again became more or less political functionaries. Lower functionaries ("employees") were subordinate to them. By the mid-nineteenth century, debate about a civil service act protecting the rights of lower functionaries became a political issue of first importance. After 1814, the employees were by no means protected against the internal reforms undertaken in response to economic decline. No appeal was possible in case of sudden dismissal. This is one of the reasons why the employees resisted, with success, the creation of an "Ecole Nationale d'Administration" in 1848. Their plea for legal protection had not been granted (Church, 1981: 289, 300). The ENA would have widened the gap, already large, between higher and lower functionaries. These circumstances did not prevent private initiatives for the training of higher officials (Chand, 1949). Finally, in 1946, the French Parliament passed a "Statut Général" or Civil Service Act, one year after the creation of the ENA (Church, 1981: 286–92).

Changes also occurred in administrative theory. There is a clear shift in the literature from general administration to administrative law. One of the last to attempt to develop a generic study of public administration in Europe was Lorenz von Stein. He was also the first to describe the modern state as an administrative state *(Verwaltungsstaat)* (Rutgers, 1990).

In the United States and Canada, things were changing rapidly as well, although in administrative thinking attention was not so much directed to administrative reorganization as to "the moral purification of public life, the deterioration of which they declared threatened the existence of a self-governing republic" (White, 1967: 19). Administrative action was still considered to be mainly a routine and simple execution of political demands. Woodrow Wilson and Frank Goodnow were the first to pick up developments in scholarly thinking on public administration, undoubtedly influenced by such Europeans as von Stein (Rutgers, 1990). Administrative practice followed quickly in English footsteps. After a U.S. government assignment, Dorman B. Eaton compiled a list of "principles and conclusions" for the U.S. civil service based on his report *The Civil Service in Great Britain* (1880) (Gladden, 1972: II, 316). At the local level the list had an immediate impact. In 1880 the City of New York installed a Civil Service Reform Association. Eaton was one of its members. Other local associations followed rapidly, and they were brought together in the National Civil Service Reform League as early as 1881 (Schiesl, 1977: 31–41). The Pendleton Act of 1883 established the first national Civil Service Commission and introduced the idea of competitive entrance examinations. The civil service system rested henceforth on the ideas of merit and nonpartisan government (Sayre, 1965: 46). In 1890 the three-member Civil Service Commission appointed approximately 10 percent of federal employees through competitive exams; in the 1970s the figure had risen to 85 percent (Saffell, 1984: 343). The Hatch Acts of 1939 and 1940 imposed stringent limitations on federal, state, and municipal employees and on the extent to which they could participate in partisan politics. In the twentieth century the Civil Service Commission transformed itself into a modern personnel agency through initiatives in such areas as position classification, equal pay for equal work, and orderly promotion ladders. They also encouraged and assisted with pre- and postentry training services.

Canada was a little ahead of the United States. Their Civil Service Act of 1868 created noncompulsory examinations for the civil service. In an amendment to this act, a nonpartisan Civil Service Commission was instituted; it is responsible for administering more competitive compulsory exams and for organizing and classifying the civil service (Kernaghan and Siegel, 1987: 467; Rowat, 1988: 54). Nowadays the Public Service Commission handles roughly 98 percent of public service appointments (Kernaghan and Siegel, 1987: 477).

In comparison with Anglo-Saxon countries, the Netherlands were rather late in improving the legal position of the civil servant. Although voices could be heard in favor of protection of the position as early as 1883, it would take until 1929 for a Civil Service Act to be passed by Parliament (van IJsselmuiden, 1988: 194–98). Open competition and entry exams had been introduced during the 1850s and 1860s (van IJsselmuiden, 1988: 128).

In Germany, despite the merit system as it had existed since the eighteenth century, entry into the public service was open only to those of the higher and educated segments of society. A bureaucratic elite arose that controlled key positions and was mainly recruited from among the nobility. The civil service grew to be inflexible and narrow (Gillis, 1968: 126). Well into the Weimar Republic, ministers found themselves confronted with an overwhelming majority of civil servants that did not adhere to the principles of neutrality and democracy (Bendix, 1977: 150). Only after 1945 did the civil service acquire legal protection.

The changes during this period can be related to the emancipation of civil servants as well as of the public at large. Civil servants no longer had merely duties, they also enjoyed rights. This was a function of growing government intervention in society. The public demanded more government services, especially in view of the social upheaval caused by industrialization. Government now started to provide more social and health services and began to exploit agencies of a technical nature (for instance gas and electricity companies at the local level). With the growth of the size of government, the self-awareness of the civil servant increased.

## PHASE 5: CIVIL SERVICE AS PROFESSIONAL SERVICE

The duties and rights of the civil servant having been well established, the civil service had found its modern manifestation. This, however, does not imply that the system was no longer subject to change. Quite the contrary: after World War II the civil service underwent major changes characterized by specialization and reorganization.

Criticism in the late eighteenth century was aimed at "illegal" practices, and it brought about major innovations. In the early nineteenth century, complaints could be heard about the increasing size of government and about bureaucratism—for instance in Prussia and the Netherlands (Hattenhauer, 1978: 212–17; van IJsselmuiden, 1988: 52). Size, efficiency, and reliability would again become objects of much criticism in our own time. Some new topics of criticism have been added.

We can understand the nature of the criticism only if we examine the national civil service system. In France, Germany, and the United States, part of the civil service developed into a highly specialized "corps" directly attached to a government (the ministerial cabinet in France, the spoils system in the United States). Such civil servants are not so much neutral as they are loyal to the government in power; they leave office when the minister does, often returning to posts in the purely administrative ranks from which they were originally recruited. Thus, at the very top of the administration, civil servants are very much political-administrative actors. This creates tension with purely "line" functionaries. Members of a French ministerial cabinet believe that the domains of politics and administration cannot be separated, whereas the directors of directorates within departments regard the two as very distinct (Heady, 1991:

181, 185, 190). In Great Britain and the Netherlands, on the other hand, the civil service developed into a neutral and loyal body of generalists that remains in office when a new government is sworn in.

Developments in the twentieth-century civil service are well documented in the literature, although the information is rather scattered (Chevalier and Loschak, 1987; Mayer, 1959; Perry, 1989). We will therefore confine ourselves to a few general observations. First, professionalization has increased tremendously through educational provisions, open exams and competition, and the provision of specialized management staff. Also, governments have increasingly employed other specialists, for example, economists, in addition to officials with a background in law (Bemelmans-Videc, 1984; Hernes, 1985: 168). Second, and more generally, government has grown in terms of personnel. This has multiplied the demands on the management of public administration itself. Two indications of these developments are the flourishing of public administration as a discipline, and an increased emphasis on multidisciplinarity (Rutgers, 1993). Both the increase in personnel and specialization have recently raised new questions about the size and, as a new topic, the representativeness of the civil service and the bureaucracy at large.

In Great Britain, criticism of the functioning of the civil service started in the early 1960s. Despite the increase of governmental activity, the civil service operated very much as it had since the nineteenth century: dealing with routine administration, arbitration when interests conflicted, and advising the minister on policy matters. Anticipation of future developments and outlining governmental responses was not perceived as part of a civil servant's duty (Birch, 1982: 165–66). The publication of the Fulton Report in 1968 seriously criticized the principles laid down in the Northcote-Trevelyan Report (recruitment immediately after education and division into administrative classes). Critics from academia and politics pointed to the lack of specialization in the civil service and the secrecy that surrounded the activities in Whitehall. Some modifications were realized, but the main structure still stands (Birch, 1982: 169–73).

The French civil service has a merit-based system of recruitment following national examinations. The national examination was introduced after World War II in answer to criticism of the prewar system of specialized exams for various offices (about 1200 different exams existed before 1945). The most important postentry training schools are the ENA and the Ecole Polytechnique. The system of recruitment and training as it exists today is still subject to the kind of criticism heard in earlier decades. Despite postwar reforms, recruitment has not been democratized. Senior civil servants are often the sons of former high functionaries, lawyers, doctors, and company directors. They generally still come from the Paris region and have been educated at the Institut d'Etudes Politiques de Paris or at some other prestigious Parisian school. Representation is very much an issue in French bureaucracy.

The same is true for the German civil service, where most high positions are filled by people from the upper middle and upper classes of society. It is interesting to note that those with legal training still hold a large majority of the key positions as compared with economists or social scientists. No major reform has recently taken place in the German civil service system.

Another indication of professionalization in Europe is that during the 1960s and 1970s public administration became established as an independent field of inquiry, freeing itself from its juridical preoccupation (König, 1970).

Developments in the United States are in some respects comparable to those in Great Britain. Criticism mounted in the 1970s: government was too large, employees were overpaid and performed poorly, there was too much red tape, and merit did not seem the criterion for promotion (McClenaghan, 1985: 433). The Civil Service Reform Act of 1978 confirmed the long-standing division of employees into classified and unclassified service. The Civil Service Commission was replaced by the Office of Personnel Management (OPM) under a director who was responsible directly to the president. The responsibility for the protection of the rights of civil servants was transferred to the new Merit System Protection Board, which was less subject to presidential control. The third new element was the creation of the Senior Executive Service (SES), consisting of the top 8,000 federal employees. The intention was that this group would form an elite within the civil service, available for assignment to a variety of positions near the center of government. This appears to have been realized to a limited extent. The civil service as a whole seems quite an open elite (Rowat, 1988: 409), so less discussion exists in the United States than elsewhere about the representativeness of the system.

The situation is quite different in Canada, where in the late 1960s an Affirmative Action Plan was developed in order to make the civil service a more accurate reflection of society. The Official Language Act of 1969 was part of this plan, making bilingualism a factor in recruitment for the civil service (Rowat, 1988: 49). More recently programs have been developed under the Action Plan to promote the recruitment of women and the handicapped. Other criticism was voiced by the D'Avignon Committee, revealing that government was ". . . viewed by managers as slow, inflexible and inefficient; by bargaining agents as misguided and inequitable; and by employees as frequently failing to ensure that their qualifications are fairly and objectively assessed" (Kernaghan and Siegel, 1987: 477).

Criticism is no longer limited to the size of bureaucracy or the civil service and its efficiency. In most countries the efficiency of government is being questioned, sometimes with reference to lack of specialization, sometimes insufficient personnel policies. A new issue is the representativeness of the system, a goal that is difficult to balance with the merit system.

Economic and demographic development have both induced changes in the character of the civil service. The public has demanded adequate service delivery. Government had entered into such a variety of services that specialization, that is, professionalization, was needed. What may also have an impact upon professionalization was the internationalization of public affairs (Raadschelders and Toonen, 1992).

## SUMMARY AND CONCLUDING REMARKS

It is commonly accepted that the structure of our contemporary public institutions is rooted in the Middle Ages, more specifically in the period 1050–1150. The most developed organization in the Middle Ages was, without doubt, the Catholic church. Its hierarchical structure and departmental organization would prove to be an example for the development of secular institutions. It took some time, however, for this to trickle down into state organization.

The origin of civil services is closely related to nation-state development in general. Civil servants were very much personal servants to the king; one could even speak of "household servants." There was still no strict distinction between the public and the private realm. There was, however, a shift in political ideology; the monarchy came to be regarded more and more as an instrument for providing for the public welfare. The separation of public and private was important for the creation of a civil service.

Equally important is the contemporary distinction between political and administrative positions. Up to the end of the eighteenth century it was common for higher functionaries to perform both political and administrative tasks. In fact, the concepts of government and administration were not yet distinct. Notions regarding the division of power were very influential in this respect. Once the fields of politics and administration had been demarcated, a modern civil service could develop.

The demarcation was of great importance in several respects. For centuries higher positions in the public/private service had been controlled by an elite. Patronage, cooptation, sinecures, and venality of offices were common and accepted practice. Although an office had not been a personal possession of an office-holder since the Middle Ages, these practices did offer ample opportunity to control succession in office. Separating office and official by the end of the eighteenth century thus underlined the fact that those who worked in administration were subordinate to those who were politically elected or appointed.

At the same time that the distinction between politics and administration occurred, a shift took place from a collegial to a bureau system, which constituted another basis for the advent of the modern civil service. For centuries, higher civil servants had belonged to the same elite as political functionaries. In the long run, the separation of political from administrative offices had another important effect on the position of higher civil servants. It appeared that they now belonged to the large mass of public servants; they therefore soon became formally distinguished from lower administrative personnel.

Closely linked with the previous factors was the call for a loyal and politically neutral official: loyal to civil society and not to a personal ruler. "Civil" no longer referred to "not military or household," but to a servant within the executive of a civil society.

Another important factor in the evolution of civil services is that of security of position. People appointed to the service of the king, the state, or the municipality did not enjoy the security of position nowadays regarded as inherent in a modern civil service system. Changes in the political climate could easily result in loss of office. The public servant had many duties and few rights. Once a position no longer depended solely upon the whims of the powerful, as of the early nineteenth century, the notion of the neutral civil servant, loyal to the state, could develop. This does not imply a similar interpretation of these notions everywhere. In Europe, "loyal" is usually regarded as politically neutral (the two concepts intertwine). Quite opposed to this is the American principle that loyalty is guaranteed either through selection of officials by election or by political "patronage." In exchange for neutrality and loyalty in the implementation of decisions, the administrative apparatus has been given security of position and the right to adequate payment and pension facilities. This process was completed when the rights and duties of higher public functionaries were laid down in a civil service act or a document of equal meaning.

Last but not least, it is important to realize that civil servants were recruited for their specific, often legal, knowledge. It was not until the eighteenth century, however, that preentry training institutions were created with a view to public service. Since then, knowledge and fitness for office have been the criteria upon which recruitment for public service is based. The professionalization of the civil service (both in terms of preparation for office as well as specialization) has had a great influence on its further development.

The issues discussed in this chapter pertain to developments in the west. The developments presented here are not a prescriptive outline. The framework does, however, provide for comparison between countries and even regions in the world. There is most certainly a case to be made for global comparison as well. It will be interesting to compare western developments with those elsewhere in order to verify the contingencies and universalities of the development of civil service systems.

We can thus list five major topics with regard to the evolution of a civil service that merit further attention:

1. The advent of civil service systems cannot be understood without attention to the influence of the church, nation-state development, and the proliferation of public tasks (departmentalization).
2. Processes of demarcation and differentiation were necessary conditions for

the evolution of modern civil service systems: politics vs. administration, office vs. official, collegial vs. bureau system, higher vs. lower functionaries, policy formulation vs. policy implementation.

3. The successful functioning of civil servants, once they were truly public servants, has been influenced by professionalization and security of position.

4. The concept of civil service was developed in relation to ideas of state and society.

5. The evolution of civil service systems in nonwestern regions should be subject to analysis and comparison.

The first three topics require empirical research: the early modern civil service came into being in the Middle Ages, processes of demarcation occurred in the late eighteenth and first half of the nineteenth centuries, and professionalization and security of position came to the forefront in the second half of the nineteenth and the first half of the twentieth centuries. This is not to say that certain developments took place at the same time everywhere. Research on the fourth topic may explain such variation since it is related to ideological developments and concerns more normative issues—not the actual historical situation but how people thought that the civil service should relate to state and society. National studies of the evolution of civil service systems should be promoted, with attention to differences in concepts of "civil service" and "civil servant" and the extent to which public, communal tasks have become governmental tasks. Furthermore, the evolution of civil service systems in the nonwestern world should be analyzed, for this may illuminate interesting differences and similarities. One might argue that a study like that of Findley (1980) on the civil bureaucracy in the Ottoman Empire will shed a different light on the contingencies of western concepts of civil service. In particular, the interaction between colonial and home administration and the impact of colonial administration on development in the "new states" requires more attention. Some material on nonwestern developments is already available (Beaglehole, 1977; Braibanti, 1966; Burke, 1969; Kooperman and Rosenberg, 1977; Lofstrom, 1973; Manchester, 1972; Misra, 1977; de Vere, 1970). There is a need for separate studies of the developments of other countries and/or regions using the first four topics outlined above. This may highlight the uniqueness and/or the universal character of the development of civil service systems. However, we reject the idea that in some respects the structure and functioning of civil services in the nonwestern world resembles the situation at an early/earlier phase in the western world.

The history of civil service systems can be understood on the basis of internal as well as external variables. Changes in the structure and functioning of higher functionaries were influenced by both considerations of efficiency as well as by the relationship between society, government, and administration. It is important to realize that government and administration came to be guided more and more by principles of hierarchy and standardization, whereas western society at large developed into an open and democratic system. It is worth investigating the extent to which the criticism of bureaucracy is brought about by the inherent tension with democracy.

Historical and contemporary comparison must always take into account the context in which specific phenomena occur. Studying development over time, juridical, political, economic, social, cultural, and even geographical conditions must be part of the analysis. If we want to compare specific administrative arrangements in time and place, it is only by reference to these contexts that we can appreciate the contingency of events.

## NOTES

1. Characteristics of bureaucratic organization by Max Weber, as elaborated by van Braam (1977):
   A) Characteristics of functioning *(legal-rationale Herrschaft)*
       1. continuous administrative activity
       2. formal rules and procedures
       3. clear and specialized offices
       4. hierarchical organization of offices
       5. use of written documents
       6. adequate supply of means (desk, paper, an office, etc.)
       7. nonownership of office
       8. procedures of rational discipline and control
   B) Characteristics of functionaries *(bürokratischer Verwaltungsstab)*
       9. office held by individual functionaries
       10. who are subordinate, and
       11. appointed, and
       12. knowledgeable, who have expertise, and are
       13. assigned by contractual agreement
       14. in a tenured (secure) position, and
       15. who fulfill their office as their main or only job, and
       16. work in a career system
       17. rewarded with a regular salary and pension in money,
       18. rewarded according to rank and
       19. promoted according to seniority, and
       20. work under formal protection of their office

## REFERENCES

Albrow, M. 1970. *Bureaucracy.* London: Pall Mall Press.

Alkemade, M. J. M., and J. C. N. Raadschelders. 1992. "Ontstaan en ontwikkeling van de ministeries van algemeen bestuur, 1798–heden." In J. N. Breunese and L. J. Roborgh, eds., *Ministeries van Algemeen Bestuur.* 2nd ed. Leiden: SMD.

Amburger, E. 1966. *Geschichte der Behördenorganisation Russlands von Peter dem Grossen bis 1917.* Leiden: Brill.

Armstrong, J. A. 1973. *The European Administrative Elite.* Princeton: Princeton University Press.

Barker, E. 1944. *The Development of Public Services in Western Europe 1660–1930.* London: Oxford University Press.

Beaglehole, T. H. 1977. "From Rulers to Servants. The I.C.S. and the British Demission of Power in India." *Journal of Developing Areas* 11, no. 2: 237–55.

Bemelmans-Videc, M. L. 1984. *Economen in overheidsdienst, 1945–1975; bijdragen van economen aan de vorming van het sociaal-economisch beleid.* Ph.D. diss., University of Leiden.

Bendix, R. 1977. *Nation-building and Citizenship.* Berkeley: University of California Press.

Berman, H. J. 1983. *Law and Revolution. The Formation of the Western Legal Tradition.* Cambridge: Cambridge University Press.

Birch, A. H. 1982. *The British System of Government.* 5th ed. London: Allen & Unwin.

Blomstedt, Y., ed. 1985. *Administrasjon i Norden paa 1700–talet.* Oslo: Universitetsforlaget.

Bödeker, H. E. 1989. " 'Verwaltung,' 'Regierung' und 'Polizei' in deutschen Wörterbüchern und Lexika des 18. Jahrhunderts." Pages 15–32 in Heyen, 1989.

Van Braam, A. 1957. *Ambtenaren en bureaucratie in Nederland.* Zeist: De Haan.

———. 1977. "Bureaucratiseringsgraad van het plaatselijk bestuur van Westzaandam ten tijde van de Republiek." *Tijdschrift voor Geschiedenis* 90, nos. 3–4: 457–77.

Van Braam, A., and M. L. Bemelmans-Videc. 1986. *Leerboek Bestuurskunde.* Muiderberg: Coutinho.

Braibanti, R., ed. 1966. *Asian Bureaucratic Systems Emergent from the British Imperial Tradition.* Durham: Duke University Press.

Brauw, W. M. de. 1864. *De departementen van algemeen bestuur in Nederland sedert de omwenteling van 1795.* Utrecht: Kemink.

Burke, F. G. 1969. "Public Administration in Africa: The Legacy of Inherited Colonial Institutions." *Journal of Comparative Administration* 1, no. 3: 345–78.

Van Caenegem, R. C. 1977. *Over koningen en bureaucraten. Oorsprong en ontwikkeling van de hedendaagse staatsinstellingen.* Amsterdam: Elsevier.

Caiden, G. E. 1971. *The Dynamics of Public Administration: Guidelines to Current Transformations in Theory and Practice.* New York: Holt, Rinehart & Winston.

Chand, B. 1949. "Political Science and Public Administration Studies." *Revue International des Sciences Administratives* 20, no. 2: 261–68.

Chester, N. 1981. *The English Administrative System 1780–1870.* Oxford: Clarendon Press.

Chevalier, J., and D. Loschak. 1987. *La science administrative.* 2nd ed. Paris: Presses Universitaires de France.

Church, C. H. 1981. *Revolution and Red Tape. The French Ministerial Bureaucracy 1770–1850.* Oxford: Clarendon Press.

Cliteur, P. B., and M. R. Rutgers, eds. 1990. *De trias onder spanning.* Groningen: Wolters Noordhoff.

Cohen, E. W. 1941. *The Growth of the British Civil Service 1780–1939.* London: Allen & Unwin.

Cremer, A. 1989. "L'administration dans les encyclopédies et dictionnaires français." Pages 1–13 in Heyen, 1989.

Debbasch, Ch. 1989. *Science administrative. Administration Publique.* 5th ed. Paris: Dalloz.

DelaMare, M. 1722. *Traité de la police.* 2nd ed. Paris: M. Brunet.

Depré, R. 1978. "Groei van de ambtenarij getoetst aan voorbeelden in België." *Bestuurswetenschappen* 32, no. 3: 163–83.

Dimock, M. E., and G. Dimock. 1983. *Public Administration.* 5th ed. New York: Rinehart and Company.

Dowdy, E. 1972. *Japanese Bureaucracy. Its Development and Modernization.* Melbourne: Cheshire Press.

Elias, N. 1982. *The Civilizing Process.* Vol. 2. New York: Uricon Books, Basil Blackwell.

Findley, C. V. 1980. *Bureaucratic Reform in the Ottoman Empire: The Sublime Porte, 1789–1922.* Princeton: Princeton University Press.

Fischer, W., and P. Lundgreen. 1975. "The Recruitment and Training of Administrative and Technical Personnel." Pages 456–561 in Ch. Tilly, ed., *The Formation of National States in Western Europe.* Princeton: Princeton University Press.

Flora, P., and A. J. Heidenheimer, eds. 1981. *The Development of the Welfare State in Europe and America.* New Brunswick, NJ: Transaction Books.

Garrett, J. 1980. *Managing the Civil Service.* London: Heineman.

Gerth, H. H., and C. W. Mills. 1946. *From Max Weber. Essays in Sociology.* Oxford: Oxford University Press.

Gillis, J. R. 1968. "Aristocracy and Bureaucracy in 19th Century Prussia." *Past and Present* 41: 105–29.

Gladden, E. N. 1966. *An Introduction to Public Administration.* 2 vols. London: Staples Press.

———. 1972. *A History of Public Administration.* London: Frank Cass.

Gosman, J. G. 1989. "De ontwikkeling van de centrale bureaucratie in Nederland." *Bestuurswetenschappen* 43, no. 1: 35–50.

Hattenhauer, H. 1989. "Geschichte des Beamtentums." In W. Wiese, ed., *Handbuch des öffentlichen Dienstes.* Cologne: C. Heymann Verlag.

Heady, F. 1991. *Public Administration: A Comparative Perspective.* 4th ed. New York: Marcel Dekker.

Henry, N. 1989. *Public Administration and Public Affairs.* 5th ed. Englewood Cliffs: Prentice Hall International.

Heper, M. 1976. "Political Modernization as Reflected in Bureaucratic Change: The Turkish Bureaucracy and a 'Historical Bureaucratic Empire' tradition." *International Journal of Middle Eastern Studies* 7, no. 4: 507–21.

Hernes, G. 1985. *Det moderne Norge. Makt og styring.* Oslo: Gyldendal Norsk Forlag.

Heyen, E. V., ed. 1989. *Formation und Transformation des Verwaltungswissens in Frankreich und Deutschland (18./19. Jh.). Jahrbuch für europäische Verwaltungsgeschichte* 1. Baden-Baden: Nomos Verlagsgesellschaft.

———. 1991. *Beamtensyndikalismus in Frankreich, Deutschland und Italien. Jahrbuch für europäische Verwaltungsgeschichte* 3. Baden-Baden: Nomos Verlagsgesellschaft.

Hinsley, F. H. 1966. *Sovereignty.* New York: Basic Books.

Hoock. J. 1989. "Economie politique, statistique et réforme administrative en France et en Allemagne dans la deuxième moitié du 18e siècle." Pages 33–45 in Heyen, 1989.

Van IJsselmuiden, P. G. 1988. *Binnenlandse Zaken en het ontstaan van de moderne bureaucratie in Nederland 1813–1940.* Kampen: Kok.

*International Institute of the Administrative Sciences.* 1983. XIXth International Congress of Administrative Sciences.

Jacoby, H. 1973. *The Bureaucratization of the World.* Berkeley: University of California Press.

Kernaghan, K., and D. Siegel. 1987. *Public Administration in Canada.* Toronto: Methuen.

König, K. 1970. *Erkenntnissinteressen der Verwaltungswissenschaft.* Berlin: Dunker und Humblot.

Kooperman, L., and S. Rosenberg. 1977. "The British Administrative Legacy in Kenya and Ghana." *International Review of the Administrative Sciences* 43, no. 3: 267–72.

Langrod, G. 1954. "Science et enseignement de l'administration publique." *Revue International des Sciences Administratives* 20, no. 4: 543–606.

Lindenfeld, D. F. 1989. "Decline of Polizeiwissenschaft: Continuity and Change in the Study of Public Administration in Germany." In Heyen, 1989.

Lofstrom, W. 1973. "From Colony to Republic: A Case Study in Bureaucratic Change." *Journal of Latin American Studies* 5, no. 2: 177–97.

Manchester, A. K. 1972. "The Growth of Bureaucracy in Brazil 1808–1821." *Journal of Latin American Studies* 4, no. 1: 77–83.

Marx, F. M., ed. 1959. *Elements of Public Administration.* 2nd ed. Englewood Cliffs, NJ: Prentice Hall.

Mayer, F. 1959. "Neuzeitliche Entwicklungen der öffentlichen Verwaltung." In F. M. Marx, ed., *Elements of Public Administration.* 2nd ed. Englewood Cliffs, NJ: Prentice Hall.

McClenaghan, W. A. 1985. *MacGruder's American Government.* New York: Allyn & Bacon.

Miller, M. 1984. "From Ancient to Modern Organization: The Church as Conduit and Creator." *Administration and Society* 15, no. 3: 275–93.

Misra, B. B. 1977. *The Bureaucracy in India: An Historical Analysis of the Development up to 1947.* New Delhi: Oxford University Press.

Mohnhaupt, H. 1989. "Vorstufen der Wissenschaften von 'Verwaltung' und 'Verwaltungsrecht' an der Universität Göttingen (1750–1830)." Pages 73–103 in Heyen, 1989.

Mosher, F. C. 1977. "The Evolution of American Civil Service Concepts." Pages 53–98 in *Democracy and the Public Service.* New York: Oxford University Press.

Nelson, W. E. 1982. *The Roots of American Bureaucracy 1830–1900.* Cambridge: Harvard University Press.

Nigro, F. A., and L. G. Nigro. 1984. *Modern Public Administration,* 6th ed. New York: Harper and Row.

Osterloh, K.-H. 1970. *Joseph von Sonnenfels und die österreichische Reformbewegung im Zeitalter des aufgeklärten Absolutismus: Eine Studie zum Zusammenhang von Kameralwissenschaft und Verwaltungspraxis.* Lübeck: Matthiesen.

Parris, H. 1969. *Constitutional Bureaucracy. The Development of British Central Administration since the Eighteenth Century.* London: Allen & Unwin.

Pawlowski, T. 1980. *On Concepts and Methods in the Humanities and the Social Sciences.* Wroclaw: University of Wroclaw Press.

Perry, J. L., ed. 1989. *Handbook of Public Administration.* San Francisco: Jossey-Bass.

Pfiffner, J. M., and R. Presthus. 1960. *Public Administration.* 5th ed. New York: Ronald Press.

Pintner W. M. 1970. "The Social Characteristics of the Early Nineteenth Century Russian Bureaucracy." *Slavic Review* 29, no. 3: 429–43.

————. 1975. "The Russian Higher Civil Service on the Eve of the Great Reform." *Journal of Social History* 8, no. 3: 55–68.

Quah, J. S. T. 1978. "The Origins of the Public Bureaucracies in the ASEAN Countries." *Indian Journal of Public Administration* 24, no. 2: 400–29.

Raadschelders, J. C. N. 1988. "Coproduction in Historical Perspective. Initiative and Participation at Local Government Level. In L. J. Roborgh, Th. A. J. Toonen, and R. R. Stough, eds., *Public Infrastructure Redefined.* Bloomington: School of Public and Environmental Affairs, Indiana University.

————. 1989. "Departementen in vergelijkend en historisch perspectief." In J. L. M. Hakvoort, and J. M. de Heer, eds., *Wetenschap over Departementen.* The Hague: VUGA.

————. 1990. *Plaatselijk bestuurlijke ontwikkelingen 1600–1980. Een historisch-bestuurskundig onderzoek in vier Noordhollandse gemeenten.* The Hague: VNG-Uitgeverij.

Raadschelders, J. C. N. and Th. A. J. Toonen, 1992. "Adjustment of Dutch Administration to European Policies." Paper presented at a conference on Administrative Modernization in Europe, Perugia, Italy.

Rosenberg, H. 1958. *Bureaucracy, Aristocracy and Autocracy. The Prussian Experience 1660–1815.* Cambridge: Harvard University Press.

Rowat, D. C. 1988. *Public Administration in Developed Democracies.* New York: Marcel Dekker.

Rutgers, M. R. 1990. "Lorenz von Stein als grondlegger van de bestuurskunde." *Bestuurswetenschappen* 44, no. 4: 286–300.

————. 1993. *Tussen fragmentatie en integratie. De bestuurskunde als kennisintegrerende wetenschap.* Delft: Eburon.

Saffell, D. C. 1984. *The Politics of American National Government.* Boston: Little, Brown & Company.

Sayre, W. S. 1965. *The Federal Government Service.* New York: Columbia University, American Assembly.

Schiesl, M. J. 1977. *The Politics of Efficiency. Municipal Administration Reform in America, 1800–1920.* Berkeley: University of California Press.

Seckendorff, V. L. von. 1976. *Teutscher Fürstenstat,* ed. Ludwig Fertig (reprint of edition of 1665), Glashütte im Taunus.

Seip, J. A. 1974. *Utsikt over Norges historie, 1814–1860.* Oslo: Universitetsforlaget.

Seysell, Claude de. 1961. *La Monarchie de France et deux autres fragments politiques,* ed. J. Pujol. Paris: Librairie d'Argences.

Sharkansky, I. 1975. *Public Administration: Policy-Making in Government Agencies.* 3rd ed. Chicago: Rand McNally.

Shinder, J. 1978. "Early Ottoman Administration in the Wilderness: Some Limits on Comparison. *International Journal of Middle Eastern Studies* 9, no. 4: 497–517.

Simon, H. A., D. W. Smithburg, and V. A. Thompson. 1970. *Public Administration.* 13th ed. New York: Alfred A. Knopf.

Starling, G. 1986. *Managing the Public Sector.* 3rd. ed. Chicago: Dorsey Press.

Swaan, A. de. 1988. *In Care of the State: Health Care, Education, and Welfare in Europe and the USA in the Modern Era.* Cambridge: Polity Press.

Thieme, W. 1984. *Verwaltungslehre.* 4th ed. Cologne: Karl Heimanns Verlag.

Tilly, Ch., ed. 1975. *The Formation of National States in Western Europe.* Princeton: Princeton University Press.

Van Riper, P. 1958. *A History of the United States Civil Service.* Evanston, IL: Row, Peterson.

Vere, A. J. de. 1970. "The Malayan Civil Service 1874–1941: Colonial Bureaucracy/ Malayan Elite." *Comparative Studies in Society in History* 12, no. 2: 149–78.

Waldo, D. 1980. *The Enterprise of Public Administration: A Summary View.* Novato, CA: Chandler & Sharp.

Walker, N. 1961. *Morale in the Civil Service: A Study of the Desk Worker.* Edinburgh: University Press.

Wansink, H. 1981. *Politieke wetenschappen aan de Leidse Universiteit 1575-±1650.* Utrecht: Hes.

Weber, M. 1980. *Wirtschaft und Gesellschaft. Grundriss der verstehenden Soziologie.* 5th ed. Tübingen: J. C. B. Mohr.

White, L. D. 1967. *Introduction to the Study of Public Administration.* 10th ed. New York: Macmillan.

Wright, M. 1969. *Treasury Control of the Civil Service 1854–1874.* Oxford: Clarendon Press.

# 5 INTERNAL LABOR MARKETS

Lois Recascino Wise

The underlying notion in the study of internal labor markets (ILMs) is that organizations create closed systems for managing human resources; this has consequences for individual employees as well as organizational efficiency and effectiveness. Internal labor markets involve the administrative policies and practices that determine the way human resources are used and rewarded within an organization. They can be broadly defined by the rules pertaining to job definition or classification, deployment, job security and membership, and reward structures and wage rules.

Differences among individuals and between groups in occupational mobility and opportunity have been one important area of research into the consequences of ILMs (Whyte, 1956; Crozier, 1971; Kanter, 1978). Studies of internal labor markets have also attempted to develop theoretical models for understanding observed variations between organizations in the rate of pay offered for equal jobs where the laws of supply and demand would predict equal wages (Kerr, 1954; Doeringer and Piore, 1971; Osterman, 1984; 1988).

Very little of the work on ILMs focuses on the public sector (DiPrete, 1989). This is ironic because in many of the elements that distinguish internal labor markets, public sector organizations are distinct. For example, civil service systems have been inclined to use highly structured job classification systems and at the same time to promote employee job security and job protection through organizational rules and sanctions. The desire for uniformity in the rules and regulations governing personnel management decisions and efforts to limit managerial discretion can be said to characterize traditional personnel management styles. This view has been particularly popular in government, perhaps because of a desire to foster an image of fair and uniform treatment of employees. In comparison, the internal labor market systems approach focuses on the effects of variations within organizations in the way human resources are used and rewarded.

As Christopher Hood points out in this volume, the current global transition in public management is closely connected with human resource management structures. Decentralization increases the significance of internal labor market systems as determinants of variations in the way members of the labor market progress in their careers and earnings. Efforts toward more decentralized and discretionary management systems are in sharp contrast with rigid and highly structured personnel management rules and wage setting practices that exist in many national civil service systems. Existing organizational rules and policies may undermine reforms and send conflicting signals to employees about what behavior or which attributes are valued in public organizations, and they may alter the distributional effects of reward systems.

The use of internal labor market systems for managing human resources serves different organizational purposes. From a management perspective, internal labor markets are functional because they allow employers to develop and retain employees with valued knowledge that would be costly to replace and that may enhance organizational productivity and efficiency. Job ladders provide for a rational progression in skills and knowledge that enables an organization to develop in-house capabilities and expertise. Like wage structures, opportunities for advancement can be used to stimulate loyalty among organizational members. ILMs may provide dissatisfied employees with alternatives to voluntary separation or exit. At the same time, greater access to the upper rungs of the career ladder or to management posts may advance social and economic equality and provide opportunities for a more pluralistic and less elitist decision-making structure, something that is particularly desirable in government organizations.

For these reasons, the absence in public administration literature of a theoretical framework for understanding the integral relationships among the rules and techniques governing human resource management in government organizations, the efficiency and effectiveness of government operations, and the well-being of public employees is striking. This study attempts to contribute to the development of a framework for understanding the importance of internal labor markets in the context of different national civil service systems. It begins with a discussion of the structure of internal labor markets in governments and the role of informal customs and rules in the way these systems operate. The next section provides a framework for comparative analysis of internal labor markets in civil service systems and identifies four key systemic factors of ILMs. The last section presents some outcomes of ILMs that impact both organizations and organizational members.

## INTERNAL LABOR MARKETS IN GOVERNMENT ORGANIZATIONS

Internal labor markets are formal components of an organization's management system. The choice of emphasis on internal or external labor market systems is a strategic management decision that defines the employment relationship within an organization and the constraints within which human resource management tasks are implemented. These choices are of particular importance in civil service systems because of the need to hold employees accountable, as McGregor (1991) observes. Moreover, the notion that government should function as a model employer is common to many cultures. This means that the employment relationship is expected to meet a higher standard, one that can serve as a model for how workers should be treated. As model employers, governments promote the concepts of fairness and equality and may also advance affirmative action policies to redress the effects of labor market discrimination in other sectors.

Internal labor markets are complex systems. It is unlikely that a single internal labor market exists, even in predominantly white-collar organizations. Rather, multiple employment systems operate simultaneously with categories of workers treated differently within an organization. For example, the rules and customs affecting clerical workers' pay and opportunities for advancement may be distinct from those affecting professional or managerial workers (Osterman, 1984: 167). DiPrete's study (1989) of the U.S. civil service system describes how, in response to increasing task complexity during the 1800s, separate career systems evolved for administrative and clerical work, sharpening the boundaries between these two areas of work.

Typically, an internal labor market is composed of a series of job ladders. On each ladder, jobs increase in technical difficulty or skill requirements with each step. In principle, the way the ladder is structured and the relationship of one job to the next in terms of difficulty and skill requirements should facilitate upward progress in the organization. In practice, the structure of the job ladders themselves may hinder employee advancement and truncate opportunities for upward mobility. For example, in systems patterned after the French civil service, work in each ministry is organized into cadres that establish rules for recruitment and promotion which are sensitive to the needs of the ministry and the conditions of the relevant profession. The result is that interdepartmental mobility is impeded by inconsistencies in job requirements even for positions with the same title and grade.

## Role of Custom and Informal Rules

Although formal rules and regulations that govern personnel management procedures are a critical component of internal labor markets, informal customs and unsanctioned practices are also key determinants of internal labor market dynamics. These informal customs may be inconsistent with organizational goals but more compatible with employee preferences for how work should be managed. For example, group pressure may dictate lower productivity rates or higher wage rates (Ross, 1948) than management would prefer.

The trend toward decentralization in public management impacts the role of custom and informal rules. Decentralization may contribute to norm drift

(Buitendam, 1991) within the public sector in that without some mechanism for uniformity, multiple decision centers cannot promulgate as uniform or consistent a norm system as a single centralized structure that sets personnel standards. In the absence of mechanisms to reinforce prevailing norms, norm drift is likely to occur and to expand the differences between working conditions and benefit allocation within the same national civil service system. Consequently, internal labor markets gain importance through decentralization.

To the extent that social discontinuities arise from decentralization and related norm drift, efforts to secure some centralizing mechanism may become increasingly apparent (Buitendam, 1991). Management may seek some standardization of norms and may be reluctant to assume responsibility for setting personnel standards and practices. Employer and trade union associations may develop mechanisms to monitor and censure practices outside some acceptable range or to reinforce prevailing standards of acceptable working conditions or salary levels (Wise, 1993). In the case of human resource management, some centralizing mechanisms may improve the possibility of achieving real productivity gains through decentralization of decision-making by reducing the costs of social discontinuities related to norm drift (Buitendam, 1991).

Custom may play an important role in explaining hiring patterns within a public agency. The case of the international civil service is instructive both in terms of the effects of customs on sex discrimination and geographic representation of the work force. As it evolved, the United Nations' goal of achieving geographic representation gained prominence over other criteria, including merit, for hiring and promoting employees. By tradition, certain positions became designated as geographic posts and, in some cases, positions were attached to specific countries or geographic areas.

Although no formal rules existed, professionally qualified women were traditionally hired into United Nations agencies at the top clerical grade or the lowest professional grade, regardless of their professional credentials. Men, on the other hand, were recruited into the second or third professional grade, and they made faster progress through the professional ranks to grade six. Initial efforts at reform launched during the 1970s made little progress against entrenched custom, but in more recent years some improvement in women's status has been apparent. Similarly, despite efforts to democratize the French upper-level civil service, research concludes that bureaucratic elites in government continue to be drawn from the ranks of the French social elite and that persons hired into mid-level positions have very little chance of advancement to top posts (Bodiguel, 1990).

Organizational culture may also establish standards that affect efficiency and effectiveness. Adherence to guidelines or tolerance for different levels of absenteeism and production quality may be a function of organizational culture, for example. In the same vein, management's ability to hire workers above entry level grades, or to promote some workers more rapidly through the system than others, reflects a less rigid culture that tolerates managerial discretion and flexibility. In other organizations, the demand for uniformity in treatment may be much stronger and managerial discretion sharply limited. Even when a new system is formally established, the prevailing culture may continue to support traditional practices. Thus, pay-for-performance schemes may fail to show any differentiation among employees in rating levels, and "merit awards" may continue to be given to the great majority of workers. The success of efforts to change organizational systems are closely linked to organizational culture.

Organizational culture is integrally related to the prevailing social culture. This places limitations on the extent to which practices can be transferred between countries or civil service systems. It is now generally understood that Japan's quality circles are effective in improving productivity because of a prevailing relationship between workers and management that typifies Japanese culture. Mobility patterns may also be determined by national customs, especially in consensus-oriented systems like those in Japan and Sweden, where workers can be ostracized and eliminated from information loops and decision-making responsibilities for not conforming. Social customs that segregate sexes, tribes, or castes also have the effect of eliminating groups from decision-making opportunities in government agencies. Where power is manipulated on the golf course, in the sauna, steam bath, or sports club, members of excluded groups are disadvantaged.

## FRAMEWORK FOR COMPARATIVE ANALYSIS

Organizational rules and regulations establish the conditions and terms of employment within an organization as well as the opportunity structure for groups of workers. Compared to other researchers, Osterman (1988) takes a more expansive approach to ILMs. He suggests that the rules defining internal labor market dynamics can be divided into four categories. This study modifies those categories slightly; here they are job definition and classification systems; deployment rules; job security rules and membership; and reward structures wage rules. The categories are useful for exploring a comparative framework for analysis of internal labor markets in public sector organizations. The discussion identifies systemic factors relevant to each of the four dimensions of internal labor markets listed in table 5.1.

### Job Definition and Classification Systems

Job evaluation systems play a significant role in defining the boundaries between work areas. From a management perspective, the structure of job tasks within an organization and the rules and regulations governing placement facilitate the development of a trained and qualified work force. Job ladders provide a rational sequence for training and development in the skills and knowledge required for increasingly difficult work within an organization and thus provide organizations with a qualified labor supply (Doeringer and Piore, 1971). The extent to which the responsibility for job classification is centrally held or decentralized to the agency level, as in the Dutch system, affects the flexibility of the system.

Rigid position classification systems, popular in civil service systems, can be seen as an impediment to employee growth and development in that they put employees in job categories that do not share common attributes or ranking factors. When white-collar work is organized into separate categories such as clerical, technical, or professional work, the top administrative and policy-making jobs in the organization are likely to be available only to those who climb the professional ladder. For those hired into clerical positions there may be no bridge job that enables them to cross over to the technical or professional category, or there may be arbitrary requirements such as licenses or certificates or some educational degree that serve as barriers to such a move. As DiPrete's (1989) research indicates, however, a certain amount of porosity typically exists within these systems, permitting some movement between job ladders among lower-level employees.

Systems can be distinguished by the extent to which jobs are broadly or narrowly defined. Although public sector organizations are generally characterized by narrow grades and relatively rigid position-ranking systems to which individuals are assigned, there are important exceptions and changes are underway. In the United States, for example, efforts to switch from the eighteen-grade white-collar classification system to six broad bands which allow management greater flexibility in assigning personnel are underway in some agencies (NAPA, 1991). In Sweden, the national schedule of thirty-five narrow grades for white-collar civil servants was replaced with a gradeless system in 1991.

The choice between broad generalist jobs and more narrowly defined specialist positions has significant implications for both employer and employee, as Kanter (1978) and others have demonstrated. Both types are found in national civil service systems. The U.S. system has been characterized by an emphasis on job specialization, although important exceptions to this pattern exist. Certain agencies within the federal government have generalist positions, and the Senior Executive Service, established in 1978, can be seen as a movement toward more flexible positions at the top level of the civil service. While specialization is valued for meeting the challenges of work in an increasingly complex society, generalist positions may provide a more circumspective view of organizational mission and activities and provide for greater flexibility in the placement of employees within an organization or in departments of the same organization.

## Deployment Rules

Movement within an organization is determined by rules affecting career advancement as well as by an organization's policies for and investments in staff development. Opportunities for promotion and job training can be seen as distributive functions of internal labor markets. From an organization's perspective, these are nonmarketable resources. They are also scarce provisions of internal labor market systems. The scarcity of these resources increases the importance of internal labor market rules and regulations in determining their allocation.

*Mobility.*

Mobility rules affect opportunities for career advancement and economic well-being. Both lateral and vertical opportunities for movement within and between departments are important vehicles for improving the career horizons of employees. Deployment rules define who is eligible for mobility opportunities and the criteria by which candidates will be assessed. Interdepartmental mobility is typically uncommon in national civil service systems. Although some countries (including the United States, France, and the Netherlands) have special programs to promote mobility among upper-level civil servants, various impediments seem to block movement within the civil service (OECD, 1990). An important exception is the Japanese civil service system, which emphasizes exposure to different agencies within an organization as part of a civil servant's career development. In addition to skill-sharing and the broadening of an individual employee's understanding of organizational operations, mobility between ministries or departments can be seen as a way to improve the overall quality of a civil service work force, particularly where hiring freezes on the one hand and reduction through planned attrition on the other have the potential for reducing staff creativity and flexibility.

Within this context, the establishment of affirmative policies or upward mobility programs within public agencies recognizes the extent to which deployment rules may serve as barriers to advancement to people who have been socially or economically disadvantaged. The choice between educational and experiential criteria for placement, for example, impacts socially advantaged and disadvantaged groups differently, as does the use of achievement and aptitude tests for hiring and promotion. Similarly, the identification or construction of bridging jobs between career ladders establishes alternative routes for mobility that extend the career horizons of public employees.

The tendency to require educational degrees and credentials limits access to professional positions and the upper rungs of career ladders. Where educational degrees are a formal requirement, the benefits of public employment fall to those who have the social advantage of advanced education. Variations exist among national civil service systems, however, in the extent to which they require high school or university undergraduate degrees for entry and advancement. Germany traditionally imposed relatively high educational requirements on its national civil servants, and historical data suggest that the trend has been toward higher credentials (Schmidt and Rose, 1985: 148). Educational attainment is used not only as a criterion for job placement but also for eligibility for training opportunities.

The United States is noteworthy among western nations to the extent that it has rejected in principle the idea of educational certification. Both national and state laws prohibit across-the-board application of educational standards. Since passage of the Civil Service, or Pendleton, Act of 1883, selection tests have been required to be job relevant and practical. When degree standards are used, employers should be able to prove that they are valid job-related requirements. The Japanese civil service selects employees on the basis of competitive exams, history of work performance, or an evaluation of work skills. The examination process employs a general test as well as specialized tests and personality tests for work (Kim, 1988).

African countries tend to link educational requirements to posts. Those patterned after the British system typically measure degree attainment, while those modeled after the French system focus on years of schooling completed (Robinson, 1990: 43–57). In some cases members of the civil service system may advance to a post without meeting the degree requirements applied to new entrants into the service. Salary premiums are attached to advanced (college baccalaureate) and specialized (i.e., engineering or science) degrees.

*Staff development.*

Job training opportunities are a critical element for employee growth and upward mobility. Firms vary in their emphasis on human resource development, and these differences have effects on employment patterns (Osterman, 1984: 183). Emphasis on training and retraining reflects a willingness to invest in people as part of the organizational value system. Civil service systems based on patronage, for example, may view employment as a short-term relationship and see little value in long-term investment. Where jobs are given out purely for their reward value, the complexity of the work and need for training may go unrecognized, even on a short-term basis. The notion of long-term employment, which characterizes many national civil service systems, is compatible with policies for investing in the training and development of employees not only for job-specific skills but also for long-term career development within the organization. Thus, there is a clear link between staff development and provisions for job security.

## Job Security and Membership

Civil service systems typically offer employees more job protection than private sector jobs and more liberal provisions for pension vesting, but there are important exceptions to this general pattern. Patronage-based personnel systems do not promise lifetime employment and may in fact encourage turnover among employees. Government cutbacks in many countries over the last decade have been associated with reductions-in-force at all levels of government. Of interest here are the criteria for establishing tenure rights, and the trade-off between individual employees' seniority and their perceived value in terms of performance rating scores or some other indicator of productivity. At the same time, factors determining eligibility for entry and the conditions of membership are affected by internal labor market structures. Organizations that emphasize the value of equal employment opportunity, for example, would be expected to use the same framework for choosing new members. The criteria for admission and the process of socialization may also impact workforce composition and the strength of internal labor market systems. Job recruitment systems, for example, may succeed in screening out people who are unlike incumbent employees in demographic characteristics or professional training. They may limit the labor pool according to geographic regions or educational institutions. The nature of the ILM would determine whether organizations attempt to recruit entry level personnel with high potential or hire more broadly across job levels and levels of experience.

Changes underway in core-peripheral workforce dynamics, especially in white-collar organizations, are also important for understanding the role of internal labor markets. Core workers are those who are promised job security and career advancement within a firm, while peripheral workers are those members of the contingent workforce who offer their services on a part-time or temporary basis, often working without fringe benefits or any pledge of job security. The general trend in industrialized societies is toward more flexible workforces, using more contingent workers. In government, this translates into more part-time and more temporary and contractual appointments.

The trend may also be associated with more restrictive conditions for pension vesting and eligibility for retirement benefits or more liberal terms for pension buyouts or pension fund portability as governments attempt to trade off their current payroll costs against their future obligation to pay out retirement benefits. Italy, for example, recently reduced early retirement pension privileges for public employees as a way of reducing the budget deficit; at the same time, U.S. officials were considering a cash payment to induce an early exist from the civil service.

Contingent workers include an increasingly wide range of occupations and are not limited to clerical workers. Computer specialists, engineers, and technicians may also be engaged on a temporary basis, but overall contingent workers are disproportionately female, young, and old. These groups largely make up the buffer that protects prime workers from reductions in force or temporary layoffs. So the overall effect of expansion in the size of the contingent work force is less equity among social groups. Great Britain, Sweden, and West Germany, for example, are countries that have experienced sharp increases in civil service part-time appointments filled mainly by women.

Osterman (1988: 63) suggests that the increased use of temporary workers can be viewed as management's attempt to transform the internal labor market status of an occupational group from stable employment with job security, training opportunities, and career development to a simple hire/fire relationship. Elements of the internal labor market may be used as an inducement by management to make certain changes more palatable to the work force. For example, plans to widen job classification categories and increase managerial discretion in placing employees might be accompanied by more opportunities for training or opportunities for greater earnings through productivity incentives. A key point in ILM research is that the utility of the framework is determined by the extent to which individual workers spend large shares of their working lives with a single employer who impacts both their social and economic well-being. Thus changes in job security rules and job tenure rates may fundamentally transform internal labor market systems (Osterman, 1992).

### Reward Structure and Wage Rules

Salaries for public employees may be attached to a specific position that an employee happens to occupy, or to the individual worker based on his or her training, competency, experience, productivity, or some other attribute. The connection between internal labor market systems and wage differentials has been examined by many researchers. Internal labor markets may create wage structures that are uniquely different from the external market. The extent to which ILMs favor people with employer-specific knowledge or skills and those with skills in great demand in the external labor market, however, appears to be indeterminate. In highly segmented labor markets, where government is the only employer for specific professional groups, employees are often disadvantaged in salary setting and wage development. Nurses and teachers, for example, may lag behind the wage rates of those with similar training and experience working in other jobs in the private sector. On the other hand, employers in both sectors appear to offer premium wages to employees who have valued organization-specific knowledge and whom they are unwilling to lose to another employer. This practice became popular in national civil service systems during the 1980s as governments began to implement different market supplements as bonuses above fixed salary levels in order to recruit and retain valued employees. Positions at the top of the promotion ladder and those with access to organizational decision-makers may have an advantage over others in gaining a wage premium for organization-specific knowledge (Cappelli and Cascio, 1991).

The determinants of pay increases and the rules affecting the distribution of organizational rewards are key elements in internal labor market systems. Reliance on pay for performance as a determinant of reward distribution may produce a different organizational culture and motivation structure than a seniority or time-in-service reward system. Moreover, organizations may rely on nonmonetary incentives to stimulate different motives and levels of commitment than performance-related pay systems.

TABLE 5.1

**Variables for Comparative Analysis of Internal Labor Markets in Civil Service Systems**

A. Job Definition and Classification Systems
Type of system(s)
Degree of managerial flexibility within the system

B. Deployment
Mobility
Criteria for placement in upper-level jobs
Structure of career ladders
Opportunity for interdepartmental mobility
Staff Development
Criteria for eligibility for training
Per capita expenditure for training and continuing education

C. Job Security and Membership
Criteria for layoff/reduction in force
Ratio of peripheral to core positions
Criteria for pension vesting and eligibility for retirement benefits
Criteria for entry and membership

D. Reward Structure and Wage Rules
Pay parity between public and private sector for equal work
Size of wage differentials within or between occupational groups
Determinants of pay rates and pay increases
Content of the reward structure
Rules affecting the distribution of rewards

These four components of ILMs are integrally related. Changes in the job definition and classification systems would directly affect the pattern of mobility within an organization and, in turn, the rate of job tenure. Opportunities for upward mobility and career growth are linked to job security and membership. Organizations that emphasize promotion from within may represent more closed personnel systems that place a greater value on offering job security and attractive retirement benefits. Deployment rules, particularly investments in staff development and in the development of challenging career ladders, are thus directly tied to the content of organizational reward structures. Similarly, reward structures and wage rules may represent a short-term strategy for human resource utilization or a long-term plan for maximizing an individual's contribution to an organization. Changes in one ILM component may force change in another. A civil service system that restricts entry and membership may be forced to increase expenditures for staff development, for example; a system that reduces job security may be required to liberalize wage policies or mobility opportunities to retain valuable workers, and so forth.

## CONSEQUENCES OF INTERNAL LABOR MARKETS

The structure of internal labor markets is related to significant outcomes for both organizations and their members. Among sociologists, internal labor markets are of particular interest because of their impact on occupational mobility and the level of social and economic equality in society. Much less attention has been given to the consequences of ILMs for the distributional issue of access to political power. Similarly, the potential impact of ILMs on organizational effectiveness and receptivity to change or innovation, as well as broader questions related to spillover effects on external labor markets have been less adequately explored. Table 5.2 provides a listing of some different outcome measures of internal labor markets.

### Impact on Organizations

Internal labor markets impact organizational efficiency. Greater flexibility in management decisions regarding personnel operations is expected to lower human resource management costs and reduce constraints that might hamper management's ability to utilize personnel effectively. Career advancement and salary incentives generated by ILMs have the goal of stimulating employee loyalty and reducing undesired turnover and replacement costs.

One motive for the development of internal labor markets lies in the use of progressive job ladders to cultivate a knowledgeable and experienced in-house workforce. Internal labor markets allow organizations to groom their own professional and managerial staff. Staff development is particularly important where organizations experience little turnover and replacement of employees. Staff development and promotion from within have the advantage of increasing the rate of accumulation of agency-specific knowledge and, in turn, an organization's capacity for learning and innovation.

Where downsizing and hiring freezes are in effect, organizational culture and capacity may become increasingly determined by the incumbent work force. It is for this reason that the Dutch civil service has embarked on a program to increase interdepartmental mobility within a workforce that is expected to become increasingly stable and in which replacement cannot be relied on for new energy.

Internal labor markets may also impact organizational culture by reducing their level of competitiveness. Risk taking, for example, can be negatively affected by the reward structures within an organization. Where rewards are linked to short-term results, employees are less likely to invest in long-term strategies that may have less tangible benefits and would result in short-term reward deprivation (Brockhaus, 1980). Payment by results and other forms of performance-based pay would be expected to reduce an individual employee's willingness to absorb the costs of a risk-based strategy (Jackson et al., 1989). Innovativeness, in turn, would be similarly impeded because innovation comes from risk taking and often involves many false starts and failures. Where the individual employee is penalized for short-term failure, his or her willingness to be innovative would be hampered.

Job security and membership rules also impact the competitiveness of an organization. Because innovations may change the way the work is performed and alter the status quo, employees who are not protected in their job may be unwilling to pursue reforms that could result in staff reductions or job changes (Fast, 1976). High turnover rates through weak job security systems would also negatively affect the level of cumulative knowledge within an organization (Kanter, 1985). Increased expertise in the product or service of an organization is accumulated by individuals and may not be formally recorded or documented.

In the same vein, staff development efforts related to deployment rules and job training opportunities would be associated with knowledge accumulation within an organization. Flexible deployment rules, interdepartmental mobility practices, and investments in staff development through job training would contribute to an employee's ability to gain expertise in an organizational process or product; the achievement of such expertise would be a platform from which innovation could be pursued.

Within an organizational context, ILMs create subsystems around different occupational groups that lower the level of uniformity within an organization. Differences in decision-making processes within these subsystems will be associated with differences in organizational outputs and standards in a variety of management areas. These subsystems may build on different preferences and value systems operating within a large organization, or a lack of uniformity in norm structures may create certain tensions between organizational units. Internal labor markets may be dysfunctional where they produce intolerable levels of norm drift within an organization, creating value conflicts between management and employees that may lead to nonproductive or even disruptive behavior. The decentralization of the human resource management function promotes variation in treatment among employees that tests the strength of the employer-employee relationship.

### Impact on Organizational Members

Public sector organizations may have a strong influence on opportunities for upward mobility within a society. Government employment has traditionally been a haven for those discriminated against by the competitive sector, particularly women. Because women and minority group members tend to occupy lower-ranking posts within an organization, barriers to advancement such as rigid requirements or the absence of clearly defined career paths for upward mobility in the organization thwart social mobility for these groups. At the same time, studies of civil service elites have concluded that barriers to upward mobility in the public bureaucracy have significant implications for the level of democracy and representativeness in a system (Bodiguel, 1990; Wise, 1990).

The extent to which an employee's skills are organization-specific may impact his or her power in the open labor market. Labor market segmentation, by sector, may have a more significant impact on labor market flows and pricing. In large welfare states and highly segmented sectors of employment, government is often a monopsonistic user of specific labor market skills. Monopsony reduces the competitiveness of workers and spawns inequities in the internal alignment of job values within an organization as well as the comparative alignment of jobs between firms or agencies. These inequities become sharper when they are attached to social groups rather than evenly dispersed throughout the workforce. Wise (1990) discusses the broad implications of inequities within the civil service for social equity in gaining access to political power and to the economic resources of public employment.

At the same time, however, research demonstrates that some organizations will pay a premium to develop and retain employees with firm-specific knowledge that it would be costly to replace. Efforts to enhance loyalty among these employees may be associated, for example, with salary premiums, training opportunities, and promotions, all of which would have the effect of increasing an employee's costs for leaving his or her current employer. Organizational knowledge may not always be rewarded favorably. Management may underestimate the value of replacing such people and, because of their lack of competitiveness on the external market, may at the same time undervalue their contribution to the organization. There is no reliable relationship between organization-specific knowledge and the price internal labor markets attach to an employee's services.

Cross-national research on opportunities for advancement within national civil service systems shows some variation among nations in opportunities for mobility. Within the context of contemporary public management reform (OECD, 1990), mobility within civil service systems is seen as an indicator of organizational flexibility; but certain factors appear to hinder career mobility between agencies of government. DiPrete's review (1989: 9) indicates that earlier research showed little opportunity for advancement from one tier to another in Spain, Italy, or Denmark. French and British workers, however, had more opportunity for transfers between job ladders. The chances for Americans to move within the organization appeared higher, and DiPrete reports that lateral entry opportunities in the U.S. civil service also advantage American public employees.

Studies of African civil service systems, which are largely patterned after the British and French systems, indicate that upward mobility opportunities are an important avenue for civil servants to increase their earning levels, and movement within a group of classes or job ladders is a characteristic of these systems.

This means that a clerical employee might be promoted into the executive class and an executive employee might join the administrative ranks. Technicians might be able to advance into the scientific class, especially if they have acquired additional education (Robinson, 1990: 56–57). Cohort studies of civil servants provide some evidence about the extent of this activity (Robinson, 1990: 125–56).

Internal labor market dynamics are reflected in the social orientation of an organization's wage structure and the system for rewarding employees for loyalty or good performance. They thus have a direct impact on the economic well-being of organizational members. The construct of social orientation pertains to the internal alignment of positions within an organization as well as differences among employees in their level of earnings. The policies of equal pay for equal work and equal pay for work of comparable difficulty would each affect the amount of social differentiation in economic well-being created by an organization's wage structure. Researchers often compare the wage gap between groups, the percentage a disadvantaged group earns relative to the advantaged group. Wise's work (1991: 572) shows the relative advantage Swedish women in the civil service have over their American counterparts, and the very strong position of Asian-Americans relative to other American minority groups.

Parity between public and private sector wage structures is influenced not only by the level of internal alignment in public sector pay but also by the point at which the wage floor and the ceiling of public sector pay is set. Governments seeking to function as "model employers" may attempt to establish a higher wage for unskilled labor in their salary structure. Parity is also affected by the frequency with which government enacts pay increases and the extent to which public sector pay rates are believed to become obsolete. Worsening economic conditions prevent governments from implementing pay revisions. During the 1970s and 1980s, some governments revised pay rates very infrequently (Paukert and Robinson, 1992: 127).

Similarly, ratios of wage spreads between the lowest and highest paid employees reflect differences in social equity. Variations in such ratios can be fairly sharp. In Great Britain, for example, the ratio was 15:1 in 1981, while in Hong Kong, the ratio for the same period was 29:1 (Scott et al., 1984). Pay differentials can also be measured by comparing earnings for segments of the workforce, for instance by quartiles.

The organizational reward system determines who is eligible for pay increases based on time-in-service, output, or acquired knowledge or skill. In this sense, the reward system sends cues to employees about the value of attributes that affect employee behavior and a worker's value outside the organization. Rewards are distributed according to the determinants of step increases within grade, the criteria for advancement, or eligibility for special opportunities for training. Reward systems may be group based, with several workers receiving the same benefits based on work cooperatively performed, or individually based. The emphasis on pay for performance and greater use of individual rewards is a common trend among civil service systems.

The grade distribution of employees within the existing grade structure also provides an indicator of social equity. In some systems some social groups are clustered in the lower ranks, while the small percentage of upper-level policy-making posts is occupied by an advantaged social group. Wise's comparison of the systems in the United States and Sweden found greater inequity in the Swedish quartile grade distribution, but in both cases women held only ten percent of the elite positions (Wise, 1990: 571–72).

TABLE 5.2

**Some Outcome Measures for Internal Labor Markets**

A. Classification and Job Definition
   Quartile distribution of social groups by grade level

B. Deployment
   Proportion of employees, by job category, experiencing vertical position change per year within same department
   Proportion of employees experiencing lateral or vertical mobility between government departments per year
   Comparison of mobility rates within government and industry for different social groups and occupations or grade levels
   Existence and relative size of budget item for staff development
   Proportion of employees receiving in-service training
   Proportion of employees participating in continuing education

C. Job Security and Membership
   Rate of voluntary separation per total employees
   Job tenure rates by job category within the organization
   Job tenure rates in government and external market by job category
   Proportion of employees experiencing reduction-in-force or layoff
   Proportion of employees vested in the retirement plan
   Selection rates by level of experience

D. Reward Structure and Wage Rules
   Size of differentials between groups in the organization and in the external market
   Existence of pay-for-performance reward structure
   Size of pay bonuses relative to annual salary

## SUMMARY

The relevance of the internal labor market framework for examining public organizations appears to be reinforced by contemporary trends in public management reform identified by various authors in this volume. In particular, cost-cutting efforts and related hiring freezes tend to produce closed personnel systems that may experience very little change in staff from year to year. At the same time, decentralization of the personnel function implies that agency-level variations in the way human resources are used and organizational incentives are distributed will increasingly account for variations in organizational performance as well as in important aspects of organizational culture.

Individual career outcomes are determined by the portals and requirements for entry into the organization, the criteria for promotion, the structure of job ladders within the organization, and the likelihood of finding a bridge from one job ladder to another. Because job tenure rates in government tend to be longer, the long-term effects on an individual's career horizons of employment in civil service systems are more significant than they might be with other employers. As a result, a single public sector employer has great potential impact on the social and economic well-being of its workers.

Moreover, movement between sectors is not always fluid; labor markets flow out of civil service systems may be more difficult than movement into or within government organizations. Thus, once a person enters the civil service, opportunities for exit may become limited. Government employees may invest in skill development and training in areas whose value is not recognized in the private sector. This, in turn, creates distortions in the broader market between the skills needed by employers and the skills available in the labor supply.

The use of internal labor markets raises important issues, not only for the dynamics of the economic system but also for the level of economic equality and political equality in a system. Opportunities for upward mobility and access to elite positions in government are important indicators of the level of democracy and social equity in a system. At the same time, the extent to which internal labor markets may facilitate or impede contemporary efforts toward more cost-efficient and accountable public bureaucracies is an important concern.

This discussion suggests that the four dimensions identified for internal labor markets are useful for research and analysis and are applicable to civil service systems. The dimensions point to the key attributes of internal labor market dynamics and provide a basis for comparing both organizational structures and the effects of those structures on members of the workforce. As such they may provide a theoretical framework for linking organizational rules and practices to the efficiency of government operations and the social and economic well-being of public employees. Future research might focus on empirical efforts to test the utility of these indicators in civil service systems. Further research is needed to develop a series of indicators to demonstrate the effect of ILMs in the public sector on both organizational productivity and employee well-being. Given the trend toward the decentralization of decision-making in public sector organizations and the expected increases in the importance of internal labor markets for explaining variations in employee earnings and status as well as the success of efforts to achieve greater productivity gains, understanding the role and function of internal labor markets in civil service systems warrants both further theoretical and empirical research.

*The author acknowledges with appreciation comments from Patricia W. Ingraham, Joop Koppenjan, Jon Quah, and James L. Perry.*

## REFERENCES

Bodiguel, J. 1990. "Political and Administrative Traditions and the French Senior Civil Service." *International Journal of Public Administration* 13: 707–40.

Brockhaus, R. H. 1980. "Risk-Taking Propensity of Entrepreneurs." *Academy of Management Journal* 23: 509–20.

Buitendam, A. 1991. "Decentralization and the Governance of Employment Relationships: Human Resource Management between Labour Market and Organization." Research Memorandum no. 413, Institute of Economic Research, Faculty of Economics, University of Groningen, Groningen, Netherlands.

Cappelli, P., and W. F. Cascio. 1991. "Why Some Jobs Command Wage Premiums." *Academy of Management Journal* 34: 848–68.

Crozier, M. 1971. *The World of the Office Worker.* Chicago: University of Chicago Press.

DiPrete, T. A. 1989. *The Bureaucratic Labor Market: The Case of the Federal Civil Service.* New York: Plenum Books.

Doeringer, P. B., and M. J. Piore. 1971. *Internal Labor Markets and Manpower Analysis.* Lexington, MA: Lexington Books.

Fast, N. D. 1976. "The Future of Industrial New Venture Departments." *Industrial Marketing Management* 8: 264–73.

Jackson, S., E. Randall, S. Schuler, and J. C. Riveria. 1989. "Organizational Characteristics as Predictors of Personnel Practices." *Personnel Psychology* 42: 727–86.

Kanter, R. M. 1978. *Men and Women of the Corporation.* New York: Basic Books.

———. 1985. "Supporting Innovation and Venture Development in Established Companies." *Journal of Business Venturing* 1: 47–60.

Kerr, C. 1954. "The Balkanization of Labor Markets." Pages 92–110 in E. Wight Bakke et al., *Labor Mobility and Economic Opportunity.* Cambridge, MA: MIT Press.

Kim, P. S. 1988. *Japan's Civil Service System.* New York: Greenwood Press.

McGregor, E. B., Jr. 1991. *Strategic Management of Human Knowledge, Skills, and Abilities.* San Francisco: Jossey-Bass.

NAPA (National Academy of Public Administration). 1991. *Modernizing Federal Classification.* Washington, DC: National Academy of Public Administration.

OECD (Organization for Economic Cooperation and Development). 1990. *Flexible Personnel Management in the Public Service.* Paris: OECD.

Osterman, P. 1988. *Employment Futures.* New York: Oxford University Press.

―――. 1992. "Internal Labor Markets in a Changing Environment." Pages 273–386 in David Lewin, Olivia S. Mitchell, and Peter D. Sterer, eds., *Research Frontiers in Industrial Relations and Human Resources.* Madison, WI: Industrial Relations Research Association.

―――, ed. 1984. *Internal Labor Markets.* Cambridge, MA: MIT Press.

Paukert, F., and D. Robinson. 1992. *Incomes Policies in the Wider Context.* Geneva: International Labour Organization.

Peters, B. G. 1985. "Sweden: The Explosion of Public Employment." Pages 203–27 in Richard Rose, ed., *Public Employment in Western Nations.* Cambridge: Cambridge University Press.

Robinson, D. 1990. *Civil Service Pay in Africa.* Geneva: ILO.

Rose, R., ed. 1985. *Public Employment in Western Nations.* Cambridge: Cambridge University Press.

Ross, A. M. 1948. *Trade Union Wage Policy.* Berkeley: University of California Press.

Schmidt, K. D., and R. Rose. 1985. "Germany: The Expansion of an Active State." Pages 126–62 in Richard Rose, ed., *Public Employment in Western Nations.* Cambridge: Cambridge University Press.

Scott, I., and J. Burns, eds. 1984. *The Hong Kong Civil Service.* Hong Kong: Oxford University Press.

Whyte, W. F. 1956. *The Organization Man.* New York: Simon and Schuster.

Wise, L. R. 1990. "Social Equity in Civil Service Systems." *Public Administration Review* 50: 567–75.

―――. 1993. "Whither Solidarity? Transitions in Swedish Public Sector Pay Policy." *British Journal of Industrial Relations* 31: 75–95.

# 6 CIVIL SERVANTS AND REPRESENTATIVENESS

Frits M. van der Meer and Renk L. J. Roborgh

Topics such as affirmative action, emancipation policies, political nominations, and the social background of civil servants have regularly captivated the public and political imagination. These themes form an integral part of the debate on so-called "representativeness" in public administration. In this debate two important questions have to be distinguished. First, should government policy be aimed at increasing the representative level of the civil service, and second, if so, how can this objective best be realized? The often poignant nature of the controversy associated with these issues is largely determined by the fact that the underlying values are considered fundamental to the persistence of the government system by both proponents and opponents alike. The accessibility, effectiveness, efficiency, legitimacy, and responsiveness of government are thought to be at stake.

It is, however, surprising that interest in the theoretical aspects of this subject has declined considerably since the mid-seventies. The absence of a clearcut definition has to be a factor. Although it is equally true for many other concepts in public administration, the various interpretations of what is meant by representativeness has been a source of profound terminological confusion (Nachmias and Rosenbloom, 1973: 590; Page, 1992: 46). The problem becomes even more acute when doing research on the meaning and significance of representativeness in comparative perspective.

Looking at the problem from a more positive angle, divergence in the meanings of representativeness can serve as a starting point for analysis. The answers to the above questions differ according to the society under discussion. To a large extent, the wide range of ideas and policies on representativeness are the result of marked differences in political, societal, and administrative values. These values, reflecting a given institutional design, have an important bearing on the function of civil service systems in the respective societies. Therefore, the issue of representativeness has a multilevel character that corresponds to the operational, collective choice, and constitutional levels discussed in the introductory chapter of this volume.

This chapter looks first at the dichotomy between active and passive representation. This distinction pertains to the behaviors of civil servants given a certain level of representativeness. Next we consider three different dimensions of representation—demographic, opinion, and interest representation. Finally the concepts of equal-opportunity and mirror image representativeness are examined. They define the way representativeness is related to society. The multidimensional approach to the above-mentioned classification scheme results in an explanatory framework that can be used for conducting comparative research in this field.

In order to formulate the outlines of such a framework it is necessary to examine the motives behind the significance of the issue. Attention must be paid to how differences in political, societal, and administrative values influence the way representativeness is perceived. Finally, the methodological implications for research in this field have to be considered.

## REPRESENTATIVENESS AND THE POLITICAL AND SOCIETAL ENVIRONMENT

It is a well-established custom in writing about representativeness to credit the coining of the term "representative bureaucracy" to the American J. Donald Kingsley (Mosher, 1982: 91; Krislov, 1974: 10), who published a study under that title in 1944. His work is primarily concerned with the discrepancy between the social background of the British civil service on the one hand and the population as a whole on the other. At the heart of Kingsley's argument lay the conviction that the "famed" neutrality and impartiality of the civil service was imaginary. He proclaimed that its attitudes and interests did, in fact, exhibit mainly middle-class bias (Kingsley, 1944: 215, 281). The term representative bureaucracy was therefore introduced as a criticism of the idea of a "neutral" civil service from the vantage point of the needs and wants of society.[1] In Kingsley's opinion, the introduction of more representativeness would alleviate this problem.

Although it is quite convenient to consider Kingsley's book as an "official" starting point for the discussion of representativeness, such an approach does embody the danger of neglecting almost identical phenomena in earlier days. It is argued that the theme of the representativeness of the civil service emerged at a relatively late stage (Krislov, 1974: 26–27). In a sense, it is misleading to presume that the issue did not exist in the period prior to World War II. Even without a label, representativeness was given ample consideration well before the beginning of the debate within the scientific and political community on the influence of permanent government officials. A comparative study of representativeness from a historical perspective undertaken by the Working Group on the History of Public Administration of the International Institute of Administrative Sciences shows that prior to World War II, attention was paid to representativeness in ten (western) countries included in the project (Wright, 1991: 2). For example, the level of political and religious representation of different groups in the civil service was discussed in the Netherlands from the end of the nineteenth century onward. This discussion can be situated within the context of a process of political and religious emancipation. As a matter of fact, criticism was not so much focused on the actual performance and outcomes of the administrative system itself (van der Meer et al., 1991). The misgivings of the political and religious groups involved were inspired by a perceived lack of equal opportunity in civil service employment emanating from the recruitment policies of the ruling liberal elites of those days. The same line of argument can be developed for many other nations, though it may involve different topics in different periods. In American public administrative history, it is often maintained that the Jacksonian revolt at the beginning of the nineteenth century can be seen as a reaction to an increasing "aristocratic" and "elitist" vein in the composition of the administration. In the United States the expression "government by the people, for the people" has been more popular than in many other countries. The notion of representativeness in civil service systems has symbolic importance both at the constitutional and collective action level.

Past and present discussions show that in various societies, there are major differences concerning the extent to which representativeness is an important issue. This "issue-like" character must be acknowledged because representativeness can be viewed both as an empirical, sociological phenomenon and as a normative or political phenomenon (van der Meer et al., 1991: 194).

Representativeness must be viewed against the background of basic concepts of the raison d'être of the state and more specifically the changing relationship between the population and the state. These fundamental concepts pertain to the system of governance and the related, appropriate institutional arrangements. In western industrialized nations, the political and administrative systems and traditions of the United States, the United Kingdom, and continental Europe show some remarkable differences. Arguments pertaining to the legitimacy and responsiveness of government action in promoting representativeness are especially relevant in the United States. In the United Kingdom and continental Europe, and with reference to the civil service and not to political appointees, neutrality is still the official credo. Compliance with political decisions is mainly relied on for external and internal control. The nature of these control mechanisms can be of a judicial nature and rooted in the German *rechtsstaat* tradition, can be inspired by administrative codes of behavior as in the United Kingdom, or can be a "civil service ethos" as is the case in France. These differences in the political, administrative, and societal setting have important implications for the content of and aspirations toward representativeness in the above-mentioned countries.

Comparative research on representativeness is rendered meaningful only by focusing on the importance that representativeness acquires in a certain political, governmental, and societal environment. A comparative perspective must therefore allow for the inclusion of substantial differences in institutional design. When assessing representativeness in one political, administrative, and societal setting, one must therefore use criteria appropriate to that situation. In fact, one of the things we can learn from studying the different meanings of representativeness across civil service systems is the assessment of the unique characteristics of systems as a consequence of the political and societal environment in which they are operating.

The treatment of representativeness in civil service systems is complicated in nonwestern contexts. Apart from the fact that the notion "nonwestern" is too broad to define differences in culture and tradition, it is important to mention the fact that relevant colonial experience must be taken into consideration, whether it be Anglo-Saxon, French, Spanish, etc. The combination of indigenous and "colonial" political and administrative culture and tradition leads to a wide variety of possible outcomes.

## THE ARGUMENTATION BEHIND REPRESENTATIVENESS

A first explanation for the increased relevance of representativeness is to be found in concern about the legitimacy of government action in relation to responsiveness. This concern drew the attention of both the political and the scientific community from approximately the middle of the twentieth century. The concept of a strict dichotomy between politics and administration dominant in both public administration and political thinking was responsible for the concern. Interest articulation and aggregation were perceived as the prerogative of the political system alone. The implementation of policy was regarded as a duty to be performed by administration. This dichotomy became meaningless with the growth of government and the increased complexity of the public sector. In the same period, a relative decline in the importance of both the normative legal study of government and the scientific, management-oriented study of government occurred. The rise in popularity of a more empirically oriented political science opened a new approach to the functioning of government. These changes resulted in an awareness of the importance of government officials as powerful actors in the policy-making process and the crucial role of the civil service for collective action.

Renewed interest in the influence of permanent government officials in the policy-making process and the attention paid to the discretionary, policy-reformulating powers of administration in policy implementation have changed the perception of the relationship between politics and the civil service. As a result, both the legitimacy and the responsiveness of the administrative branches of government toward the wishes and needs of both the public and politicians have come under question. Civil servants are not regarded as mere executors of policy decisions, they are thought to have ample resources and room to maneuver for influencing decision-making. It can be inferred that civil servants can incorporate their own interests into decision-making.

However, the pursuit of interests constitutes only one aspect of the problem. Another elementary function performed by the civil service consists of collecting information necessary for the policy-making process. Thus, if the composition of civil service is narrowly based, the possibility arises that only selective signals from society will be received and transmitted to the administrative system.

The danger described above is not only immanent in the policy advisory capacity of the civil service at the collective choice level; it can be considered especially relevant during policy implementation at the operational level. The implementation of legislation containing vague legal norms may cause a certain degree of ambivalence about the "correct" manner of adjudication in the sense of a "correct" interpretation of these implicit norms (Dijkstra, 1991: Mayntz, 1982: 214–16). Consequently, the interpretation of the objectives of a certain policy depends on the attitude, expertise, role conception and, ultimately, the values of the official concerned. Officials may prove accessible and responsive only to the wishes and needs of the particular segment of society to which they belong.

The perception that there are serious shortcomings in the formal administrative and political control mechanisms for limiting abuse of power by civil servants is essential to understanding the role of representation (Meier and Nigro, 1976: 459). Representation is viewed as a substitute for formal controls. The assumption is that the legitimacy of public administration is impaired by inadequacies in formal controls and that responsiveness is less than desirable. The acceptance of government action can be secured or increased by greater representativeness in the civil service. The connection between promoting a more representative civil service and guaranteeing the legitimacy of government action can be understood as follows: the inclusion of the whole societal spectrum in the civil service guarantees that relevant signals will be received. In order to avoid middle-class bias, the attitudes of civil servants should be in accordance with the opinions held in society. When the composition of the civil service is more or less in accordance with that of society in terms of its demographic composition, opinions, and interests, then acceptance and control of administrative activities will increase. The idea is that in this way representativeness becomes a valuable check on the use or abuse of power by the civil service. Representativeness would therefore fill the gap in control over the civil service. The improvement in the perceived loyalty of the civil service to society is a key element in legitimacy and responsiveness arguments. Representativeness is seen as a way of assuring administrative responsibility (Mosher, 1982: 93).

One problem associated with the notion of responsiveness is the question of responsiveness to whom. A first obvious answer would be responsive toward society at large. This notion is implicit in most of the recent literature on representativeness. But as we have seen, it is not a foregone conclusion. Earlier we noted Kingsley's remark about responsiveness toward dominant groups in society. The operationalization of "groups" should not be limited to class-oriented groups, as Kingsley writes. Besides this responsiveness toward societal groups, a sensitivity toward the party (or parties) or government in power could be mentioned. Responsiveness and its different manifestations depend very much on ideas intrinsic to a particular system concerning the relationship between "rulers and ruled." It is obvious that the different expressions of responsiveness could easily conflict.

The view of representation encountered in the United States is more egalitarian than in European countries. But in addition to a more formal reliance in continental Europe on control mechanisms rooted in the *rechtsstaat* tradition, or administrative codes of behavior, and on a civil service ethos, there is another element that is important for understanding the differences. Political and administrative systems in the United States are more strongly characterized by pluralism than is the case in Europe. Notwithstanding the fact that recent changes in Europe that have been induced by administrative reform show a certain tendency toward a greater pluralism, there are still marked differences between the European and American systems with regard to the relations between administration and society, politics and administration. In the United States, pluralism makes the question of legitimacy and responsiveness a more urgent issue. Government officials in the various agencies are given more autonomy to deal with relevant segments of the population. The integrative parts of the political administrative system are less well developed in comparison with European systems. As a consequence, the American civil servant is less oriented toward general government policies (or "public duty") and more toward a specific policy field and its clients (Self, 1977: 169–74).

In addition to arguments derived from the legitimacy of government action and civil service responsiveness, another line of argumentation must be considered. The "equal opportunity" argument should be seen in relation to the composition of the civil service in the period before World War II. The idea behind a consideration of equal opportunity (sometimes embodied in constitutional rules) is that individuals, irrespective of the groups to which they belong in society, ought to have an equal opportunity to be appointed to administrative positions. The mere fact of equal opportunity enhances the legitimacy of public administration. In this connection, it is argued that public sector employment is a kind of public right to which everyone in society should have access. In some countries (for instance the Federal Republic of Germany or the Netherlands) this right has even been embedded in the constitution. From a normative standpoint, public service is seen as a good opportunity for citizen involvement and development of the public interest. The advantage for the citizen lies in a personal realization of her or his contribution to the public service. A parallel may be drawn to democracy in its classical sense and democracy in nineteenth-century Great Britain as a school of thought for the citizens (the collective interest). In continental Europe, dominated by the Weberian philosophy of neutrality, this vision can be encountered in the public spirited motivation of the civil servant.

To summarize, in analyzing differences in representativeness across civil service systems we have to explore to what extent representativeness is an issue in relation to responsiveness on the one hand and equal opportunity on the other. The first sense involves doubts about the effectiveness of political, legal, and democratic controls on the civil service (Meier, 1975: 528). Policy on representativeness can also be inspired by the desire to realize a greater degree of equal opportunity. It is not, of course, an either/or situation. Both elements may be observed in one particular civil service system simultaneously. However, it is necessary to find out where the emphasis is placed, because this has important consequences. In order to examine these consequences, attention has to be focused on the various modes of expression representativeness can take.

## A TYPOLOGY OF REPRESENTATIVENESS CONCEPTS RELATING TO CIVIL SERVICE

Levels of representativeness can be studied from three different angles. The first rests on a demarcation of passive and active forms of representativeness. The second rests on demographic, idea or opinion, and interest representation; representativeness in relation to this trichotomy reflects the extent to which opinions and interests held in the civil service correspond with those displayed in society. Finally, a distinction can be made between equal opportunity and mirror image representativeness.

The concepts of active and passive representativeness were first introduced by Frederick C. Mosher. The dichotomy relates to the level of activity displayed by civil servants that is dependent on a certain degree of representativeness. Representativeness pertains to the personal or sociological characteristics of government officials. A civil service is considered to be representative when the personal characteristics of civil servants mirror the structure of society. Passive or descriptive representativeness does not involve behavioral attributes of civil servants. The active form of representativeness, on the other hand, implies government officials actively pursuing goals that are in tune with the interests of their "constituency." A major point of discussion is whether and under what conditions passive representativeness leads (or should lead) to actual patterns of behavior, that is, to active representativeness. Before going into this relationship we have to deal with a second division, namely between the degree of demographic representation; the degree of representation with respect to societal opinions; and the degree of interest representation (van der Meer et al., 1991: 195). These concepts above show a considerable degree of similarity to

Mosher's. The difference between them is that the latter classification defines precisely what is represented rather than how actively representation is pursued or manifested.

The degree of demographic representativeness plays a major role in discussions about the operation and outcomes of recruitment procedures in civil service systems in most western and many nonwestern nations. In this particular manifestation of representativeness, the composition of the civil service in comparison to the segmentation existing within society is emphasized. The demographic structure of the civil service can be broken down into a number of areas, such as education, ethnicity, gender, language, origin, religion, political affiliation, and socioeconomic background (van der Meer et al., 1991: 195; Van Riper, 1958: 552; Mosher, 1982: 12). Which themes are considered relevant depends, as noted earlier, on the stratification of society and the working of the political and administrative systems.

Opinion representativeness refers to congruence between views and values in society on the one hand and views in the civil service on the other. Interest representativeness basically implies that the civil service has objectives identical to those of groups in society. If this is the case, we might speak of policy congruence between the civil service and the population. In an active interpretation of interest representativeness, policy congruence would mean that civil servants would act as sponsors for the interests of groups to which they are attached. A more active political role for government officials does emerge.

Interest participation can take two forms. Interests can be pursued by individual government officials or interest representation can be incorporated into organizational design (Meier, 1993: Romzek and Hendricks, 1982: 75–81). In countries where the clientele organization principle is dominant, active representativeness can become manifest, though one crucial condition must be met: government officials must perceive the interest groups that are operative in their functional area as their own constituency.

We have mentioned that a relationship is assumed to exist between passive and active forms of representativeness. Meier (1993) points to socialization experiences as an explanation in theory for representative bureaucracy. Socialization experiences are related to personal background. Shared socialization patterns would lead to similar policy-relevant attitudes and therefore to policy decisions similar to those that the populace would make if it participated in all decisions (Meier, 1993: 8–9; Meier and Nigro, 1976: 458–60).

From this perspective, demographic representativeness can be considered synonymous with passive representativeness. Opinion representativeness refers to similarities in policy attitudes; interest representativeness is to be seen as an equivalent for active representativeness.

This line of argument is summarized on table 6.1. On the vertical axis, a distinction is made between passive and active representativeness; there is a parallel division between demographic, opinion, and interest representativeness.

TABLE 6.1

**Different Types of Representativeness in
Relation to the Level and Type of Activity Employed**

Inclusion of the Societal Spectrum

|  | Low | High |
|---|---|---|
| **ACTIVE** — Interest | Elitist | Participatory |
| Opinion | Narrow-based | Wide-based |
| **PASSIVE** — Demographic | Inequality | Equality |

*Level and Type of Activity*

These two demarcations pertain to the level and type of activity. The horizontal axis represents the level of inclusion of the societal spectrum. This continuum ranges from low to high. The figure can be read both vertically and horizontally. The horizontal, demographic scale shows a division between systems characterized by a low to a high degree of equality in terms of inclusion of societal groups. On the opinion scale we can see a continuum from a narrow to a broad base of societal opinion. On the interest scale we can see a continuum from elitist to participatory interest inclusion. In a vertical direction we get two clusters of characteristics that are polar opposites on the continuum of civil service systems.

With respect to the (vertical) relationship between personal background and shared policy attitudes, it has to be noted that the suggested connection is open to debate (Page, 1992: 170–71). Research on the socialization of individuals casts serious doubt on the general validity of such a relationship. The crucial issue is whether demographic background is as important as has been suggested. Does it determine the future role (and therefore the articulated values) of a civil servant in his or her working life? In other words, do organization members derive their values, opinions, and goals from the societal background they originated from and do they thus influence the functioning of the organization? Alternatively, does conformity to the dominant culture within the organization emerge as a result of postentry socialization and, more specifically, of enculturation? In an often quoted essay on socialization through the life cycle, Orville C. Brim argues that socialization in childhood is not sufficient to enable individuals to fulfill the various roles they must perform during later phases in life. We have little empirical knowledge about the effects of pre- and postentry socialization on the values of individuals acting as members of the civil service.

Comparative research should therefore concentrate on the question of which factors influence the convergence of passive and active representativeness and under what conditions they are operative (Brim, 1966). Mosher has suggested a number of factors that might be of some help: "the length of time in the organization, or the time distance from his background; the nature and strength of the socialization process within the organization; the nature of the position . . . ; the length and content of preparatory education, the strength of associations beyond the job and beyond the agency" (Mosher, 1982: 13). This is not an exhaustive list and elements could be added, but the list does include a number of intervening variables affecting the relationship between active and passive representation.

In close resemblance to the factors Mosher mentions, Meier (1993) formulates a number of hypotheses.[2] As the effects of these factors may differ depending on societal order, they present an interesting avenue for comparative research. It is evident that consequences may differ according to a particular governmental and societal order. For instance, if the neutrality of the civil service is regarded as official doctrine, an effort is undertaken to prevent such relationships.

A final observation should be made about whether a lack of opinion or even interest representation would necessarily be the result of a failure to achieve a high degree of demographic representation. Research has shown that although the civil service is not considered a true mirror of society in a demographic sense, a remarkable correspondence can be noticed between opinions held in the civil service and in society (Lewis, 1990: 226–27).

To conclude, major differences can be observed between active and passive forms of representativeness. The weak relationship between demographic background, opinions, and interest representativeness causes severe methodological problems. What persons say (opinions) does not necessarily agree with what persons do (interests). Neither of these are necessarily determined solely by their educational or demographic background. For this reason each concept of representativeness requires its own approach and methodology.

## THE MICROCOSMIC AND EQUAL OPPORTUNITY APPROACHES TO REPRESENTATIVENESS

A mirror image or microcosmic approach is implicit in the discussion of passive and active representation in the previous section. The essence of a microcosmic perspective on civil service systems is that the composition of the civil service should correspond to the proportional size of groups within society. This does not automatically correspond to an equal opportunity perspective on representativeness. Central to this last approach is impartiality during the process of recruiting candidates who meet the requirements necessary to fill a civil service post. In this section, the relationship between microcosmic and equal opportunity representativeness is discussed.

There is some skepticism about the feasibility of creating true mirror image representativeness. An important restriction stems from the fact that government organizations are in need of expert personnel for achieving their objectives (Krislov, 1974: 47–52, 62). The growing need for specialized knowledge is extensively portrayed in Max Weber's analysis of bureaucracy in *Wirtschaft und Gesellschaft* and can also be found in the concept of merit bureaucracy (Weber, 1976: 128). Krislov, however, argues that the extent to which a compromise has to be sought in order to retain a representative composition of the civil service poses no serious problems. Looking at size and diversity of government employment, a near complete inclusion of the societal spectrum could be achieved (Krislov, 1974: 81).

However, there is a serious flaw in Krislov's reasoning. It is deceptive to speak about civil service employment in a generalized way. In analyzing the nature of government employment, we have to disaggregate government tasks (Rose, 1984: 15–20). Government tasks comprise a wide range of activities extending from services to industrial activities. Looking at it from the perspective of legitimacy and responsiveness, the discussion of representativeness does not have equal relevance for the whole range of government activities. In the past, discussions of the representativeness of the civil service have been preoccupied predominantly with the composition of the higher civil service. Higher civil servants are considered to possess a preeminent influence in the policy-making process. This picture has been modified by more recent implementation research, which has highlighted the importance of lower-ranking officials and especially of those officials who have been called "street-level bureaucrats." The qualifications necessary to perform specialized tasks in the service sector, both at the level of policy-making and implementation, are spread unevenly among the different layers of society due to differences in educational background.

However, it should be noted that under certain conditions, mirror image representativeness can be seen as guaranteeing the acceptance of government action, even if professional standards are impaired. We spoke earlier about a merit or Weberian bureaucracy. These kinds of administrative systems are mainly concentrated in western nations with a particular administrative history and tradition. In a very fragmented society with, for instance, a very uneven distribution of economic and political power as well as education, combined with a not fully developed democratic system, mirror image representativeness in the form of a quota system could improve the functioning of government through greater acceptance of government action. This could be the case, for instance, in multinational states in the third world.

Given the fact that a certain level of expertise and professionalism is necessary for entry into the civil service, the question arises as to whether all the members of society who meet those demands actually have an equal opportunity of being appointed. If informal recruitment criteria are excluded and only functional requirements are taken into consideration, we may speak of equal opportunity representativeness. Equal opportunity does not imply a society-wide equality of opportunity. The discrepancy between the need for expertise and professionalism on the one hand and the practice of recruitment based on "equal opportunity" and "microcosmic" criteria on the other is the result of the socioeconomic and closely related educational stratification of society.

With respect to the notion of equality, it must be said that setting quotas in order to achieve mirror image representativeness can endanger equity as seen from the angle of equal opportunity. Certain groups or individual members of a group have to be discriminated against in order to realize equality in a different and more general societal perspective.

Table 6.2 shows different combinations of levels of mirror image and equal opportunity representativeness in civil service systems.

In a civil service system where a high degree of mirror image and a low level of equal opportunity are combined, representativeness can be characterized as group discrimination. The demographic characteristics of the group to which a person belongs is used as a discriminatory factor to achieve microcosmic inclu-

TABLE 6.2

**Combinations of Mirror Image and
Equal Opportunity Representativeness**

Equal Opportunity

|  |  | Low | High |
|---|---|---|---|
| **Mirror Image** | **High** | Group discrimination | Non-discrimination |
|  | **Low** | Personal/systematic discrimination | Functional discrimination |

sion. This implies that people are not judged solely on the basis of functional requirements. By using a quota system, some groups (or group members) are treated as more "equal" than others. In this situation, the two meanings of equality are inconsistent. A combination of lows on both scales means that "full" discrimination is taking place during the recruitment process. The term "full discrimination" implies that selection is not based on either functional or group characteristics but on informal recruitment criteria devised to maintain a "ruling elite." A low level of mirror image and a high level of equal opportunity representativeness indicates that a system can be characterized as exhibiting functional discrimination. The only relevant criteria for recruitment are the necessary job requirements. When both mirror image and equal opportunity levels are high, we may call a system nondiscriminatory. As we have pointed out earlier, this presupposes the existence of an open society.

## SUMMARY

This chapter has raised the issue of how to do research on the representativeness of civil service systems from a comparative perspective and has pointed out that a distinction must be made between active and passive representativeness on the one hand, and demographic, opinion, and interest representativeness on the other. It has also made a distinction between mirror and equal opportunity representativeness. Examination of the connection between these different expressions has shown their relevance for studying civil service systems. The resulting divisions can be helpful for answering the two central research questions: What forms does representativeness take in a civil service system? and, What explanatory variables determine particular patterns of representativeness? With regard to the second question, we must look to political, administrative, and societal values, norms and rules for explanatory variables. Social structure is also likely to be an important variable. These cultural and structural elements will serve to explain the different forms of representativeness and the extent to which it can be considered significant.

## NOTES

1. It should be stressed, however, that Kingsley believed "bureaucracy" should represent the dominant forces in society and not be a microcosm of society (see Meier, 1975).

2. Meier's first hypothesis, however, does not concern the relations between passive and active representation. It merely points to the type of issue which reaches the political agenda in a given governmental system. In this respect, it corresponds to Wright's classification.

## REFERENCES

Birch, A. H. 1980. *Representation.* London: Pall Mall.

Brim, O. C. 1966. "Socialization through the Life Cycle." In Orville C. Brim and Staunton Wheeler, eds., *Socialization after Childhood.* New York: John Wiley & Sons.

Denhardt, R. B. 1984. *Theories of Public Administration.* Pacific Grove: Brooks-Cole.

Dijkstra, G. S. A. 1991. *Wetgeving en omvang van het gebruik van rechtsbescherming.* Deventer: Kluwer.

Heady, F. 1991. *Public Administration: A Comparative Perspective.* New York: Marcel Dekker.

Kingsley, J. D. 1944. *Representative Bureaucracy.* Yellow Springs, OH: Antioch.

Krislov, S. 1974. *Representative Bureaucracy.* Englewood Cliffs, NJ: Prentice Hall.

Lewis, G. B. 1990. "In Search of the Machiavellian Milquetoasts: Comparing Attitudes of Bureaucrats and Ordinary People." *Public Administration Review* 50: 220–27.

Mayntz, R. 1982. *Soziologie der öffentlichen Verwaltung.* 2nd ed. Heidelberg: Möller Juristischer Verlag.

Meer, F. M. van der, and R. L. J. Roborgh, 1991. "Civil Servants and Representative Bureaucracy." Paper presented at the annual meeting of the American Society for Public Administration, Washington, DC.

Meer, F. M. van der, J. C. N. Raadschelders, R. L. J. Roborgh, and Th. A. J. Toonen. 1991. "Representativeness and Bureaucracy in the Netherlands." In Vincent Wright, ed., *The Representation of Public Administration.* Brussels: IIAS.

Meier, K. J. 1975. "Representative Bureaucracy: An Empirical Analysis." *American Political Science Review* 69: 526–42.

———. 1991. "Representative Bureaucracy: What We Know." Paper presented at the annual meeting of the American Society for Public Administration, Washington, DC.

———. 1993. "Representative Bureaucracy: A Theoretical and Empirical Exposition." *Research in Public Administration* 2: 1–36.

Meier, K. J., and L. N. Nigro. 1976. "Representative Bureaucracy and Policy Preferences: A Study in the Attitudes of Federal Executives." *Public Administration Review* 36: 458–70.

Mosher, F. C. 1982. *Democracy and the Public Service.* 2nd ed. New York: Oxford University Press.

Nachmias, D., and D. H. Rosenbloom. 1973. "Measuring Bureaucratic Representation and Integration." *Public Administration Review* 33: 590–97.

Page, E. C. 1992. *Political Authority and Bureaucratic Power. A Comparative Analysis.* 2nd ed. New York: Harvester-Wheatsheaf.

Peters, B. G. 1988. *Comparing Public Bureaucracies: Problems of Theory and Method.* Tuscaloosa: University of Alabama Press.

———. 1984. *The Politics of Bureaucracy.* 2nd ed. New York: Longman.

Rich, H. 1975. "The Canadian Case for a Representative Bureaucracy." *Political Science* 27: 97–110.

Romzek, B. S., and J. S. Hendricks. 1982. "Organizational Involvement and Representative Bureaucracy: Can We Have It Both Ways?" *American Political Science Review* 76: 75–82.

Rose, R. 1984. *Understanding Big Government. The Programme Approach.* London: Sage.

Self, P. 1977. *Administrative Theories and Politics: An Enquiry into the Structure and Process of Modern Government.* 2nd ed. London: Allen & Unwin.

Subramaniam, V. 1967. "Representative Bureaucracy: A Reassessment." *American Political Science Review* 61: 1010–19.

Suleiman, E. N. 1974. *Politics, Power and Bureaucracy in France: The Administrative Elite.* Princeton: Princeton University Press.

Van Riper, P. 1958. *A History of the United States Civil Service.* Evanston, IL: Row, Peterson.

Weber, M. 1976. *Wirtschaft und Gesellschaft.* 4th ed. Tübingen: Mohr.

Wright, V. 1991. "Representative Bureaucracy: Some Introductory Comments." In Vincent Wright, ed., *The Representation of Public Administration.* Brussels: IIAS.

# PART THREE
# CONTEXT

In the introductory chapter we emphasized that civil service systems serve not only instrumental roles as personnel systems, but that they have governance and constitutional roles as well. The link between civil service and wider contexts was reinforced by B. Guy Peters in his discussion of the difficult methodological problems involved in studying administrative systems embedded in broader social and political systems. Part 3 is devoted to a more detailed examination of context and its implications for civil service systems.

In chapter 7, William P. Hojnacki addresses one of the most vexing dilemmas facing civil servants, the conflict between being politically responsive and professionally responsible. A variety of collective choice mechanisms and operational rules are used to simultaneously integrate and buffer politics and administration in civil service systems. These mechanisms and rules determine the scope and depth of the penetration of political regimes into administrative systems.

Whether or not politicization is a major factor within civil service depends on the values, norms, and traditions governing particular situations. Hojnacki explores the variations in these factors and their consequences across national systems. He uses two broad ideal types in his analysis: that of the classical, independent civil service, establishing and implementing an agenda on behalf of the political regime, and that of the civil service dominated by the political regime, carrying out the political agenda of the latter.

Social control is the process by which individuals, groups, and organizations attempt to make the performance and operation of civil service systems conform to standards of behavior or normative preferences. In chapter 8, Michael Hill and Desi Gillespie assert that apart from political control from above, control of the civil service by the public is important because of the difficulty of discerning policy-making and policy implementation. Hill and Gillespie focus on formal collective choice mechanisms for facilitating public input and control of civil servants. These mechanisms intersect with structures internal to civil service—such as professional standards, procedural rule systems, and hierarchy—in shaping the civil service control.

Another important contextual factor regulating civil service systems is public opinion—the views held by elites and the mass public about the civil service. Public opinion about the performance and prestige of the civil service is important for its potential to shape governance, and for civil service to function as a mediating institution. In chapter 9, Hal G. Rainey tries to sort out what we know about public opinion regarding civil service, how it is shaped, and what effects it has. He addresses several key questions, among them: What are the factors upon which the public judges the quality and performance of the civil service? How does public opinion affect the structure and performance of civil service systems?

Rainey's approach is largely inductive. He reviews research on public opinion of civil service in developing a general model. He notes that public opinion has received surprisingly little attention in theories of public administration. In the general model, Rainey argues that perceptions of civil service are driven by various factors, including social and political context, demographics, individual respondent differences, and general political attitudes. Rainey's framework reinforces a central theme of this book, namely, that civil service systems are complex phenomena that must be studied at multiple levels of analysis.

# 7 POLITICIZATION AS A CIVIL SERVICE DILEMMA

William P. Hojnacki

On the assumption that the role of any society's civil service system is an evolving one, the first objective of this chapter will be to put into some perspective the place of civil service politicization in the evolutionary process. A second, related objective is to begin developing a theoretical framework suitable for cross-national comparisons of civil service politicization. The term civil service politicization lacks precise definition. As it is used here, however, it refers to the levels and types of political activity undertaken by civil servants, as well as to attempts by others to politically influence the behavior of civil servants (Aberbach and Rockman, 1987).

The question of civil service politicization is an important one because it represents, or at least reflects, a dilemma faced by most societies today, especially those whose governments claim to be based on democratic principles (Kaufman, 1969). The dilemma is that civil servants often face a conflict between being politically responsive and professionally responsible (Almond and Powell, 1966: 152–58). The prevailing view in most countries is that civil servants should be politically neutral (Gordon, 1982: 50–51). Yet civil service systems are part of government, and government is by definition a political enterprise. Further, no society can lay claim to following democratic principles if it does not have an active and vibrant political process, one in which all components of government, including the civil service, are at least indirectly responsible to the people being governed. Thus, to the extent that democracies require a large dose of politics, Mosher's notion of the central question facing public bureaucracies—how can a professional civil service be made compatible with democracy? (Mosher, 1968: 3)—must be extended to ask how politics can be made compatible with the responsibilities of civil servants.

In attempting to put civil service politicization into a theoretical perspective that can address the responsibility/responsiveness dilemma, some basic questions must be raised. First, assuming it is possible to distinguish between political and nonpolitical activity, we need to ask what kinds of activity actually constitute civil service politicization, and, relatedly, does politicization encompass all of those activities that can be classified as political in nature? Second, under the politicization umbrella, we need to ask what constitutes appropriate and inappropriate behavior on the part of civil servants. Finally, we need to ask what civil service systems are doing, or in some cases ought to be doing, to ensure that both civil servants and those who interact with them behave in appropriate ways in terms of their politically oriented activities.

Addressing these questions will provide a starting point for constructing a theoretical framework. We make no pretense, however, to answering them definitively here. Instead, our goal is the more modest one of attempting to use these questions to help identify the variables on which future research can be based. Raising such questions is necessary because although there are several studies such as those on the political dimensions of public administration by Almond and Powell (1966), Kaufman (1969), Aberbach and Rockman (1987; 1988), and others, there have been few attempts to isolate civil service politicization as a distinct area of inquiry. Two exceptions are Aberbach, Putnam, and Rockman's *Bureaucrats and Politicians in Western Democracies* (1981) and the volume edited by Dogan, *The Mandarins of Western Europe: The Political Role of Top Civil Servants* (1975). Both of these efforts, however, are somewhat dated. In short, there are few guideposts to help in theory development. It would appear, then, that we need to start, as Peters suggests in his contribution to this volume, by deciding what it is we want to know about civil service politicization.

Peters offers his own suggestions. In his work here, he reflects on an early effort (1988) in which he identified four possible dependent variables that could point to at least some of what we want to know about administrative systems from a comparative perspective: people, structures, behavior, and power. Although these are not necessarily appropriate for a focused assessment of civil service politicization, his four possibilities are a good starting point.

In terms of politicization, civil service systems function quite differently in different parts of the world, and for good reason. They have evolved from different administrative and political traditions, reflect different societal values, and are guided by different constitutional and governmental arrangements (McLennan, 1980: 8–24). Those differences, as other contributions to this volume indicate, make comparative analysis difficult. In order to make such comparisons more manageable, it is necessary, as has been done with other attempts at comparative analysis, to establish the parameters of politicization, that is, to draw the line between politicized and nonpoliticized activities and then to identify and isolate, at least in general terms, a set of variables common to different societies (Wiatr, 1988).

Using Peters's suggestion, but modifying it somewhat for present purposes, two dependent variables will be considered—people and behavior. These two variables have been chosen on the assumption that the level and type of civil service politicization in any society is the result of first, who serves, and second, how they behave after they have been selected. Structure (broadly defined to include constitutional provisions) and political and administrative tradition are treated as independent variables. These choices are, of course, arbitrary and subject to dispute, but they do represent at least one set of common points of reference. They would seem to allow us to give at least a preliminary answer to the question of what it is we want to know about civil service politicization from a comparative perspective.

## POLITICIZATION REDEFINED

As was stated at the outset, there is no precise definition of the term civil service politicization. One of the difficulties in offering a definition and one of the reasons why it will not be attempted here is the use of the term in much of the literature on public administration. Many authors, including Aberbach and Rockman (1987; 1988), tend to view politicization as synonymous with a violation of the principle of political neutrality. Political activities that are seen as proper and legitimate, such as the exercise of the political skill necessary to be a good public manager, are not always included under the politicization umbrella (Pfiffner, 1992). Hence, views of what actually constitutes politicization often appear to be more dependent upon what different observers view as appropriate and inappropriate behavior than on any particular set of political acts or activities (Aberbach, Putnam, and Rockman, 1981).

The notion adopted here is that politicization ought to be treated essentially as a neutral term referring to the political behavior of civil servants, one that encompasses a particular range of activities, some of which may be considered appropriate while others may not. Politicization is an extension of politics in general.

It is a form of human behavior that includes the use of political means to achieve political ends. As Plano and his colleagues state, "It is commonly identified with the exercise of influence, the struggle for power, and competition among individuals and groups over the allocation of rewards of 'values' within a society" (Plano et al., 1973: 291). Civil servants function in a political world. From virtually any perspective, the environment in which civil servants function is highly politicized. As Aberbach and Rockman state, "The issue, therefore, is not whether organizational politics occurs or not but, rather, the size of the stage on which it is played, and relatedly, the number of actors involved in the play" (Aberbach and Rockman, 1987: 486).

From this preliminary discussion of what constitutes civil service politicization, two dimensions of politics seem to be more critical than others. One dimension is that set of political activities engaged in by civil servants themselves, for example, the behavior they exhibit when dealing with the political system of which they are a part. At issue is the extent to which the work civil servants undertake of their own volition, within the policy process from initiation to implementation, is legitimate and proper (Medeiros and Schmitt, 1977: 3–32). This work can be further refined into two distinct but interrelated sets of activities. One set of activities involves the things civil servants may do to try to influence the substance of public policy. Included here are such things as trying to influence the selection of policymakers, either by running for office themselves or by campaigning for sympathetic candidates or by direct involvement in the policy-making process itself (i.e., lobbying of one form or another). The second set of activities is what civil servants do after policies have been established and are ready to be implemented, that is, the use of political means such as power-brokering, negotiations, and compromises, to carry out what are ostensibly their legitimate policy implementation responsibilities (Aberbach and Rockman, 1988).

The second dimension is what others do in a political way to influence the behavior of civil servants (Plano et al., 1973: 291–92). These others may either be inside or outside the confines of government. They could be elected or politically appointed government officials who try to get civil servants to advance their particular political agendas, or they could be outside representatives of interests that try to "lobby" or influence the outcome of the administrative decision-making process (Riggs, 1988).

Returning to the question of civil servants being included in the policy-making and implementation process, in virtually all countries some involvement by high-level civil servants in the creation of policy initiatives is considered, under most circumstances, to be appropriate (Riggs, 1988). Civil servants are, after all, the foremost experts in their chosen fields. What is open to question is the type of involvement they exhibit, who is directing this involvement, and how far the involvement carries forward beyond the policy formulation stage (Pfiffner, 1992: 48–65). Most societies have, at least formally, established principles that guide the involvement of civil servants in the policy-making process. Most countries, for instance, forbid civil servants from running for office, at least while they hold active civil service appointments, and from blatant lobbying or participation in the affairs of political parties (Heady, 1987). Such restrictions are, however, subject to differing interpretations and are not always enforced. In France, civil servants may take leave of their posts to serve in the legislature, as if they could forget from which agency they came (Rohr, 1991). And in several states in the United States it is possible for civil servants in one local jurisdiction to run for public office in a different jurisdiction (Hojnacki, 1983: 133–43).

The proper role of civil servants becomes even less clear when they participate in policy formulation. The line between appropriate and inappropriate behavior may be thin indeed (Newland, 1987). Presumably, it is appropriate in most countries for a politically appointed official to ask a civil servant to draft a legislative proposal in the civil servant's area of expertise; but it is inappropriate for the same civil servant to draft the same proposal without being requested to do so. The issue becomes one of who controls the policy process and how civil servants respond (Heady, 1979: 128–31).

In terms of the propensity of civil servants to behave to political ways while they are carrying out their legitimate duties, there are only a few standards available to govern civil service behavior, and practice varies considerably from country to country. Given the programmatic responsibilities that come with such positions, the fierce competition for scarce resources, and the need to satisfy the demands of fickle legislators and executives, including those who attempt to exercise inappropriate political influence on administrative agencies, it is understood in most societies that in order to be a good administrator, one must also be a good politician (O'Toole, 1987: 17–20). But, where does appropriate behavior end and inappropriate behavior begin? The question is one of how far an ambitious administrator can go in the name of serving the public good before his or her private agenda subverts the agenda established through the political process (Dwivedi and Olowv, 1988).

The second dimension of politics that impacts on public administrators is the propensity of groups and individuals both inside and outside of government to seek to influence the behavior of civil servants. Although the relationships that develop between civil servants and outside interests are often identifiable and, in most countries, highly regulated, these links cannot be ignored in any discussion of civil service politicization.

Indeed, it can become a very serious concern if administrators have the capacity to act (either legitimately or not) in highly political ways while carrying out their assigned administrative duties. A good deal depends on how much discretion individual civil servants show in making politically sensitive decisions and how much flexibility they have in carrying out these decisions (Rohr, 1988). Civil servants often feel a need to keep happy those individuals and groups that have a vested interest in the work their agency or bureau is doing (Nakamura and Smallwood, 1980: 7–12). Most civil servants are keenly aware that the very existence of the unit for which they work is often heavily dependent upon external political support.

Different agencies, bureaus, departments and, more importantly, the staffs to make them operational, exist only because there is (or was) sufficient demand generated through the political process to create them in the first place and maintain them thereafter (Cochran et al., 1982: 1–14). In spite of the myth that bureaucracies once created exist in perpetuity and continue to grow uncontrollably, there is, in fact, considerable evidence to show that once an agency loses its base of public support, it will either wither away or change its focus to a field for which public support exists and demands are generated (Rubin, 1985: 1–19). These political demands come from different constituencies of varying strengths within society. It is these constituencies that work through the policy process to ensure that their agency, bureau, or department has both the authority and the funding needed to function effectively (Nakamura and Smallwood,

1980: 31–44). Hence, these constituencies have a major stake in what civil servants do and how they do it. Civil servants and various constituencies easily become dependent upon each other for the successful pursuit of their own interests (Almond and Powell, 1966: 74–79).

The relationship between civil servants and different configurations of constituencies is an area in which more research needs to be done. Although there is an abundance of literature on both organizational behavior and the political process from a multitude of perspectives, there have been few attempts to focus on links between public organization and political processes (Karl, 1987). Two key questions that need to be addressed are: How much external political support does a public agency or bureau need in order to successfully carry out its legitimate administrative mission? And, How far can civil servants go in nurturing this support within the confines of the principle of political neutrality?

A viable and stable political regime, regardless of the level of democratic decision-making it employs, takes its public policy cues from a mixture of civil servants, special interest groups, and directly from the population at large (or at least elitist elements within it). It is folly to ignore the links that exist between segments of the society being governed (however they may be organized and express themselves) and civil servants (Palumbo and Maynard-Moody, 1991: 13).

To summarize, civil servants function in a politically charged atmosphere. Pressure to act in ways that could be considered political comes from at least three different sources. One is internal. Agencies and bureaus want to survive, and the civil servants who control them want to succeed. It takes political skill to accomplish both. Second, elected and politically appointed public officials have their own political agendas and often look to civil servants to help achieve them. Third, external interests also have a political agenda, and they often consider civil servants as natural allies. It is virtually impossible to be a successful high-level civil servant in any society without being political in some way. Even though most countries provide ways to monitor and control the political behavior of civil servants, distinguishing between appropriate and inappropriate behavior can be a difficult task.

## POLITICS AND THE FUNCTION OF PUBLIC MANAGEMENT

The idea that civil servants should be politically neutral is antithetical to the view that they have a political role to play, but it is highly consistent with conventional wisdom about how civil servants should go about carrying out their responsibilities. This is a view that has its roots in the classic administrative systems that evolved in Germany and other western European countries; it is now generally accepted throughout the world (Heady, 1991: 92–93). The view that civil servants should be politically neutral, that is, that they should not be involved in the political process, is recognized as the ideal code of behavior in virtually all modern political systems (Heady, 1979: 167–70); it is the ideal strived for in most other countries as well (Morgan, 1991). It was articulated as part of Weber's "ideal type" bureaucracy (1978). Woodrow Wilson (1887) in his classic essay, "The Study of Administrations," emphasized what he perceived to be the distinction between politics and administration; as Palumbo and Maynard-Moody state (1991: 24), "this distinction has shaped the intellectual history of the profession." The idea that public administration is much more closely aligned with business management than with politics has been carried forward. There seems to be an assumption that political involvement corrupts and detracts from sound business management practices and thus that the "public good" is less well served.

Most modern political systems have taken this view as a license to attempt to isolate or insulate their civil servants from politics of any kind. The normal approach is to appoint civil servants on "their merits" based on competitive, ostensibly nonpolitical exams. Once employed, they tend to enjoy an elaborate protective network that is designed, in large measure, to keep external and internal political forces at bay (Hummel, 1977: 176).

Operationally, bureaucracies are supposed to function like their counterparts in the private sector, and civil servants are supposed to follow sound business management practices. The prevailing ethos is that the further civil servants are kept from politics the better (Pfiffner, 1992). Regardless of their personal viewpoints, good civil servants are loyal to whatever political regime is in power and neither try to influence how that regime functions nor subject themselves to influence from outside sources (Aberbach and Rockman, 1988: 606–609).

There is clearly a gap between what is ideally expected of civil servants in terms of their political behavior and what appears to occur operationally in most places around the world. It is this gap that represents the dilemma civil servants face in many countries. Most societies do, however, manage to resolve this dilemma operationally (Newland, 1987). In some countries, for instance modern-day Great Britain, civil servants behave close to the norms identified in the ideal, Weberian model, at least in terms of maintaining a degree of political neutrality (Arnold, 1988). In countries such as the United States and a number of developing countries, the dilemma is resolved operationally by simply tolerating some types of political activity on the part of civil servants (Kaufman, 1969). An understanding of how different countries resolve this dilemma operationally is an important part of putting the concept of politicization into perspective for comparative analysis.

Of the different aspects of politicization, the most controversial frequently emanate from the collision that inevitably takes place when the civil service and the political regime meet, that is, at the point of interaction between high-level civil servants and elected and appointed public officials representing the ruling political regime (Aberbach and Rockman, 1988). Although Heady, in a comparative assessment of political system/administrative relationships (1991: 448–50), identified six different types of configurations, in very general terms these can be consolidated into two (Lutrin and Settle, 1976: 326). In one scenario, the political regime dominates the civil service. In this scenario the civil service loses a large portion of its independence and instead serves as an arm of the ruling political regime carrying out its political agenda. In the second scenario, the opposite is true. The civil service maintains a highly independent existence and uses its power to establish and implement its own agenda on behalf of the political regime (Riggs, 1988).

The United States, prior to the adoption of the Pendleton Act of 1883, was an example of the first scenario (Maranto and Schultz, 1991: 39–59). What occurred in the Soviet Union and eastern European countries prior to the downfall of communism could be considered an example of the second scenario (Rice, 1992). Other extreme examples can be found in the developing countries of Asia, Africa, and Latin America (McLennan, 1980: 341–78).

Although many countries may tilt in one direction or the other, most countries, especially those with modern political systems, do not go to such extremes (Heady, 1991: 91–92). Of these two scenarios, as far as most countries are concerned, the possible political dominance of the civil service by political regimes seems to be of greater concern than the possible dominance of the political regime by the civil service (Aberbach and Rockman, 1988).

Political history appears to be important. France and Germany, for instance, came closer than most other countries to separating the activities of civil servants from the day-to-day operation of political regimes (Heady, 1991: 92–93). The dichotomy between policy-making and policy implementation that developed in these two countries, came about, however, more as a result of practical necessity than by conscious design. Both experienced long periods of political instability during which the type of government and the approach changed frequently (Almond and Powell, 1966: 149–68). The two civil service systems became stabilizing forces in their respective societies by keeping their distance from often volatile political situations while carrying out their duties professionally. Further, the political regimes were often too weak or preoccupied with other matters to impose their will on the civil service successfully. The relationship has been identified by Heady (1979: 170–72) as the *classic administrative model* and is practiced, with some variations, by virtually all of the countries in continental western Europe.

The continental experience is easily contrasted to the experiences of the United States and Great Britain. In the United States and Britain, the dichotomy between policy-making and policy implementation is less well established and evolved quite differently. Unlike France and Germany, Britain and the United States were early converts to democracy and have had more than two centuries of political stability (Almond and Powell, 1966: 128–48). There was little cause for their civil service systems to develop independently of the ruling political regimes. With the exception of India, similar statements could be made about most of the nations that evolved out of the British political experience, including Canada, Australia, and New Zealand (Deutsch, Dominguez, and Heclo, 1981: 59–86, 158–82). Further, in most of the English-speaking world the civil service became a significant instrument in establishing democratic institutions, something that did not occur until later in western Europe. The civil service became, especially in the formative years of democratization, an extension of the political regime that controlled the government. Civil servants were expected to behave politically (Almond and Powell, 1966: 128–48).

Britain was one of the first modern states to give real political power to an elected parliament. This development spurred the creation and institutionalization of political parties, which then used their powers of appointment as rewards for loyal support and to ensure that votes would be delivered in the next election (Dragnich, 1961: 50–65, 76–101). Similar developments occurred in the United States. A major difference between the British and American systems was that in Great Britain patronage positions were reserved for the nobility and representatives of the upper classes. In the United States the major beneficiaries of the patronage system were the lower classes, which came to depend on political jobs for their livelihood (Maranto and Schultz, 1991: 27–38). Patronage appears to be a factor in many developing countries as well. Patronage in developing countries, however, may or may not be linked to a process of democratization (Almond and Powell, 1966: 63–72).

India is different from other countries that evolved from the British tradition because its civil service system evolved from the administrative organization created for the semipublic East India Company rather than from the British government itself. The East India Company, a trading company chartered in 1600 that became the dominant mercantile force in the Far East, adapted its administrative structure from the German bureaucratic model (Hall, Albion, and Pope, 1961: 207, 454). It was this model, in turn, which served as the basis for reform of the British civil service system in the mid-1850s.

It is interesting to note that the civil service in India is often seen as alienated from the population it is supposed to serve. It has been identified as an instrument of British colonial rule, and its composition of upper-class, well-educated individuals has served to separate it from the mass of India's population. It is closely linked to the Indian National Congress political party that has ruled India since independence in 1947 (McLennan, 1980: 346–47).

In the classical administrative systems that evolved in western Europe, patronage is at most a minor factor. Because these systems feature civil service systems that evolved as independent entities within the respective political structure, they were able to erect significant barriers between the civil service and the forces controlling the various political regimes (Heady, 1979). Patronage in this model is seen as a form of intrusion by political functionaries into the professional realms of the civil service.

One consequence of this view is a disdain for political accountability. As has been said about the French civil service, high-ranking officials see themselves as public administrators, not public servants (Heady, 1991: 194). To the extent that the evolution of different political systems seems to have influenced the relationship between political decision makers and civil servants, these two models, the classic administrative model and the British patronage model, serve to define the historical extremes. Most of the nations with modernized political systems developed their own relationship somewhere in between and are continuing to cope with the responsibility-responsiveness dilemma. Although Mosher has argued that it is possible for civil servants to be both politically accountable and professionally responsible (Mosher, 1968: 1–23), these roles are not automatically compatible (Daniel and Rose, 1991). In most instances, one or the other dominates. When patronage is a factor, political loyalty tends to take precedence over professional responsibility. When patronage is eliminated, political responsiveness can be relegated to a distinctly secondary responsibility (Almond and Powell, 1966: 98–127).

It is difficult to make generalizations about these two broad models as they apply to the developing countries in Asia, Africa, and Latin America, but there is some evidence to indicate that the civil service systems of these countries are coming to embrace one model or the other (Montgomery, 1986). It would appear that the countries of the Pacific Rim that have enjoyed a measure of recent economic success are also developing a cadre of professional civil servants who are beginning to function in ways consistent with the traditional administrative models. These countries include Taiwan, Korea, Singapore, and to a somewhat lesser extent Indonesia and Malaysia (Shin, 1993). At the same time, countries that have not experienced a great deal of economic success, most notably the Philippines and many of the nations in Africa, appear to be moving toward a different model (Bräuchli, 1992). Many of these countries seem to be emphasizing a high degree of responsiveness in terms of how their civil service systems deal with both internal and external political pressure. As Morgan points out in his contribution to this volume, many of these countries have highly developed patronage networks.

It would appear that in a number of countries that have experienced a sustained period of political instability, for example, Chile, Brazil, Liberia, and Nigeria, the civil service has come to play a stabilizing political role (McLennan, 1980: 306–66). In some cases, civil service systems have come to dominate the policy process (Lutrin and Settle, 1976: 362–64).

Such developments, according to Riggs (as noted in Heady, 1991: 428), quite possibly impede the establishment of a viable political system. In other developing countries the reverse seems to be true; through patronage and by other means, the political leadership makes the civil service little more than an extension of the political regime in control of the country (Morgan, 1991). Many of these countries are politically quite unstable, and most lack the prerequisites for a working constitutional democracy. Public policy can come from a number of different sources, including the military and the upper level of the civil service (Montgomery, 1986: 407–13). It would appear that the major concern in most developing countries is, indeed, development. Whether policy is initiated and administered by civil servants on their own or as agents of political decision makers is less important than the outcome of that policy. In any case, concerns that civil servants are violating the principle of political neutrality are not often expressed.

The task is different in the emerging democracies of central and eastern Europe, but the issues are similar. What they are trying to do is remove policy-making responsibilities from the bureaucracy while enhancing its ability to be an effective policy implementing area of the government (Rice, 1992). There can be little doubt that during the last several years of communist rule, the major force in both policy-making and policy implementation in these countries was the communist-led bureaucracy that was almost immune to political pressure from any source. There were diminishing ideological concerns, and there was almost no distinction made between policy-making and policy implementation (Rice, 1992).

In attempting to privatize the economy, decentralize the bureaucracy (and thus the delivery of basic services), and establish government based on democratic principles, eastern European countries have also created a need to deal with the rules and responsibilities of the civil servants who will remain with the government. They will face the same questions of who controls the policy-making and policy implementation process that other societies face (Seroka, 1992).

This brief assessment suggests that political history can go some way toward providing an explanation of the relationships that develop between civil servants and political regimes; but history alone cannot account for all of the differences that exist from country to country. At the same time, to the extent that the level and type of political activity of a civil service is a product of historical trends, other historical experiences should also be documented (Ashford, 1991). A historical perspective could be helpful, as Morgan indicates in his chapter on trends in some developing countries. Just as, for a variety of reasons, India has deviated from the political norms associated with other countries that emerged from the British political experience, there may well yet be undiscovered trends at work in a number of recently independent countries that could guide future civil service behavioral patterns in one direction or another.

## CONSTITUTIONS AND GOVERNMENT STRUCTURE

The constitutional and governmental structure of any country is unique. Constitutional and legal provisions are relatively more important in some countries than in others. Some countries, such as the United States and Britain, have a long history of respect for a constitutional/legal system (Heady, 1987: 9–16). As Morgan points out, in other countries—including those in central and eastern Europe and many developing countries that only recently became independent—the tradition of relying on constitutional and legal traditions for guidance is not so deeply ingrained.

In the United States, more so than in virtually any other country, the Constitution and the resulting legal system go a long way toward explaining the differences between civil service behavior in America as compared with other countries. It is probably the single most important factor in determining the character of American public administration (Stillman, 1988). In addition, much of what the American Constitution provides is antithetical to the basic principles of the classical administrative systems that evolved in western Europe. But while the classic administrative system has come to represent the ideal model for professional administrative behavior world-wide, the American Constitution comes close to being a model for constitutions world-wide (Burger and Neuhaus, 1984: 220–26). Many countries, including Germany, France, Nigeria, and Japan, have adopted one or more of the provisions of the American Constitution. Clearly, among the causes of the responsiveness-responsibility dilemma are the sometimes conflicting requirements of the model classical administrative system on the one hand and the American constitutional model on the other hand (Heady, 1987).

There are three major constitutional provisions that serve to separate the American civil service from those in other countries. The first, and perhaps most important, is the constitutionally defined separation of powers that divides the government into distinct legislative, executive, and judicial branches (Woll, 1971: 7–18). Most constitutional democracies are organized as parliamentary systems without an independent executive, and the civil service thus reports to the legislative leadership. In the United States, at least at the national level, most of the bureaucracy reports to the executive and has only informal relationships with the legislature.

A second critical constitutional provision is the American federal system (Cigler, 1990: 642–43). Although countries such as Canada, Germany, India, and Nigeria also function as federal structures, none is quite like the United States, particularly in terms of how the civil service functions (McLennan, 1980: 27–45). With fifty states and 80,000 semiautonomous units of local government, each with its own approach to public administration, the United States features, in reality, a mosaic of different civil service approaches. There are many places left in the United States where the approach to public administration is closer to that practiced in some underdeveloped countries than it is to that practiced in Britain, Japan, or on the European continent (Hojnacki, 1983: 133–43).

The third constitutional provision that is important to the operation of the civil service in the United States is the emphasis on individual rights, in particular, the first amendment protection of free expression (Riggs, 1988). This provision is viewed (at least in principle) as fundamental, and it is one the American government has aggressively attempted to export to all the world. Civil servants are citizens, too, and although there have been a number of statutes passed in an attempt to limit the political participation of civil servants (Benda and Rosenbloom, 1992: 25–47), and although this legislation has been upheld by the U.S. Supreme Court as constitutional, many American civil servants do not feel the same compulsion to avoid political activity felt by their counterparts elsewhere in the world. Further, the Constitution requires that other citizens have access to decision makers, including those in the civil service (Garnett, 1987). Future research will need to address constitutional systems from a comparative perspective in order to examine the impact of constitutional arrangements on the political behavior of civil servants.

It would appear that the system of government organized under the United States Constitution serves to promote at least some level of civil service politicization (Newland, 1987). The separation of powers arrangement which creates independent legislative and executive branches of government but requires them to cooperate in policy matters means that a good deal of political give and take must take place before serious matters can be resolved. The civil service, responsible to the executive branch but dependent upon the legislature, inevitably gets caught in the process (Rourke, 1984: 339–63). Further, the federal system disperses authority and thus encourages "creative" administrators at the various levels of government. In addition, the emphasis on civil liberties, especially free expression, means that civil servants must regularly encounter citizen groups and a wide range of special interests.

In a similar, if less profound way, the constitution of the French Fifth Republic has partly redefined the way the French civil service functions (Rohr, 1991: 287–94). Prior to the establishment of the Fifth Republic in 1958, France functioned as a parliamentary democracy in a way similar to Italy (Elia, 1989: 11–14). Its civil service functioned along classical administrative lines, keeping its distance from the turmoil around it. With the advent of the Fifth Republic, which in part copied the American presidential model, the president of France assumed new powers, and the role of Parliament in policy-making was reduced. These changes have had the effect of concentrating such powers as legislative initiatives, administrative control, and oversight in the executive branch of government. In short, in creating the Fifth Republic with enhanced presidential power based on the American experiment, France also increased the potential for bureaucratic politicization similar to that in the United States. As Quermonne and Rouban say, "France has been partly challenged by the new, increasingly political role adopted by administrative institutions and their capacity to regulate lobby pressures" (Quermonne and Rouban, 1986: 397).

Germany and Japan both function under constitutions that were adopted with a good deal of American influence following the end of the second world war.

In Germany, the executive branch, under the direction of a chancellor, has been able to assume power independent of the legislature. Further, most of the politically appointed German ministries have relatively small staffs and the bureaucracy has thus been able to achieve a good deal of independent political power in terms of policy formulation (Dragnich, 1961: 276–83).

In Japan the new constitution virtually incorporated the old administrative system, which meant that the bureaucracy retained a large measure of policy-making power (Pempel, 1992: 8–13). Of more importance than the constitution in terms of the behavior of the civil service is the administrative reform movement that began in earnest in the early 1980s. One objective of this broad review of national policy was to restructure the relationships between the civil service and the parliament, and to allow parliament to take back some of its policy-making authority (Wright and Sakurai, 1987: 121–31). It appears to be an attempt to make a constitutional change without changing the constitution.

In Great Britain it is difficult to separate constitutional/legal restrictions on the behavior of the civil service from those that have guided the civil service for more than a century. To be sure, there is a large body of British law focused on the civil service but, beyond the early reform legislation that served to establish the civil service and define its role, there is little evidence to indicate that this body of law is objectionable to the current generation of civil servants (Dragnich, 1968: 109–11).

In terms of guiding the political behavior of civil servants, constitutional/legal concerns seem to be relatively less important in developing countries than in industrialized countries. Former colonies of European powers tend to adopt the administrative structures of their former rulers. In few cases, however, are these administrative systems totally appropriate for the society in which they exist. Imposed administrative systems are seldom able to adjust to the unique cultural and ethnic relationships that exist in most developing countries. Many of these countries regularly experience coups and function for extended periods of time under military juntas or civilian dictators (McLennan, 1980: 181–223). Many governments have suspended their constitutions or have openly violated various constitutional provisions. It would appear that in a large number of cases, constitutionalism and the legal system which flow from constitutional arrangements are held in low regard by both governmental officials and the public at large (Umeh, 1992: 57–70). Morgan, in this volume, and other observers of public administration in developing countries find that although civil servants pay lip service to principles of modern public administration as it is understood in western countries, in practice, local customs and traditions play a more important part in steering their behavior.

Clearly, the constitutional/legal system of the United States is important in determining the political behavior of civil servants. The institutional arrangements organized under the U.S. Constitution clearly encourage rather than discourage administrative politicization (Coleman, 1982: 326–42). And, to the extent that certain American constitutional provisions are exported to other countries, there is also a tendency to alter the traditional responsibilities of the civil service in those countries.

The propensity of other nations to adopt provisions of the American constitutional system is an area that needs further research. We do not yet know the full extent to which the Constitution is having an impact on other parts of the world. The mere longevity of the U.S. Constitution and the political system of Great Britain is an indicator of their appropriateness as the basic laws of these two nations. The impact of constitutional/legal provisions in other countries is not so apparent. Countries with modernized political systems, even those with a history of political instability, tend to support constitutionalism (Heady, 1991: 188–89). But the jury is still out on the impact of constitutional/legal arrangements in developing countries (Morgan, 1991).

## OPERATIONAL TRADITIONS

Beyond identifying a few historical trends and noting how some constitutional and legal provisions seem to either encourage or discourage certain types of activities, it is difficult to isolate other factors that are both common to most countries and serve to influence the political behavior of civil servants (Riggs, 1988). Identification of such factors is, of course, necessary for long-range theory building, but as yet we lack the database to proceed.

No two civil service systems, even those in a region that shares a common history and legal tradition, are the same (Heady, 1987). Indeed, as Hojnacki (1983) has noted for the United States, and Lutrin and Settle (1976: 364–66) have noted for Italy, even in the same country civil servants from different regions are likely to behave differently. Although there are some standards that most societies seem to embrace, at least in principle, these standards are often interpreted and applied differently. Both the standards and various interpretations of them can best be put into perspective by reviewing civil service political behavior on a case-by-case basis.

In most societies there is a prohibition against the direct participation of civil servants in the electoral process, at least while they are serving in their professional capacity. This prohibition means they cannot work in election campaigns, provide financial support, or make political speeches. This rule, however, is not universally applied, and it is violated regularly at the subnational level in the United States (Lutrin and Settle, 1976: 254–55).

Beyond the prohibition against involvement in recognizable and highly visible electioneering (defined as it is in different ways), there are few other easily identifiable standards that cut across nations. Most countries do try to limit civil service involvement in the policy process; but different countries undertake this task in different ways, and some are obviously more successful than others.

The British have apparently gone further than most in protecting the civil service by isolating it from very deep involvement in the policy process. Upper-level civil servants, at least, still come primarily from Oxford and Cambridge, are relatively well paid, and hold positions of high status. They can achieve the equivalent of tenure, and the promotion and position assignment system is designed to protect them from reprisals by members of the Parliament, including those in the cabinet (Deutsch, Dominguez, and Heclo, 1981).

At the same time, even high-level, career administrators keep their distance from the political side of the policy process. The British Civil Service has a reputation for being unquestionably loyal to whatever government happens to be in power. The uniquely British office of "Permanent Secretary" has the task of bridging the gap between career administrators and the political, policy-making individuals in each of the ministries (McLennan, 1980: 344–46). The essence of the British standard comes as close to the Weberian model as any system in the world. The British system can be readily contrasted to the American system.

The major difficulty in the United States appears to be the constitutionally mandated separation of powers that, with some important exceptions, excludes Congress from any formal involvement in program administration (Rohr, 1988: 167–68). For its part, Congress, primarily because of the ombudsman's role that most congressmen and senators play with administrative agencies (in addition to their legislative responsibilities), finds it very much in its own interest to stay involved in certain aspects of program administration. Hence, Congress has been historically very reluctant to try to deal with civil service politicization (Riggs, 1988: 344–45).

In writing the system of checks and balances into the American Constitution, the framers sought to enhance political give and take, not to discourage it. Their goal, as Hamilton pointed out in *The Federalist,* no. 9, was to ensure that no single constituency could gain effective control over either the policy-making or policy implementation process (Rossiter, 1961: 71–76). The system as it was established by the Constitution requires a high degree of interaction between the executive and legislative branches of government. Most of this interaction, however, occurs at the subcabinet agency level (interacting with congressional committees and subcommittees) (Rohr, 1988: 167–70).

One important difference between the United States and other nations is the depth of political control exercised by the executive branch. In Britain, Japan, and most of the countries with classical administrative systems, the political control exercised by the elected government extends only to the top level of the bureaucracy, where individuals are likely to have had professional administrative experience. In this context, most policy initiatives tend to be negotiated between senior civil servants and the politically selected ministries before the initiative is brought forward (McLennan, 1980: 126–28).

In the United States, political control by the executive branch tends to extend at least four levels into the various administrative agencies, and often the individuals who fill these positions are appointed primarily because they represent one constituency or another; they may or may not have a large degree of public administration experience. It is not unusual in the United States for the president or one of his political appointees to announce a policy initiative without consulting any career civil servants from the affected agency (Aberbach and Rockman, 1987: 489–93). Few attempts to change policy direction undertaken in this manner are likely to result in the total loyalty of the affected civil servants. It would appear, then, that executive branch attempts to control the policy process often have the opposite effect. In excluding key civil servants from decisions concerning policy initiatives, members of the executive branch risk encouraging these civil servants to seek the assistance of Congress, where support can usually be found at the committee and subcommittee level (Nakamura and Smallwood, 1980: 53–65).

In the U.S. federal civil service, especially at the higher levels, the loyalty of administrators can be divided in three or four ways simultaneously (Benveniste, 1983: 31–36). As professionals, the vast majority are loyal to the agency for which they work and to the administration that is controlling the policies of the agency. But when the administration begins promoting policies that are perceived as violating the agency's basic mission, that loyalty can be shifted to the agency's advocates in Congress, and perhaps directly to the constituents the agency is supposed to serve (Kettl, 1992: 94–109). Cabinet level secretaries and politically appointed agency heads often have little real power to enforce loyalty to particular policies and programs. On the other hand, disgruntled administrations can frequently use the press to counter unpopular initiatives from the administration. Information is often released prematurely, and civil servants will often serve as "anonymous sources," providing the press with background information on various policy initiatives (Rubin, 1981: 170–80).

To a large extent then, operational standards in the United States provide at least a window of opportunity for American federal civil servants to become involved in the policy process (Rohr, 1988: 167–68). It would appear that neither the executive branch nor Congress has control over the public policy process in the same way it exists in other nations (Coleman, 1982: 256–57).

Great Britain, on the other hand, seems to do a better job of keeping policy-making out of the hands of the bureaucracy and under control of the Parliament, although appearances may be somewhat misleading since much of what occurs inside the British civil service is not subject to the same kind of public scrutiny found in the United States. The British civil service still has a reputation of strong loyalty to whatever political party happens to control Parliament (McLennan, 1980: 125–31). One important fact is that individual members of Parliament play a more purely legislative role than do individual members of Congress in the United States. Members of Parliament seldom have the opportunity to go directly to administrative agencies to intercede on behalf of constituent interests (Deutsch, Dominguez, and Heclo, 1981).

The British constitutional/legal system appears to discourage political maneuvering on the part of civil servants (Arnold, 1988: 726–33). Great Britain has a unitary form of government that features an essentially two-party system with a high degree of party discipline. True policy initiatives almost always come through the leadership of the majority party at the national level, a relatively small group of individuals. Even civil servants who are politically inclined find it difficult to get an audience for their ideas (McLennan, 1980: 125–31). For career civil servants, there is a great deal of incentive to go along with the policies of the controlling political party and very little incentive to chart their own policy direction. The resultant lack of civil servant influence in the policy process also serves to discourage lobbying by various private interests. Thus, it would appear that the ethos of loyalty to the "powers-that-be" has a pragmatic foundation that is largely absent in the United States and, to a lesser degree, on the European continent (Dragnich, 1961: 115–18). Unlike France, there is little opportunity in Britain for civil servants to move into high-level private sector positions, and there is little advantage in trading a career in the civil service for one in electoral politics.

In France and Germany, the traditional role of the civil service as a professional enterprise aloof from politics (at least partisan battles) has been altered somewhat in recent years, but it remains largely the norm. Although the origins are different, the pattern in Japan is similar to that of France and Germany.

In Germany, the traditional operating standards established during the days of Prussian dominance remain the norm and public administration is an important function. Prior to reunification, civil service employment involved up to 20 percent of those employed in the country (Heady, 1991: 208).

As a federal republic, Germany features decentralized policy-making and policy implementation. Less than 10 percent of the people employed in the public service work for the federal government. The government appears to maintain effective control of the policy process, at least in broad general terms. The civil service, however, retains a good deal of discretion, and there can be little doubt that within the broad policy framework of the federal political system, the civil service, as Heady states, is "actively and extensively engaged in policy-making functions"; the federal ministries are too small and their tasks too large for the case to be otherwise. Heady (1991: 213–16) also quotes Mayntz and Scharpf: "the Federal bureaucracy does not attempt to actively circumvent executive control and to impose upon the political executive a course of action developed according to its own pretenses" (Heady, 1979: 191). The only conclusion that can be drawn here is that in the German civil service, the long-standing tradition of professionalism in operational ethics remains intact but may be in danger in the future. There appear to be precious few other constraints on politicization of the civil service; and in the absence of such constraints, politicization in the form of participation in the policy process could become a more serious concern in the future than it is in the 1990s.

There are two sets of factors that may encourage change in the German system. One is internal. The "new breed" of German civil servant is less willing than his or her predecessor to accept the traditional approach to public administration. The second is external. As the country experiences high levels of immigration and attempts to reintegrate Germans from the East, there appears to be increasing pressure from various private interests to influence policy-making and policy implementation. Heady (1991: 212–18) has noted changes in the attitudes of some segments of the German civil service.

In France, concern over civil service politicization is justifiably somewhat greater than it is in Germany. France too is experiencing pluralization, and change appears to be occurring more rapidly. The French civil service seems to be moving much more rapidly toward direct political entanglement through involvement in the policy process than the German civil service. The key to this difference is the constitution of the Fifth Republic and, in particular, the provision adopted in 1962 which split administrative responsibilities between the president and the prime minister. This split executive arrangement had the effect of putting the civil service in the middle, and of encouraging bureaucratic maneuvering in ways that are similar to what occurs in the United States but alien to the traditional French experience. The French are also experiencing an increase in pressure on the civil service from various special interests (Rohr, 1991).

An important critical difference between the American and French administrative experience is that in France civil servants have played a legitimate and visible role in public policy formulation, something explicitly denied to American civil servants. Like their American counterparts, French civil servants cannot, while they are serving in an administrative capacity, engage in partisan politics. Indeed, unlike their American colleagues, they are even prohibited from writing or making public speeches on policy issues while they are serving in an administrative capacity. However, it is very easy for French civil servants to take leave from their administrative duties to run for public office, and large numbers choose to do so at various points in their careers. From 1958 through 1986, 33 percent of the members of the National Assembly came from the civil service; and all of the first eleven prime ministers in the Fifth Republic came from the civil service (Rohr, 1991: 283–90). Thus, civil service involvement in the policy process has been a fact of French political life for some time, although it exists in a highly controlled environment.

Of greater current concern in France is the traditional tendency of the civil service to respond to policy initiatives outside the established political process. As Quermonne and Rouban state: "The higher civil service in France has been so closely involved with top-level government policy making, social reforms, and economic development that the political and administrative worlds are now merging" (Quermonne and Rouban, 1986: 398). It would appear, based on evidence they provide, that legitimate French political authorities are in some danger of losing effective control of the policy-making process.

In Japan, the administrative system and tradition are similar to those in Germany, but the question of politicization is similar to that in France. As in Germany and France, the civil service in Japan evolved independently of other parts of the political system. Entrance into the civil service is highly competitive, and as in Britain, most of the recruits come from only the most prestigious universities, especially Tokyo University. Civil servants enjoy high status, are well paid, and are shown a great deal of professional courtesy. The Japanese civil service has maintained a strong reputation for professionalism, but the standards of operational ethics do not include a strict prohibition of involvement in policy matters. Indeed, there is evidence to indicate that the civil service exercises considerable influence on the policy process (Pempel, 1992: 2–24). As in Germany and France, some members of the civil service resign their positions in order to run for public office (Pempel, 1992: 19–22). The Japanese Diet has never had full control of public policy process in modern times. The civil service, although embracing a long tradition of professionalism, has also served as an initiator of public policy. As Pempel (1992: 19) states: "Because the Japanese bureaucracy has been so closely linked to political leadership, it provides an important contrast to countries where bureaucrats and politicians are presumed to have rather separate and antagonistic roles." The political role of the civil service has been a matter of concern in Japan for some time. As in France, there has been a high level of interaction historically between the civil service and the politically appointed ministries. The tradition of professionalism comes from the period of prewesternism. Suffice it to say that the movement to stimulate administrative reform in the early 1980s came primarily (but not exclusively) from concern over the political role of the civil service (Schleginger and Chandler, 1993).

The operational approach used in developing countries is another matter altogether. It is very difficult to make generalizations concerning operational standards in developing countries because there is a great deal of diversity among these countries. Some have been independent nations for many years, while for others independence is a recent occurrence. Some have been making significant economic progress, others continue to struggle. Some have close ties to developed western countries, others have significant economic and political differences with the west. Some are politically stable, many are not (Hojnacki, 1993). All of these differences have an impact on the organization and operation of the various civil service systems.

In the countries of central and eastern Europe, and especially in the states of the former Soviet Union, civil service systems basically need to be reinvented. Although economic and political changes have occurred very rapidly in this region of the world since 1988, changes in the administrative structures have not. Administrative agencies continue to be run by the same bureaucrats and operate according to the same basic procedures as before (Witt, 1993). With the possible exception of Poland, policy decisions, especially at the regional and local levels, are made and implemented in much the same way as they were under communist rule. In Poland, however, there is evidence that populism, extending into the local bureaucracies, is starting to take hold (Owen, 1992). Here there is some concern that civil authorities may lose control altogether.

Moving to a different part of the world, standards in India are very close to those observed on the European continent; the Indian civil service plays an important role in both initiating public policy and assuring that it is adopted (Dwivedi and Jain, 1988: 205–14). Civil servants are a highly elite group, recruited—as in Japan and Britain—from only the best schools. As a rule, they do not engage in day-to-day political affairs, but the civil service leadership is tied closely to the dominant political elites and is directly involved in the policy process. One concern is that the civil service is removed form the mass of India's population and that it does not enjoy a high level of popular support (McLennan, 1980: 346–47).

Indonesia, a former Dutch colony, has a slightly different problem with its civil service. Up until the late 1950s, Indonesia suffered through an extended period of political instability. The civil service was not well trained or highly respected, with the result that government services were poorly administered (McLennan, 1980: 358–59).

During the 1980s, with a major push for economic development underway, the quality of the civil service began to improve. Like its counterparts in Taiwan and Singapore, however, it became an extension of the political regime of President Suharto. Basic policy came to be created and implemented through a strong civilian-military cabinet system, of which the civil service is a part, and the country has enjoyed a level of economic success (Brauchli, 1993). The Indonesian civil service does not follow the principle of political neutrality.

In sub-Saharan Africa, a variety of different approaches to managing civil service systems appear to exist. Many of the countries have only recently become independent, and their civil service systems are modeled on those of the former colonial power. As Morgan points out in this volume, however, what is chosen to be adapted from the previous regime may be highly selective. In many of these countries, the colonial power departed without leaving a well-trained civil service. The problem was particularly acute in those colonies under the control of France, Belgium, and Portugal (McLennan, 1980: 362–72). Former British colonies faired somewhat better.

In Nigeria, the largest country in sub-Saharan Africa, the civil service, organized on the British model, has played an important policy-making role, both during the periods of civilian rule and under the military junta. The Nigerian civil service, especially as it is diffused to the state government level, lacks the discipline of its British counterparts; but it is one of the stabilizing forces in an otherwise volatile political system (Heady, 1991: 351–53; Montgomery, 1986: 407–13). As in other developing societies, the responsibility and accountability of Nigerian civil servants is divided between the government ministries for whom they work and the tribal and religious groups from which they come.

The developing nations of Latin America are different from the developing nations of Africa for two important reasons. One of the reasons is that, with the exception of Brazil, they share a common language and cultural tradition; the second is that most of them have existed as independent nations for many decades. Their economic problems, however, are similar to those of Africa. The civil service systems tend to be more highly developed and institutionalized than those in Africa, but they are often no more efficient or less corrupt (McLennan, 1980: 350–60; Morgan, 1991). Many South American countries have been governed by highly elitist civilian and military regimes. As was the case in Germany and France in the previous century, the civil service system often provides a measure of stability; it continues to provide reasonable services in the absence of stable political leadership.

Civil service systems in developing societies are quite vulnerable to politicization. In some cases, this politicization is viewed as a necessary step toward speeding up the process of economic development. In other cases, it is seen as a way of spreading democratic government. In still other cases, it can be seen as nothing more than a way for a political regime to extend its power and authority.


## CONCLUSION

The purpose of this chapter has been to establish a theoretical framework for cross-national comparison of civil service politicization. Although there are some common standards of civil service behavior to which most societies subscribe, they are interpreted and applied differently in different parts of the world. More importantly, these standards, for instance, the principle of political neutrality, cannot account for all of the tasks that civil servants are asked to perform—tasks that vary considerably from country to country.

The difficulty in dealing with the question of civil service politicization is, first, defining the type of behavior that is to be scrutinized, and secondly, putting this behavior into a meaningful sociopolitical context. The behavior of civil servants in any given society follows a pattern that is unique to that society. This pattern is conditioned by the size and diversity of the society, by its historical political development, by the society's constitutional and legal system, and by whatever operational traditions emerged over time. As the observations of both developed and developing nations show, as society changes, so do the behavioral patterns of civil servants. In countries such as Great Britain, which has a stable political system of long duration and a relatively homogeneous population, the civil service reflects the society and changes very slowly. In central and eastern Europe, change has come very quickly.

It would appear that the people who serve in various civil service organizations around the world and their behavior can be used as distinct, dependent variables in assessing civil service politicization from a comparative perspective. It would also appear that in terms of guiding the behavior of civil servants in different countries, the most important elements are their constitutional systems and the organizational arrangements of their governments.

Some progress has been made, but not all of the possible common historical trends or common elements in constitutional or government organizations have been identified here. Rainey, Hill, and Gillespie, in their chapters in this volume, have made notable progress in identifying societal influences on civil servants. But there is more to be done. Civil servants, regardless of the society in which they function, face pressures from a variety of sources.

Civil servants everywhere are more than just implementors of policies determined by other people in other places. They must also be responsive to legitimate political decision makers and sensitive to the needs and desires of the citizens who make up the constituency their particular agency, bureau, or department is supposed to serve. Further, civil servants are a special interest group unto themselves. They have a stake in any set of public policies that touches their own field of endeavor and often feel the need to defend their own turf. They will behave in political ways to the extent they feel they must and to the extent the ruling political regime requires it of them. One of the major criticism leveled against civil servants is that they are too bound to rules, regulations, and procedures, that in essence they are not political enough. Whether they are overly political or not political enough, it would appear that in most circumstances they meet both their professional obligations and the expectations set for them by the polity for which they work.

It would appear that civil service politicization does not, in itself, threaten a political system, at least as long as there is an effort to maintain professional standards. Civil service politicization might, however, be viewed as a symptom of problems within the umbrella political system. However involved the bureaucracies of the Soviet Union or the other countries of central and eastern Europe may have been in creating public policy, they did not cause the downfall of those political systems. As in most places, bureaucrats carried on as was expected of them.

If politicization is becoming an increasing problem in liberal constitutional democracies, it is because of the dilemma created by the requirements of democracy on the one hand, and the objectives of administrative responsibility on the other. But the problem will have to be solved by the political systems in question, not by the civil service systems within them.

## REFERENCES

Aberbach, J. D., and B. A. Rockman. 1987. "Comparative Administration: Methods, Muddles, and Models." *Administration and Society* 18: 473–506.

————. 1988. "Mandates or Mandarins? Control and Discretion in the Modern Administrative State." *Public Administration Review* 48: 606–11.

Aberbach, J. D., R. D. Putnam, and B. A. Rockman. 1981. *Bureaucrats and Politicians in Western Democracies.* Cambridge: Harvard University Press.

Almond, G. A., and G. B. Powell Jr. 1966. *Comparative Politics: A Developmental Approach.* Boston: Little, Brown & Company.

Arnold, P. 1988. "Reorganization and Regime in the United States and Britain." *Public Administration Review* 48: 726–33.

Ashford, D. E. 1991. "History and Public Policy vs. History of Public Policy." Review of Francis G. Castres, ed., *The Comparative History of Public Policy. Public Administration Review* 51: 358–63.

Benda, P. M., and D. H. Rosenbloom. 1992. "The Hatch Act and Contemporary Public Service." In P. W. Ingraham and D. F. Kettl, *Agenda for Excellence: Public Service in America.* Chatham, NJ: Chatham House.

Benveniste, G. 1983. *Bureaucracy.* 2nd ed. San Francisco: Boyd & Fraser.

Bräuchli, M. W. 1992. "Filipinos Look to Takeover of U.S. Base as Spark for a Badly Lagging Economy." *Wall Street Journal,* 25 June.

Burger, P. L., and R. J. Neuhaus. 1984. "To Empower People." In D. C. Korten and R. Klauss, eds., *People Centered Development: Contributions toward Theory and Planning Frameworks.* West Hartford, CT: Kumarian Press.

Cigler, B. 1990. "Public Administration and the Paradox of Professionalism." *Public Administration Review* 50: 637–49.

Cochran, C. E., L. C. Meyer, T. R. Carr, and N. J. Cayer. 1982. *American Public Policy: An Introduction.* New York: St. Martin's Press.

Coleman, F. M. 1982. *Politics, Policy and the Constitution.* New York: St. Martin's Press.

Daniel, C., and B. J. Rose. 1991. "Blending Professionalism and Political Activity: Empirical Support for an Emerging Ideal (Research Note)." *Public Administration Review* 51: 438–41.

Deutsch, K. W., J. I. Dominguez, and H. Heclo. 1981. *Comparative Government: Politics of Industrialized and Developing Nations.* Boston: Houghton Mifflin.

Dogan, M. 1975. "The Political Power of the Mandarins." Pages 3–24 in M. Dogan, ed., *The Mandarins of Western Europe: The Political Role of Top Civil Servants.* New York: John Wiley & Sons.

Dragnich, A. N. 1961. *Major European Governments.* Homewood, IL: Dorsey Press.

Dwivedi, O. P., and Dale Olowv. 1988. "Bureaucratic Morality: An Introduction." *International Political Science Review* 9: 163–66.

Dwivedi, O. P., and R. B. Jain. 1988. "Bureaucratic Morality in India." *International Political Science Review* 9: 205–14.

Elia, L. 1989. "The Marshall Plan and the Evolution of Democracy in Italy." *Italian Journal* 3: 11–14.

Garnett, J. L. 1987. "Operationalizing the Constitution via Administrative Reorganizations: Oil Cans, Trends and Proverbs." *Public Administration Review* 47: 35–44.

Gordon, G. J. 1982. *Public Administration in America.* New York: St. Martin's Press.

Hall, W. P., R. G. Albion, and J. B. Pope. 1961. *A History of England and the Empire-Commonwealth.* 4th ed. Boston: Ginn & Company.

Heady, F. 1979. *Public Administration: A Comparative Perspective.* 2nd ed. New York: Marcel Dekker.

————. 1987. "American Constitutional and Administrative Systems in Comparative Perspective." *Public Administration Review* 47: 9–15.

————. 1991. *Public Administration: A Comparative Perspective.* 4th ed. New York: Marcel Dekker.

Hojnacki, W. P., and Lloyd Rowe. 1983. "Local Government in Indiana: A Study of Contrasts." Pages 109–44 in *Politics and Public Policy in Indiana: Prospects for Change in State and Local Government.* Dubuque, IA: Kendall/Hunt.

————. 1993. "A Comparative Perspective of Managing Economic Development: Some Alternative Models." Paper presented at the conference on Creative Responses to Economic Development in Industrial Communities, Flint, MI.

Hummel, R. P. 1977. *The Bureaucratic Experience.* New York: St. Martin's Press.

Karl, B. D. 1987. "The American Bureaucrat: A History of a Sheep in Wolves' Clothing." Public Administration Review 47: 26–34.

Kaufman, H. 1969. "Administrative Decentralization and Political Power." *Public Administration Review* 29: 3–15.

Kettl, D. F. 1992. "Micromanagement: Congressional Control and Bureaucratic Risk." *Agenda for Excellence: Public Service in America.* Chatham, NJ: Chatham House.

Lutrin, C. E., and A. K. Settle. 1976. *American Public Administration: Concepts and Cases.* Palo Alto, CA: Mayfield.

Maranto, R., and D. Schultz. 1991. *A Short History of the United States Civil Service.* Lanham, MD: University Press of America.

McLennan, B. N. 1980. *Comparative Politics and Public Policy.* North Scituate, MA: Duxbury Press.

Medeiros, J. A., and D. E. Schmitt. 1977. *Public Bureaucracy: Values and Perspectives.* North Scituate, MA: Duxbury Press.

Montgomery, J. D. 1986. "Bureaucratic Politics in Southern Africa." *Public Administration Review* 46: 407–13.

Morgan, E. P. 1991. "Rethinking Civil Service Systems in Developing Countries: An Outline of Research Considerations." Paper presented at the American Society for Public Administration Conference, Washington, DC.

Mosher, F. C. 1968. *Democracy and the Public Serivce.* New York: Oxford University Press.

Nakamura, R. T., and F. Smallwood. 1980. *The Politics of Policy Implementation.* New York: St. Martin's Press.

Newland, C. A. 1987. "Public Executives: Imperium, Sacerdotium, Collegium? Bicentennial Leadership Challenges." *Public Administration Review* 47: 45–56.

Ortona, G. 1989. "New Trends in the Traditional Balance of the Italian Political System." *Italian Journal* 3: 21–23.

O'Toole, L. J., Jr. 1987. "Doctrines and Developments: Separation of Powers, The Politics-Administration Dichotomy, and the Rise of the Administrative State." *Public Administration Review* 47: 17–23.

Owen, C. J. 1992. "Local Government in Plock: An American Observation." Paper presented at the 51st annual meeting of the American Society for Public Administration, Chicago, IL.

Palumbo, D., and S. Maynard-Moody. 1991. *Contemporary Public Administration.* New York: Longman.

Pempel, T. J. 1992. "Japanese Democracy and Political Culture: A Comparative Perspective." *P.S.: Political Science and Politics* 25: 2–24.

Peters, B. G. 1988. *Comparing Public Bureaucracies: Problems of Theory and Method.* Tuscaloosa: University of Alabama Press.

Pfiffner, J. P. 1992. "Political Appointees and Career Executives: The Democracy-Bureaucracy Nexus." *Agenda for Excellence: Public Service in America.* Chatham, NJ: Chatham House.

Plano, J., M. Greenburg, R. Olton, and R. E. Riggs. 1973. *Political Science Dictionary*. Hinsdale, IL: Dryden Press.

Quermonne, J.-L., and L. Rouban. 1986. "French Public Administration and Policy Evaluation: The Quest for Accountability." *Public Administration Review* 46: 397–406.

Reischauer, E. O. 1981. "Japan." In K. W. Deutsch, J. I. Dominguez, and H. Heclo, eds., *Comparative Government: Politics of Industrialized and Developing Nations*. Boston: Houghton Mifflin.

Rice, E. 1992. "Public Administration in Post-Socialist Eastern Europe." *Public Administrative Review* 52: 116–24.

Riggs, F. W. 1988. "Bureaucratic Politics in the U.S.: Benchmarks for Comparison." *Governance: An International Journal of Policy and Administration* 1: 347–79.

Rohr, J. A. 1988. "Bureaucratic Morality in the United States." *International Political Science Review* 9: 167–78.

————. 1991. "Ethical Issues in French Public Administration: A Comparative Study." *Public Administration Review* 51: 283–97.

Rossiter, C. 1961. *The Federalist Papers*. New York: New American Library.

Rourke, F. 1984. "The President and the Bureaucracy." M. Nelson, ed., *The Presidency and the Political System*. Washington, DC: CQ Press.

Rubin, I. S. 1985. *Shrinking the Federal Government: The Effect of Cutbacks on Five Federal Agencies*. New York: Longman.

Rubin, R. L. 1981. *Press, Party, and Presidency*. New York: W. W. Norton & Company.

Seroka, J. 1992. "Enhancing Public Management Competence on the Local Level in Post Socialist East Central Europe." Paper presented at the 51st annual meeting of the American Society for Public Administration, Chicago, IL.

Shin, R. 1993. "The Role of Industrial Policy Agents: A Study of Korean Intermediate Organization as a Policy Network." *International Review of Administrative Sciences* 59: 115–30.

Stillman, R. J., II. 1988. "The Future of the American Constitution and the Administrative State after the Bicentennial: Some Reflections" (book reviews). *Public Administration Review* 48: 813–15.

Umeh, O. J. 1992. "Capacity Building and Development Administration in Southern African Countries." *International Review of Administrative Societies* 58: 57–70.

Weber, Max. 1978. "Bureaucracy." In Jay M. Shafritz and Albert C. Hyde, eds., *Classics of Public Administration*. Oak Park, IL: Moore.

Weher, M. 1978. "Essays on Bureaucracy." In Francis Rourke, ed., *Bureaucratic Power in National Politics*. 3rd ed. Boston: Little, Brown & Company.

Wiatr, J. 1988. "Introduction: Political Leadership from a Comparative Perspective." *International Political Science Review* 9: 91–94.

Wilson, W. 1887. "The Study of Administration." *Political Science Quarterly* 2 (reprinted in Jay M. Shafritz and Albert C. Hyde, eds., *Classics of Public Administration*. Oak Park, IL: Moore, 1978).

Witt, H. 1993. "Foreign Investors Fail in Quagmire of Unsettled Ukraine." *Chicago Tribune*, 6 July.

Woll, P. 1977. *American Bureaucracy*. 2nd ed. New York: W. W. Norton & Company.

Wright, D. S., and Y. Sakurai. 1987. "Administrative Reform in Japan: Politics, Policy, and Public Administration in a Deliberative Society." *Public Administrative Review* 47: 121–34.

# 8 SOCIAL CONTROL OF CIVIL SERVICE SYSTEMS

Michael Hill and Desi Gillespie

It is difficult to arrive at a definition of the "social control of civil service systems" that does not embrace the whole range of major questions about political and judicial institutions. In many presentations of constitutional theory, the notion of social control over civil services is subsumed under the concept of political control. Civil services are seen as instruments that (a) support democratically elected politicians in the making of policy, and (b) implement policy. However, that formulation has been challenged by evidence that civil servants often have a direct influence upon the policy-making process (Hill, 1972) and by demonstrations that the policy/implementation or politics/administration division is essentially permeable and that much policy is in practice *made* during the implementation process. Such evidence suggests that there may be grounds for conceptualizing social control as an issue separable from political control. Nevertheless, that view may be countered by the assertion that, while limits to political control may be demonstrable, they merely constitute evidence of a problem to which political solutions must be found. Hence, at one level, the case for being concerned with social control over civil services may be seen as based upon the existence of a set of problems involved in securing adequate political control.

However, there is an alternative view which predates democratic politics, and still survives because of deficiencies in the political process itself—the opportunism and narrow time horizon of elected politicians, etc.—which sees civil servants as having responsibilities and duties that may override those imposed by their political masters. This is a view of the social obligations of civil servants embodied in Confucian ethics and reasserted in various ways in modern considerations of the relationship between bureaucracy and democracy (see, e.g., Weber's classic discussion of this issue [Weber, 1947]). Its modern form appears in a concrete way in efforts to formulate codes of ethics for civil servants which postulate social responsibilities over and above any subservient relationship to politicians (Sisson, 1959; First Division Association, 1972). It is manifest in efforts to professionalize civil services and in concerns about the responsibilities of already professionalized groups that enter into public employment (e.g., in health services and education).

Hence, alongside concerns about political control there may be other concerns about ways to achieve social control. One of these involves an attempt to establish a "representative" bureaucracy in which the social profile of society is reproduced in the public service. While this has been regarded principally as an issue about the social class origins of civil servants, there is no reason not to widen the concern to turn attention to issues about their ethnic origins, gender, regional origins, and so on. This is a theme explored at greater length elsewhere in this book; it can be given no more than passing attention here. Another alternative evident in discussions of civil service and professional ethics concerns the value systems of public servants. In this formulation, the crucial values are seen principally as entailing a recognition of the responsibility to act impartially and to separate public and private interests (as in Weber's formulation of the characteristics of rational/legal bureaucracy). Yet, in practice this theme is not altogether separable from the representative bureaucracy theme. Impartiality in a social context where consensus is absent may be better guaranteed by an organization in which no specific interest has a monopoly of power than by adherence to abstract principles of service. This leads us to a third form of social control, as opposed to direct political control, which is, in our view, more important than the first two. It is, moreover, a form that is likely to lend crucial reinforcement to the other two, both of which are fragile in contexts in which bureaucratic self-interest is likely to be a powerful phenomenon. This third form of social control consists of building into systems of government opportunities for the public to exercise direct influence on bureaucratic behavior.

The two principal forms of influence open to individual members of the public are (a) opportunities to ventilate grievances, and (b) opportunities in addition to "normal" political activity to participate in policy decision-making and implementation. In contemporary debate about control over the civil service, two related issues are also given attention. One of these is the extent to which it is possible to build into accountability systems requirements to provide the public with information, particularly information on policy outputs. The other is the extent to which the public can be enabled, once in receipt of such information, to make market-type choices about public services that would enable them to exercise the simplest and most fundamental kind of influence, that entailed in using the "exit" rather than "voice" option (Hirschman, 1970).

In this chapter we are going to give central attention to what we see to be the two key mechanisms of social control over civil services, the ventilation of grievances and the exercise of participation. In a concluding section we will widen the discussion to examine not only issues of information and feasibility and uses of the "exit" option, but also to connect the whole discussion to issues of political control, representative bureaucracy, and civil service ethics.

While social control may be a matter of influence over the creation of policy itself, it is primarily concerned with devices to enable ordinary, largely unorganized citizens to influence the direct impact of public policy processes upon themselves. This means a concern with those processes at, or close to, the implementation end of the policy implementation chain, processes which are likely to be the responsibility of civil servants rather than politicians, insofar as such a distinction can be made. This tends to comprise:

(a) interpretations of policy, where challenges may be made about the extent to which civil service actions are in conformity with the law which authorizes them
(b) discretionary behavior, where citizens perceive a possibility of exercising influence in their own favor or of preventing unfavorable interpretations
(c) delegated policy-making, where there is some scope for citizens to influence the detailed, low-level elaborations of a broader policy framework.

These three areas of decision-making are interrelated and may tend to be indistinguishable to the citizen.


## CITIZEN PARTICIPATION

We have argued that there are various ways by which the citizen can influence or affect decisions made by civil servants at different levels. The types of influence may be classified as follows: (i) political action, (ii) participatory behavior, and (iii) the invoking of grievance procedures. There is much scope for overlap in the activities of the citizen in the first two of these categories. Politics in any democracy requires some degree of participation on the part of its electorate while participation itself is often an attempt to become part of the political process (Pateman, 1970; Richardson, 1983). This section will look at the political/participatory means open to the citizen by which he/she can influence what is essentially the administrative branch of the state.

The means can be divided into three categories:

(a) direct contact between the citizen and the civil servant he or she hopes to influence;
(b) the usual methods of liberal democracy in which the citizen periodically elects a delegate to represent his/her views to a higher body;
(c) a situation somewhere between the first two, where the citizen plays an active role within an interest or pressure group and where delegates from that group to the higher body may be accountable to their members.

### The Participation/Decentralization Model

It is clear that for participation by the individual to have any significance in the decision-making process, there must be a high degree of decentralization of power from higher-level to lower-level political and administrative bodies. Thus, decentralization is a necessary, if not a sufficient, condition for giving meaning to citizen participation.

Only direct contact between the citizen and the civil servant provides scope for effective participation in the activities of a public bureaucracy. Hence the size and complexity of the modern state means that such participation can only take place at the lowest levels in the process. In the quest for some ideal form of participation based on the imagined Athenian model, this is necessarily a limitation in the modern state. As Richardson (1983) has argued, it is more appropriate to use a more modest criterion for the assessment of successful participation than that represented by the top of Arnstein's ladder (Arnstein, 1969). This means that the individual must have some chance of having an impact on detailed decisions that affect him/her directly. In practice, this means those decisions which are likely to be delegated to civil servants at comparatively low levels. Delegation is therefore important for facilitating participation.

Once delegation exists, participation may be facilitated by the extent to which it is formally recognized, that is by the provision of information which enables the level of responsibility to be identified. Other forms of recognition that support participation include the provision of evidence on the way in which policy has been implemented—publication of audit reports and data about decisions, for example. Ideas of this kind have figured in current British suggestions for a "citizens' charter."

In carrying out comparative studies of participation, it is likely to be difficult to explore involvement outside formally devolved powers and formal rights to participation. In many societies, citizens have informal contact with their political leaders, who use that contact as a way of keeping in touch with public opinion. Appointed officials may also be accessible in this way, particularly in small communities. Such systems are obviously open to various forms of abuse by the politician, official, or citizen. But our doubt about informal influence mechanisms is based on the fact that they do not readily lend themselves to comparative analysis except in an anecdotal fashion. This represents a problem for comparative research as it would be foolish to discount their significance (Barrington, 1991).

### Voting as a Participatory Activity

To many lay observers, political participation means little more than the act of voting at election time for a delegate to represent their views to a higher political assembly. This form of indirect democracy, while it is a form of political activity, does not require the citizen to be an active participant in day-to-day decision-making. He/she entrusts the representative with the power to judge what is in the best interests of the electorate. There is no recall or sanction of the representative other than the chance to choose a different candidate at the next election. Furthermore, since people often vote for a party irrespective of the candidate, and since a candidate is usually selected by a relatively small number of the party faithful, the elector is one step further removed from having any real influence over the representative (Richardson, 1983; Lukes, 1974).

In democracies the general direction of policy is determined centrally by the government, with agencies at lower levels having power to make decisions within a determined policy framework. The civil service and its actors, at whatever level in this scenario, see their activities as predetermined by the designs of their political masters. Even when there is a high degree of decentralization, the scope for individual initiative on the part of the civil servant is fairly limited.

For the citizen, then, this would seem to imply that in order to influence or exercise any control over the administrative branch, he or she can only do so by choosing an appropriate representative who will in turn set the ground rules under which the civil service operates. To expect to achieve much this way is recognizably a naive view of the political process, widely challenged by evidence on the "postparliamentary" nature of much decision-making (Richardson and Jordan, 1979; Jordan and Richardson, 1987).

There is, however, an interesting issue here about the extent to which it is possible to have an initiative and referendum system which opens up to public participation quite detailed "administrative" issues. The nearest exemplar of this system is that of Switzerland (see Steinberg, 1976). One author has noted, for example, a federal referendum dealing with quite specific issues about vehicle size and length and a cantonal referendum on whether schools should continue to open on Saturdays.

### Activities of Pressure/Interest Groups

The third road open to the citizen who wishes to cross the line between being a passive subject of policy decisions and an active participant in the political process which leads to those decisions is to take part in pressure group politics. The group involved may be an ad hoc grouping formed to lobby on a single or a small number of issues, or it may be a multipurpose body. Among the latter are professional bodies with both legal status and obligations. These may well see themselves as embedded in the machinery of the state and as having rights, including particular rights of access to the administration, granted to them as a consequence of their statutory recognition and regulation.

The nature of the interest group model for citizen participation combines elements of the direct and the indirect democratic examples described above. In this model, the individual may not meet the decision-makers or the bureaucrats face-to-face, although he/she may do so as  a member of the group. However, through the group he/she is in a position to articulate views to the higher body on a regular and formal basis rather than merely through the ballot box at infrequent intervals. If this is regarded as the appropriate approach to the social control of civil service, it is important to recognize that it raises issues about (a) the extent to which pressure groups are granted a recognized status in "corporate" or "postparliamentary" systems, and (b) the extent to which members are really able to participate to ensure that their officials can speak on their behalf.

The first issue again touches on a major subject, difficult to handle in brief, about the extent to which participatory rights are a recognized part of the political system or are rights that have to be continually fought for and tend to be distributed inequitably. In other words we are dealing here with another of the major issues of comparative politics, and there are wide differences, for example, between the highly participatory systems of the Netherlands and Scandinavia, and systems like the United Kingdom where it is very questionable whether the political and administrative system is really open to a wide range of groups.

The second issue takes us into the debate about intra-organizational democracy originally opened up by Michels (1915). Many people today are members of societies or associations in which they play some role, from merely paying dues to holding elected office. Often these people are represented by officers of the society in consultative meetings with governmental departments, but these meetings frequently take place without the knowledge or concern of the members. Participation may be particularly low where many members have joined the organization because it offers specific personal benefits (breakdown coverage in the case of motoring organizations, for example, or free admission to stately homes, as in the case of the National Trust). On the other hand, many people join organizations primarily because they have a function within the political system and membership can require some degree of active participation (single issue lobbies such as antiabortion or antinuclear groups are key examples here). Trade unions and professional organizations are mixed types in this respect, playing valuable political roles but also offering protection and fringe benefits to members as individuals. Their political importance has, of course, brought them particular attention.

If these organizations are to be effective vehicles for participation, it is essential that the accountability of the representatives of the group be maintained and that the activities of those representatives be monitored with the sanction of immediate removal from their posts for transgressors. To the individual member this may not be as satisfying as direct contact with the political system and its civil servants, but it could ensure that members' views are fairly represented and not just at election time. If these concerns are translated into the context of a comparative study, a complex of questions arises about the extent to which different types of organizations in different countries can be said to pass what we might call the "Michels test" of effective internal democracy. We regard these issues about pressure groups as ones that should be taken into account in a comparative study of the social control of civil services, but to do so effectively requires work both on the major questions linked by the corporatism/postparliamentary democracy debate and on the issues of the internal accountability of pressure groups. Since these are two major issues, it may be better to leave them aside to concentrate on the lower-level individual participation issues mentioned above.

### Private Provision of Public Services

Finally, we must consider the scope for participation of the citizen in those services which are not supplied directly by government but by private agencies acting on behalf of the government. With privatization a growing phenomenon in many western societies, we need to see whether this means that the power of the citizen to influence the policies of this sector (the "new civil servants") remains. It may be argued that market mechanisms will solve the problem, offering scope for "exit" rather than "voice" (Hirschman, 1970). That this is not possible, particularly in the case of monopolistic suppliers such as water or gas companies, is obvious. It may thus be asked if, when a service is being supplied not by the state but by a private "agent of the state," it is possible to produce a contract between the state and its agent which would ensure that accountability is maintained by guaranteeing the rights of the citizen to participate in the decision-making process. There may be levels of participation which do not correspond with levels of normal democratic accountability. There are some interesting research questions about their effectiveness in practice.

### Difficulty of Comparing Systems

Cross-country study of social control of the civil service is not a simple exercise. Much of the influence exercised over both politicians and bureaucracies takes place in an informal manner (Barrington, 1991), and an anthropological study of decision-making would undoubtedly make interesting reading. However, it may well prove exceptionally difficult to make cross-national comparisons. It would appear, therefore, that even when considering only the formal processes for decision-making and for influencing decision-makers, the problem of comparison is a difficult and complex one. How much more complex it would be if consideration were given to informal methods of achieving similar ends.

It is probably necessary to confine comparisons to a comparatively small area of policy activity, such as control over schools or hospitals, specific areas of environmental control, etc. Even with such restrictions, wider questions tend to require attention, for example, that of relevant financial control mechanisms and funding arrangements.

## GRIEVANCE PROCEDURES

Citizens' redress of grievances offers an alternative avenue for social control over public services, in various respects more attainable then direct participation, but not without difficulties and merging at the edges with participatory devices. The concept has its roots in legal arguments about the extent to which citizens can challenge the act of the "sovereign." The original concept that the king can do no wrong has been interpreted in republican and democratic constitutions as meaning that policy decisions by legitimate policymakers must be deemed proper in legal terms and that they can be challenged only by using the political process to change the law. An American judicial ruling makes this point:

> A sovereign is exempt from suit, not because of any formal conception or obsolete theory, but on the logical and practical ground that there can be no legal right as against the authority that makes the law on which the right depends. (Justice Holmes in Kawananakoa v. Polyblank, 205 US 349 at 353 [1907], quoted in Craig, 1990)

What occurred in the evolution of administrative law, on the other hand, was the notion that the king's servants could be wrong in their interpretation of the law (or even that the king could misdirect himself). This issue was, of course, further complicated by the fact that being wrong could mean merely misinterpreting the law and by extension misusing the discretion the law conveys, but it could also mean willfully disregarding the law. In the latter case, public servants may in fact be committing a criminal offense, and it has normally come to be regarded as appropriate for them to be liable for criminal prosecution.

The field of administrative law has therefore tended to be regarded as concerned with legal errors where criminality is not involved. It focuses essentially on interpretation of policy. What follows from this is that, in a modern world in which policy is very complex and policy implementation depends on the interpretation of complex regulations and the exercise of extensive but fettered discretionary powers, there are many difficulties in drawing lines between a challenge to a policy and a challenge to the way in which it has been implemented. Moreover, there are further difficulties that arise where a policy itself may be shown to be self-contradictory or to be incompatible with either the constitution, or common law principles, or another policy. Understandably, a citizen who has a grievance may be confused as to whether he or she can merely challenge a policy, probably through political processes, or whether there is a basis for a challenge either to the legality of that policy or to the way in which the policy has been interpreted. Such confusion is not helped by the fact that questions of political strategy may influence decisions about how to make a challenge (in other words challenges may be made through the courts not because cases can be won there but because this offers an opportunity to win publicity and make a political point).

These, then, are some of the definitional problems to be faced by comparative study of grievance procedures. Broadly, the aim here is to confine attention to the narrower uses of administrative law as a form of social control over civil servants, that is, of the "sovereign's servants," who from time to time—normally without criminal intent—misinterpret, misunderstand, or over-amplify their powers. This is, obviously, a within-system view of the issue: the aggrieved citizen often sees merely a decision with consequences that seem to be unfair or merely undesired. It could be argued that a good grievance process needs to recognize this fact and operate in ways that help with the identification of bad laws it has no power to overrule. There are obvious questions here about links with participatory devices. The process may also need to operate in ways that even losers recognize as just.

## Types of Grievance Procedures

For purposes of comparative study, grievance procedures in public administration can be divided into:

(1) procedures built into other, more general legal structures dealing with a wide range of civil law disputes (these are characteristic of American and British procedures);

(2) specific administrative courts (e.g., the French *Conseil d'Etat*);

(3) administrative tribunals, under the overall surveillance of courts and independent of the agencies they oversee;

(4) specialized investigatory commissions (ombudsman systems) which are independent of the administrative agencies they oversee (Stacey, 1978). These bodies report to legislatures and tend to be alternatives to, not substitutes for, courts and/or tribunals;

(5) tribunals which are not independent of the agencies they claim to oversee;

(6) investigatory commissions which are not independent of the agencies they claim to oversee.

In any specific system there will tend to be hybrid cases. Hence, in Britain, tribunals tend to be partially but not wholly independent of the agencies whose work they oversee. Those agencies may be involved in their organization and staffing and may be consulted on tribunal membership, yet the tribunals are not accountable to them and their work is supervised by the independent Council on Tribunals. There is, overall, a general issue about the extent to which any specific procedure is independent, or is seen to be independent by people with grievances.

In outlining the typology of grievance procedures, reference was made to the likelihood that some procedures will be in a subordinate or superordinate relationship to others. Some questions for comparative study involve the different ways these hierarchies are organized. In addition to issues of judicial hierarchy there are issues involving political hierarchies. It is possible, particularly in the case of investigatory devices, that accountability will be to a legislature or executive rather than to a judicial body. There are connections to be made here, both with policy-making systems and with participatory devices. An investigatory system that draws into its deliberations organizations and individuals beyond the original "combatants" may more accurately be described as a participatory device than as a grievance resolution mechanism.

### Types of Issues

It is important to try to develop a typology of issues in terms other than the substantive nature of the grievances. It might be useful to relate this to policy typologies—regulatory policy, redistributive policy, etc.—but it is probably most useful to try to develop a typology based upon possible outcomes or remedies. Hence individuals may be seeking (or may get, whether they seek it or not) one or more of the following:

- reversal of the decision
- compensation
- an apology
- assurance that a different decision will be taken next time (for themselves)
- assurance that a different decision will be taken next time (for others)
- a complete change of policy
- an outcome that it is not in the power of the complained about agency to give (even with a change of policy) inasmuch as it results from an interaction between its policies and the policies of others
- an explanation of why and how the decision was taken.

What people seek depends upon what is feasible; for example, if someone dies as a result of a hospital error, reversal of the decision is not possible. This is obviously related to the kind of policy adopted and its consequences. It may also be related to limits imposed upon the grievance system by the legal framework in which it operates. But it is also important to bear in mind that, once again, we find the policy versus policy implementation issue coming up here. Some interventions seek to change policy, others do not. This depends both upon the issue and the person's aspirations. Moreover, some concepts of where the policy/implementation boundary lies may be more flexible than others (we have here the issue of the extent to which the remedy of a grievance may include a de facto reversal of policy where its consequences are deemed to be a reversal of its intentions or a violation of some superordinate law).

This concern with types of issues can be related back to the concern with different ways grievances may be handled. A matrix can be developed in which some fits may be better than others—ombudsman procedures to secure future improvements, courts and tribunals to secure reversals and compensation, for example.

The question of fit cannot be resolved as simply as that, however; there are other considerations, among them issues of cost. Clearly, costs of invoking grievance procedures fall upon (a) those with grievances, (b) those they complain about, (c) the grievance procedures, and (d) anyone else drawn to participate by giving evidence, etc. Costs must not be classified in only money terms. Participants in these procedures are likely to have to give time, and they may suffer inconvenience, embarrassment, or even public ridicule. For administrative agencies costs may include delays and the need for elaborations and safeguards that affect the efficiency of their work and thus the quality of service they give to others (see Dunleavy, 1991, for an analysis of processes like these as "positive externalities").

### Summary

As suggested in the discussion of participation, any broad cross-national comparative exercise needs to work in a fairly broad-brush way, focusing on formal procedures that may or may not work satisfactorily in practice. The broad considerations for such work on grievance procedures involve the following questions:

- Are procedures general or policy specific? If they are policy specific, which policy areas are included?
- What sorts of institutional devices are used?
    General courts
    Specific administrative courts
    Policy specific independent tribunals
    Ombudsmen
    "Internal review systems"
    Possible combinations of systems.
- What kinds of constraints upon use can be identified?
    Limited jurisdictions
    Limited access
    Cost barriers to activation.

### CONCLUSION

We have distinguished two principal kinds of social control over civil services. They are: (a) devices which provide opportunities for citizen participation in low-level policy-making of the kind which is likely to be delegated to civil servants; and (b) devices which enable citizens to ventilate individual grievances about civil service actions.

Citizens may be invited to participate when all they want is the rectification of a specific grievance. Or they may find that all they can do is raise a specific case when they want to open up wider questions of policy and principle. Recent research suggests that on both the official and the public side there is considerable confusion about the extent to which grievance procedures are expected to contain discontent in a narrow way or to open up policy delivery systems to review (Lewis, Seneviratre, and Cracknell, 1989; Karn et al., 1991; McCarthy et al., 1992).

The two systems of control interact, and in doing comparative research, we will encounter institutions that are hybrids. Both kinds of systems raise important substantive questions about effectiveness, in particular about the relationship between individual grievances and the wider political processes that may have generated them. There are some important comparative questions here about the actual impact on opportunities for social control over the actions of civil servants of movements that purport to facilitate "decentralization" or "consumerism" or to give citizens "rights."

Faced with this complicated mixture of definitional questions and important issues about the extent to which civil services can really be open to social control, this discussion has inevitably been a general ground-clearing exercise in identifying ways of analyzing control processes comparatively. All of them are ultimately related to the broader paradigms of policy, and any effort at social control may be related back to the wider context of the political and legal framework in which a civil service operates.

For the purposes of comparative study, it is important to recognize the way in which cultural and institutional contexts influence the extent to which detailed decision-making is delegated to civil servants and provides opportunities for political and judicial interference in that delegated action. The very difficulty of working comparatively with the concept of civil service highlights this point. For comparative purposes, the concept of the civil service is taken to embrace the whole range of public service at the central and local level, including the activities of professionals in public services such as education and health care. This goes far beyond the definition of civil service conventionally used in some countries, including that used in the national base of the authors of this paper. If we relate this to the concerns about representative bureaucracy, it raises issues about the extent to which it is just as important to be concerned about the ethnic origins, gender, and class background of, for example, doctors and teachers as about those of top bureaucrats. Lipsky's street level bureaucrats probably also need to be "representative" if the social accountability he desires is to be achieved (Lipsky, 1980).

Efforts to limit the scope of the civil service in some countries can be taken, in part, to be devices for facilitating social control—by identifying areas of state activity that may come under alternative localized control systems more accessible to citizens. But they may also be seen as making social control more difficult by removing areas of state activity from direct political scrutiny. Thus, in the United Kingdom, we are presented with competing political interpretations of the privatization of services hitherto run directly by the state. The process has been defended as opening up avenues for participation by way of consumer choice, making feasible the operation of new forms of control through the availability of the "exit" option mentioned in the introduction to this chapter. Alternatively, they have been attacked as removing services from direct political influence. There is an important tension here, and it needs further exploration. In this context the availability to the public of more information about services will assist in the effective use of grievance procedures and the extension of participation. However, the availability of exit and treatment of the public as retail consumers does not encourage either the levels of identification necessary for close participation on the consumer side, or the development of community service ethics on the provider side.

As suggested in the introduction, the conceptual issues with which this paper is concerned raise the widely debated issue of the distinction between politics and administration. Research on street-level bureaucracy and discretion has indicated the difficulty involved in making this distinction (see discussion in Ham and Hill, 1983: chaps. 8 and 9), but it continues to have importance for control, both political and social, over public sector decisions. For the purposes of comparative study there are some interesting issues about different attempts to draw the boundary between politics and administration and the implications of this for control over civil servants. Our discussion has concentrated on two approaches to social control that assume the politics/administration split has been successfully made and citizens can be invited to relate to the latter through low-level participation devices and through grievance mechanisms. But the use of both approaches raises, as we have seen, questions that concern the very fabric of politics. The issue then becomes one of securing ways in which both social and political control over civil services can somehow be integrated. The democratic ideal is one in which these lower  levels of social control become essential feedback mechanisms for the ultimate form of social control—political control. The alternative is to give up on this democratic ideal. The concern then tends to be with either the creation of a socially responsive civil service using some combination of the notions of representative bureaucracy and civil service ethics, or with the establishment of a system that provides feedback to consumers who have an exit option. Our contention is that both of these alternatives, while they can be used to supplement the approaches we have discussed, are severely limited—the former because there is an inherent contradiction in the notion of a representative elite, the latter because in many public service contexts the exit option is logically very limited and inadequate. However weak the democratic ideal, the most satisfactory approach to social control over civil services lies in the existence of devices of the kind we have described, devices that can be tied into the wider political control system.

## REFERENCES

Arnstein, S. R. 1971. "Eight Rungs on the Ladder of Citizen Participation." In E. S. Cahn and B. A. Passett, eds., *Citizen Participation Effecting Community Change.*, London: Praeger.

Barrington, T. J. 1991. "Local Government in Ireland." In R. Batley and G. Stoker, eds., *Local Government in Europe: Trends and Developments.* London: Unwin Hyman.

Craig, P. P. 1990. *Public Law and Democracy.* Oxford: Clarendon Press.

Dunleavy, P. 1991. *Democracy, Bureaucracy and Public Choice.* Hemel Hemstead: Harvester-Wheatsheaf.

First Division Association. 1972. "Professional Standards in the Public Service." *Public Administration* 50 (Summer): 167–82.

Ham, C., and M. Hill. 1983. *The Policy Process in the Modern Capitalist State.* Brighton: Harvester-Wheatsheaf.

Hill, M. 1972. *The Sociology of Public Administration.* London: Weidenfeld & Nicholson.

Hirschman, A. O. 1970. *Exit, Voice and Loyalty.* Cambridge: Harvard University Press.

Jordan, A. G., and J. J. Richardson. 1987. *British Politics and the Policy Process.* London: Unwin Hyman.

Karn, V., et al. 1991. *Voicing Grievances and Getting Redress.* Report to the Economic and Social Research Council (Great Britain).

Lewis, N. M. Seneviratre, and S. Cracknell. 1989. *Complaints Procedures in Local Government.* Sheffield: University of Sheffield.

Lipsky, M. 1980. *Street Level Bureaucracy.* New York: Russell Sage.

Lukes, S. 1974. *Power, a Radical View.* London: Macmillan.

McCarthy, P., et al. 1992. *Grievances, Complaints and Local Government.* Aldershot: Gower.

Michels, R. 1915. *Political Parties.* London: Constable.

Pateman, C. 1970. *Participation and Democracy.* Cambridge: Cambridge University Press.

Richardson, A. 1983. *Participation.* London: Macmillan.

Richardson, J. J., and A. G. Jordan. 1979. *Governing under Pressure.* Oxford: Martin Robertson.

Sisson, C. H. 1959. *The Spirit of British Administration.* London: Faber and Faber.

Stacey, F. 1978. *Ombudsmen Compared.* Oxford: Clarendon Press.

Steinberg, J. 1976. *Why Switzerland?* Cambridge: Cambridge University Press.

Weber, M. 1947. *The Theory of Social and Economic Organization.* Trans. A. M. Henderson and T. Parsons. Glencoe, IL: Free Press.

# 9 PUBLIC OPINION TOWARD THE CIVIL SERVICE

Hal G. Rainey

This chapter reviews research on public opinion toward the civil service and proposes a framework for accessing such opinion. The framework includes concepts that support analysis of major dimensions of public opinion toward the civil service of a nation. There have been relatively few attempts at a comprehensive analysis of the formation of public attitudes toward civil service. A number of surveys have asked respondents whether civil servants work hard and work well, for instance, but few studies have attempted to develop analytical insight into the reasons for such opinions. The framework of this discussion draws heavily, therefore, on the limited number of studies currently available and on research on related topics such as public opinion concerning taxes and public services. It also draws on Bekke, Perry, and Toonen's concept of operational, collective choice and symbolic levels of civil service systems (see chap. 1). It also includes an array of concepts and components that could contribute to a comprehensive conceptualization of the issue. Finally, the chapter will present a reduced version of the framework that could be more feasible as a basis for a survey.

## ADMINISTRATIVE THEORY AND PUBLIC OPINION TOWARD THE CIVIL SERVICE

In spite of its importance, public opinion about the civil service has seldom received explicit attention in theories of public administration or in administrative theory more generally. The theoretical implications, however, loom very large. Most public administrative theory and general administrative theory concerns the performance of the administrative branch of government implicitly or explicitly, with the civil service as one major component of this administrative machinery. Public administration theorists usually assume that civil servants perform crucial functions. Public opinion concerning this performance therefore takes on great importance.

On the other hand, many journalists, political scientists, and political officials treat the civil service as relatively unimportant and seldom worthy of serious attention (Hill, 1992). Still other theorists and observers argue that the civil service performs very poorly. In recent decades concern over the legitimacy and efficacy of the civil service has spread virtually throughout the world (Bekke, Perry, and Toonen, 1991; Goodsell, 1985; Hill, 1992). Such negative views often vary between the implication that the civil service indeed plays a crucial role even if it discharges it poorly, and the position that the civil service has little importance—that is, that civil servants do little, that this involves some waste, but that generally civil servants figure only vaguely in important political developments.

As the review of research below demonstrates, such ambivalent or conflicting views of the civil service appear as commonly among citizens as among scholars and officials. We will see that citizens' views of public agencies, administrators, and employees are often complex, shifting, and ambivalent, and that they are driven by general images and stereotypes rather than by valid evidence. Citizens have difficulty arriving at well-justified, objective assessments of the civil service, although the civil service clearly plays a symbolic role in a nation, as pointed out by Bekke, Perry, and Toonen in this volume. This would imply that there is a weak connection between actual performance of the civil service and public perceptions. This in turn raises important theoretical and practical questions about the link between performance and public perception of that performance. The limited evidence available suggests the very plausible interpretation that this link is indirect and attenuated. General opinion about the civil service is therefore subject to influence by general stereotypes and other symbolic processes. At the same time, individuals also respond to their own experience and to more specific evidence in forming opinions about relatively specific aspects of civil servants and their performance. A conceptual framework is needed in order to account for both possibilities. In developing that framework, we should first look carefully at such evidence as is available.

## RESEARCH ON PUBLIC ATTITUDES TOWARD THE CIVIL SERVICE

The elaborate literature on public opinion offers an abundance of valuable insight. Public opinion researchers have not, however, produced general theories of public opinion. Their work tends to concentrate on models and conceptual frameworks for the explanation of public opinion in particular topic areas or about particular referents (see e.g., Stimson, 1991; Erickson, Luttbeg, and Tedin, 1991; Beck, Rainey, and Traut, 1990).

Nevertheless, a considerable body of relevant research provides valuable evidence to support the development of a conceptual framework for a fairly comprehensive analysis of public opinion toward the civil service. The framework can then be reduced to proportions feasible for a social survey. Numerous studies have assessed public opinion concerning such related matters as taxes, public services, general confidence in government, confidence in the executive branch of government, the performance of government and government agencies, and waste in government. Relatively few studies have asked people directly about civil servants, the civil service, or government agency managers and employees (Foster and Snyder, 1989: 82).

Some of the surveys which do ask about civil servants simply report the general level of opinion about them or some aspect of their performance, with little analysis of the determinants of these opinions. In some other studies, attitudes about government  employees have served as predictors for other attitudes, such as support for tax reduction initiatives (Sears and Citrin, 1985: 209). Occasional major studies of public opinion toward civil servants and their performance have analyzed the determinants or correlates of such opinions (Katz et al., 1975; Kilpatrick, Cummings, and Jennings, 1964a). In addition, some reviews and compilations of surveys provide useful conclusions about the patterns of survey results (Foster and Snyder, 1989; Goodsell, 1985; Lipset and Schneider, 1987).

### General Public Opinion—Just How Unfavorable?

Although limited in numbers, surveys in the United States and other western countries often find unfavorable attitudes toward the civil service. This pattern coincides with the general decline in survey measures of confidence in governmental and societal institutions as well as related developments such as tax resistance in numerous countries over the last several decades (Peters, 1984: 32; Dalton, 1988; Lipset and Schneider, 1987; Sears and Citrin, 1985: 1).

The survey questions indicating this decline in confidence in many institutions often suggest declining confidence in the civil service as well. Those implications are not entirely clear, however, because of the phrasing of the questions. For example, one prominent measure of confidence in institutions asks respondents for ratings of their confidence in a set of institutions, one of which is "the executive branch of government" (Lipset and Schneider, 1987; Smith, Taylor, and Mathiowetz, 1980). The problem is, of course, that the executive branch in most nations include the chief executives and many politically appointed officials. How these ratings of the executive branch reflect on attitudes toward the career civil service is not clear (Citrin, 1974; Smith, Taylor, and Mathiowetz, 1980).

Similarly, another prominent measure of confidence, the University of Michigan political cynicism scale asks questions that may reflect on the civil service but do not directly focus on it. Those questions ask respondents about whether the government is run by a few big interests looking out for themselves, whether government wastes a lot of money, whether the people running the government know what they are doing, whether you can trust government, whether the people running the government are crooked. Responses to these questions have become much more unfavorable in the last several decades (Smith, Taylor, and Mathiowetz, 1980), and these responses apparently have relations to attitudes about the civil service. Katz et al. (1975) report fairly strong correlations between the political cynicism scale and scales about general attitudes toward government service (e.g., prompt, fair service), negative stereotypes about the bureaucracy, and bureaucratic helpfulness. Sears and Citrin (1985) also report strong relations between items from the cynicism scale and both the perception of waste in government and the perception that government workers are overpaid; these perceptions were related in turn to stronger support for Proposition 13 during the California tax revolt in the 1970s.

In addition, responses on the waste in government question of the political cynicism scale have been sharply deteriorating for thirty years (Lipset and Schneider, 1987: 17; Smith, Taylor, and Mathiowetz, 1980: 47). Responses to various surveys, including many cited below, suggest that the public often attributes much of waste in government to the bureaucracy. More direct questions about the public bureaucracy elicit many negative opinions, although the responses also tend to reflect the ambivalence and complexity of opinions about government in the United States and elsewhere.

Civil service systems differ across nations, obviously, but they also show similarities because nations often imitate features of the civil service systems of other countries (Kingdon, 1990; Smith, 1984). The implications of these similarities and differences for public opinion are hard to predict. Dalton (1988) cites two surveys of confidence in institutions in the United States, Great Britain, France, and Germany, with "the civil service" as one of the institutions. In spite of the differences among these countries, the surveys found roughly equivalent levels of confidence in the civil service systems. Between 35 and 55 percent of respondents expressed confidence in the civil service. In each of the four nations, this placed the civil service among the lower half of the institutions rated but above several others, such as major companies, the press, and labor unions.

The variations among the four countries in levels of confidence, while not large, would have been difficult to predict. While one might have predicted that the West German civil service would receive a relatively high vote of confidence (Peters, 1990: 184; Dalton, 1988: 232), it received the lowest among the four nations—35 percent of respondents expressed confidence. While American experts often cite superior features of European civil service systems (Smith, 1984) and scholars and journalists regularly refer to negative stereotypes of the civil service in the United States, the percentage of respondents expressing confidence was highest in the United States—55 percent.

Other fairly direct questions about civil service or government agencies or operations also elicit unfavorable responses. In a comprehensive review of survey results about the public bureaucracy in the United States, Foster and Snyder (1989) found that numerous surveys had discovered unfavorable opinions about management in government, including widespread perceptions that government agencies are managed inefficiently. Similarly, numerous polls in the late 1970s and 1980s found high percentages of Americans favoring reduction in the number of federal employees and reductions in their pay. Kilpatrick, Cummings, and Jennings (1964a) found that higher-level professional and executive respondents outside the U.S. federal service had unfavorable views of the public service.

In the most comprehensive study of the attitudes of service recipients of U.S. federal government agencies, Katz et al. (1975) also found unfavorable opinions among a fairly high percentage of respondents on such criteria as doing a good job, giving prompt service, taking care of problems, considerate treatment, fair treatment, and avoiding mistakes. Katz et al. (1975) also found that high percentages of respondents felt that compared to government, business performs more efficiently, attracts better people, has employees who work harder, and otherwise performs better. Other studies report similar findings (Foster and Snyder, 1989; Lipset and Schneider, 1987).

### Ambivalence, Complications, and More Favorable Attitudes

Surveys also find conflicting results on many points, patterns of favorable attitudes toward the civil service and public agencies, and apparent ambivalence on the part of respondents. In the United States, for example, survey respondents consistently support a strong role for government, even in surveys where they express some unfavorable views of the sort we have described. Foster and Snyder (1989), while noting strong support for a federal role in handling many issues and that some surveys detected quite favorable views of government agencies, found it ironic that respondents also support decreases in federal employment. Similarly, survey respondents often express preference for more public services but no higher or even lower taxes (Beck et al., 1987; Beck, Rainey, and Traut, 1990). Lipset and Schneider (1987) report declining levels of confidence in governmental institutions and a tendency for survey respondents to regard private business as more efficient and effective than government. However, they also find declining confidence in business and strong support for a major role for government.

The study by Kilpatrick, Cummings, and Jennings (1964a) also found that the general public expressed many favorable views of federal employees, and that favorable views substantially exceeded unfavorable ones. Many respondents rated federal civil servants high on character, honesty, and interest in serving the public. The Katz et al. (1975) study also found many favorable opinions about public agencies and employees and an interesting pattern of ambivalence in respondents' attitudes. They found that many respondents gave more positive

ratings to specific encounters with public bureaucracies than to public bureaucracies in general. They concluded that attitudes about bureaucracy are organized on two levels—a more general, ideological or stereotypical level, and a
more specific, pragmatic level.  The more general attitudes are influenced by
general stereotypes and ideological orientations, while the more specific pragmatic attitudes are formed on the basis of more specific experiences and contexts.

Sears and Citrin (1985) also found that what they called "symbolic predispositions" were among the strongest predictors of support for the California tax
revolt. By symbolic predisposition they mean a general, long-standing attitudinal orientation toward a referent of such a general nature that it takes on a symbolic character, such as government in general, another race, political ideology,
or a political party.

Similarly, Beck, Rainey, and Traut (1990) found that citizens' satisfaction with
local services and taxes showed a strong correlation with general attitudes
toward the community, such as general evaluations of community leaders and
general satisfaction with the community as a place to live. The correlation was
stronger, moreover, for ratings of local services than for attitudes toward taxes.
For tax attitudes, respondents' impressions of their own financial well-being
played a stronger role as predictors. The pattern is consistent with the findings
of Katz et al. (1975). It suggests that citizens' general attitudinal dispositions—
general satisfaction with nation or community, general ideological or stereotypical attitudes—determine responses to general evaluative questions where
referents are relatively diffuse or remote. On the other hand, for more specific
questions citizens draw on more specific information and experiences when it
is available—an encounter with the agency, a tax bill in relation to current
finances. Studies of public opinion toward the civil service must be designed to
detect and analyze such divergent types and sources of opinion.

## Determinants of Public Opinion toward the Civil Service

In spite of the scarcity of theory and research, several studies have analyzed
determinants of public opinion toward the civil service (although they did not
necessarily use the term civil service). These studies suggest that some evaluative attitudes about the civil service, especially the more general ones, will be
influenced by more general, long-standing, stereotypical or ideological predispositions. These relationships can follow complicated, not necessarily predictable patterns. For example, in the United States, confidence in government
does not show the straightforward relationship to political ideology that one
might expect; that is, one might expect that persons identifying themselves as
left-liberal would express more support for government than persons self-identi-
fied as right-conservative. Yet both extreme liberals and extreme conservatives
express low confidence in government, with "slightly conservative" respondents

expressing the highest confidence of any group (Lipset and Schneider, 1987: 317). We must therefore expect complicated relations, but the studies reviewed earlier support that general political attitudes such as political cynicism (trust in government), ideology, and party identification should still appear in any framework of potential determinants of attitudes toward the civil service.

While various studies indicate the importance of such generalized attitudes, researchers have debated their nature and strength as determinants of other attitudes. For example, noting that other researchers contend that confidence in government scales mainly reflects a general national "mood" that affects attitudes toward many institutions, Smith, Taylor, and Mathiowetz (1980) report evidence that many respondents discriminate more carefully than that. They point out that individuals discriminate among institutions to some extent and that they express the lowest confidence in institutions that appear to be the main source of the most significant problems at a given time. Similarly, studies cited above indicate that respondents often discriminate to some degree between departments and agencies, levels of government, societal institutions, and types of public programs. Thus, in addition to being sensitive to very general, symbolic, stereotypical, and ideological predispositions, a framework for analyzing attitudes toward the civil service needs to take into account variations among levels of government, types of agencies and programs, and levels of individual experience and information about them.

Demographic variables such as age, gender, race, income, and education exhibit a variety of relationships to attitudes toward the civil service in a variety of studies. Overall, however, they have not shown consistent, strong relationships to views of the public service (Katz et al., 1975; Foster and Snyder, 1989; Beck, Rainey, and Traut, 1990; Sears and Citrin, 1985). Family background (father's occupation, socioeconomic level of the family) has shown a relationship to choice of a career in public service in studies in the past. Whether or not one is employed by government, or whether one has a family member in public employment, also shows a significant relationship to some attitudes about government and the public service (Sears and Citrin, 1985; Kilpatrick, Cummings, and Jennings, 1964a). In spite of complicated research findings for some of them, demographic variables usually figure importantly in interpretations of results, either as predictive variables or as controls, and they need to be represented in the framework.

### Interpretive Communities as a Methodological and Conceptual Alternative

The emphasis on demographic variables in the model follows the pattern of contemporary survey research in using demographics as indicators of various political, economic, and social interests on the part of the respondents. In recent research on the impact of literature and mass communications, researchers have also begun to analyze the influence of interpretive communities on responses to messages from the media (see, e.g., Jensen, 1990). The concept of interpretive communities draws on critical theory perspectives and emphasizes the active role of audiences in interpreting mass communications.

Students of interpretive communities argue that recipients of messages or communications from texts, mass media, or other sources engage in active interpretation of the message content. In this process, recipients may draw on alternative or opposing frames of reference and may resist or reinterpret messages. In so doing, they will be influenced by their political and social interests, which will be mediated by social groups in which they participate or which they use as reference groups. This concept of interpretive communities certainly adds to our conception of how public opinion forms and moves beyond the static and indirect implications of relying on demographic indicators. However, the identification of various types of interpretive communities appears to be still in the formative stages. In addition, studies of interpretive communities usually use ethnomethodological approaches involving closer and more interactive contact with smaller groups of respondents that are participating as focus or action groups (Jensen, 1990). This involves the typical complications that arise in making inferences about general public opinion from small samples.

A focus on interpretive communities, then, represents an interesting methodological alternative or complement to a broad social survey, and such a focus can be considered in planning assessments of the civil service in different nations. Moreover, this approach suggests inclusion in surveys of more questions about the attitudes of the respondent's reference groups. Critical theorists and qualitative researchers might find such a compromise repugnant, but as an example of such a procedure, Cho (1992) successfully employed a measure of prestige of the civil service that involved questions about how the members of the respondent's community felt about the prestige of the civil service. Variables of this nature are included in the framework proposed below.

## The Difficult Problem of Predicting National Differences

One would expect that national differences with respect to such variables as those already discussed would have an important influence on opinions about the civil service. Yet there is very little literature or research that can serve as a basis for clear predictions about how nations would differ on such opinions. Peters (1984: 44) concludes that "the evidence of citizens' attitudes toward the public bureaucracy is spotty in the developed countries, but it is extremely difficult to find for less-developed countries."

Our review of research noted only one study that compared nations on attitudes toward the civil service (Dalton, 1988: 235). Peters (1984) cities two additional studies. One of these found that respondents in Mexico felt much less able to influence administrative decisions than respondents in Germany and Great Britain. The other found that respondents in India, as compared to a sample of U.S. citizens, were more willing to take government jobs but were much more negative about corruption in their public bureaucracies and the way they were treated in their encounters with them.

To complicate the problem of limited evidence, the existing evidence often fails to accord with what one might expect from discussions of national differences. One way to form some expectations or hypotheses about the effects of national differences would be to extrapolate from findings or assertions about other aspects of the government or the administrative system, such as political culture, political trust, or administrative power. Yet the available empirical research often refutes the propositions that one might form this way. For example, Peters (1984) suggests that one might categorize societal cultures using Bendix's distinction between entrepreneurial and bureaucratic cultures. This distinction in turn would have important implications for the public bureaucracy and administrative culture. Peters suggests that Great Britain represents an entrepreneurial culture, while Germany provides a prime example of a bureaucratic culture. As a result, in Germany "bureaucracy and its emphasis on authority relationships is a natural and acceptable form of public organization" (Peters, 1984: 41). In the United Kingdom and the United States, Peters suggests, bureaucratic authority is considerably less acceptable; a more important role for bureaucrats has been much more readily accepted in Germany than in the United Kingdom. Yet in the comparative survey of confidence in institutions summarized by Dalton (1988: 235), German respondents were considerably *less* likely to express confidence in the "civil service" (35 percent) than were respondents from the United Kingdom (48 percent) and the United States (55 percent). Germans also expressed lower levels of confidence in the police and the armed services. Such an apparent anomaly might have many reasonable interpretations, but it certainly illustrates the difficulty of predicting responses about the civil service from other assertions or conceptions about national differences.

The comparative findings on India and the United States mentioned above illustrate a similar complication. Respondents in some less-developed countries such as India and Korea may express concern about corruption and other problems with their civil servants. They may also, however, regard civil service positions as well compensated, prestigious, and influential, and may therefore express a high regard for civil servants in response to certain types of questions (Cho, 1992).

Far from undercutting the need for consideration of national differences, however, these difficulties in making a priori predictions suggest the value of comparative research. The suggestions about differences among categories of nations advanced by Peters (1984) and by Heady (this volume) establish a conceptual rationale for conducting comparisons, as opposed to a straight comparison of individual nations. For example, Peters (1984: 55) suggests that one might categorize nations according to levels of administrative power, based on their location of the dimensions of political trust and trust for others within the population. In societies such as that of the United Kingdom where there is high political trust and trust in others, administrative power will be low because it is limited by the strength of other political and social institutions. Nations such as Italy, France, and third world countries fall at the other extreme, with low trust on both dimensions; administrative power is high because the public bureaucracy fills the void of authority and power left by other institutions. Still other countries can be classified as intermediate on the dimension of administrative power. Researchers conducting comparative studies of public opinion toward the civil service could easily group nations according to these categories using Peters's examples. They could analyze whether such distinctions show a relationship to perceptions of the civil service.

Similarly, in another chapter of this book, Heady proposes a set of configurations of civil service systems. He distinguishes between ruler trustworthy, party controlled, policy receptive, and collaborative configurations, and provides examples of nations in each category. As indicated in the framework that follows, such categories could readily be used in designing and analyzing research on public opinion in order to test for systematic variations among such categories.

Obviously, one can also compare individual nations on the results of survey research and other forms of inquiry such as focus groups. In view of the sorts of complications and unanticipated findings mentioned above, researchers could analyze such differences using the framework described below instead of advancing a set of propositions about variations among nations and groups of nations.

## BROADER FRAMEWORKS FOR ASSESSMENT OF PUBLIC OPINION

Existing research provides support for the suggestions already made about the nature of public opinion toward the civil service, for example, about the difference between opinions about specific encounters and opinions about more general, distant referents. However, the research provides no overarching framework to guide us in deciding what we want to know about public opinion toward the civil service. Researchers have taken an ad hoc approach of assessing whether opinion is favorable or unfavorable in general, or in relation to general performance criteria, or in relation to specific encounters with civil servants.

For a broader framework of theoretically important issues about the civil service, we can draw on the several levels of analysis of the civil service that Bekke, Perry, and Toonen develop in the first chapter of this book. They distinguish between three interrelated but separate levels or "worlds of action," including the operational level, the collective choice level, and the constitutional choice level. They depict these levels as relating to the civil service as an operational personnel system, the civil service as a component of the pattern of institutional rules for collective action in a nation, and the civil service as a source of general symbols. Research on public opinion toward the civil service can usefully analyze the relationship of public opinion to these three levels or roles of the civil service.

This framework conforms in interesting ways to some aspects of the research reviewed earlier. As mentioned above, the research suggests that the attitudes of many survey respondents toward governmental bureaucracies appear to be organized on at least two separate levels—a more general symbolic and stereo-typical level, and a more specific level derived from actual experiences. These two levels correspond fairly well with the operational and constitutional choice levels. While the collective choice level does not readily correspond to variables used in the research reviewed above, it raises the interesting question of how such beliefs and perceptions figure in public opinion toward the civil service. Bekke, Perry, and Toonen define the collective choice level as pertaining primarily to the rules in the system. As indicated in the framework to follow, respondents can be questioned about their beliefs about rules governing the civil service system. Such beliefs can be examined both as an indication of the accuracy of such beliefs among respondents, but also for their relations to the other levels.

## A FRAMEWORK FOR ANALYSIS OF PUBLIC OPINION TOWARD THE CIVIL SERVICE

Table 9.1 presents a conceptual framework of dimensions for the assessment of public opinion toward the civil service and of factors with potential influence on such opinions. The components of the framework are based on the research reviewed in the preceding sections. Appendix A provides much more detail on the variables and dimensions within general components of the framework presented in table 9.1.

The framework is based on the assumption that a large-scale attitudinal survey would make up one major component of an assessment of opinion toward civil service. The framework, however, attempts a degree of comprehensiveness that most opinion surveys could not cover. It also includes factors, for instance, many of the macrosocial and political context factors in table 9.1, that an opinion survey could not very well assess.

The framework reflects a fairly comprehensive approach, incorporating many of the variables from the research reviewed earlier as a way of conceptualizing the issue in its full complexity. To simplify too quickly can lead to oversights. As the preceding review of research has shown, attitudes toward the civil service can involve both general symbolic or stereotypical attitudes, as well as attitudes

TABLE 9.1

**A Framework for Analysis of
Public Opinion toward the Civil Service**

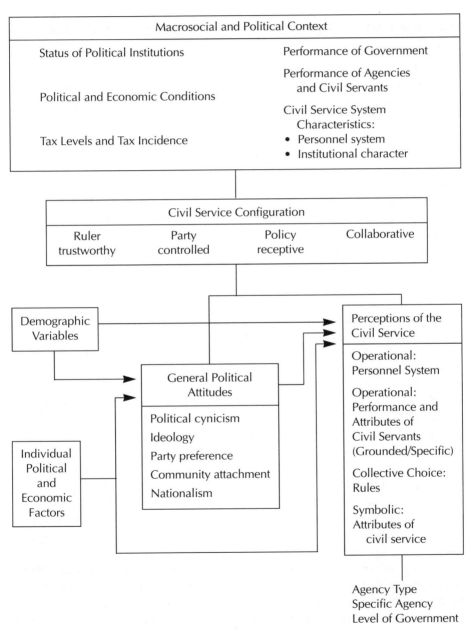

toward more specific referents grounded in more specific experiences and evidence available to citizens. A survey concentrating only on symbolic and stereotypical impressions of the civil service would miss the latter types of attitudes. The framework incorporates both, as well as factors that influence both.

### Last Things First: The Dependent Variables—Perceptions of the Civil Service

The framework treats perceptions of the civil service as dependent variables and includes factors that have the potential for influencing such perceptions. One possible strategy for an assessment of public opinion, however, would omit many of the variables to the left of the "Perceptions of the Civil Service" component and concentrate on these perceptions. They are, after all, the main points of concern. In that sense, the last component on the extreme right of the table plays the most important role and receives attention first here.

As indicated on table 9.1 and appendix A, the "Perceptions of the Civil Service" component includes variables referring to the levels of analysis discussed by Bekke, Perry, and Toonen (chap. 1). They conceive of the operational level as the specific operational features of the civil service system, that is, such matters as recruitment, training, and performance appraisal. Table 9.1 also includes as an operational-level set of variables the respondents' perceptions of their experiences with civil servants, grounded in their actual experience. This expands the operational level to include the actual operation-level activities and behaviors of civil servants from the viewpoint of citizens (i.e., the respondents). The reason for including this set of variables should be obvious in view of the importance—in the research reviewed above—of the distinction between attitudes grounded in specific experiences and attitudes toward more distant or general referents such as "the federal bureaucracy in Washington." It will be very useful to examine the relations between such attitudes and the respondents' attitudes and beliefs about the operating procedures, rules, and general symbolic characteristics of civil service systems.

Space limits preclude a full discussion of the conceptualization of these operational-level components, their measurement in research, and their differentiation from other concepts in the framework. Appendix B, however, proposes some questionnaire items for use in survey research or other forms of research that indicate what these components mean and how they might be measured. The questions pertaining to the characteristics of the personnel system are based on the examples that Bekke, Perry, and Toonen (chap. 1) used in defining that level.

Similarly, the collective choice level in the framework refers to rules of the civil service system, following Bekke, Perry, and Toonen's conception. Appendix B proposes questionnaire items based largely on their examples. "Symbolic Level" refers to respondents' perceptions of very general or symbolic characteristics of the civil service system. In the framework and the proposed questions in appendix B, these are conceived primarily in terms of general performance attributes of the civil service and its contribution to national or public well-being. Bekke, Perry, and Toonen give very few examples of their concept of the symbolic level, but this approach appears consistent with theirs. They give general examples concerning the symbolic impact of pay-for-performance and the merit system, and appendix B includes questions about such matters. Again, a full discussion of the rationale for these sets of variables and their measurement is not possible here, but appendix B gives clear suggestions about how the framework proposes to use them.

## Determinants and Influences on Perceptions of the Civil Service

The framework implies that all components and variables to the left of the "Perceptions of the Civil Service" component have causal priority and act as influences on such perceptions. Of course one could reverse this assumption. One could argue, for example, that widespread perception of waste or corruption in the civil service aggravates political cynicism. No available research firmly resolves causal precedence. The ordering in the figure is reasonable for the planning of research.

### Macrosocial and political context.

The framework assumes the existence of a context in each nation that influences perceptions of the civil service and other components of the framework. Obviously the institutional traditions and political and economic conditions in different nations and at different times in the same nation can influence the other variables in the framework. For example, crises, scandals, and bad economic conditions can influence responses on questionnaire items about the other variables. In the United States, both political cynicism (confidence in government) responses and ratings of confidence in various institutions in the United States have been affected by the Watergate scandal, economic recessions, and other difficult conditions (Smith, Taylor, and Mathiowetz, 1980; Lipset and Schneider, 1987).

Relatedly, government, government agencies, and civil servants vary in performance and characteristics. Civil service systems vary in their attributes, such as their characteristics as a personnel system—for example, pay levels, bases of compensation, recruitment, and selection—and in their institutional character— for example, patronage rules, institutionalization of merit criteria, and representation of subpopulations (Bekke, Perry, and Toonen, 1991).

As discussed earlier, one cannot confidently predict variations among nations and groups of nations, but surveys designed on the basis of this framework can certainly provide evidence about such variations. Heady's configurations of civil service systems in this volume are included in table 9.1 and appendix A to illustrate that researchers could examine variations among such groupings.

*Demographics and individual-level variables.*

As discussed earlier, demographic variables have not always figured as strong, consistent predictors of other variables in this framework. In many studies they have played important roles as predictive or control variables. In addition to typical demographic variables, certain individual-level variables have exhibited a relationship to other variables in the framework or have obvious potential relevance. These include individual financial, political, and economic characteristics, such as whether one receives or has recently requested particular public services, political knowledge and participation, status as a public employee, and home ownership. Some of these can easily be conceived of as demographic variables. Other studies, however, have treated some of these variables as distinctive influences on other variables in the framework because they reflect personal and political interests and incentives more directly than some of the typical demographic variables (see, e.g., Sears and Citrin, 1985).

As suggested in the earlier discussion of interpretive communities, research on them usually involves ethnomethodology or at least directly interactive qualitative methodology. Even in a survey, however, one can utilize questions about the attitudes of the respondents' reference persons and groups. Such a component is included in this part of the framework, as indicated in appendix A.

*General political attitudes.*

The framework conceives separately a group of attitudinal variables akin to those which some researchers treat as "symbolic," general, long-standing predispositions (Sears and Citrin, 1985). As described in the review of research, such generalized political attitudes have shown important relationships to various attitudes toward taxes, public services, and public bureaucracy in various studies (Beck, Rainey, and Traut, 1990; Katz et al., 1975; Sears and Citrin, 1985).

*The desirability of comparative bases and common methods.*

Those interpreting survey research results typically face a problem in interpreting the meaning of a given percentage response to a particular question. It is good that 75 percent of the clients of a public agency express satisfaction with services, or worrisome that the remaining 25 percent express dissatisfaction? (Katz et al., 1975: 114–15). Variations in question wording and response choices also complicate interpretation of results of different surveys and often account for the anomalous and conflicting findings of different surveys.

Cross-national surveys, of course, confront even greater complications, given such challenges as translation of the questions into different languages. Using questionnaire items that have performed well in previous surveys as well as data from previous studies or even data banks can provide some comparative bases. Comparative bases for results, and common question wording, can provide some help in confronting the interpretational problems of cross-national survey research. To the extent possible, surveys and other studies should draw on well-developed, previous questions and procedures. The framework in table 9.1 takes its form largely from previous studies and the variables and questionnaire items that have figured meaningfully in them. Appendix A further illustrates a preliminary effort to operationalize many of the variables in the study with questionnaire items from previous research.

*Reducing the framework for survey research.*

The more comprehensive framework illustrates the complexity of the factors involved in analyzing public opinion toward the civil service, but the framework can readily be reduced to proportions more feasible for a social survey. Appendix B, for example, illustrates one alternative for such a reduced version. Researchers can readily adopt other alternatives, depending on the resources available. For example, a more elaborate survey could follow the Katz et al. (1975) procedure of grounding questions about contacts with civil servants in specific instances identified by the researchers. Also following the example of Katz et al. (1975), researchers could ask batteries of questions such as those illustrated in the lower sections of Appendix B about different encounters with different agencies or programs.

In conclusion, in spite of the many complications and challenges that public opinion researchers often face, valuable research on public opinion toward the civil service appears feasible and worthwhile. The framework and questions described here are proposed as useful for such research. The scarcity of such research, and especially of internationally comparative research, is unfortunate, in view of the value of an improved understanding of citizens' beliefs and attitudes about the general value and role of the civil service in their society, and the specific, practical influence of the civil service in their lives.

*I gratefully acknowledge the valuable criticism and comment on the original draft of this paper by Peter Hupe, James L. Perry, and Johan Olsen, and other participants at the Comparative Civil Service Conference. Peter Hupe, as discussant of my paper at the conference, provided a critique on which I have drawn in revising aspects of the conceptual framework.*

*APPENDIX A*

**Variables and Dimensions for Components of the Framework for Analysis of Public Opinion toward the Civil Service (see table 9.1)**

| Macrosocial and Political Context |
|---|
| National economic conditions |
| National and local political conditions |
|     Current crises? |
|     Current stability/instability? |
|     Scandal? |
| Long-term political history and institutional traditions |
|     Status of government and government officials |
|     Status of political institutions |
| Media treatment and coverage of governmental issues |
| Levels of taxation/tax incidence/tax effort |
| Performance of government |
| Performance of specific government agencies and programs |
|     Efficiency |
|     Effectiveness (internal process, outcome, impact) |
|     Representativeness |
|     Responsiveness |
|     Fairness/reasonableness/due process |
|     Accountability |
|     Legality |
| Performance of civil servants |
|     Same criteria as above, for agencies and programs |
|     Ethics/integrity |
|     Innovativeness/caution |
|     Responsiveness/helpfulness |
|     Courtesy |
| Civil service system characteristics |
|     Personnel system (examples) |
|         Compensation bases and levels |
|         Recruitment and selection practices |
|     Institutional character (examples) |
|         Institutionalization of merit norms |
|         Patronage |
|         Representation of groups and subpopulations |

| Civil Service Configuration | | | |
|---|---|---|---|
| Ruler trustworthy | Party controlled | Policy receptive | Collaborative |

| Demographic Variables |
|---|
| Age |
| Educational level |
| Occupation |
| Government employee? |
| Professionalization/specialization |
| Income |
| Race/ethnicity |
| Regional/subnational locus |
| Family/parental background (Parents or relatives in civil service? Parents or relatives in private industry or professions? Socioeconomic status of parents) |

| Individual Political and Economic Factors |
|---|
| Knowledge of government |
| Political participation |
| Attitudes regarding the public interest |
| Current service recipient? |
| Recent contact/service request/quality of interaction |
| Level of individual's taxes (objective and perceived) |
| Policy and program preferences/supportiveness |
| Personal economic status and expectations |
|     Perceived financial and employment security |
|     Perceived financial well-being |
|     Anticipated financial well-being |
| Attitudes of reference persons and groups |

| General Political Attitudes<br>(Long-standing, "symbolic" predispositions) |
|---|
| Community attachment or disaffection |
|     Community a good place to live |
| National attachment or disaffection |
|     Nation a good place to live |
|     Nationalism |
| Political cynicism |
|     Confidence in government |
|         Local, state/regional, national |
|     Waste in government? |
|     Leaders care/listen? |
| Political ideology |
| Party preference |

| Perceptions of the Civil Service |
|---|
| Perceived Performance of Public Bureaucracy<br>    Efficiency<br>    Effectiveness (internal process, outcome, impact)<br>    Representativeness<br>    Responsiveness<br>    Fairness/reasonableness/due process<br>    Accountability<br>    Legality<br><br>Perceived Performance of Public Agencies<br>    (same criteria as for public bureaucracy, above)<br><br>Perceived Performance/Characteristics of the Civil Service<br>    (Primarily General and Symbolic Perceptions)<br>    (same criteria as above, for public bureaucracy)<br>    Innovativeness/caution<br>    Responsiveness/helpfulness/courtesy<br>    Efficient/wasteful<br>    Hardworking/lazy<br>    Overpaid<br>    Ethical/corrupt<br>    Overstaffed<br>    Effective/ineffective<br>    Prestigious<br>    Stable and reliable<br>    Fair<br><br>Perceived Performance/Characteristics of Civil Servants<br>    (Primarily Emphasizing Specific Encounters)<br>    (criteria similar to those above) |

*APPENDIX B*

**One Possible Reduced Version of the Framework
for Use in a Social Survey**

*Demographic Variables* (all those listed in appendix A)

*Individual Political and Economic Factors*
Selected from appendix A:
Personal economic status and expectations
Contacts/service requests/character of interaction with civil servants
Attitudes of reference persons and groups

*General Political Attitudes*
National attachment/disaffection
Political cynicism
Political ideology
Party preference

*Perceptions of the Civil Service*

Instructions: Think of the large group of people who work for national agencies and programs as their permanent careers. Think of this group as a whole, as the civil service. Five-point, agree-disagree response choice format:

Constitutional Choice (Symbolic) Level: Perceived general performance and attributes of the civil service

The civil service is stable and reliable.
The civil service is competent.
They perform their tasks effectively.
They work for the good of the nation.
The civil service helps to make the nation stable and secure.
The civil service helps to make this nation a place where one can expect to be treated fairly.
They help to make the nation a better place to live.
They are corrupt and dishonest.
The civil service is very prestigious.
They are paid well.
They work hard.
To get their jobs, civil servants must show that they are highly qualified.
To be promoted, civil servants must show that they are very qualified for a promotion.
Those who are hired in the civil service are those who most deserve it, based on their knowledge and skill.
Those who are promoted are those who most deserve it, based on their knowledge and skill.
The pay that civil servants receive depends on how hard they work and how well they perform.
The people I know feel that the civil service is very prestigious.

Collective Choice Level: Perceptions about the civil service as a system of rules for collective action

In the civil service, there are laws and rules that require that all groups in the nation will be represented in government.

In the civil service, there are rules and laws that say how civil servants should do their work.

Even if politicians try to get them to do special favors for their friends, civil servants obey rules and laws, not the politicians' requests for special favors.

Civil servants do not follow rules; what happens in the civil service is determined by politics.

When someone needs something from a civil servant, whether they will get it depends more on their political influence than on what the rules and laws say.

To get a civil service job, you have to be a member of an influential political party.

If you have a civil service job, there are rules that give you a lot of job security.

Operational Level: Perceptions of the civil service as a personnel system (item labels would not appear in the survey)

Recruitment:

When there is a job opening in the civil service, they recruit widely to fill the position.

The only way to get a civil service job is to be in a privileged position.

Selection:

When a person enters the civil service, they enter it as a career.

In the civil service, there are tests and procedures to determine who is the most qualified for a job.

Job Evaluation:

A civil servant's rank and pay is something they take with them, it does not depend on the position they hold.

A civil servant's rank and pay depends on the position they hold. If they change positions in the civil service, their rank and pay may change.

Performance Appraisal:

In the civil service, they carefully evaluate a civil servant's performance to determine whether the civil servant should get a pay raise.

Operational Level: Perceptions of the performance and attributes of civil servants, based on encounters and specific instances

Instructions: Think of the people who work for the national government with whom you have dealt in seeking or getting services from the government. We refer to these as civil servants. Think of how these people behaved and how they were when you dealt with them. Five-point, agree-disagree response choice format:

They really took care of my problem.

They were courteous.

They tried to help me.

They were careful to avoid mistakes.

They demanded a bribe.

They treated me fairly.

They did not care about me.

They seemed lazy.

## REFERENCES

Beck, Paul A., and Thomas R. Dye. 1982. "Sources of Public Opinion on Taxes: The Florida Case." *Journal of Politics* 44: 172–82.

Beck, Paul A., Hal G. Rainey, and C. Traut. 1990. "Disadvantage, Disaffection, and Race as Divergent Bases for Citizen Fiscal Policy Preferences." *Journal of Politics* 52: 71–93.

Beck, Paul A., Hal G. Rainey, K. Nicholls, and C. Traut. 1987. "Citizen Views of Taxes and Services: A Tale of Three Cities." *Social Science Quarterly* 68: 223–43.

Bekke, Hans A. G. M., James L. Perry, and Theo A. J. Toonen. 1991."The Need for Comparative Research on Civil Service Systems." Paper presented at the Conference on Comparative Civil Service Systems, Leiden/Rotterdam, Netherlands, October 17–19.

Cho, Kyoung Ho. 1992. "Modelling Antecedents of Organizational Commitment in Korean Public Organizations." Ph.D. diss., University of Georgia.

Citrin, Jack. 1974. "Comment: The Political Relevance of Trust in Government." *American Political Science Review* 68: 973–88.

Dalton, Russell J. 1988. *Citizen Politics in Western Democracies*. Chatham, NJ: Chatham House.

Erickson, Robert S., Norman R. Luttbeg, and Kent L. Tedin. 1991. *American Public Opinion*. New York: MacMillan.

Fesler, James W. 1984. "The Higher Civil Service in Europe and the United States." In Bruce L. R. Smith, ed., *The Higher Civil Service in Europe and Canada: Lessons for the United States*. Washington, DC: Brookings Institution.

Fish, Stanley. 1980. *Is There a Text in This Class? The Authority of Interpretive Communities*. Cambridge: Harvard University Press.

Foster, Gregory D., and Sharon K. Snyder. 1989. "Public Attitudes toward Government: Contradictions, Ambivalence, and the Dilemmas of Response." Pages 71–94 in the Volcker Commission, *Leadership for America: Rebuilding the Public Service*. Lexington, MA: Lexington Books.

Goodsell, Charles T. 1985. *The Case for Bureaucracy: A Public Administration Polemic*. 2nd ed. Chatham, NJ: Chatham House.

Hill, Larry B. 1992. "Taking Bureaucracy Seriously." Pages 15–58 in Larry B. Hill, ed., *The State of Public Bureaucracy*. Armonk, NY: M. E. Sharpe.

Hood, Christopher, and Andrew Dunsire. 1981. *Bureaumetrics: The Quantitative Comparison of British Central Government Agencies.* Tuscaloosa: University of Alabama Press.

Jensen, Klaus B. 1990. "Television Futures: A Social Action Methodology for Studying Interpretive Communities." *Critical Studies in Mass Communication* 7: 129–46.

Katz, Daniel, Barbara A. Gutek, Robert L. Kahn, and Eugenia Barton. 1975. *Bureaucratic Encounters: A Pilot Study in the Evaluation of Government Services.* Ann Arbor: Survey Research Center, Institute for Social Research, University of Michigan.

Kettl, Donald F. 1989. "The Image of the Public Service in the Media." Pages 95–112 in The Volcker Commission, *Leadership for America: Rebuilding the Public Service.* Lexington, MA: Lexington Books.

Kilpatrick, Franklin P., Milton C. Cummings, and M. Kent Jennings. 1964a. *The Image of the Federal Service.* Washington, DC: Brookings Institution.

———.1964b. *Source Book of a Study of Occupational Values and the Image of the Federal Service.* Washington, DC: Brookings Institution.

Kingdon, J. E., ed. 1990. *The Civil Service in Liberal Democracies.* London: Routledge.

Ladd, Everett Carll. 1983. "What the Voters Really Want." Pages 114–25 in J. L. Perry and K. L. Kraemer, eds., *Public Management.* Palo Alto, CA: Mayfield.

Lipset, Seymour M., and William Schneider. 1987. *The Confidence Gap: Business, Labor, and Government in the American Mind.* Baltimore: Johns Hopkins University Press.

Morgan, E. Philip, and James L. Perry. 1988. "Re-orienting the Comparative Study of Civil Service Systems." *Review of Public Personnel Administration* 8: 84–95.

Peters, B. Guy. 1984. *The Politics of Bureaucracy.* New York: Longman.

———. 1988. *Comparing Public Bureaucracies: Problems of Theory and Method.* Tuscaloosa: University of Alabama Press.

Peters, L. R. 1990. "West Germany." In J. E. Kingdon, ed., *The Civil Service in Liberal Democracies.* London: Routledge.

Reif, Karlheinz, and Ronald Inglehart. 1991. *Eurobarometer: The Dynamics of European Public Opinion.* New York: St. Martin's Press.

Sanders, Ronald P. 1989. "The 'Best and Brightest': Can the Public Service Compete?" Pages 157–63 in The Volcker Commission, *Leadership for America: Rebuilding the Public Service.* Lexington, MA: Lexington Books.

Sears, David O., and Jack Citrin. 1985. *Tax Revolt: Something for Nothing in California.* Cambridge: Harvard University Press.

Smith, Bruce L. R., ed. 1984. *The Higher Civil Service in Europe and Canada: Lessons for the United States.* Washington, DC: Brookings Institution.

Smith, Tom W., D. Garth Taylor, and Nancy A. Mathiowetz. 1980. "Public Opinion and Public Regard for the Federal Government." Pages 37–64 in C. H. Weiss and A. H. Barton, eds., *Making Bureaucracies Work.* Beverly Hills, CA: Sage.

Stimson, James A. 1991. *Public Opinion in America: Moods, Cycles and Swings.* Boulder, CO: Westview Press.

U.S. Merit Systems Protection Board. 1987. *Working for the Federal Government: Job Satisfaction and Federal Employees.* Washington, DC: U.S. Merit Systems Protection Board.

U.S. Merit Systems Protection Board. 1990. *Why Are Employees Leaving the Federal Government?* Washington, DC: U.S. Merit Systems Protection Board.

Volcker Commission, The. 1989. *Leadership for America: Rebuilding the Public Service.* Lexington, MA: Lexington Books.

# PART FOUR
# CONFIGURATIONS

In parts 2 and 3, the contributors provided substantive details about the evolution, structure, and context of civil service systems. The goal of part 4 is to synthesize these elements into a gestalt for civil service systems.

In search of the gestalt, the authors of the two chapters in part 4 use an approach akin to ideal types, a methodological tool discussed approvingly by Peters in chapter 2. The device is configuration analysis. Configuration analysis seeks to identify commonly occurring clusters of attributes that are internally cohesive. It is usually assumed that a relatively small number of configurations can be used to characterize a large portion of a population.

The first example of the configuration approach is Ferrel Heady's "Configurations of Civil Service Systems." He uses five dimensions to describe variations in civil service systems: (1) relation of civil service to the political regime; (2) socioeconomic context of the civil service system; (3) focus for personnel management functions in the civil service system; (4) qualification requirements for civil service membership; and (5) sense of mission of civil servants. These dimensions reflect important aspects of civil service systems from the operational, collective choice, and constitutional worlds of action introduced in chapter 1. Heady's analysis identifies qualitative variations in each of the five dimensions.

More traditional analytic approaches might stop with the five dimensions or cross-classify the dimensions into an exhaustive array of types. Instead, using the logic of the configurational approach, Heady identifies four common configurations of civil service systems: ruler trustworthy, party controlled, policy receptive, and collaborative. Ruler trustworthy civil service systems are characterized by conformity to ruler expectations, high status, corporate identity, and sense of mission as pivotal policymakers. Party controlled configurations manifest the political party as the primary reference point in the society, downplay professional qualifications, and exhibit a vague sense of mission. Policy receptive systems, the configuration representative of the largest number of countries, are characterized by pluralist and competitive environments, appropriate credentials for entry, and allegiance to constitutional and legal obligations. The fourth configuration, collaborative, is characterized by a sense of mission that is geared toward avoiding the alienation of the political leadership and toward maintaining their support, competencies for adequate administrative performance, and deference to authority.

In chapter 11, E. Philip Morgan also develops configurations, but his construction of types is motivated by an interest in explaining civil service systems in developing countries. Morgan identifies developing countries as those that emerged from colonial hegemony after the mid-nineteenth century. He includes among them the newly independent republics of the former Soviet Union.

Morgan describes the contexts for civil service systems in terms of four dimensions: level of institutionalization of the nation-state, aggregated public attitudes toward the state, degree of professionalism/politicization, and tension between process and outcomes. From these dimensions he identifies four macro-institutional environments or fields. Morgan concludes his analysis with a consideration of the dynamics of civil service systems moving across fields.

We believe both Heady and Morgan's specific configurations and their general strategies have considerable potential for comparative research. In the concluding chapter, we discuss how their contributions can be used to guide future comparative civil service system research.

# 10  CONFIGURATIONS OF CIVIL SERVICE SYSTEMS

Ferrel Heady

The purpose of this chapter is to explore the utility, for comparative study of civil service systems, of a holistic approach designed to identify configurations of civil service systems with shared attributes that might enhance comparative research.

## CONFIGURATION AS A CONCEPT

The concept of configuration as used here has been developed in recent years for the comparative analysis of organizations, principally by Danny Miller, Peter H. Friesen, and Henry Mintzberg (Miller and Mintzberg, 1983; Miller and Friesen, 1984). Their basic assumption is that organizational entities have a natural tendency to coalesce into what they term "configurations" or "quantum states." The crucial advantage of their "approach of configuration" is that "a relatively small number of these configurations are believed to encompass quite a large fraction of the population of organizations" (Miller and Friesen, 1984: 1).

Configurations may be derived in two ways. Conceptual configurations are "defined on the basis of a theoretical framework or a synthesis of the literature." Empirical configurations "are the products of statistical analyses of multivariate data on large samples of organizations." A crucial difference is that conceptual configurations are "defined in advance, while empirical configurations emerge from the quantitative analysis of data—from the building of taxonomies" (Miller and Friesen, 1984: 4).

The objective is to present a conceptual configuration of civil service systems, using the approach outlined by Miller and Mintzberg (1983; rev. as chap. 1 in Miller and Friesen, 1984: 10–30). Their contention is that methods traditionally used in studying organizations encourage analysis rather than synthesis. Analysis tends to "focus on simple relationships among few variables in search of direct causation." Synthesis favors "developing or isolating composites" in the form of "gestalts," "archetypes," or "configurations," defined as "commonly occurring clusters of attributes or relationships . . . that are internally cohesive, such that the presence of some attributes suggest the reliable occurrence of others." The ultimate aim of synthesis is to generate sets of configurations "that collectively exhaust a large fraction of the target population of organizations or situations under consideration. . . . This allows many organizations to be classified using only a few distinguishing attributes, and then permits the prediction of many other organizational features or relationships simply by making reference to the configurations" (Miller and Friesen, 1984: 11, 12).

An illustrative example is the typology of organizational structure presented by Henry Mintzberg (summarized in chap. 3 of Miller and Friesen, 1984: 68–86), which suggests five configurations: simple structure, machine bureaucracy, professional bureaucracy, divisionalized form, and "adhocracy." The claim is that such configurations are useful if they do in fact reflect reality by demonstrating the occurrence of "common, internally homogeneous clusterings of attributes or relationships, a relatively small number of which can account for a large fraction of the population of organizations" (Miller and Friesen, 1984: 20). The assumption is that research from the perspective of synthesis "will lead to more complete, more accurate, and more useful theories by which to comprehend our complex world of organizations" (Miller and Friesen, 1984: 30).

## CIVIL SERVICE SYSTEMS AS A FOCUS

The entities considered here are civil service systems as a distinct and identifiable form of organization. I define civil service systems as "mediating institutions that mobilize human resources in the service of the state in a given territory." This modifies a definition proposed earlier by Morgan and Perry (1988: 85–86) by dropping a reference to "authorized by constitutional rules," because in some circumstances relations between rulers and ruled may differ from those laid out in a formal constitutional document.

As Morgan and Perry comment, this definition suggests that these organizations are derived from relations among rulers and the ruled, that they act as bridges between the state and specific administrative organs, and that they have a dominant concern with human resources. It is also consistent with the definition used by Morgan in chapter 11 of this volume.

For greater utility in making comprehensive global comparisons, one crucial consequence of this definition must be that the civil service system is regarded as less inclusive than the public service system or total public bureaucracy in a polity: it excludes the military component of the bureaucratic apparatus by compartmentalizing the civil and military services. It is therefore essential that the relationships between civil and military bureaucracies be dealt with in the comparative analysis of national civil service systems. This is particularly important in the numerous instances among developing nations where military and civil professional bureaucrats constitute the core of the ruling political elite.

## VARIABLES FOR DESCRIBING CONFIGURATIONS

One of the guidelines stressed by Miller and Friesen (1984: 7–8) in their comments on the nature of configurations is that there is no one best set of variables or elements that should be used in describing all sets of configurations. The variables chosen should depend on the problems being researched and the kinds of predictability sought. They refer to the work of Hall (1972) and suggest that a thorough characterization of organizational configurations would include variables "describing their technology, environment, type of personnel, structure, process, and organizational output," but would stress that the possibilities are endless and that the prime consideration is that the variables chosen interrelate to produce predictive configurations.

With such latitude available, it is obviously unlikely that there will be consensus on the selection of variables for use in the configuration approach to the comparative study of civil service systems. I do not offer my list of variables as the only one, or even as the best one, merely as an appropriate one. One consideration taken into account is the value of being able to tie together as closely as possible the wide variety of research targets, methods, and techniques set forth in this volume.

There is evidence of agreement on, or at least common usage of, several properties of civil service systems that have promise for comparative research purposes. Morgan and Perry concluded (1988: 89) that civil service systems need to be described in terms of at least four parameters or properties: rules, structures, roles, and norms. Saying that they "represent a mixture of categories from traditional institutional analysis and more recent behavioral research," they proposed that these "become the building blocks for theory about civil service systems." Without offering detailed analyses as to the meaning attached to each property, they gave these brief explanations as to the meaning of each category: rules ("assigned guides for conduct or constraints that social systems use to structure behavior"), structure ("the organizational arrangements of civil service systems"), roles ("the set of activities expected of a person occupying a particular social position"), and norms ("values internal to the system which ground the rules and roles").

I will not attempt such an elaboration, but will only undertake to correlate these properties, as I understand them, to one or more of the variables suggested for use in arriving at comprehensive configurations for civil service systems. The intent is not to equate each variable to a corresponding property, but to provide a connection or tie-in between variables and properties. The variables are presented as a means for placement of specific national civil service systems along selected dimensions which, when combined, point toward probable configurations of these systems. There may be and presumably are numerous other ways in which these four basic properties and others can be studied on a systematic comparative basis. My assumption is that, at a minimum, each variable deals with some relevant aspect of an associated property.

The variables or dimensions are as follows: (1) relation of the civil service system to the political regime; (2) socioeconomic context of the civil service system; (3) focus for personnel management functions in the civil service system; (4) qualification requirements for entering and performing as a member of the civil service system; and (5) sense of mission held by members of the civil service system. The principal correlations of variables with properties are: variables (1) and (2) with rules, variable (3) with structures, variable (4) with roles, and variable (5) with norms.

In conformity with the process already described and drawing upon the existing literature, these variables will be considered one by one as a means of deriving a set of conceptual configurations for civil service systems that will be subject to verification or modification based on further consideration and subsequent research efforts. On a continuum for each variable, several points will be suggested as the most useful for placement of a civil service system with regard to that variable.

## RELATION TO THE POLITICAL REGIME

In any existing national polity, the civil service system operates in a context that is affected significantly by the character of the political regime. This relationship may conform to stipulations laid out in a formal constitutional document, or it may reflect a reality that deviates from such constitutional norms. The characteristics of the current relationship are likely to change when and if there is a shift in the nature of the political regime. In developing countries where the civil service is weak, regime instability and frequency of regime shifts are likely to have a destabilizing effect on the civil service system, whereas in cases where the civil service is strong, its position may be consolidated under such circumstances, as has happened historically in Germany and France. The key question that needs to be addressed is that concerning the responsiveness of the civil service system to the political elite exercising effective power in the existing political regime. A secondary question is how long this type of responsiveness has been present, and what the prospects are for it to continue.

An emphasis on the link between the civil service system and the political regime does not imply that the nature of the political regime is necessarily the most important determinant of bureaucratic behavior, but merely that this factor will always be present and is likely to be significant. Case by case and cross-national exploration of other factors, such as historical bureaucratic tradition and the legacy from colonialism, are also important in determining the relative impact of a variety of factors on the functioning of particular systems (Heady, 1991: 87, 88). Moreover, the precise nature of the regime-civil service system linkage itself requires much more concentrated and sophisticated study.

In the array of nation-states in the contemporary world of the late twentieth century, taking into account the pattern of distribution among political regimes, the most likely variations in civil service system responsiveness may be found at one or another point along this continuum:

| Ruler responsive | Single party responsive | Majority party responsive | Military responsive |

"Ruler responsive" refers to a situation in which political power resides in the hands of a ruler or ruling group possessing sufficient legitimacy to exercise effective control over the civil service system. In Weberian terms, the basis for the claim to legitimacy rests either on traditional or charismatic grounds. This relationship is much less prevalent now than it was historically. The most common examples are surviving monarchies that still maintain direct and comprehensive decision-making capabilities that can demand compliance. Iran under the shah is a recent example; Saudi Arabia, Morocco, and Brunei are current ones. Iran after the revolution of 1979, at least during the lifetime of the Ayotallah Khomeini, also qualifies, with the traditional claim to legitimacy having a strong religious base. Charismatic rulers at the national level are more of an exception, particularly since my intention is to exclude those whose professional background is in the military bureaucracy, or who place their major claim to power on leadership of a dominant political party.

Ruler responsiveness means generally that the civil service system is closely curbed and controlled, and that its members enjoy relatively little discretion in the making of policy. The regime may be ultimately dependent on the capacity of the civil service to conduct civil affairs in a way that copes adequately with the complexities of modern life, but the fate of individual civil servants is highly dependent on retaining the confidence of the ruler or his political subordinates.

Regimes dominated by a single political party that insists on and is capable of exercising a political power monopoly are presently declining in number. The demise of communist single-party regimes has been a remarkably swift and unanticipated phenomenon, but the same tendency is evident among regimes where the single party has more of a nationalist orientation. Nevertheless, dominant party regimes that permit no party competition or only token competition continue to function in many parts of the world and are unlikely to disappear.

In such circumstances, the civil service system, even though it has usually been kept organizationally separate, is as a practical matter a subservient organ of the party. Decisions as to the structure and operation of the civil service are party decisions arrived at by officials of the party, with very little participation or influence from members of the civil service system, at least in their capacity as civil servants and not in their often concurrent roles in the party apparatus. Party policy is official or state policy, and the obligation of the civil service as part of the state machinery is to implement that policy without question.

The situation changes in a political regime that permits and in fact has active competition among political parties for the exercise of political power. The obligation of civil service responsiveness is primarily and ultimately to the governing party or coalition of parties, whether the system is a parliamentary or a presidentialist one. The main difference is the normal expectation that over time there will likely be shifts in party control, leading to corresponding shifts in civil service system responsiveness.

The characteristics of this responsiveness differ significantly between parliamentary and presidentialist regimes. In parliamentary systems, controls over the civil service are unequivocal and effective because of the absence of competition between the executive and legislative branches as a result of a constitutional separation of powers. The governing party, acting through the cabinet, can put into operation and maintain a merit-based career personnel system and can compel prompt compliance with its policies from civil servants.

In presidentialist systems, policy direction and compliance capabilities are more diffusely distributed among the executive, legislative, and judicial branches. This results in cross pressures on the civil service as to accountability, with a weakening of presidential control. Presidentialist regimes are more likely to utilize patronage in staffing the civil service, with patronage appointees being replaced frequently if patronage is linked with the practice of rotation in office, or retained indefinitely but without permanent status. Even when a merit approach has been installed for civil service staffing, as in the United States at the national level since the civil service reforms of the last century, it is subject to statutory change and does not reach to the top levels of the service. Moreover, different parties are often in control of the executive and legislative branches. As a consequence of these factors, civil service responsiveness to changes in party electoral support are often partial and relatively slow. Only if a party is dominant in both the legislature and the presidency, and only if patronage is the primary basis for staffing the civil service, will nonresponsive civil servants be promptly dismissed and control over the civil service be unequivocal.

Nevertheless, the essentials in the pattern of relations between the civil service system and the regime are similar in all these variations among polyarchal competitive polities. Ultimately, the expectations and the reality is that civil servants must recognize their duty of compliance with shifts in party political power. If the civil service system is a meritocracy, such responsiveness tends to be a product of the socialization process among civil service professionals, combined with the knowledge that effective disciplinary measures can be brought to bear against them, particularly in a parliamentary setting. In a nonmerit patronage situation, the need to conform is even more evident and pressing.

Obviously, this category will include a large proportion of existing civil service systems, especially among developed countries, pointing toward the utility of identifying subcategories, although this is not undertaken here.

The fourth responsiveness relationship occurs in the numerous instances during recent decades in which military professionals have come to form the ruling political elite, usually in recently independent nations following an extended period of colonial domination. This pattern became established earliest in Latin America, where independence came sooner, but has spread rapidly since World War II in other geographical regions. The prevalence of such regimes seems to ebb and flow on a cyclical basis, the current trend being downward; but this may be only temporary and numerous cases of such regimes must be anticipated in the foreseeable future. The basic cause is an imbalance inherited from colonialism between the bureaucracy as an institution and what Riggs (1973: 28–29) terms the "constitutive system" (including an elected assembly, an electoral system, and a party system), offering opportunities and temptations for professional bureaucrats to move into political dominance with the justification that this is the only alternative to political instability.

Usually such regimes are coalitions of military professionals and civil service professionals, but for obvious reasons the civilians are apt to be the junior partners and must conform to controls imposed by their military colleagues. Because collaboration with civilian bureaucrats is nearly always a necessity for continuity in a military regime (Heady, 1991: 289), the restrictions may not be rigorous or extensive, provided the civilians do not threaten military supremacy. Consequently, the dilemma of civil servants may be merely to adjust as necessary while maintaining as strong a role as possible in the bureaucratic coalition. The hard reality, however, is that the civil service system in such a regime is a tool in the hands of military rulers while they retain political power.

## SOCIOECONOMIC CONTEXT

Another environmental factor important in characterizing civil service systems is the socioeconomic context in which they function. The basic differentiation here has to do with the approaches taken in the polity to decision-making on socioeconomic issues and how these options impact on the civil service system, using this continuum:

| Traditional | Pluralist competitive | Mixed | Corporatist | Planned centrally |
|---|---|---|---|---|

"Traditions are implicit rather than explicit rules that govern behavior" (Ouchi, 1980: 139). In numerous societies, the most common way of reaching decisions continues to be acceptance of what emerges from generally accepted interactions among individuals and groups in a "clan" type of association that relies extensively on socialization as a means of control. The political leadership in such a society may be formally unfettered in the exercise of power, but monarchs as well as subjects are limited by traditions that restrict their options. Servants of the crown or monarch in such a society have even less leeway, because they do have a traditional societal duty to obey their leader without question. Consequently, civil servants in this setting generally play a passive role unless they are confident of being backed unreservedly by the ruler. Societal change usually takes place slowly and incrementally, except when it is initiated from above by leaders whose legitimacy is well established. This pattern is associated with polities usually considered less modernized or developed, and the number of them has been decreasing in recent decades.

The second category refers to a pattern for socioeconomic decision-making that relies heavily on market forces and the outcome of competition among individuals and groups. Pluralism is valued and encouraged. Political parties and organized interest groups are allowed wide latitude in pursuing their objectives, and societal decisions are assumed to emerge from this process of interaction, with minimal interference from political authorities except to maintain a level playing field for the contestants. These characteristics are associated with contemporary advanced capitalist democracies in Western Europe and North America. Civil servants themselves are participants in this pluralist milieu, being allowed, for example, to organize into trade unions for the pursuit of civil service goals. These activities are subject, of course, to the basic obligation of the civil service system to comply with public policy directives from political sources.

The "mixed" category is intended to encompass instances of a deliberate combination of limited pluralism and enhanced governmental regulation and/or competition in the socioeconomic sphere. The spectrum here is wide, including, since World War II, new governmental programs for social reform in the United States, Scandinavian social welfare states, nationalized industries under socialist or labor governments in France and Great Britain, and perhaps current experiments moving toward a market system in countries of Eastern Europe and the former Soviet Union. The status of civil service systems is somewhat ambiguous in these varying circumstances, but is not fundamentally different from the situation in the more pluralist environment just described.

Corporatist socioeconomic systems are designed to control and channel representation of interests by placing the state in the central mediating and deciding role among competing groups. This orientation has European roots, particularly in Italy and the Iberian countries, but has been most pronounced in recent decades in Latin America. The power of the state is extended over major societal forces, and a process of depoliticization is fostered and sometimes imposed. The dominant ruling political elite is usually a combination of military and civilian officials. The former group ordinarily has the upper hand, but civilian technocrats are essential to provide the necessary expertise and are thus in a strategic position to support or undermine the system. This gives the higher civil service an unusual opportunity to be near the center of power. Prime examples of this orientation were Brazil between 1964 and the mid-1980s, and Peru from 1968 to 1980. Such cases are now on the decline.

The final grouping of "centrally planned" socioeconomic systems is also diminishing as the result of the disintegration of the Soviet Union and its sphere of influence in Eastern Europe and elsewhere. The prime current example is clearly the People's Republic of China, but the pattern is replicated elsewhere, as in Cuba and North Korea. In these cases, a monopolistic single party is completely in charge. Political pluralism is entirely illegitimate, and interest groups are not allowed to organize or become active. Here the high-ranking party bureaucrat is obviously more important as a policymaker than the high-ranking civil servant in the state apparatus. However, as in the corporate category, it is the expertise in the hands of these higher state civil servants that may turn out to be one of the decisive factors in the future of the system.

## FOCUS FOR PERSONNEL MANAGEMENT

One indicator of the structural character of a civil service system is the placement within the overall governmental system of primary responsibility for exercising the personnel management functions essential for civil service operations. Normally there will be in place constitutional and/or statutory specifications reflecting the major policy decisions that have been made as to system design and dealing with such basic matters as staffing, status, tenure, discipline, political activity, retirement, and so forth. Within these boundaries, considerable discretion remains in the day-to-day application of these policies and in the adoption of rules filling in policy gaps. This variable considers some of the major options that have been chosen for assignment of responsibility for these personnel management functions. Each option has ramifications affecting other aspects of the civil service system. The following continuum indicates major alternatives available:

| Chief | Independent | Divided | Ministry- |
| executive | agency | | by-ministry |

The tendency in situations where the civil service system is kept under tight rein by the ruling political elite—whether it be a monarch, a single political party, or military officers—is to locate personnel functions directly within the office of the chief executive or in a unit directly and fully under executive control. This not only contributes to mastery over the selection and behavior of civil servants, but also facilitates rapid or drastic changes of policy that might be desired. Hence such an arrangement was to be expected in early civil service systems rooted historically in European absolutist monarchies; but it is also the preference in more recent dominant party and bureaucratic elite regimes.

A tenet of the civil service reform movement beginning in the middle of the nineteenth century was that the integrity of a civil service system based on merit called for personnel management to be lodged in the hands of an independent agency insulated from direct political interference. A prime example was the civil service commission in the United States from 1883 to 1978. This model was widely copied, not only at state and local government levels in the United States, but in many other countries as well, either by voluntary adoption or by imposition, for instance in Japan, as part of post–World War II occupation reforms. As time passed, it became subject to increasing scrutiny and skepticism on the grounds that it fostered a negative rather than a positive approach to personnel management, protecting merit in the selection process at the price of dulling personnel management as an administrative tool.

A divided, usually bifurcated, assignment of responsibility was the remedy frequently substituted for complete reliance on an independent agency. Great Britain has preferred this approach since the Northcote-Trevelyan reforms of the 1850s, although the prime minister is ultimately responsible for control over the civil service. Initial recruitment of civil servants is done by a commission, and other personnel management functions are divided between the prime minister in his capacity as the minister for the civil service and the treasury. The 1978 reforms in the United States divided these functions between an Office of Personnel Management and a Merit Systems Protection Board. In France, where decentralization on a corps or ministry basis had earlier been the mode, reforms in the mid-1940s introduced the still existing National School of Administration as a common training center for incoming higher administrators. Various other forms of division in personnel management duties are in place or may be devised.

Decentralization of personnel functions on a ministry-by-ministry or department-by-department basis (or alternatively on the basis of a variety of professional groups or corps) is another much used option, subject of course to conformity with basis constitutional or statutory requirements. The earlier French pattern, before it was modified as mentioned, was adopted in many former French colonies or countries influenced by French administrative practices. Italy and several other continental European countries continue to prefer this general arrangement, with variations as to details in its application. It is appropriate for any polity in which the ruling political elite has ample control over the appointment, retention, and behavior of ministry or department heads.

## QUALIFICATION REQUIREMENTS

Determination as to qualities required for entrance into and retention in the civil service system usually rests on one of the grounds indicated by the following continuum (based on varying degrees of involvement by bureaucrats in decisions as to their own qualification requirements), combined with what is considered at least minimum competence to perform assigned duties:

| Patrimony | Party loyalty | Party patronage | Professional performance | Bureaucratic determination |
|---|---|---|---|---|

Typically in historical empires and occasionally even now in instances where strong dynasties still function, a role in the civil service is provided at the discretion or whim of the ruler. An opportunity to serve the regime is among the favors that can be granted to subjects regarded as deserving of the honor. Long after a distinction had been recognized between the king's household and the royal service, the privilege of becoming a civil servant continued to be treated essentially as part of the royal patrimony, to be bestowed or withheld at the will of the ruler. The key expectation in the relationship is that the civil servant will be trustworthy. When reliability is in doubt, so is the future of the civil servant. In such patrimonial civil service systems, once this qualification has been met, there may be wide variations in other competencies sought, ranging all the way from minimal concern about ability to carry out duties to insistence on professional education and training as exemplified in various Chinese dynasties, the absolutist monarchies of Prussia, and perhaps some of the present-day regimes of this type. The fundamental feature of civil service roles is that they are set by and may be easily and drastically changed by decree of the ruler. The primary task of civil servants is to cultivate and maintain the confidence of royal officials.

In many contemporary polities, party loyalty has replaced ruler allegiance as the touchstone of eligibility for membership in the civil service. In these single or dominant party political systems, party claims to a monopoly on policy-making and execution make it imperative that civil servants pass whatever tests of party loyalty may be imposed and that they suffer not only loss of status or position for falling short, but suffer in other ways as well, including imprisonment, banishment to the countryside, or death. With the passage of time after establishment of party control, the obvious need for competence as well as party loyalty is likely to lead to growing emphasis on professional expertise and an effort to achieve a balance between being "red" and being "expert." In a showdown, however, expertise gives way to party loyalty. This pattern has recurred repeatedly in both Communist and non-Communist party regimes, the most recent example being China before and since the Tiananmen Square crisis. In these circumstances, the behavior of civil servants who want to remain in the civil service is overwhelmingly determined by what is required of them by the current party line as to their roles.

A party patronage civil service along the lines of the pre–Civil War pattern found in the United States is becoming increasingly rare, at least at the national level. It may persist at lower governmental levels, or in segments of the civil service, but its twin justifications based on maintenance of party vitality and universal capability to perform the work of government are now less persuasive. Where the prerogative of a victorious party in an election to replace incumbent civil servants with deserving party faithful has been preserved, however, and rotation in office is considered desirable, the impact on bureaucratic behavior is no less impressive. The civil servant who owes his or her post to patronage recognizes clearly how qualification for appointment and for continued service is measured, and acts accordingly.

I have used "professional performance" as the designation for what appears to me to be the most prevalent basis for civil service qualification and role performance in contemporary democracies. This pattern combines a selection process designed to require and measure technical competence in the performance of duties with an obligation as part of the socialization of the professional civil servant to carry out neutrally and impartially the policy directives of political decision makers. Of course, I am speaking of central tendencies and not isolated exceptions, and I acknowledge that there are strongly held views that this is more illusion than reality. Also, it is my intention to recognize the prevalence and legitimacy of widespread and frequently decisive participation by civil servants in the making of policy choices. The crucial issue is whose judgment ultimately prevails. The conclusion of most recent researchers in Europe and elsewhere is that bureaucrats are contributors to but not the dominant makers of public policy (Dogan, 1975; Aberbach, Putnam, and Rockman, 1981; Suleiman, 1984; Rowat, 1988; Heady, 1991). Thus, I am assuming that most of the civil services in parliamentary and presidentialist democracies can be placed in this category, although the stress may be on generalist professionalism (as in Great Britain) or on specialist professionalism (as in the United States). "Bureaucratic determination" is the final option, referring to the dominant source of influence in the setting of civil service qualification and performance standards in cases where bureaucrats themselves are the major wielders of political power. Of course, bureaucratic self-interest is pursued when the opportunity presents itself in all bureaucracies; but it can usually be contained when bureaucrats are subject to external controls. In bureaucratic elite regimes, as already indicated, those most influential are apt to be military rather than civil bureaucrats, and their perceptions of self-interest are likely to differ from those of civil servants. In both the military and civil services, the actual priorities adopted may vary over a wide range of options, as indicated by the long-standing debate as to whether, under any circumstances, bureaucratic elites can be expected to exercise leadership in movement toward greater balance among political institutions. The crucial requirement for placement here is that bureaucrats of some type have the opportunity to determine how civil service professional and performance standards should be set and evaluated.

## SENSE OF MISSION

This dimension refers to values internal to the system, values that form the sense of mission most commonly held by members of the civil service. Of course, not all members of any civil service will ever have an identical sense of mission because of variations due to rank in the system, ministerial or corps affiliation, geographical location, seniority, individual personality characteristics, or other factors. All that can be expected is identification of views about the mission of the civil service that are widely concurred in and have a significant impact on overall bureaucratic performance. Such internally held values may often be expected to counteract other external factors and thus lessen what their effects might otherwise be. Concepts of "stateness" (Heper, 1987), "organizational culture" (Schein, 1985), and "the derivative middle class" (Subramaniam, 1990) as well as studies of these phenomena have a bearing on this variable that cannot be explored in any detail here.

The following continuum is suggested for placement of civil service systems as to their most widely shared sense of mission:

Compliance    Cooperation        Policy         Constitutional    Guidance
                              responsiveness    responsiveness

The compliance category includes any instance in which the overwhelming motivating factor is an urge to conform without question to directives from a controlling political elite recognized by members of the civil service as fully capable of punishing for deviant behavior. The type of political regime may vary over a wide range. What is critical is the pervasiveness of control and recognition of it by civil servants. The setting may be, for example, a despotic state, a single-party state with a doctrinaire agenda, an entrenched patronage system, or a military dictatorship such as that in Guatemala under Ubico or Uganda under Idi Amin. These are subservient civil service systems, with the policy preferences of individuals or groups in the civil service having little relevance for policy outcomes.

If cooperation properly identifies civil service mission, the key motivator is a desire to take whatever course of action will be acceptable to effectual political superiors, while retaining to the maximum extent feasible a significant role for input from the civil service in making important policy decisions. Caution against jeopardizing civil service status is a crucial consideration, even though the political leadership may frequently be highly dependent on the civil service for performing essential functions to ward off political instability. Preservation of civil service self-interest takes precedence over all other factors when this is the mind-set among civil servants, but the actual degree of participation in policy-making available to the civil service may vary over a wide range.

When policy responsiveness is accepted as the essential mission of the civil service, this usually reflects the combined consequences of civil service professionalization and acceptance of an obligation to respond reliably to political leadership from outside the civil service. This sense of mission does not preclude exploitation of whatever opportunity for policy input is available to civil servants within these boundaries, depending on factors such as, for example, the type of minister heading a ministry in Great Britain, the viability of "iron triangle" relationships in the United States, or the possibilities of combined efforts with former bureaucrats currently serving as ministers or legislators in Japan or France. The understood presumption here is that, within a short period of time and with minimal distortions of initial intent, policy shifts adopted by political officials will be carried out in practice by appropriate members of the civil service.

A civil service with constitutional responsiveness exists in the rare instances when responsiveness to a constitution or legal system is preferred by civil servants over responsiveness to policy set by political officials. This priority in responsiveness is more likely to be accepted by individuals or small segments of the civil service than to be the generally prevailing sense of mission. Such tendencies were encouraged by the "new" public administration movement in the United States beginning in the 1970s. "Whistleblowers" who disregard hierarchical supervision and appeal to outside sources for support of their views about what is in the public interest are typical of civil servants so motivated. Newland (1987) has discussed some of the factors leading to this form of linkage between such civil servants and what they regard as the general public interest or "high civic culture." Wamsley et al. (1990: 25), beginning with their "Blacksberg Manifesto" of the early 1980s, have argued that public administration should be viewed as "governance rather than merely management administration in the public sector," and they have urged a more active normative role for public administrators. Riggs (1991) attributes this orientation to career officials in the American presidentialist system who are frustrated by contradictory mandates from the executive, legislative, and judicial branches.

A civil service with a guidance mission views itself as entitled to assume and carry out a leadership role in the political system to the maximum extent permitted by circumstances. Civil servants see themselves as the most legitimate and best-equipped group for setting and achieving societal goals. With this sense of mission, civil service claims may sometimes be pushed to an extent that endangers or even destroys the preexisting power position of the civil service. The rationale for this self-perception does not follow any uniform pattern. In the unlikely circumstance that past events might have converted civil servants themselves into a governing political elite, it is easy to understand that this would be accepted and justified as the way things ought to be. In a military–civil service coalition, civil servants may have the professional capabilities plus the power standing to be crucial decision makers even though operating under the cover and protection of some kind of military front; and this may be a favorable enough situation to satisfy their sense of mission. A common historical circum-stance was that servants of a traditional powerful ruler viewed themselves as agents of the monarch entitled to obedience from a subject population, as illus-trated during the Tokugawa era in Japan by the adage: "Officials honored, the people despised." Such cases are now rare, but the carryover from the absolutist past to contemporary bureaucratic self-perceptions is still evident not only in Japan, but in Germany, France, Turkey, and other nation-states where long-exist-ing bureaucratic prerogatives continue to influence current behavior and may even provide a basis for a future reassertion of claims to political power. A more common explanation is the transference, after independence, from colonial to national civil servants of the prerogatives, perquisites, and social status enjoyed earlier by officials representing the former imperial power. This legacy of colo-nialism is particularly strong among civil servants in African and Asian countries that had been colonized for long periods by Great Britain and France. Such a sense of mission widely shared among civil servants is a powerful motivator, and its impact deserves much deeper investigation than has taken place so far.

## DERIVED CONCEPTUAL CONFIGURATIONS

What groupings or configurations of civil service systems can be anticipated as the outcome of interactions among variables such as these? Do such configura-tions provide a basis for placement of a high proportion of existing civil service systems, as the "approach of configuration" anticipates they should? What are some examples of civil service systems tentatively assigned to each of these con-figurations? Several conceptual configurations suggested to me by this review of the literature of the field will be briefly identified and characterized. Table 10.1 summarizes this effort to categorize civil service system configurations.

The first configuration is *ruler trustworthy* civil service systems. Their prime characteristics are conformity to ruler expectations and preoccupation with retaining their reputation for reliability. The price civil servants pay in such a system is that their status is insecure even when they have been professionally trained and occupy positions of great responsibility, and that the circumstances under which they are appointed and retained and their instructions as to policy may change rapidly and drastically. On the other hand, members of such a civil service are apt to have high status in society generally, often have a strong sense of corporate identity, and are likely to share a sense of mission in which they view themselves as central shapers of policy as long as they retain the ruler's trust. Examples are countries such as Saudi Arabia, Morocco, Jordan, and Brunei with orthotraditional political regimes ruled by monarchs, and Iran with a neotraditional regime under religious leadership.

*Party controlled* civil service systems form a second configuration. The main reference point in the polity for members of such a civil service is the political

TABLE 10.1

**Configurations of Civil Service Systems**

| *Variables* | Ruler trustworthy | Party controlled | Policy receptive | Collaborative |
|---|---|---|---|---|
| Relation to political regime | Ruler responsive | Single party or majority party responsive | Majority party responsive | Military responsive |
| Socioeconomic context | Traditional | Corporatist or planned centrally | Pluralist competitive or mixed | Corporatist or centrally planned |
| Focus for personnel management | Chief executive or ministry-by-ministry | Chief executive or ministry-by-ministry | Independent agency or divided | Chief executive or ministry-by-ministry |
| Qualification requirements | Patrimony | Party loyalty or party patronage | Professional performance | Bureaucratic determination |
| Sense of mission | Compliance or guidance | Compliance or cooperation | Policy or constitutional responsiveness | Cooperation or guidance |
| *Examples* | Saudi Arabia Iran Brunei | China Cuba Egypt | France Great Britain United States | South Korea Indonesia Ghana |

party as a political institution, because this is the source of both civil service empowerment and control. The requisite element is that political party leaders are capable of and willing to exert decisive direction over civil service qualifications and performance, most often in a socioeconomic context of corporatism or central planning that needs the civil service as an agent to execute party policies. The party may be a single party monopolizing political power, a dominant party unlikely to relinquish power in the near future, a party victorious in the electoral process in possession of patronage tools to coerce civil servants, or in some instances a governing party or coalition of parties temporarily able to bring about civil service compliance even though the long-term rules of the political game do not condone such manipulation. In these circumstances, external controls are pervasive and effective, civil service careers are hazardous, unquestioning party loyalty has priority over professional qualifications, and the civil service as a corporate body has a weak and vague sense of mission beyond its inescapable obligation to comply with party mandates while they are enforceable. It must be either completely compliant or at least cooperative whenever necessary. Contemporary examples are Communist Party regimes such as the People's Republic of China and Cuba, and other single party or dominant party regimes such as Egypt, Tanzania, Mexico, Malaysia, and Singapore.

A third configuration is made up of *policy receptive* civil service systems. They are usually found in a political, social, and economic environment that is pluralist and competitive. As already indicated, entrance into these systems is dependent on appropriate preparation as determined by measures of merit; tenure status is achieved after a period of probation; and service is normally on a career basis unless the civil servant takes the initiative in leaving. In tandem with these protections, members of the civil service, as part of their professional preparation, are socialized to defer on policy matters to political officials outside the ranks of the civil service itself, or to invoke as an alternative an overriding constitutional or legal obligation to explain their actions, thus acknowledging the ultimate primacy of extrabureaucratic over bureaucratic political institutions. Within these boundaries, specific systems may exhibit preferences for a variety of operational options. Examples are generalist versus specialist claims of competence at the time of initial appointment, rank versus position as a basis for determining status in the system, placement of the dividing line between political appointees and career officials in the departments or ministries, the range of political activities permitted to civil servants, and so forth. Important though these options are, the choice among them does not usually affect placement of a civil service system within this configuration.

My assumption is that the largest population among the various configurations will be found here, enhancing the importance of subclassifications and comparisons among examples of these subgroups. This task is not undertaken here, but a tentative possible breakdown would be into classic continental European examples with long-established professional services committed to conformity with legal obligations as formulated in the political sphere (such as France, Germany, Belgium, the Netherlands, Switzerland, Austria, and Italy, plus the Scandinavian and Iberian countries), noncontinental parliamentary system examples (such as Great Britain, Canada, Australia, New Zealand, Japan, and several smaller states in the Caribbean), and presidentialist systems with civil services based essentially on merit (such as the United States and a few other countries in Latin America, Africa, and Asia).

A fourth configuration is what I will term *collaborative* civil service systems. Here the dominant sense of mission is the modest one of following a pattern of conduct that will not jeopardize the existing opportunities of civil servants to be participants in the political process. This requires first of all that they acquire competencies for adequate administrative performance, and then that they succeed in meeting operating demands placed on the civil service. Beyond that, the main concern is to retain support from the political leadership, which is most likely to consist of fellow bureaucrats who are military professionals. Cooperation is relatively easy and mutually beneficial, but the civil servants are the ones who are most at risk and hence they are inclined to move cautiously. Action is guided by a strategy of deference rather than exercise of initiative. However, the socioeconomic context is likely to favor corporatism or central planning, often requiring the placement of civilian technocrats in strategic posts, and encouraging them to develop a guidance mentality conditioned by the basic necessity of satisfying the ultimate holders of political power.

Examples of contemporary collaborative civil service systems drawn from different geographical regions are South Korea, Indonesia, Ghana, Algeria, and Guatemala. Numerous other instances occurred in recent decades before political shifts took place toward greater competition and pluralism.

The configuration approach does not anticipate that all civil service systems can be placed in one of these configurations. The intent is a more limited one of providing categories that will account for a high proportion of the population of cases. Recognition must be given to instances of systems that do not now fit into any of these configurations, as well as to the possibility that new configurations may emerge in the future.

What are some illustrative cases of systems falling outside of these configurations? Sometimes ongoing political transition is so drastic and unpredictable as to raise doubts about any current attempt to categorize. The most obvious current examples are the former republics of the USSR (whether or not they are in the new Commonwealth of Independent States), and the countries of Eastern Europe. Another is the Republic of South Africa during the process of dismantling apartheid and moving toward greater access to the political arena by disenfranchised groups. Polities with a history of pendulum-like swings at frequent intervals from one to another form of political regime, with consequent inconsistent impacts on their civil service systems, make up another group. Currently, important members are Brazil, Nigeria, and Turkey.

Sometimes the political situation is so chaotic that any analysis is risky, as is presently the case in Haiti and Zaire.

Possible future configurations can be envisioned. For instance, if all the new national entities emerging out of the former Soviet Union power bloc should end up with civil services having common unique characteristics, this group might be numerous enough to form a new configuration. Another possibility deserves mention, although there are no current cases and none are likely to occur. This potential group would consist of controlling civil service systems, referring to a situation in which members of the civil service are themselves also occupants of positions of political power enabling them to exercise effective direction of the political system in addition to their administrative responsibilities. A recurring theme in the literature on bureaucracy is the danger of bureaucratic usurpation of political power (Heady, 1991: 426–27). Opportunities are greater for military bureaucrats, as demonstrated by the historical record and by the contemporary scene, but civil servants may also have the potential for gaining the upper hand, Developing countries would seem to present the most likely prospects, but this is a concern often expressed by critics who are apprehensive about the expansionist urges of already active civil servants with a strong sense of mission in developed countries such as Japan, France, or Germany. The extremely unsettled political situation in the former Soviet sphere presents the most recent setting for such an unlikely eventuality. Whatever the probabilities may be, these are potential developments requiring attention in a comprehensive program of comparative research on civil service systems.

## MOVING FROM CONCEPTUAL TO EMPIRICAL CONFIGURATIONS

The configuration approach used here assumes that configurations can be derived either conceptually or empirically. The suggested configurations are conceptual ones, based on a synthesis and interpretation of the existing literature on civil service systems. Their utility depends on whether or not they describe actual civil service systems based on more detailed and systematic analysis of available empirical data. The obvious next step is to verify or modify these configurations through organized case-by-case research on a variety of national civil services, leading to empirically derived configurations that may or may not be identical or similar to these conceptual configurations. This should be a major objective of future research efforts.

## REFERENCES

Aberbach J. D., R. D. Putnam, and B. A. Rockman. 1981. *Bureaucrats and Politicians in Western Democracies.* Cambridge: Harvard University Press.

Dogan, M. 1975. "The Political Power of the Mandarins." Pages 3–24 in M. Dogan, ed., *The Mandarins of Western Europe.* New York: John Wiley & Sons.

Hall, R. H. 1972. *Organizations: Structure and Process.* Englewood Cliffs: Prentice Hall.

Heady, F. 1991. *Public Administration: A Comparative Perspective.* 4th ed. New York: Marcel Dekker.

Heper, M., ed. 1987. *The State and Public Bureaucracies.* Westport, CT: Greenwood.

Miller, D., and H. Mintzberg. 1983. "The Case for Configuration." Pages 57–73 in Gareth Morgan, ed., *Beyond Method.* Beverly Hills, CA: Sage.

Miller, D., and P. H. Friesen. 1984. *Organizations: A Quantum View.* Englewood Cliffs: Prentice Hall.

Morgan, E. P., and J. L. Perry. 1988. "Re-orienting the Comparative Study of Civil Service Systems." Review of Public Personnel Administration 8, no. 3: 84–95.

Newland, C. A. 1987. "Public Executives: Imperium, Sacerdotium, Collegium? Bicentennial Leadership Challenges." *Public Administration Review* 47, no. 1: 45–56.

Ouchi, W. G. 1980. "Markets, Bureaucracies, and Clans." *Administrative Science Quarterly* 25: 129–41.

Riggs, F. W. 1973. *Prismatic Society Revisited.* Morristown, NJ: General Learning Press.

———. 1991. "Bureaucracy and the Constitution." Unpublished manuscript.

Rowat, D. C., ed. 1988. *Public Administration in Developed Democracies.* New York: Marcel Dekker.

Schein, E. H. 1985. *Organizational Culture and Leadership: A Dynamic View.* San Francisco: Jossey-Bass.

Subramaniam, V. 1990. "Appendix: The Derivative Middle Class." Pages 403–11 in V. Subramaniam, ed., *Public Administration in the Third World: An International Handbook.* Westport, CT: Greenwood Press.

Suleiman, E. N. 1984. *Bureaucrats and Policy Making: A Comparative Overview.* New York: Holmes & Meier.

Wamsley, G. L., R. N. Bacher, C. T. Goodsell, P. S. Kronenberg, J. A. Rohr, C. M. Stivers, O. F. White, and J. F. Wolf. 1990. *Refounding Public Administration.* Newbury Park, CA: Sage Publications.

# 11 ANALYZING FIELDS OF CHANGE:
## CIVIL SERVICE SYSTEMS IN DEVELOPING COUNTRIES

E. Philip Morgan

In 1988 Morgan and Perry put forward an argument that the theoretical foundations of bureaucratic behavior, particularly the links between administrative and constitutional systems, were not, in fact, well understood (87). They made the case that since civil services exhibit configurations, properties, perform functions, and reflect doctrines that vary over time and space, they deserve to be studied systemically.

In the spirit of the stock-taking and innovative goals of this volume, the following discussion presents a characterization of the range of civil service systems in developing countries. The exercise entails conceptualizing the context as well as selected properties of civil service systems in a search for empirical illumination of relationships between politics, administration, and civil society.

Notwithstanding the great variety among countries one might identify as "developing," there are certain dynamics that are common to many and are defined by the exigencies of economic restructuring and popular demand for institutional reform. The particular configuration of causes, attendant adjustments, and reforms differs, of course, from country to country. But in most cases, whether we speak of the liberalizing socialist countries of Central Asia, of states in Central America undergoing reconstruction following civil war, or of recovering poor countries in the African Sahel, the civil service system is both the subject and the object of change.

The institutional reforms are of two types: (a) those relating to the constitutional order, and (b) those focused on improvement of performance. One has its antecedents in the history of and ideas about governance (the state, government, public law, citizenship and other social rules), the other in experience and ideas about organization and management.

The desire for reforms relating to a revision of the rules of governance expresses itself in the popular demand for democracy, openness, and accountability in countries across the globe. The focus is on the rules of the political process and the role of the state in civic life. Who has the right, that is, the authority, to exercise power over whom, and according to what rules? The institutions that represent the answer to that question are enshrined in basic laws (constitutions or covenants), statutes, political conventions, rituals and symbols—what Riggs (1991) has called the "constitutive system."

The reforms associated with improving economic performance have to do with reducing the role of the state in the economy to that of facilitator, getting the budget under control, and inducing professional commitment from civil servants. "Reform" is often used to refer to reduction of the public sector wage bill, and by extension, to the size of the civil service establishment. Of course, cutbacks alone are not reforms. But if they are accompanied by revision of pay and employment conditions and a rationalization of administrative arrangements that improves organizational performance, cutbacks can be regarded as part of a reform strategy (World Bank, 1991: 7). Cutback, coordination, and productivity measures can be reformist to the extent that they are systemic, or that they establish incentives for efficiency and results where these have either never existed or where they have been displaced by other values (e.g., the private appropriation of public resources).

By defining the context for a comparison of civil service systems in terms of these two classes of institutional reforms, we evoke parallel streams of theory pertinent to understanding systems in transition: the body of political ideas informing the constitutive system on the one hand, and theories of administration, management, and organization on the other. The existence of parallel theoretical traditions also poses the question of whether and how they intersect. The answer lies in the character of civil society, which is the corpus of social arrangements defining state/society relations and public/private domains of relative autonomy. Understanding how civil society mediates the interplay between the normative and positivist principles in a civil service system will tell us much about the properties, functions, and performance of *classes* of civil service systems.

In the west, the end of absolute rule in the eighteenth century was signaled by a separation of public and private spheres; royal prerogative no longer included a claim on the fruits of individual labor (Woods, 1993: 79; Raadschelders and Rutgers, chap. 4 of this volume). Moreover, as the nineteenth century evolved, civil society became differentiated as an effect of markets. Liberalism, both political and economic, became the general organizing principle. (For our purposes, the notion of more or less "dominant organizing principles" will serve as shorthand for civil society.)

Such are the antecedents of the organizing principle that mediates the two bodies of theory informing public administration in the west. To be sure, the evolution of civil society in France and the United States has been different, with the legacy of the state in France remaining more robust than that of the market. In Kaufman's terms (1956), the core values of hierarchy and meritocracy in France have remained more salient than those of representation. It also goes without saying that history is dynamic, the tension between politics and administration representing a continuous feature of public affairs (Rosenbloom, 1993). Nonetheless, the modalities of public and private, the state and the individual are institutionalized in both countries within a limited range of variation.

Efficiency comes out of this tradition, too. The early dominant value of representativeness (participation) in the United States was balanced over time by the need for results (neutral competence or meritocracy as embodied in the civil service, and some concentration of both authority *and* responsibility, also known as executive leadership or hierarchy; Kaufman, 1956). Regarding the legacy of the market organizing principle, the efficiency imperative in administrative practice derived from the constraint of scarce resources. Organization and management arrangements are instrumental in securing value-for-money. This distinction between the normative context of governance and the positivist roots of management, mediated by variously dominant and changing organizing principles, provides the groundwork for understanding civil service systems in other places and cultures.

## CHARACTERIZING CIVIL SERVICES IN THE DEVELOPING WORLD

In order to identify and characterize the variation in institutional configuration, rules, and functions obtaining in the civil service systems of developing countries, we must simplify in various ways. First, we shall identify as developing countries those which emerged from colonial hegemony after the mid-nineteenth century, including the newly independent republics of the former USSR. Within this group we shall stipulate a primary interest in those that are pre-industrial and face acute scarcities of both resources and organizational capacity. With the exception of never-colonized Ethiopia and Thailand, all such countries adopted a formal apparatus of governance modeled after the former colonial power, whether the United Kingdom, France, Spain, Portugal, Japan, or the USSR (to name only the major imperial powers). This legacy of governance included a centralized, if truncated, civil service and the accompanying legal codes: civil, administrative, and criminal. These structures have become attenuated in many developing countries over time. Today the civil service in much of the pre-industrial group is an arena of ambiguity and confusion. More often than not, indigenous social arrangements divert public resources to parochial ends, in keeping with a residuum of Weberian principles of legal rationality (Adamolekun, 1993).

By looking at developing countries' civil service systems comparatively, we remind ourselves that the civil service is both an arena and an instrument in the simultaneous pursuit of a range of values. Efficiency is only one of these, and it seldom ranks high. In countries where patron-client relations dominate and a clearly separate public sphere does not exist, we can say that civil society has yet to evolve some organizing principle that mediates the normative and the positivist. In such a situation, what is going on (process) may be more important to the actors (and to our understanding) than what happens (outcomes), a prospect of enormous empirical importance to those contemplating "reform" (March and Olson, 1983). The most ardent positivist reformer cannot substitute hard budget constraints for a political formula. In a patronage society, rules of financial and administrative management are subordinated to a social system based on obligation and exchange.

## The Integral State

After independence, many countries expanded considerably the role of the state as a guide to and centerpiece of a national development strategy, arrogating to the state a monopoly on resource allocation in the interests of national integration and economic development. This "integral" or hegemonic state, whether civilian or military, created a civil service that was supposed to behave as a secular, rational policy instrument in the delivery of "development" through government agencies or state-owned enterprises.

A few countries, for example, Taiwan and South Korea, have managed to create an effective integral state, delivering high economic performance in exchange for compliance. To be sure, compliance resulted from a shared sense of vulnerability to military invasion in both cases. But the governments of both countries also invested heavily in both agricultural and industrial production, as well as in human resource development. An elite civil service has been fundamental to their success. The Korean civil service, like that of Japan, is small. It exalts technical competence and recruits only from top universities and is, accordingly, very hierarchical.

Forty years after the war, prosperity has enabled the Korean public to think about freedom and participation. The middle class has come to interpret the seamless relationship of privilege between the governing elites and the business elites of the megacorporations as a possible threat to that prosperity. The middle class, no longer just university students, criticize what they see as restricted access to resources, particularly credit for smaller firms and entrepreneurs who are not tied into the *chabol* network. The elite civil service is under attack as an instrument of the establishment and is the target of popular demands for reform (Chung and Jun, 1991). These calls for reform include a greater role in policymaking for representative institutions and less autonomy for the Economic Planning Board, for example, and for the executive in general. Civil society in both Taiwan and Korea has evolved to the point where the organizing principles of political and economic liberalism are about to be substituted for those of executive leadership and security.

## The Patrimonial State

In most other developing countries the integral state has been less successful.

Internal centrifugal forces of social pluralism, combined with an absence of the strategic advantages of Korea and Taiwan, has resulted in attempts to retain a monopoly on power and resources through a system of patronage (Young, 1991). Patrimonialism as a system of rule includes:

> appropriation of public offices as the elite's prime source of status, prestige, and reward; political and territorial fragmentation through the development of relationships based on primordial and personal loyalties; and the use of private armies, militias, and mercenaries as chief instruments of rule. (Willame, 1972: 2)

In Africa, patrimonialism has been manifest principally in clientage based on clan, ethnic, or religious criteria. It is combined with support for a "strong central government on the implicit grounds that this was needed to ensure control over the economy in order to ensure an equitable share for everyone" (Dia, 1993: 12).

The civil service in patrimonial states is not as concerned with actions or outcomes as with servicing patronage networks. Public servants are caught between the instrumental values of their education and professional training on the one hand, and the traditional imperatives of social obligation on the other. Delivering the public goods and services that a position calls for is in competition with, or is displaced by, intra- and interorganizational social and political relationships.

Sometimes the political aspects of these relationships are quite subtle; "tradition" itself becomes a term of expediency. The exploitation of public resources for private purposes might be cloaked in traditional or religious legitimacy, for example, in the historical entitlement of local elites to resources in exchange for stewardship as protectors of the community. In other cases, religious leaders become political brokers; Muslim clerics in Senegal, for example, stand between the government, the market, and the rural peanut farmers on whose produce so much depends. They have enormous influence over the implementation of any pricing policies directed at groundnut production (Boone, 1988).

## The Custodial State

In still another generic configuration the civil service endures as the principal institutionalized agent of the state in an otherwise turbulent political environment. This is common in situations where the political culture of the higher civil service derives from an absolutist past, but because of endemic instability, whether military or civilian, takes on a custodial character: "We are (responsible for) the state." This is the case, for example, in France and Turkey. This is also frequently characteristic of military regimes in Latin America in which the civil service remains civilian and acts as the principal mediating or brokering agent between the junta and corporate groups such as unions and the church.

The above patterns of linkage between the civil service and the state or regime provide a general framework for comparison, but they do not suffice for differentiating between and among civil service systems themselves. We need further conceptual disaggregation of properties of civil services and contexts if we are to capture the dynamics of a normative order, positivist principles of management, and dominant organizing principles as a set of theoretical categories.

## TOWARD A FRAMEWORK OF CIVIL SERVICE SYSTEMS

Given the great complexity and variation in our empirical field, we need a heuristic device in order to isolate potentially interesting relationships. We shall stipulate several parameters and their relationships as a way of ordering the universe, illustrating them impressionistically. The framework is generally relevant to all countries, but commentary will focus primarily on developing countries.

One parameter important to understanding the civil service system in any given country, and one in which there will be considerable variation, is the *level of institutionalization of the nation-state*. Institutionalization must be validated by its empirical cohesiveness and shared commitment to basic procedures and practices (not simply by international juridical standing). Values range between the highly institutionalized state, for example, France and Brazil, and an inchoate state, for example, Zaire and Afghanistan. An inchoate state is one in which a territory might enjoy international juridical standing but is otherwise without broad-based citizen identification or commitment to the state as an entity or to institutional proxies such as deliberative or judicial bodies. This suggests another dimension: an affective scale of *aggregated public attitudes toward the state*, where symbols of authority evoke positive or negative responses. The term pro-state here refers to beliefs in the legitimacy of state competence. Its obverse is the preference for strict limits on the domain of government action. In table 11.1 we represent these two parameters as continua, plotting a few countries in the appropriate quadrants to illustrate the point.

The attitude dimension, taken as is, would measure only the most ad hominem reactions to symbols of the state. However, measures could be designed to illuminate citizen expectations of, and/or satisfaction with, state performance regarding the economy or political freedom. In addition, by differentiating between the state, government, and bureaucracy, and by developing measures that discriminate among these in eliciting respondent opinion, one can capture more empirical subtlety as to the perceptions of the civil service and its relationship to other institutions.

TABLE 11.1

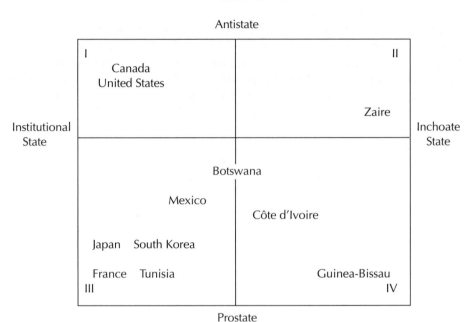

Antistate

| I | | II |

Canada
United States

Zaire

Institutional
State

Inchoate
State

Botswana

Mexico

Côte d'Ivoire

Japan    South Korea

France    Tunisia                          Guinea-Bissau
III                                                    IV

Prostate

Revisiting the continuum describing the level of institutionalization of the state, we could achieve more theoretical power by further differentiating what is meant by "inchoate." Inchoate refers to a state or condition of incoherence, of a lack of definition or clarity. It can be associated with endemic instability, or with scattered pastoral populations, or with repressed historical antagonisms. The nature of the barriers to institutionalization of a state consciousness and identity would affect what measures a regime might take to overcome them. For example, fragmentation due to ethnic pluralism might put a premium on representativeness in political and administrative institutional design; but experience has shown that this has to be balanced with hierarchy and administrative capacity if genuine institutional development is to occur.

Moving to parameters more directly characterizing the civil service system, there are many countries in which there is tension between process (what is going on) and outcomes (what happens), between concerns with symbols, rules, and rituals of various kinds and the need for results. If we view this tension as a continuum, we would locate the U.S. closer to the process pole, for instance, and France closer to the outcomes pole. Americans are perceived by Europeans as obsessed by process as an instrument of limited government, prone to define goals simplistically in terms of procedures (elections). Most African countries would be even closer to the process end of the continuum than the United States, while South Korea and Japan would be closer to the French in keeping with their disposition toward performance.

Adding another property common to civil service systems, that of *degree of professionalism* and its obverse, *degree of politicization* or responsiveness to the powerful as distinct from the public, we confront the tension between values of competence and selective representation. The neutral competence of a South Korean civil service embodies the value of meritocracy. The personal interference of the powerful in the allocation of benefits so common in Africa is exceeded only by the excesses of party intervention into public administration by various regimes pursuing radical idealism, whether socialist (Peoples' Republic of China) or fascist (the Third Reich). "Responsiveness," to be sure, can be a laudable relationship between a capable civil service and a legitimate government; but more often it characterizes situations such as those identified above.

TABLE 11.2

Value of Process

| | Profession-alism | | | | Political Respon-siveness |
|---|---|---|---|---|---|
| | I<br><br>United States | | II<br><br>Nigeria | | |
| | Hong Kong<br><br>France<br>III | | China (1949–66)<br><br>IV | | |

Value of Outcomes

Using France and Japan as the prototype professional civil service systems, for example, we would locate them in quadrant III indicating high results orientation and high professionalism, as with two of their "legacies": South Korea and Tunisia. The U.S. civil service would be located in quadrant I further toward the political responsiveness pole, and further toward process or symbolic action. Many African countries would be plotted even further up in quadrant II, a field defined by the process and politicization scales.

If we superimpose the two matrices on one another as in table 11.3, we begin to generate some hypotheses about comparative civil service systems (CSSs) merely by plotting locations on a continuum:

Those countries with strong state traditions have more results-oriented, professional CSSs.
Countries with more antistate or unformed state identities have CSSs more preoccupied with processes.
The more inchoate the nation-state, the more likely aggregated opinion will be antistate.
The more inchoate the nation-state, the more likely the CSS will be politicized.
The more patrimonial the state, the more likely aggregated opinion will be antistate.
The more patrimonial the state, the more likely the CSS will be politicized.
The more patrimonial the state, the more likely the CSS will be preoccupied with process at the expense of results.

TABLE 11.3

|  | Antistate | Process |  |
|---|---|---|---|
| I | | | II |
| | PRAGMATIC | PATRIMONIAL | |
| Profession-alism | | | Political Responsiveness |
| | | V | |
| Institutional State | | | Inchoate State |
| | POSITIVIST | ABSOLUTIST | |
| III | | | IV |
| | Prostate | Outcomes | |

Testing these general propositions would shed some light on the dynamics of civil service systems in different macro-institutional environments. We might achieve even richer empirical patterns if we were to answer questions with respect to the modal systems in each of the four fields:

1. What is the modal mix of constitutive (normative)-administrative (positivist) principles in each field?
2. Is there a dominant or modal organizing principle in each field?
3. What are the salient features, functions, and performance elements of the modal civil service system in each field?
4. Is the range of variation in each field more important than the mode?

### Quadrant I—the Pragmatic Field

The modalities of the field designated by quadrant I include the practical fact that the state is a valued entity, an institution, combined with a general skepticism about state power and activist government. Procedures and rituals reflect the primacy of participation or process over outcomes. Similarly, the hierarchy one associates with strong executive leadership is unstable given the preoccupation with process, giving way to pressures for participation and distribution. The salient organizing principles are those of economic and political liberalism.

A career in the civil service is not held in high esteem by the public or business elites. At the same time, positivist values do extend to the expectation that the civil service will be competent, if limited in jurisdiction. Recruitment is by and large based on merit, and compensation and promotion are subjects of frequent review for consistency and fairness. Public and private spheres of activity are distinct, but there is a domain of overlap which varies with the business cycle as well as the party in power at any given time. The civil service is a very small percentage of total employment in keeping with skepticism about state power and monopoly on resources.

The United States and Canada occupy the pragmatic field. Although there are currently no developing country cases, we will address those prospects below.

### Quadrant II—the Patrimonial Field

The field designated patrimonial is characterized by patron-client relations in the allocation of resources and opportunities. Social and symbolic actions dominate the official arena where, for all practical purposes, there is no distinction between public and private domains. There is rarely any genuine executive leadership, only elite power. Accordingly, modal public attitudes toward the state are matter-of-fact since official positions are seen as opportunities for accumulating wealth and power rather than for achieving a larger public purpose. There is a pragmatic resignation to the reality that access to resources requires bargaining through this fragmented clientage system. This fact also constitutes the modal organizing principle in patrimonial systems.

Recruitment of general cadres to the civil service takes place via these same social networks. The higher civil service will recruit from the universities and professional institutes, but mobility within the service will be circumscribed by the extent to which officers hold to principles of neutral competence as opposed to yielding to the interests of sponsors or patrons. The culture of high patrimonialism leaves the dedicated professional in an isolated, even vulnerable, position. This corrupts the career concept of public service, of course, but both cadres and higher civil servants have few options to do better elsewhere in the economy, despite the eroding purchasing power of their wages, because public employment is such a high percentage of total wage employment. Budget estimates become fantasies, expenditure constraints are feeble, especially in a world of multidonor financing. However, in the changing environment with which we began, the requirements of economic adjustment have begun to limit some of these excesses.

Countries occupying this field include Afghanistan, the Gulf States, Zaire, and others in sub-Saharan Africa.

### Quadrant III—the Positivist Field

The positivist field includes the successful integral states, those which have established traditions of strong state identities and accomplishment. They have strong executive leadership and an elite technocratic civil service. Representative institutions exist, but outcomes are not sacrificed to process. Public and private spheres are distinct, but the domain of overlap is much larger in the positivist field than that in the pragmatic field. The scope of state involvement in the economy is wide. Strategic industries are the subject of state ownership or joint ventures or of official financing. The modal organizing principle in the positivist field is that of guided liberalism, where the guidance is more or less *dirigiste* (directive), depending on the country.

The modal civil service in the positivist field is small, technically competent, and enjoys high prestige. Recruitment is from a narrow band of elite universities or institutes, and promotion is largely merit based. Compensation is also highly rationalized, but it tends to include a large component of nonwage allowances and benefits (in comparison to the pragmatic system). The culture of the civil service reinforces the privilege and obligation to give one's best to the state, an esprit which is important in countries where governments rise and fall rather frequently. The higher civil service is the custodian of the state, regardless of what happens in politics or economics.

Cases include South Korea, Tunisia, Turkey, Singapore, and Mexico, among others.

### Quadrant IV—the Absolutist Field

The absolutist field is so labeled because executive leadership dominates other values, such as representation, and tends to be authoritarian. The historical version of absolutism is a monarchy like that of Louis XIV in France, with a distinct modernizing agenda. This has its contemporary parallels in Morocco and perhaps Jordan, systems with a mix of positivist norms for the civil service, but with power still subject to patronage. Such cases would cluster near the patrimonial border of the absolutist field.

In the twentieth century, however, absolutism tends to repose in radical leaders or parties, who arrogate to themselves the broadest scope of action. Although it takes a positivist view of the state and uses authoritarian means to achieve results, executive action is often uncertain and erratic in terms of policy direction because the state itself is weak or inchoate. The absolutist field is characterized by regimes attempting to legitimize themselves through accomplishments at the same time they are using measures which defer or undermine public confidence. There is no modal organizing principle in the absolutist field, since fragmentation and a political vacuum are precisely what authoritarian measures are meant to rectify.

The civil service in the absolutist field is a direct instrument of executive leadership. It does not purport to be neutral; rather, recruitment, promotion, and reward are tied to perceptions of loyalty and commitment to the persons or policies of the government or party. Precisely because of the weakness of the state, the civil service is left guessing what "the line" actually is as an uncertain leadership often changes course without notice in an attempt to direct development or mandate the achievement of a new goal. The notion of career is more a matter of astute alliances and chance than competence.

Examples of this type include Toure's Guinea (1958–84), the People's Republic of China (1949–66), contemporary North Korea, and Guinea-Bissau.

### Variation within versus across Fields

It has become clear by now that variation within fields is great. Marginal cases in each of the four fields tend to cluster toward the middle of the respective continua, suggesting they could be in one of several fields (V). Sorting that out would require specific empirical investigation. Perhaps those cases represent a separate field. For our purposes, however, it is enough to explore the significance of the global differences between fields.

### FIELDS OF CHANGE: FROM STATICS TO DYNAMICS

Although this heuristic exploration has been an exercise in statics, we did begin by saying we wanted to see what we might learn by comparing civil service systems in developing countries that are facing similar imperatives to change: financial crisis and popular demands for political reforms. We observed earlier that while going through a difficult period of adjustment

South Korea was poised to adopt liberal organizing principles over the next few years, thus moving from the positivist field toward the pragmatic. One might make a similar argument for Taiwan. In both cases the balance of core values informing the civil service system is changing from the primacy of executive leadership supported by a competent administrative hierarchy to a formula elevating the value of representativeness, or participation. If the relationship between leadership and public participation really changes, as the last election suggests, how will the civil service adjust? As Heady observes (in chap. 10 of this volume), a pragmatic subordination of administrative behavior is not the only response; bureaucratic authoritarianism justified by the higher civil servant's view of state interests is another.

The People's Republic of China might be moving from the absolutist to the positivist field. Although economic liberalism is not being combined with political liberalism in equal proportions, the requirements of the positive state promoting liberal economic development requires that the civil service become sophisticated in matters of foreign exchange, central banking, and trade. This need for professional competence could gradually push out the purely political functionaries. Both Spain and Portugal have made the transition from absolutism to positivism in the past twenty years with salutary adjustments by the public services to facilitate economic liberalization.

There are also numerous cases of movement from the patrimonial field to either the positivist or pragmatic. There are a cluster of countries in French-speaking West Africa which have experienced popularly mandated "national conferences" in which basic political reform was the agenda. Popular congresses in countries such as Benin, Congo, Mali, and Togo had in common the aspiration to agree on a new set of rules that would result in more open, accountable government. In a few cases, early results suggest the effort was successful in that military leaders stood down and permitted new, representative political leaders to take over. Whether movement of these cases is into the positivist or pragmatic fields will be determined in large measure by the civil service system. They say they welcome openness and accountability and want to be free of patrimonial bondage, but they also come from the doubly reenforcing traditions of patronage networks *and* the French tradition of centralized, elite civil services. Nonetheless, change is coming.

We could go on with anecdotal illustrations. But it is quite possible that we are seeing some real convergence from both patrimonial and absolutist types to points somewhere along a continuum between the pragmatic and the positivist. Where any given country will be on that continuum will have more to do with pluralism at home (both social and political), which affects the representation value, and the perceived quality of executive leadership, in setting a program of action. In either case the civil service system will mediate between the two to deliver that program.

## CONCLUSION

Is there a sequence to such institutional developments? Do the above propositions, if they were to test out empirically, mean that one class of institutional questions (e.g., the constitutive system) must be resolved before the other can be (administrative system)? Is the message that western democracies resolved their differences over sources of authority and crafted a constitutive system which then allowed them to turn to concerns with efficiency? Does it mean that since many developing countries have yet to settle on a normative order, attempts to install the values of efficiency and rationality, to build a civil service on the foundations of management (when that of law does not yet exist), are premature?

It was, after all, Leonard D. White's famous dictum in the 1920s that signaled at least the coequal standing of management and public law in the U.S. civil service system: "the study of administration should start from the base of management rather than the foundation of law" (White, 1955). When confronted with the inchoateness of "soft" states and the patrimonial or absolutist behavior of developing country government officials, one must ask if White was wrong.

The answer, of course, is contingent. History suggests that such matters did not get addressed and resolved sequentially (see the discussion by Raadschelders and Rutgers in chap. 4 of this volume). Louis XIV, the prince of the age of absolutism, created a cadre of fiscal officers (further developed and institutionalized by Napoleon) long before there were any durable representative institutions in France (Barker, 1966). Similarly, in the Japanese and Ottoman imperial courts and empires, the rules were made at the center of the imperium while a small, efficient administrative machine carried them out. Far from resolving the constitutive questions before administrative efficiency was achieved, the civil service system has been the one enduring state institution amidst multiple crises and frequently changing constitutive systems in France and Turkey (Heper, 1985: 106). Finally, the implications of our own exercise reinforce the contingent character of such institutional changes—there is no sequence.

What we can say, conceptually at least, is that the set of values and institutions that inform and shape a civil service system appear to come in a finite set of patterns. What we must still find out is the extent to which that is true empirically, and whether these patterns contain other clues to the direction of change.

*The author is grateful for the comments of many colleagues, in particular those of Ladipo Adamolekun, J. W. Bjorkman, Maria Chan Morgan, James L. Perry, and Richard Stillman II.*

## REFERENCES

Aberbach, J. D., and B. A. Rockman. 1988. "Mandates or Mandarins? Control and Discretion in the Modern Administrative State." *Public Administration Review* 48: 606–12.

Adamolekun, L. 1993. "A Note on Civil Service Personnel Policy Reform in sub-Saharan Africa." *International Journal of Public Management* 6: 38–46.

Balogun, M. J., and G. Mutahaba, eds. 1989. *Economic Restructuring and African Public Administration.* West Hartford, CT: Kumarian Press.

Barker, E. 1966. *The Development of Public Services in Western Europe: 1660–1930.* Hamden, CT: Archon Books.

Bates, Robert H. 1988. "Lessons from History, or the Perfidy of English Exceptionalism and the Significance of Historical France." *World Politics* 40: 499–516.

Bebler, A., and J. Seroka, eds. 1990. *Contemporary Political Systems: Classifications and Typologies.* Boulder, CO: Lynne Rienner.

Boone, Catherine. 1988. "State Power and Private Interests: Politics, Markets and Economic Crisis in Senegal." Paper presented at the American Political Science Association, September.

Caiden, G. E. 1991. *Administrative Reform Comes of Age.* Hawthorne, NY: Walter de Gruyter.

Chow, K. W. 1991. "Reform of the Chinese Cadre System: Pitfalls, Issues and Implications of the Proposed Civil Service System." *International Review of Administrative Sciences* 57: 25–44.

Chung, C. K., and J. S. Jun. 1991. "The Irony of Cutback Reform: the Korean Experience During a Period of Turbulent Transition." *International Review of Administrative Sciences* 57: 45–57.

De Merode, L. 1991. "Civil Service Pay and Employment Reform in Africa: Selected Implementation Experiences." Washington, DC: World Bank.

Dia, Mamadou. 1993. "A Governance Approach to Civil Service Reform in sub-Saharan Africa." Technical Paper no. 225. Washington, DC: World Bank.

Farazmand, Ali, ed. 1991. *Handbook of Comparative and Development Public Administration.* New York: Marcel Dekker.

Heady, Ferrel. 1991. *Public Administration: A Comparative Perspective.* 4th ed. New York: Marcel Dekker.

Heper, Metin. 1985. "The State and Public Bureaucracies: A Comparative and Historical Perspective." *Comparative Studies in Society and History* 27: 86–110.

Kaufman, Herbert. 1956. "Emerging Conflicts in the Doctrines of Public Administration." *American Political Science Review* 50: 1057–73.

March, James G., and Johan P. Olsen. 1983. "Organizing Political Life: What Administrative Reorganization Tells Us about Governing." *American Political Science Review* 77: 281–96.

Montgomery, John D. 1989. "Comparative Administration: Theory and Experience." *International Journal of Public Administration* 12: 501–12.

Morgan, E. Philip, and James L. Perry. 1988. "Re-orienting the Comparative Study of Civil Service Systems." *Review of Public Personnel Administration* 8: 84–95.

Nunberg, Barbara, and John Nellis. 1990. "Civil Service Reform and the World Bank." Working Paper no. 422. Washington, DC: World Bank.

Peters, B. Guy. 1989. *Comparing Public Bureaucracies: Problems of Theory and Method.* Tuscaloosa: University of Alabama Press.

Perry, James L., and S. Y. Tang. 1987. "Applying Research on Administrative Reform to Hong Kong's 1997 Transition." *Asian Journal of Public Administration* 9: 113–31.

Riggs, Fred W. 1991. "A Neoinstitutional Typology of Third World Politics." In *Contemporary Political Systems: Classifications and Typologies,* ed. A. Bebler and J. Seroka. Boulder, CO: Lynne Rienner.

Rosenbloom, David H. 1993. "Have an Administrative RX? Don't Forget the Politics!" *Public Administration Review* 53: 503–507.

Sangmpam, S. N. 1993. "Neither Soft nor Dead: The African State Is Alive and Well." *African Studies Review* 36: 73–94.

Subramaniam, V., ed. 1990. *Public Administration in the Third World: An International Handbook.* Westport, CT: Greenwood Press.

White, Leonard D. 1955. *Introduction to the Study of Public Administration.* 4th ed. New York: Macmillan.

Willame, Jean-Claude. 1972. *Patrimonialism and Political Change in the Congo.* Stanford, CA: Stanford University Press.

Woods, Dwayne. 1993. "Civil Society in Europe and Africa: Limiting State Power through a Public Sphere." *African Studies Review* 35: 77–100.

World Bank. 1991. "The Reform of Public Sector Management: Lessons of Experience." Unpublished draft, Country Economics Department, Public Sector Management and Private Sector Development Division, Washington, DC.

Young, Crawford. 1991. "State Decline and Democratic Rebirth." Paper presented at a symposium in honor of J. Gus Liebenow. Bloomington, IN.

# PART FIVE
# CHANGE &
# TRANSFORMATION

National civil service systems have endured a series of shocks in recent years in countries as diverse as the United States, the United Kingdom, Australia, Guinea, and Chile. The origins of these shocks have been both internal and external. In some countries they have been delivered by the electorate through democratic elections, in others by international financial agents. In yet others the sources of stress have involved changes in working methods and administrative technology. Part 5 explores the nature of the upheavals that have affected civil service systems in the last decade, the ecology of these upheavals, and the direction of future developments. The three contributions complement one another in providing insight into three highly interrelated aspects of reform: its content, determinants, and diffusion.

In chapter 12, Patricia W. Ingraham focuses on three questions about civil service reform: Who or what is it that initiates reform and why? What reforms are presently on national agendas? and Are the reforms likely to succeed? She argues that most reforms represent one of two traditions: the governance tradition that devotes attention to civil service as a mechanism for effective governability and political legitimacy, and the management tradition in which civil service is judged mainly in terms of efficiency and economic rationality. The stronger tradition is the management tradition. But there are also efforts to improve relational problems between civil service and government and to strengthen the responsiveness of the civil servant to political officials.

Like Ingraham, Christopher Hood is interested in understanding the content of reforms. He focuses on "new public management" (NPW), a group of administrative doctrines that were influential in reforms in Organization for Economic Cooperation and Development (OECD) countries. He abstracts seven dimensions along which these reforms vary, including degree of control by output measures, level of disaggregation of public organizations into self-contained units, and amount of competition across units. Many of the generic changes he identifies directly influence civil service rules through changes to pay systems, level of control by central civil service units, and level of competition for services such as training.

Hood investigates not only the dimensions of NPM but the determinants of change. His aim is to suggest a possible agenda for systematic comparison and to show that some of the common explanations of the rise of NPM are hard to sustain even from a relatively brief inspection of the cross-national data that are available. Hood suggests several changes that future research must also incorporate, among them better measures of the independent and dependent variables and multidimensional analysis of causal explanations.

John Halligan's analysis in chapter 14 complements the Ingraham and Hood chapters by addressing the question of how the content of reforms may be influenced by the diffusion of ideas across national boundaries. He looks at the diffusion of reforms from two different perspectives. One focuses on how diffusion among countries influenced the reform program in a single national system, specifically, how Australia borrowed from other countries in assembling its comprehensive civil service reform package in the 1980s. The other dissects a specific reform, the Senior Executive Service, as it diffuses among several national systems. The look at diffusion from two perspectives increases the power of Halligan's analysis and permits him to draw useful generalizations.

# 12 THE REFORM AGENDA FOR NATIONAL CIVIL SERVICE SYSTEMS: EXTERNAL STRESS AND INTERNAL STRAINS

Patricia W. Ingraham

As we approach the end of the twentieth century, there is no region in the world whose nations express satisfaction with public bureaucracies and civil service systems. The turbulence in eastern Europe, in Africa, and in Latin America creates a heightened awareness of political and institutional change. The consistent efforts of industrial democracies to reform government throughout the 1970s and 1980s is additional testimony to a generalized sense that something is "not right" with government and public institutions.

A wide variety of economic, political, and social conditions have created the environment for civil service reform efforts. Some of the conditions are long-term; the need to perform "major surgery" or administrative institutions inherited from the colonial period is a consistent impetus for reform throughout Africa, for example (Mutahaba, 1989). Some influences are economic; there is no question that declining budgets and cutback management have altered the face of many national governments. Other influences and events were unanticipated and sudden, indeed stunning. Eastern Europe faces enormous new challenges as its nations attempt to fashion institutions capable of implementing necessary social and economic changes.

In other nations and regions of the world, pressures for reform emerged from the political process—the United States, Great Britain, New Zealand, and the Netherlands fell into this category in the 1980s. As Peters (1988) and others note, "conviction politics" created a new prism through which to view government and its many activities. Ronald Reagan provided an apt slogan for the new view when he proclaimed that "Government is not the solution to the problem; government *is* the problem."

Despite the disparity in national contexts and influences on reform, there is remarkable commonality of policy ideas that influence reform content. Privatization, for example, has profoundly different meanings and implications for the United States, Angola, and Poland; privatization reforms are, however, underway in all three nations. Decentralization, devolution, and deconcentration are nearly universally present. So too are more "technical fixes," such as performance appraisal and pay for performance. This commonality has been attributed to more constrained opportunities for innovation (Hogwood and Peters, 1983), more constrained policy space (Grindle and Thomas, 1991), more complex policy problems, and simple policy diffusion (Ingraham and Peters, 1988). Whatever the cause, it is significant both that the range of policy options appears to be limited and that a similar set of options is assumed to work in a variety of national contexts and public institutions.

It is not the purpose of this chapter to assess the potential for success of the many civil service reform efforts now underway, or of national agendas for future action. Rather, the aim of this analysis is more simple—to identify the major problems that reforms address, to specify the reforms most often chosen to solve the problems of public bureaucratic institutions and civil service systems, and, when possible, to identify the theoretical foundations of the reform design and effort.

The chapter asks three sets of questions: 1) What is it about civil service systems that is perceived to be problematic? Who or what is it that initiates or demands reform and why? 2) What major civil service reform initiatives are currently or are likely to be on national agendas? and 3) Do the reforms "fit" with what we currently know about civil service systems and their fundamental capabilities? In other words, are reforms likely to succeed? In whose terms is success likely to be defined?

## WHAT IS PROBLEMATIC ABOUT CIVIL SERVICE SYSTEMS?

### Background

Aberbach and Rockman (1988: 423) argue that the "three analytic building blocks of comparative administration are structures (organizations), actors (executives and various species of bureaucratic officialdom) and actions." The previous chapters in this book describe both the significance and the remarkable difficulties of comparing and measuring those building blocks. Civil service systems—the laws, regulations, underlying values and norms about the role of public bureaucracy in government, and the management and problem-solving environment created—are an integral yet oddly elusive influence on each of the blocks. Civil service systems determine the composition, the character, the quality, and the effectiveness of the public service. They are fundamental to the nature of public organizations, but they are not synonymous with them. To fully understand reform in civil service systems, therefore, the systems themselves must be separated from the organizations, actors, and actions that they shape.

Further, analysis of civil service systems and of reforms must extend beyond the narrow technical terms of personnel management. Technical reforms, while often a part of the total reform agenda, mask or do not describe political, economic, and social objectives and components of civil service systems. As Raadschelders and Rutgers describe in chapter 4, multiple and often conflicting objectives are present in most systems. Some of those objectives relate to governance; some relate to personnel management and efficiency; while still others relate to financial or political accountability.

In 1989, for example, the member nations of the OECD agreed to pursue national politics designed to "establish sound public budgetary positions and promote efficient public management" (OECD, 1989: 10). It was noted that this resolution recognized for the first time the link "between public sector performance and the overall performance of the national economy," and that "Structural adjustments must, therefore, include reform of the public management system among their targets" (OECD, 1989: 10).

The juxtaposition and intermingling of managerial and larger social, economic, and political objectives reflects two different and generally distinct theoretical traditions. The governance tradition is described in chapters 5 and 9 of this volume: the civil service is a creature of the state and its political institutions. In many ways, however, it also shapes them. As a result, it is fundamental to the development and strength of those government institutions that provide the link between government and the governed (in whatever fashion). Heady notes (chap. 10 of this volume, for example, that

> In any existing national policy, the civil service system operates in a context that is affected significantly by the character of the political regime. . . . The key question that needs to be addressed is that concerning the responsiveness of the civil service system to the political elite exercising effective power in the existing political regime. A secondary question is how long this type of responsiveness has been present, and what the prospects are for it to continue.

The other reform tradition is more accurately reflected in Hood's discussion of the new public management: civil service systems are about efficiency and effective management, often more closely related to private sector management objectives and practices than broader governmental purpose. While the theoretical foundation of the latter—frequently summarized by the term "managerialism"—is much less rich than that surrounding the role of public bureaucracy in governance, there is a substantial literature describing both the foundations of the tradition and the set of reforms emerging from its assumptions about civil service systems (see Rainey, 1991: Appendix; Pollitt, 1990; Aucoin, 1990).

The significance of these different theoretical foundations is profound for civil service systems and civil service reform. They cast the civil service in dramatically different roles in society; they create vastly different expectations for performance and measures of successful performance; not surprisingly, they shape both problem definition and proposed reform solutions in different, and essentially incompatible, ways.

The following section is an effort to identify the dimensions of civil service systems that have most frequently been identified as problematic. As even a brief description makes clear, the multidimensional nature of problem defini-tion—the external stress and internal strain of civil service systems—has mud-dled the potential for clear and effective solution.

## Why Is Reform on National Policy Agendas?

Particularly for the past twenty years, there has been extensive dissatisfaction with the performance of public bureaucratic organizations and the civil service systems that fuel them. That is true whether one speaks of the elite administra-tive cadre that defines the identity of the French civil service, the unrepresenta-tive and bloated Italian service, the failures of civil service systems in Africa and elsewhere to provide personnel necessary for nation building and economic development, or the genuine and long term dissatisfaction with government performance that preceded reforms in the United States, the United Kingdom, Australia, and New Zealand.

In a time when many politicians and citizens demand smaller, leaner, faster, more flexible, and more responsive public organizations, civil service systems have been targets of reform on many levels. Politics and economics have both played substantial roles in bringing reform to the agenda. At least from the time of the oil shocks in the 1970s, most of the nations of the world have operated in economic circumstances different from those of the previous two or three decades. While the demand for government services continued to be high, the ability to pay for them was reduced.

In addition, widespread citizen dissatisfaction with government and its insti-tutions created new performance and accountability pressures. Peters (1988: 72) summarizes: "The comfortable world of government and public policy of the 1960s and 1970s has been transformed into a much more anxious and treacherous place." As Rainey observes in chapter 9, citizens transferred their frustrations about government in general onto public organizations and civil ser-vice systems, the most obvious manifestations of government activity.

In developing nations, the need for concrete and effective economic develop-ment, often in the face of overwhelming odds, has created an even more pro-found dissatisfaction. Dwivedi and Henderson (1990: 15) observe that

> The role of bureaucracy in national development cannot be overemphasized. . . . All development programs require considerable direct involvement and participation by the bureaucracy at all stages of their formulation and implemen-tation. . . . It will not be inappropriate to suggest that officials brought up in the colonial administrative culture and wedded to the Weberian model of bureaucracy are totally unfit for the responsibilities of development administration.

Similarly, the nations of eastern Europe find themselves encumbered by large and rigidly bureaucratic state institutions as they begin the effort to rebuild. For them, modernization necessarily implies debureaucratization and elimination of many outmoded and burdensome state organizations, even while building new ones (Siemienska, 1991).

In the mangerialist tradition, the OECD (1990: 9–10) attributes much of the current attention to reform to the newly recognized need to compete effectively in the international market:

> The need to cope with the rapid globalization of the economy and to maintain international competitiveness has added a powerful new incentive for undertaking public sector institutional reform. International issues are no longer the exclusive responsibility of organizations which have traditionally fulfilled this role. . . . All government ministries, even regional and local ones, must develop a capacity to follow, understand and deal with issues of international origin . . . which now penetrate all aspects of national society and economy. This has become an important consideration not only for members of the European Community in the context of 1992, but for those outside it as well.

Both constrained economic resources and the need to remain economically competitive to stave off further instability, then, play an important part in the current trend toward civil service reform. The perception that poor or ineffective management of government services and organizations contributes to economic problems is common. Political leaders have been quick to argue that reform is central to a more efficient, more productive government.

### Who or What Puts Reform on the Agenda?

Reform has been incorporated into policy agendas in a number of ways. Some western democracies—notably those in the Anglo-American tradition—have a fairly long history of formal reform commissions and studies and frequent diffusion of findings and recommendations. The Hoover Commissions and the Ash Council in the United States, the Fulton Commission in the United Kingdom, the Glassco, Lambert, and D'Avignon Commissions in Canada, and the Coombs Commission in Australia were all efforts to "objectively" gain political attention for government reform. This tradition is so strong in the United States that, for the past one hundred years, there has been a new reform commission approximately every seven years (Ingraham, 1992).

Strongly in the managerialist tradition, the United States, Canada, the United Kingdom, and Australia have often employed explicitly private sector analyses of civil service problems, such as the Grace Commission in the United States and the Rayner Scrutinies in the U.K. These analyses are significant for the extent to which they view public and private organizations as similar, as well as for their reliance on private sector techniques and practices for problem solution.

Elected officials have also criticized civil service systems for being insulated from political direction and for lacking accountability. Ronald Reagan and

Margaret Thatcher are the leading—and perhaps the most notorious—examples, but the issue is on the agenda for nearly every western nation. The tensions, both theoretical and practical, are particularly evident here. The underlying rationale for many reforms aimed at greater responsiveness is that stronger hierarchical controls are necessary. Rose (1988: 6) observed, for example, that "Mrs. Thatcher . . . increasingly acted on the assumption that the British government is a hierarchy, with herself at the top." Certainly the "Administrative Presidency" described by Nathan (1983) was, at heart, a classic hierarchy. Mascarenhas (1990: 89) notes that "reforms currently being implemented (in Australia and New Zealand) seem to encourage the subordination of higher civil servants."

The tension between the two theoretical reform traditions and their practical outcomes is perhaps most obvious here. While tighter political control is an objective in these and many more countries, many of the managerial reforms already adopted or on the agenda could have quite the opposite impact. That is, managerialism may, as Aucoin (1990), Peters (1991) and others have noted, advocate separating civil servants from policy so they may concentrate on management. At the same time, however, it recommends greater authority, flexibility, and discretion for individual managers. These outcomes would be in obvious tension with the demand for increased political control (particularly if that control is to be achieved through traditional hierarchical means). Quite clearly, this tangling of greater responsiveness with greater discretion creates problems for reform outcomes.

From these somewhat muddy roots, a number of reforms have emerged. There has often been a "flavor of the month" quality to the reforms; the popularity of a reform appears to be based more on its availability than on its fit with the problem at hand. The peculiar processes of policy diffusion are well described by Halligan elsewhere in this book. Overall, however, there is little evidence of hard analysis of a reform before it is initially transferred from one national setting to another. There appears to be an almost global belief that common bureaucratic problems are amenable to common solutions. Halligan's point that policy learning and redesign often occur after transference is an important one, however.

There is also considerable commonality in design activities, or, more accurately, absence of design activities. The summary description of the Scandinavian experience has much wider applicability:

> Reform programmes are more a collection of reform ideas than unified strategies for change. . . . Reform programmes emphasize the efficiency approach without formulating the operational goals which such an approach demands. . . . Decision-makers are more concerned with avoiding a fiasco than with achieving success. . . . (Laegread, 1990: 45)

The inherently political nature of civil service reform has precluded serious attention to policy design in most national settings. Further, the mix of theoretical reform traditions has often produced reforms whose component parts were in conflict. Finally, the popularity of policy diffusion in the area of civil service reform has contributed to a general tendency to choose a solution before a problem is clearly specified and to base expectations for reforms on political symbols and demands, rather than on careful analysis of civil service structures.


## THE REFORM AGENDA

### What Are the Major Reform Initiatives?

There are various ways of categorizing the broad set of institutional reforms currently "on the plate." Broadly, the reforms include (1) budgetary and financial reforms; (2) structural reforms; (3) procedural or technical reforms; and (4) relational reforms (Ingraham and Peters, 1988). Each of these sets deals with the internal workings of public organizations as well as with external relationships. Each set approaches the problem of the civil service from a slightly different perspective; in each case, however, there is no doubt that the problem is the civil service.

*Budgetary and financial reforms.*

These reforms have to do with improved planning and coordination of budgetary issues, but it is well understood that greater regularity and visibility inside the bureaucracy improves potential for direction by those outside the organization. The reforms have also had some success in achieving and holding to budgetary cutbacks, but the earliest reforms in this set preceded the budget shocks of the 1970s. Canada, for example, introduced Planning, Programming and Budgeting Systems in 1968, about the same time as the United States. A new, more rigorous, and more quantitative reform, Operational Performance Measurement System, was introduced in the mid-1970s. Dwivedi and Phidd (1990: 138) note that the basic philosophy of this system was "that if an operation was not measurable, it did not exist." Management by objective systems was frequently introduced in combination with budgetary reforms. Dunsire (1990) observes that during roughly the same period, Britain introduced Program Analysis and Review, the Financial Management Initiative, and MINIS, an information management system intended to improve priority-setting. Australia created Forward Estimate Systems, Running Cost Systems, and Portfolio Budgeting, all part of the Financial Management Improvement Programme (Hede, 1990). A recent publication of the Organization for Economic Cooperation and Development demonstrated the widespread occurrence of these reforms: fourteen of the twenty-two nations reporting were currently involved with some level of budgetary or financial reform (OECD, 1990).

*Structural reforms.*

Among the most complex reforms are those related to structure and size of government. There are four related sets in this category: structural reorganization at the center; decentralization away from the center; privatization and other "off-loading" reforms; and downsizing, or "rightsizing" as it is now frequently known.

*Structural reorganization at the center.*

Despite the very clear popularity of this reform, there is consensus that it often does not make much difference (March and Olsen, 1983; Arnold, 1986). The simple frequency with which the reform occurs is one indicator of that general lack of success. Frequency is also a tribute, however, to lack of clearly defined objectives for reorganization strategies. Many analysts relate the frequent occurrence of reorganization to a perception on the part of elected officials that existing structures impede political objectives (see Arnold, 1986; Pollitt, 1990). Further, reorganization is obvious and dramatic, qualities that make it a clear candidate for the symbolic action often demanded by political officials. Only rarely, however, are political and bureaucratic timetables congruent. Organizational change processes generally do not accommodate to the electoral cycle (Gaertner and Gaertner, 1984). Nonetheless, the appeal to elected officials is consistent; structural changes are symbolic and important in the often ephemeral world of bureaucratic change (March and Olsen, 1983). Smith (1988: 69) provides the following assessment of the British case:

> The pattern of ministerial departments is a changing one, with new ones being set up and existing ones terminated by abolition or merger. Reorganization usually follows general elections. Between 1960 and 1979 twenty-eight new departments were created and thirty-one were dismantled. These changes were concentrated in election years. The five election years of the period 1960–81 accounted for sixty-one percent of the new creations and fifty-six percent of the abolitions.

Two other "hotbeds of reform," Australia and New Zealand, have dramatically reduced the number of central departments. Other reorganization reforms have been directed specifically at the management of the civil service system. Both the United States and the United Kingdom created new organizations to administer and monitor the civil service system; the United Kingdom has since abolished the Civil Service Department, and the U.S. Office of Personnel Management, created by the Civil Service Reform Act of 1978, has been under nearly constant attack (Lane, 1992). New Zealand abolished its central personnel authority in 1988 and now operates with department level decision-making.

*Decentralization and deconcentration.*

Another part of efforts to debureaucratize public institutions has been the breaking down or transfer of functions from the center to regional or local governments, or to quasi-public organizations. Peters (1988: 13) argues that decentralization effectively bridges the two theoretical traditions that most often shape reform:

> [It] is a way of coping with problems that is more acceptable than most. . . . decentralization touches on a number of important themes in democratic theory. . . . (and) in managerial theory. . . . decentralization appeals to conservative ideologues who consider returning policies "to the people" (or to the market) to be the most efficient means of solving problems. . . . It is a major component of schemes for "modernization" of the public sector.

Among the benefits ascribed to decentralization are improved efficiency (smaller administrative units), improved public access and information (government closer to the people), and, therefore, better control and accountability. Deconcentration, which passes operating responsibility but not necessarily decision-making responsibility to lower levels, aims at basically the same objectives (Peters, 1988). Many examples of both are present on national reform agendas.

The "Next Steps" initiative in the United Kingdom is a leading case. After the report of the Fulton Commission in the late 1960s triggered what Hennessy (1990: 203) described as a "debate of almost theological proportions" about the British civil service, reforms have been consistent, but relatively modest in their impact. A scrutiny of the impact of those reforms, titled *Improving Management in Government: The Next Steps*, was released in 1987. The report described little real or long-term pressure for improving performance, too much standardization, and little emphasis on service delivery. It also noted—again—that Whitehall rewards the policy advising function more than the management function. To solve these problems, the report recommended splitting off "agencies" that would have executive responsibility for service delivery and effective management within policy guidelines set by the parent department. Staff were to be trained in managerial techniques and processes, and the overall activity was to be monitored by a high-level project manager. Early evaluations were quite positive; by 1990 about 15 percent of the total civil service staff were employed in the thirty-three agencies created to that time (Hede, 1991: 10). The agencies created vary widely in structure, function, and size (from about 50 staff members to over 35,000) and provide a natural laboratory for examining the outcome of the reforms in different organizational settings.

New Zealand has a similar, but more extensive decentralization effort, in which substantial managerial authority is transferred to the department and bureau level and in which the "chief executive" of each department has "independent authority in most areas of personnel management, such as appointments, promotion and discipline" (OECD, 1990: 80). Pay rates can also be delegated, and all bargaining occurs at the department level. The Netherlands, France, Finland, and Denmark are undertaking substantial decentralization efforts. The "debureaucratisation initiative" in Denmark, established in 1988, is intended to accelerate and simplify decentralization efforts (OECD, 1990: 37–39).

A variation on the theme is found in some of the research and demonstration projects launched under the auspices of the Civil Service Reform Act of 1978 in the United States. Although the act provided for delegation of examining and some other authorities from the central personnel agency to the departmental level, that delegation has really only occurred in the demonstration projects. More flexible pay schemes, recruiting and retention bonuses, profit sharing, and other innovations have dramatically increased agency discretion and managerial authority and flexibility in a limited number of agencies. Intensive evaluation of these efforts provides valuable data for comparison with unreformed organizations (Ingraham, 1991).

Finally, it is important to note that decentralization reforms are frequent in developing nations as well. Mutahaba writes that, in East Africa, decentralization has been undertaken to improve organizational effectiveness, to increase responsiveness of bureaucracies to citizens, and to promote national development (Mutahaba, 1989: 72). He observes that there has been little concrete analysis of various efforts, but the apparent consensus is that decentralization has not achieved the desired objectives. He concludes that "efforts to decentralize authority and responsibility. . . . were constrained not so much by poor choice of organizational systems, but by the lack of political will to decentralize on the part of the central leadership . . ." (Mutahaba, 1989: 105). Without a strong and integrated center from which to decentralize, many developing nations have expressed the same frustration and dissatisfaction.

### Privatization and off-loading.

If the previously discussed reforms recur frequently, privatization has been very nearly a siren song. Both definitions of the reform and activities associated with it vary. The movement of previously public functions and services into private hands appears relatively straightforward, but as Lundqvist (1988) notes, efforts to operationalize the concept for measurement or comparative purposes have been problematic. Further, the issues raised by lack of accountability in a heavily privatized or "contracted out" system are significant.

As a reform, privatization combines state and managerialist traditions in both problem definition and proposed solution. It is clearly part of the intense debate regarding the proper role and scope of government. Both Margaret Thatcher and Ronald Reagan simply challenged the notion that government belonged in all the areas in which it was active in the late 1970s. Pollitt (1990: 139–40) observes that privatization represents "the fellow traveler with efficiency—entrepreneurship. . . . [It represents] a new model of government in which hitherto core public services would actually be provided, on contract, by risk-taking, entrepreneurial private sector organizations. The much diminished public service would then become an enabler rather than a provider, its role reduced to one of specifying and monitoring of contracts." In some federal agencies in the United States, there are as many—or more—contract employees working for the agency as there are civil servants. Whether the practice actually reduces the size of government is clearly debatable (Kettl, 1993).

Issues such as these, however, have generally been brushed aside by the desire to reduce the role of government (Kettl, 1988; 1993). The singular enthusiasm of the United Kingdom in this regard is reflected in its report to the OECD on public management reforms:

> The Privatisation Programme is one of the key elements in the government's strategy to promote efficiency, increase incentives and widen share ownership. . . . Transferring state businesses into private ownership. . . . allows employees to take a direct stake in the companies in which they work, leading to major changes in attitudes, and gives everyone an opportunity to own a real share in the nation's assets. (OECD, 1990: 112)

As an alternative reform, New Zealand, Finland, and other countries have adopted corporatization policies, in which ownership is retained by the government but more "businesslike" procedures are installed. New Zealand's government reports that the State Owned Enterprises operate "on an equal footing with comparable private sector companies and have achieved substantial productivity gains, returning dividends to the government as shareholder" (OECD, 1990: 79). Still other countries, such as the Netherlands with its slogan, "Fewer civil servants, but a better service," have utilized privatization as one part of an effort to reduce the size of government.

The nations of eastern Europe have obviously also turned to privatization as a cure for some of their bureaucratic problems. Privatization in this context, however, involves very different problems: a private sector, to which government functions may be privatized, must be created. Further, as massive functions are off-loaded, the size and composition of the national bureaucracies will change dramatically. With little of the managerial fervor that has infected many western nations, and with virtually no experience in eliminating bureaucratic functions, state bureaucracies appear to be reverting to the oldest and most revered of civil service practices: seniority. Because older, male party members have the greatest seniority in virtually all cases, the state is likely to retain the persons least likely to support and manage the change effort (Siemienska, 1991).

*Rightsizing.*

Downsizing or rightsizing reforms are closely related to privatization and other off-loading reforms just discussed. They are strongly anchored in both economic reality and political ideology. Further, although they seem to be rather dramatic in the context of the past twenty years, they are old bureaucratic reforms. Hood and Dunsire (1989) note that, at least since the time of de Tocqueville's analysis of government, the size of public employment and expenditure has been decried. They also find, however, that in the United Kingdom, "the era of retrenchment in the 1920s meant severe and sustained reductions in both; but. . . . from the mid 70s to the mid 80s, government spending was severely cut only temporarily and then resumed its long-term upward climb. . . . staffing cuts. . . . seem to have been set on a marked downward trend . . ." (Hood and Dunsire, 1989: 19–20). Comparable analyses are not available for other countries, but there is some evidence that the same would be true at the central government level in other nations. OECD reports, for example, that "Canada achieved a reduction of 2000 person years in the federal public service in 1988/89 and a further reduction of about 1000 is anticipated in 1989/90. Ireland, Japan, and the Netherlands also reported further reductions in public employment" (OECD, 1990: 13).

Very clearly, the massive central bureaucracies will be downsized in eastern Europe; the burden of central government machinery is heavy for developing nations as well. The costs of cutbacks are significant for both of these groups of nations. As noted above, state bureaucracies in eastern Europe will become increasingly less representative of society and more out of touch with new policy directions when they are cut back. In Africa and other developing areas, Grindle and Thomas (1991: 157) argue that

> . . . in states in which national integration was a priority, powerful (bureaucratic) positions were often apportioned among ethnic, linguistic, or religious groups . . . major elements had a share in and benefitted from state power . . . and had some interest in maintaining the integrity of the state. . . . The reforms of the 1980s undercut the opportunities to build and maintain such political bases. . . . (further) policy reforms that removed state bureaucracies and allowed the private sector to replace them shifted power and influence to non-Africans.

These are cases in which current reforms will be part of the need for different reforms in the future.

*Technical reforms.*

To a large extent, the reforms discussed so far have attempted to change characteristics of public bureaucracies and civil service systems without fundamentally altering core components of the systems (those nations that decentralized human resources management to the department or agency level are exceptions). Another set of reform activities addresses the more technical aspects of personnel administration and compensation. These reforms also speak to external dissatisfaction with the civil service. They also, however, respond to a different problem: the inability of many contemporary civil service systems to perform even the most rudimentary tasks for which they are responsible, such as recruiting, rewarding, and retaining employees critical to the effective functioning of government. In the United States, the Volcker Commission (1989) noted that this "quiet crisis" confronting the public service threatened the ability of government to deliver key services. In the United Kingdom, Ireland, the Netherlands, Sweden, and elsewhere, the ability to attract qualified applicants to the public service has been identified as a significant problem (OECD, 1990). Many of the "technical reforms" on national agendas are directed at these and similar problems.

### Simplification and flexibility.

There is an increasing trend toward more flexibility in recruiting personnel, in methods and levels of compensation, in classification, and in training and development of existing and future managers. Simplification has been a key objective in many of these efforts. Its primary thrust has been the elimination of unnecessary paperwork, of superfluous rules and regulations, and of unnecessarily long time periods of activities such as hiring (Peters, 1988). Attention is just beginning to focus on rigid and outdated classification systems (NAPA, 1991).

The need to adapt to a changing labor pool in many western nations (see, for example, *Public Service 2000* in Canada; and *Civil Service 2000* in the U.S.) and to more actively pursue equal employment opportunity objectives have been other incentives for technical reforms. The OECD (1990: 13) summarizes:

> Developments in 1989 included an agreement in Belgium between the government and the public service unions on a single statute for public servants; the Public Service 2000 initiative in Canada [with] moves toward a less complicated personnel management regime; and a new statute for civil service managers in Portugal that involves more broadly based recruitment and increased responsibility. . . . [pay initiatives] include a revised pay structure and the introduction of performance appraisal for senior executives in Australia; allocation of more funds for flexible salaries in Denmark; and experiment with performance bonuses in Finland; introduction of performance related pay for some senior management grades in Ireland; development of the flexible pay system in the Netherlands; progress with rationalization of the pay system in Portugal; efforts to develop a performance bonus system in Turkey; and development of performance-related pay and flexible pay structures in the United Kingdom.

*Pay flexibility and pay for performance.*

As the above summary indicates, pay-for-performance systems are among the most common reforms. There are a limited number of cases—New Zealand and Australia appear to be the leading examples—in which these pay-for-performance schemes are "capstone" reforms; that is, basic system reforms have preceded the introduction of more discretionary and flexible pay systems. In other cases, such as the United States, the United Kingdom, and Ireland, pay for performance has simply been grafted onto existing civil service structures and pay systems.

There is also great variation in the extent to which the performance appraisal process is viewed by employees as clearly linked to reward. Perry's work in the United States indicates that a very formal and standardized system has produced high levels of dissatisfaction (Perry, 1992). In the Netherlands, on the other hand, an informal and decentralized system has apparently produced higher levels of employee satisfaction; but some dissatisfaction with levels of funding and other components of the system remain (OECD, 1991). Almost all nations report, however, that ratings are inflated; that is, nearly everyone gets a high rating. Additional variation is found in the source and level of funding for the performance awards, in the extent to which awards are one time bonuses or are added to base pay, and in the number of employees eligible to receive the awards.

With the exception of the limited number of initiatives directed at equal employment opportunity, the technical reforms currently on national agendas are closely related to the managerialist influence—they are intended to make public sector management systems look more like those of the private sector. Recent research in the United States demonstrates that the perception of the private sector and the reality of the private sector experience are often quite disparate (National Academy of Science, 1991). The reality is rarely documented, however, and widely accepted perception drives the reforms.

*Relational reforms.*

The final set of reforms relies on the full range of efforts just described to achieve its objective: improved responsiveness of public bureaucracies and civil servants to political officials. These reforms are completely the creature of politics, but they are informed by both reform traditions. If there is a political leader who feels that the public bureaucracy has been both adequately responsive to political direction and efficient in carrying out its duties, he or she has not gone on record with that observation.

Reforms in this category are essentially directed at limiting the policy role of the civil service and injecting political direction more frequently and more intensively into public bureaucratic organizations. Peters writes: "Even in countries such as the United Kingdom with a long tradition of an apolitical and largely respected and influential civil service, attempts have been made to impose greater political control and to involve outsiders, generally private sector executives. In countries such as France and West Germany, where civil servants have been more identified with political parties, the importance of that identification appears to have intensified" (Peters, 1988: 101). In the Australian context, Halligan notes that one aspect of the "managerial revolution" was the establishment of reforms which "facilitated stronger government control of the public service by redistributing power both between politicians and public service and within public service" (Halligan, 1990: 50–52).

The primary reform in this group is the Senior Executive Service, or a similar group of higher civil servants. Such a group was created in the United States by the Civil Service Reform Act of 1978. In Canada, the Management Category was created in 1981, and the *Public Service 2000* initiative will add additional flexibility to that group. Australia and New Zealand both adopted national Senior Executive Services in the 1980s; the concept is under discussion in other countries. In these reforms, the civil service "elite"—a small group of the most senior and expert civil servants—leave behind many of the traditional protections of the civil service system to operate under terms of a contract. They compete for rather substantial financial bonuses and their performance evaluations are often conducted by political ministers or executives. They are considered generalist managers and may, therefore, be moved about inside the agency or department or between agencies. Increased responsiveness to political direction is emphasized in these reforms. The combination of evaluation by political superiors, potential receipt of financial bonuses, and absence of civil service sanctuary enhances that responsiveness but, advocates argue, also increases efficiency. In turn, improved responsiveness and management focused more closely on political objectives is critical to achieving many of the other reforms outlined in this paper.

## CONCLUSION

Given the extensive nature of reform activities and the diverse problems they are supposed to address, what conclusions can be reached about the endeavor? At a minimum, they would include the following:

1. The pattern of adoption has varied, but most nations deal with more than one reform at a time. Some nations, such as Australia and New Zealand, "staged" the reforms, building from a reformed base to more technical efforts such as pay for performance. Others, such as the United States, adopted several reforms—not all of which were compatible—at one time. A decade after adop-

tion of the Civil Service Reform Act, important inconsistencies are still being sorted out (Ingraham and Rosenbloom, 1992).

2. Evaluation of both strategies is extremely limited and it is not clear which approach to reform will be more successful. Australia's reforms are still young and it is too early to draw firm conclusions. The United States has over a decade of experience with comprehensive reform, but the formal evaluation of its outcomes was eliminated by the Reagan budget cuts in the early 1980s. Further, many of the effects of the reforms were overwhelmed by the political and economic environment of that time. Clearly, however, variations in design, planning, and implementation strategy will be significant to eventual outcomes (Ingram and Schneider, 1988). The widespread diffusion of similar civil service reform policies has obscured the role that problem definition and analysis may have played in individual nations and that must be systematically analyzed.

3. Different roles for national governments and different theoretical traditions about those roles—as well as that of the public bureaucracy in governance—have been one important influence in shaping civil service systems and reforms. In many cases, that governance tradition has been combined with another, related to managerial effectiveness and efficiency. The two are frequently not compatible and their combination produces internally inconsistent and contradictory reforms.

4. Neither of the above reform traditions have paid close attention to the reality of the civil service systems and structures they intend to change. Many have, in fact, reformed only at the fringes of complex and rigid civil service structures. Critical components, such as recruitment, classification, and pay, have often not been addressed. The reforms that have been adopted have attempted to create flexibility and discretion that conflict sharply with the rigidities created by complicated civil service laws and regulations. This is particularly true in western industrial democracies, but it is also the case in developing nations that have been subject to imposition of western reform models as a condition of international aid.

5. At present, there is very little comparative information about the civil service base from which the reforms proceed. What are the primary functions the system is created to serve? What are the most critical characteristics of each national civil service system? What are the most consistent sources of variation? What are the incentives to change, to be flexible, to be responsive? How do critical functions differ between industrialized and developing nations? Which laws and regulations must be altered if effective change is to occur? These fundamental questions are important to understanding the fit between the reform and the system in which it will operate—or die. It seems to be a matter of common sense, but if base systems are not reformed or if they create or reward behavior opposite to that intended, success is unlikely.

6. Despite great surface similarity in civil service reform policy ideas and terms, there is little rigorous comparison of actual policy content. Pay for perfor-

mance appears frequently on national policy agendas; while overall objectives may be the same, there are vast differences in the policy as it is currently operating in the Netherlands as compared to the United Kingdom, for example.

7. The disparity between perceived problems and proposed solutions created by the interaction of the different reform traditions in disparate national settings suggests that the chances for clear success of any set of reforms are very limited. Politics is responsible for the mixing and matching of traditions and expectations; in the final analysis, all reform efforts will be judged by political criteria. The match between political objectives and timetables and the realities of institutional reform is often not a good one.

8. Not all that is important about civil service reform will lend itself to measurement. The relationship between political culture and administrative culture is well recognized, but elusive. It assumes a central significance, however, to the potential success or failure of many of the reforms in the mangerialist tradition. There are many reasons why government is different from the private sector, and there is adequate evidence of difficulties in transferring policy from one to the other to make one skeptical of future claims (Perry and Kraemer, 1983; Pollitt, 1990). Techniques that flourish in one culture may wither, be overgrown, or simply be inappropriate in another. There is a need to better analyze the fit, not only in terms of processes and techniques, but in terms of fundamental values and ideas about government.

9. Finally, it is necessary to recognize the political and economic environments of the reforms and their inevitable influence on reform longevity and outcomes. Pollitt says it well: "there are obvious structural tensions between the dynamics of the political process and the requirements of a programme of broad-scope cultural and organizational change. In brief, such a programme would require the commitment of substantial resources over a period of time— say ten years—which easily exceeds the normal span of political attention" (Pollitt, 1990: 182). Effective reforms aim for greater effectiveness and productivity, but also recognize political and economic constraints and destabilizing effects. They must create and retain a broad base of support, not only among elected officials and citizens, but among members of the public service as well. Reforms which exclude or ignore these realities may create different civil service systems in the short term, but they will not contribute to more effective governance.

## REFERENCES

Aberbach, J. D., and B. A. Rockman. 1988. "Problems of Cross-National Comparison." In *Public Administration in Developed Democracies*, ed. D. C. Rowat. New York: Marcel Dekker.

Aberbach, J. D., R. D. Putnam, and B. A. Rockman. 1981. *Bureaucrats and Politicians in Western Democracies.* Cambridge: Harvard University Press.

Arnold, P. 1986. *Making the Managerial Presidency: Comprehensive Reorganization Planning, 1905–1980.* Princeton: Princeton University Press.

Aucoin, P. 1990. "Administrative Reform in Public Management." *Governance* 3: 115–37.

Beltran, M. 1988. "Spain." In *Public Administration in Developed Democracies,* ed. D. C. Rowat. New York: Marcel Dekker.

Boston, J. 1987. "Transforming New Zealand's Public Sector: Labour's Quest for Improved Efficiency and Accountability." *Public Administration* (Winter): 423–42.

Caiden, G., and N. Caiden. 1990. "Towards the Future of Comparative Public Administration." In *Public Administration in World Perspective,* ed. O. P. Dwivedi and Keith Henderson. Ames: Iowa State University Press.

Crozier, M. 1964. *The Bureaucratic Phenomenon.* Chicago: University of Chicago Press.

Dunsire, A. 1990. "Policy Developments and Administrative Changes in the United Kingdom." In *Public Administration in World Perspective,* ed. O. P. Dwivedi and Keith Henderson. Ames: Iowa State University Press.

Dunsire, A., and C. Hood. 1989. *Cutback Management in Public Bureaucracies: Popular Theories and Observed Outcomes in Whitehall.* Cambridge: Cambridge University Press.

Dwivedi, O. P., and K. Henderson. 1990. State of the Art: Comparative Public Administration and Development Administration." In *Public Administration in World Perspective,* ed. O. P. Dwivedi and K. Henderson. Ames: Iowa State University Press.

Dwivedi, O. P., and R. Phidd. 1990. "Political Management in Canada." In *Public Administration in World Perspective,* ed. O. P. Dwivedi and Keith Henderson. Ames: Iowa State University Press.

Efficiency Unit. 1988. *Improving Management in Government: The Next Steps. Report to the Prime Minister.* London: Her Majesty's Stationery Office.

Gaertner, G. H., and K. N. Gaertner. 1984. "Civil Service Reform in the Context of Presidential Transitions." In P. W. Ingraham and C. Ban, eds., *Legislating Bureaucratic Change: The Civil Service Reform Act of 1978.* Albany, NY: State University of New York Press.

Grindle, M., and J. Thomas. 1991. *Public Choices and Policy Change: The Political Economy of Reform in Developing Countries.* Baltimore: Johns Hopkins University Press.

Halligan, J. 1990. "What is the SES Concept?" *Canberra Bulletin of Public Administration* (July): 50–52.

Hede, A. 1990. "Queensland's Senior Bureaucracy: Comparisons with Models of the Senior Executive Service." *Canberra Bulletin of Public Administration* (July): 147–52.

————. 1991. "The 'Next Steps' Initiative for Civil Service Reform in Britain: The Emergence of Managerialism in Whitehall?" *Canberra Bulletin of Public Administration* (January).

Hennessy, P. 1989. *Whitehall.* London: Secker & Warburg.

Hogwood, B., and B. Guy Peters. 1983. *Policy Dynamics.* Brighton: Harvester-Wheatsheaf.

Hood, C. 1989. "Public Administration and Public Policy Intellectual Challenges for the 1990s." *Australian Journal of Public Administration* (December): 346–58.

Ingraham, P. W. 1991. "A Preview of the Experience with Pay for Performance in the United States." Paris: OECD.

————. 1992. "Commissions, Cycles and Change: The Role of Blue Ribbon Commissions in Reform." In P. W. Ingraham and D. F. Kettl, eds., *An Agenda for Excellence: The American Public Service.* Chatham, NJ: Chatham House.

Ingraham, P. W., and B. G. Peters. 1988. "The Conundrum of Reform: A Comparative Analysis." *Review of Public Personnel Administration* (Fall): 3–16.

Ingraham, P. W., and C. Ban, eds. 1984. *Legislating Bureaucratic Change: The Civil Service Reform Act of 1978.* Albany, NY: SUNY Press.

Ingraham, P. W., and D. Rosenbloom, eds. 1992. *The Promise and Paradox of Bureaucratic Reform.* Pittsburgh: University of Pittsburgh Press.

Ingram, H., and A. Schneider. 1988. "Systematically Pinching Ideas: A Comparative Approach to Policy Design." *Journal of Public Policy* (January/March): 61–80.

Keeling, D. 1972. *Management in Government.* London: Allen & Unwin.

Kettl, D. 1988. *Government by Proxy.* Washington, DC: CQ Press.

————. 1993. *Sharing Power: Public Governance and Private Markets.* Washington, DC: Brookings Institution.

Laegread, P. 1990. Changes in Norwegian Public Personnel Policy." In Organization for Economic Cooperation and Development, *Flexible Personnel Management in the Public Sector.* Paris: OECD.

Lane, L. 1992. "The Office of Personnel Management: Promise and Performance." In P. W. Ingraham and D. Rosenbloom, eds., *The Promise and Paradox of Bureaucratic Reform*. Pittsburgh: University of Pittsburgh Press.

Lundqvist, L. J. 1988. "Privatization: Towards a Concept for Comparative Policy Analysis." *Journal of Public Policy* (January/March): 1–19.

March, J., and J. Olsen. 1983. "Organizing Political Life: What Administrative Reorganization Tells Us about Government." *American Political Science Review* 77: 281–96.

Mascarenhas, R. C. 1990. "Reform of the Public Service in Australia and New Zealand." *Governance* (January): 75–95.

Meny, Y. 1988. "France." In *Public Administration in Developed Democracies*, ed. D. C. Rowat. New York: Marcel Dekker.

Mutahaba, G. 1989. *Reforming Public Administration for Development*. West Hartford, CT: Kumarian Press.

Nathan, R. 1983. *The Administrative Presidency*. New York: John Wiley & Sons.

NAPA (National Academy of Public Administration). 1989. *Privatization: The Challenge to Public Management*. Washington, DC: NAPA.

———. 1991. *Modernizing Federal Classification: An Opportunity for Excellence*. Washington, DC: NAPA.

National Academy of Science. 1991. *Performance Appraisal and Pay for Performance*. Washington, DC: National Academy Press.

National Commission on the Public Service. 1990. *Leadership for America: Rebuilding the Public Service*. Lexington, MA: Lexington Press.

Nef, J. 1990. "Policy Developments and Administrative Changes." In *Public Administration in World Perspective*. ed. O. P. Dwivedi and K. Henderson. Ames: Iowa State University Press.

OECD (Organization for Economic Cooperation and Development). 1983. *Recent Trends in Performance Appraisal and Performance Related Pay Schemes in the Public Service*. Paris: OECD.

———. 1990. *Flexible Personnel Management in the Public Service*. Paris: OECD.

———. 1990. *Public Management Developments Survey—1990*. Paris: OECD.

Olsen, J. 1983. *Organized Democracy*. Bergen: Universiteten Farleget.

Perry, J. 1992. "Merit Pay in the Federal Government." In P. W. Ingraham and D. Rosenbloom, eds., *The Promise and Paradox of Bureaucratic Reform.* Pittsburgh: University of Pittsburgh Press.

Perry, J., and K. Kraemer. 1983. *Public Management.* Mountain View, CA: Mayfield.

Peters, B. G. 1988. *Comparing Public Bureaucracies: Problems of Theory and Method.* Tuscaloosa: University of Alabama Press.

————. 1991. "Government Reorganization: A Theoretical Analysis." Paper presented at the annual meeting of the Canadian Political Science Association, Kingston, Ontario.

Pollitt, C. 1990. *Managerialism and the Public Services.* Cambridge: Basil Blackwell.

Rainey, H. 1991. *Understanding and Managing Public Organizations.* San Francisco: Jossey-Bass.

Rose, R. 1988. *Loyalty, Voice or Exit? Margaret Thatcher's Challenge to the Civil Service.* Strathclyde: Centre for the Study of Public Policy.

Rose, R., et al. 1985. *Public Employment in Western Nations.* Cambridge: Cambridge University Press.

Rowat, D. C. 1988. "Comparisons and Trends." In *Public Administration in Developed Democracies,* ed. D. C. Rowat. New York: Marcel Dekker.

————, ed. 1988. *Public Administration in Developed Democracies.* New York: Marcel Dekker.

Siedentopf, H. 1988. "Western Germany." In *Public Administration in Developed Democracies,* ed. D. C. Rowat. New York: Marcel Dekker.

Siemienska, R. 1991. "Dismantling the Bureaucracy." Lecture, State University of New York at Binghamton.

Smith, B. 1988. "The United Kingdom." In *Public Administration in Developed Democracies,* ed. D. C. Rowat. New York: Marcel Dekker.

Weltenall, R. 1988. "Australia." In *Public Administration in Developed Democracies,* ed. D. C. Rowat. New York: Marcel Dekker.

# 13 EXPLORING VARIATIONS IN PUBLIC MANAGEMENT REFORM OF THE 1980s

Christopher Hood

As Ingraham indicates in chapter 12, students of public administration during the 1980s were much preoccupied with the famous "paradigm shift"—that is, the apparent move away from what is now seen as a traditional, progressive-era set of doctrines of good administration, emphasizing orderly hierarchies, depoliticized bureaucracy, and the elimination of duplication or overlap (Ostrom, 1974), and toward what has sometimes, for want of a better term, been described as the "New Public Management" or NPM (see Aucoin, 1990; Hood, 1987; 1990a; 1990b; 1991; Hood and Jackson, 1991; Pollitt, 1990). NPM is shorthand for a group of administrative doctrines that figured prominently in the agenda for bureaucratic reform in several OECD countries beginning in the late 1970s.

The term new does not, of course, imply that the doctrines of NPM appeared for the first time in the 1980s. On the contrary, many NPM doctrines are repackaged versions of ideas that have been in public administration since its beginnings; and some commentators have characterized public management reform doctrines of the 1980s as a return to themes articulated by Woodrow Wilson, Frederick Winslow Taylor, or even earlier writers, particularly in the attempt to distinguish between policy-setting and service delivery activities (Overman, 1984: 277–78).

Nor should New Public Management be confused with the so-called New Public Administration movement that flowered briefly in the United States in the late 1960s and early 1970s but achieved no real mainstream influence (Marini, 1971). NPM is an altogether different cultural product. If New Public Administration reflected a culture of what Mary Douglas (1982) and her followers (Thompson, Ellis, and Wildavsky, 1990) called "egalitarianism" or "sectarianism," NPM was an uneasy combination of "individualism" and "hierarchism."

As an administrative philosophy, NPM has been variously described (Aucoin, 1990; Hood, 1991; Osborne and Gaebler 1992; Pollitt, 1990), and Ingraham discusses some of the elements involved in chapter 12 of this volume. In spite of variations, most writers have identified a set of dimensions of change that include the following:

(1) variations in the degree of *hands-on management* (that is, the degree of active control of public organizations by visible top managers wielding discretionary power);

(2) variations in the degree to which public organizations operate with *explicit and measurable* (or at least verifiable) *standards of performance* in terms of the range, level, and content of services to be provided;

(3) variations in the degree to which public organizations are controlled by *output measures* (particularly in pay-based, on-the-job performance rather than rank or educational attainment);

(4) variations in the degree to which public organizations are *disaggregated* into separate, self-contained units, rather than operating as a single aggregated unit;

(5) variations in the degree to which organizations within the public sector formally *compete* with one another and with private organizations for the pursuit of particular tasks, rather than having semipermanent, "ascribed" roles;

(6) variations in the degree to which organizations within the public sector conduct business or use management practices that are broadly *similar to or different from* those employed in the private corporate sector;

(7) variations in the degree to which public sector management stresses *discipline and parsimony* in resource use.

These seven dimensions, drawn from debates in the 1980s over the alleged paradigm shift in public administration, give us a point of entry for looking at cross-national variations in public management reform in OECD countries, though they are of course much narrower than the broad regime categories developed by Heady in chapter 11. At first sight, they have an ephemeral air. They could be considered to be historically and culturally specific to the "New-Right" 1980s, and perhaps already to be passing away in what some have claimed to be the "postmanagerial" 1990s. Against that view, it could be argued that many of these dimensions have a more than ephemeral importance. For example, the extent to which the public sector is insulated and clearly separate from the private sector in matters of handling business and staff (items 4 and 6 above) picks up Douglas's (1982: 183–254) well-known "group" dimension, and the extent to which administrative tasks are differentiated and laid out in an orderly manner (items 3 and 5 above) picks up her "grid" dimension.

Similarly, many of the dimensions pick up areas of recurring debate in public administration (see Merkle, 1980; Downs and Larkey, 1986). The debate between legalists and Confucians in the Chinese mandarinate over 2,000 years ago, for instance, turned in part on items 2 and 3 (see Kamenka, 1989: 38–39). Items 1, 6, and 7 were of central importance to the cameralists, the first systematic students of public administration in Europe (Small, 1909). Such items as 2,

3, 5, 6, and 7 were central to the English utilitarians' philosophy of good public administration (Hume, 1981). Classic late nineteenth-century American doctrines of progressive public administration were much concerned with items, 3, 4, 5, and 6 (Ostrom, 1974). In that sense, many of these dimensions run through centuries, if not millenia, of public management debates, although the particular doctrines that are in good standing at any given time certainly vary.

As an administrative philosophy, NPM involves advocacy of change in each of these seven dimensions, as summarized in Table 13.1 below. But of course, there is no logical necessity for a public management system to change in all seven dimensions at once, and a high degree of variation is possible. Indeed, rather than thinking in terms of dichotomies—particularly of the traditional-modern type, it may be more helpful to conceive of more than one possible direction of public management reform within these dimensions, for instance in the contrast between the pragmatic/hierarchical style of the United Kingdom and the dogmatic/individualist style of New Zealand (Hood, 1990c).

## CROSS-NATIONAL VARIATIONS IN PUBLIC MANAGEMENT REFORM EMPHASIS IN OECD COUNTRIES IN THE 1980S

Debate rages as to how far New Public Management involved changes of substance as well as changes in style; the extent to which it had positive or negative consequences, or indeed any consequences at all, for ordinary citizens (see Keating, 1989; Martin, 1988; Nethercote, 1989; Scott, Bushnell, and Sallee, 1990); and why it became an attractive philosophy in the 1980s (Spann, 1981; Hood and Jackson, 1991). Like all policy reversals, it attracts debate as to whether the change was chiefly prompted by interests (see Dunleavy, 1985) or by ideas or ideology (see Merkle, 1980); whether it reflected deep-rooted changes in the sociotechnical system (as in discussion of postindustrial society, post-Fordism, the fifth Kondratiev cycle, etc., by authors such as Piore and Sabel [1984] and Jessop [1988], and whether it stemmed from economic competition between states for comparative advantage in low-cost, high-efficiency public services (OECD, 1990: 9).

Equally interesting, but rather less discussed, is the extent to which OECD countries *varied* in the extent to which they adopted New Public Management doctrines in the 1980s. Osborne and Gaebler (1992: 328ff) speak of a global revolution in the adoption of NPM; but even from casual observation, it is clear that some countries have laid more emphasis on these ideas than others and that NPM styles have varied even within the same "family groups" of countries (see Hood, 1990c). For example, whereas in Australia, the United Kingdom, and New Zealand there has been a tendency to decentralize personnel management (hiring, promotions, job classification, etc.) to line departments away from central personnel agencies, there has been no equivalent movement in

TABLE 13.1

## Doctrinal Components of New Public Management

| No. | Doctrine | Meaning | Typical justification |
|---|---|---|---|
| 1 | Hands-on professional management of public organization | Visible managers at the top, free to manage by discretionary power | Accountability requires clear assignment of responsibility, not diffusion of power |
| 2 | Explicit standards and measures of performance | Goals and targets defined and measurable as indicators of success | Accountability means clearly stated aims; efficiency needs "hard look" at goals |
| 3 | Greater emphasis on output controls | Resource allocation and rewards linked to performance | Need to stress results rather than procedures |
| 4 | Shift to disaggregation of units in the public sector | Unbundle public sector into corporatized units organized by products, with devolved budgets and dealing at arm's length with each other | Make units manageable; split provision and production, use contracts or franchises inside as well as outside the public sector |
| 5 | Shift to greater competition in public sector | Move to term contracts and public tendering procedures | Rivalry as the key to lower costs and better standards |
| 6 | Stress on private-sector styles of management practice | Move away from military-style public service ethic to more flexible pay, hiring, rules, PR, etc. | Need to apply "proven" private sector management tools in the public sector |
| 7 | Stress on greater discipline and parsimony in public sector resource use | Cutting direct costs, raising labor discipline, limiting compliance costs to business | Need to check resource demands of public sector and do more with less |

*Source: adapted from Hood, 1991: 4–5*

Japan, where the National Personnel Authority was, if anything, strengthened over the 1980s (though admittedly its powers over departments with respect to such items as promotion have always been weak). Whereas pay-for-performance doctrines have taken hold in countries such as Sweden, Denmark, New Zealand, and the United Kingdom, there has not yet been an equivalent movement in Germany.

To go beyond casual observation of this type, we need a systematic set of benchmarks or measuring rods to help distinguish between the positions of different countries in the seven NPM-related dimensions indicated above. We need both a reliable method of locating a country's initial state at the start of the period in question and the extent of movement over the period (given that a "backward" country might show dramatic change, yet still be behind an apparently "static" country that started from a different initial state). The difficulties of constructing such measures have been discussed by Peters in chapter 2, and at present, we do not have a cross-national information source that could show either sort of variation with any real reliability. The literature in the area is long on anecdote but short on systematic comparison and comes close to being a "data-free environment."

All we have is isolated fragments and relatively low-grade comparative data. For instance, management schools and consultants have done some comparative survey work on pay flexibility that embraces public sector management (e.g., the Cranfield/Price Waterhouse surveys of ten European OECD countries in 1990 and 1991 [see Hegewisch, 1991]). The OECD Public Management Service (PUMA) is attempting to provide cross-national indicators, such as its Public Management Reports from 1987 to 1992. The set of public management profiles PUMA has started to develop (OECD, 1992) may help to improve the documentary position for future work.

In the absence of a systematic data base, a rough indication of direction of change among the OECD countries can be gained by looking at the country reports submitted to the OECD's survey of public management developments in 1988 and 1990, supplemented in 1991 (OECD, 1988; 1990; 1991). Obviously, such a source has to be treated with the greatest caution, because clearly the data is seriously contaminated in a number of familiar ways. It lacks depth and rigor; it reflects what the OECD's particular correspondents in each country thought it relevant or politic to record (although there was, of course, a general checklist issued by PUMA for these exercises), rather than what a single observer might have noted. Moreover (at least until the OECD profiles are further developed), it indicates what was on the government agenda for change rather than the initial endowment of each system.

However, for lack of anything better, the OECD public management reports can give us a rough indication of the officially perceived agenda of public management change in the 1980s, and serve as a starting point for discussion of variations. For the analyses in tables 13.2 to 13.5, the country reports for 1988 and 1990 were carefully examined for references to directions of change, and a rough score was awarded to each country under each of the seven points of public management doctrine that were mentioned above as components of New Public Management. A score of 2 was given for developments reported as being in place on each of the dimensions, 1 for developments under active discussion or experimentation, and 0 for nothing reported in the area.

Clearly, such an exercise is only useful for identifying the most obviously distinctive cases: no other differentiation can be made with any confidence. The extremes were taken as cases whose overall scores (summed up across all seven dimensions) were more than one standard deviation away from the mean. The high and low cases identified by this method fitted well enough with other impressionistic views of variation in NPM during the 1980s to serve as a basis for discussion of what might be responsible for putting a country at one or the other of the extremes.

## EXPLAINING THE VARIATIONS

The development of NPM in the OECD countries in the 1980s might be interpreted in a number of different ways; for instance, it might be seen as a convergence process, as a policy-diffusion process, as a contingency-variation process, or as some mixture of all three. If it were a convergence process, we might expect the countries that were most "backward" at the start of the period to make the most rapid strides, so that the gap between the "leaders" and the "laggards" would tend to narrow over the period. If it were a diffusion process, we might expect to identify ways in which the ideas were borrowed from one country by another (as in the standard model of the development of epidemics) or by a mass propaganda type of diffusion from key international sources, such as the OECD or the World Bank. If it were a contingency-variation process, we might explore factors acting to accentuate or retard the development of NPM in particular cases.

These perspectives are not mutually exclusive. A diffusion or convergence perspective introduces an element of dynamism into the analysis that is missing from conventional contingency approaches. But a contingency approach may help to explain buffers or aggravators as a way of understanding uneven development. Four basic explanatory factors are explored in this section, following some conventional accounts of the rise of NPM.

### "English Awfulness"?

Some commentators (notably Pollitt, 1990) have written about NPM as if it were a distinctly Anglo-American phenomenon of the Reagan/Thatcher era. Even on the basis of the OECD public management reports alone (with all their admitted limitations), this view seems difficult to sustain. If nothing else, it ignores the high degree of emphasis placed on NPM in Australia, New Zealand, and Hong Kong (see, for instance, Keating, 1989; Nethercote, 1989; Scott, Bushnell, and Sallee, 1990; Sturgess, 1989; Yeatman, 1987).

However, it might be possible to generalize the view of NPM as an Anglo-American idea resulting from what Frank Castles ironically calls "the awfulness of the English" (Castles, 1989; Castles and Merrill, 1989: 181–85). It is noticeable, for example, that according to this exercise, the high scorers on NPM emphasis are mostly English-speaking countries (and hence clearly candidates for English awfulness à la Castles). The low scorers, on the other hand, are all non-English-speaking countries.

Moreover, an English awfulness explanation might fit with a convergence or diffusion approach to the development of NPM; according to Castles's (1989) analysis, English-speaking countries lost the formerly distinctive "high, direct employment" feature of public management between the 1960s and the 1980s, and NPM could be interpreted as part of that process of coming into line with non-English-speaking countries. In addition, the diffusion of NPM could be expected to go ahead more powerfully (particularly through the actions of management consultants and accountants) across countries with the same language and similar legal traditions.

For all that, it seems too simple to put NPM down to English awfulness alone. For example, Sweden appears as a high scorer on NPM emphasis, which would be particularly damaging for an interpretation built on a Castles-type English awfulness factor. Moreover, Denmark, the Netherlands, and France are cases that lie very close to the high boundary on NPM emphasis (i.e., they are just less than one standard deviation above the mean), and two of them (Denmark and the Netherlands) reported strong development of variable pay in recent years to the 1990 Price Waterhouse/Cranfield project (Hegewisch, 1991: table 3). Non-English-speaking high scorers on NPM during the 1980s clearly deserve some close analytic attention.

### Party Politics

Some commentators have interpreted New Public Management as a product of the New Right and the 1980s reaction against big government and state-led egalitarianism and welfarism (Pollitt, 1990). Are the doctrines "owned" or particularly associated with political parties at one end of the political spectrum rather than the other? If we are concerned to explore this issue, it is relevant to ask whether, and if so, how "party matters" in the development of NPM in the 1980s. This question is a traditional and important preoccupation for cross-national political science.

It is also a notoriously complex one (see von Beyme, 1984), and here we can only gain a first approximation. As a rough indication of political incumbency during the 1980s, a score of +1 was given to each OECD country for each year of incumbency in government by a political party to the right of that country's political spectrum, and a score of −1 for each year of incumbency by a party to the left of *that* spectrum. A score of 0.5 was given for each year of incumbency by a center-right coalition, and −0.5 for each year of incumbency by a center-left coalition, with 0 for a grand coalition (as in the Austrian case).

Such an exercise is clearly very crude. Scoring political incumbency presents many problems, familiar in the "Does politics matter?" debate over macroeconomic policy. There is no established method or convention for comparing degrees of "rightness" and "leftness" across countries. Obviously, too, there are different qualities of rightness and leftness (for example, participatory versus hierarchical emphases in socialism). Presidential and federal systems clearly cause complications (for example, the United States would count as "right" only in presidential terms). There is a substantial amount of bunching of coalition/proportional representation system cases in the middle, so that the most distinctive cases tend to be non-proportional representation systems (e.g., France and Japan), which may get disproportionate weight in the analysis. It could well be argued that a better test would be a series of before and after looks at cases of *change* in government. All such a scoring exercise does is to give us a first idea as to whether OECD countries were governed during the 1980s mainly by parties from their left, their right, or their center.

However, even this admittedly crude exercise seems to be enough to cast considerable doubt on the popular idea that NPM was closely associated with incumbency by "right" governing parties in the 1980s, as table 13.2 suggests. Sweden is the most obvious "misfit," showing apparently high NPM emphasis in the 1980s but scoring fairly high for "left" political incumbency with eight years out of the decade under Social Democratic governments. At the other extreme, there are unambiguously "right" cases, such as Japan and Turkey, that seem to score distinctly low on the NPM emphasis scale.

On this evidence, it would appear that the influence of the New Right on NPM developments is at best fairly indirect, and that those developments fit better with a diffusion model (of the mass-propaganda type) than with a simple contingency model in which party incumbency has much weight. But the party-matters hypothesis used above lacks a dynamic dimension, and it may be that a modified party-matters model could be constructed in which the dynamics of party competition play a greater part. One way to do so would be to draw on Scharpf's (1987) conception of "nested games," with a "party competition" game played between incumbent and challenger parties, and a "public management game" played between governments and the bureaucracy (substituted for Scharpf's macroeconomic policy game played between governments and unions). With such a model of party competition dynamics, it would be quite conceivable that incumbent social-democratic governments (such as those in Sweden or New Zealand in the 1980s) might go just as far as "bourgeois" governments (and possibly even further) in public management reforms, because they have nowhere else to go and need to work harder to establish credibility in this area with wavering middle-class voters (adapting Scharpf's ideas of asymmetrical choice by this group). At least we seem to need something more than a simple New Right political incumbency model to explain why the doctrines were unevenly diffused and to identify which were the "leaders" and which the "laggards."

## Past or Current Economic Management Performance

New Public Management is sometimes described as a response to fiscal stress and government overload. If so, we might expect NPM to be most strongly developed in countries (such as Greece or New Zealand) with a history of relatively poor macroeconomic performance on the conventional indices of GDP growth, public debt levels, inflation, and unemployment rates. Such a factor might significantly cut across party-political inputs into public management policy to increase the likelihood of NPM development in a particular country.

However, it is far from clear exactly how macroeconomic conditions are linked to public management policies, and what kind of macroeconomic performance record ought to count. On the first point, NPM is, as noted above, often interpreted as a desperate response to fiscal stress—for example, in its introduction of more flexible public sector pay systems as a means of motivating staff without increasing the overall public pay bill in conditions of high unemployment, depressed wages, and pressure on public spending and debt levels. On the other hand, it is sometimes said that NPM reflects boom conditions as well, for example, by introducing more flexible pay systems in order to make public bodies more able to compete with private sector employers in tight labor market conditions. Which of these explanations more plausibly fits the data? Or could it be that in some cases *both* statements might be true, so that we might expect the "medium" macroeconomic performers to show less NPM emphasis than the cases at either end of the macroeconomic performance spectrum?

On the second point, it could plausibly be argued that we might expect the link between good or bad macroeconomic performance and public management doctrines to be established with a time lag; new management principles would thus reflect a history of past economic success or failure rather than the current position. Such a view would fit the popular perception of NPM as a reflection of 1970s macroeconomic chickens coming home to roost. On that assumption, if we rank OECD countries according to their performance on the four conventional macroeconomic indicators in the post–oil shock era of the 1970s (i.e., 1974–79), and again pick out the extremes as those which are more than one standard deviation away from the mean, we can explore whether there is any apparent relationship between the economic basket cases or suc-

TABLE 13.2

**NPM Emphasis and Political Incumbency**

| . | Political incumbency emphasis | | |
|---|---|---|---|
| NPM emphasis | "Left" | "Center" | "Right" |
| High | Sweden | Australia<br>Canada<br>New Zealand | United Kingdom |
| Medium | France | Austria<br>Denmark<br>Finland<br>Italy<br>Netherlands<br>Portugal<br>United States[1] | |
| Low | Greece<br>Spain | Germany (Fed. Rep.)<br>Switzerland | Japan<br>Turkey |

*Sources: analysis based on OECD PUMA reports and on political incumbency data for OECD countries drawn from Gorvin (1989) and* Keesing's Contemporary Archives[1]

cess stories of the 1970s and the degree of NPM emphasis in the 1980s. Table 13.3 gives an indication of where the cases fall in such an analysis.

In fact, popular wisdom notwithstanding, it is not clear that there is any automatic relationship. True, some of the runaway macroeconomic success stories of the 1970s were in the "low NPM emphasis" group, as might be expected. Countries such as Japan and Germany (the former Federal Republic) are in this group. But not all of the high performers of the 1970s are in the group, nor are all the economic basket cases of the 1970s (in terms of overall scores on GDP growth per capita, CPI growth, and unemployment) in the "high NPM emphasis" group.

Even if we remove the assumption of lag, and relate degrees of NPM emphasis to economic performance (on the same basis) throughout the 1980s, the same puzzles arise, as can also be seen from table 13.3. Particular aspects of

---

1. It is, of course, a moot point whether the United States should be counted as "center" or "right" in this exercise. It is usually treated as essentially unclassifiable and left out of the analysis in "does party matter" comparisons. Given its separation of powers, it is here counted as a center-left coalition for 1980, a center-right coalition for 1981 to 1986, and a centrist coalition for 1987 to 1990.

TABLE 13.3

**NPM Emphasis and Economic Performance, 1974–79 and 1980–88**

| Economic performance category | NPM emphasis 1980s | | | | | |
|---|---|---|---|---|---|---|
| | High | | Medium | | Low | |
| Economic era | 1974–79 | 1980–88 | 1974–79 | 1980–88 | 1974–79 | 1980–88 |
| High | | | | | | Japan |
| Medium high | Sweden | Sweden (4) | France Austria (1) Norway | Austria Norway Finland | Germany (Fed. Rep.) Japan | Germany (Fed. Rep.) |
| Medium and mixed | New Zealand (4) Australia | Canada Australia (4) U.K. (4) | Ireland | | Greece (4) Spain Turkey (1) (3) (4) | |
| Medium low | U.K. Canada | | Italy Portugal | Italy Portugal (4) Ireland (4) | | Greece (4) Spain (4) Turkey (4) |
| Low | | New Zealand (1) (4) | | Switzer-land (4) | | |

*Source: analysis based on OECD Historical Statistics*[2]

**KEY TO ECONOMIC PERFORMANCE INDICATORS:**
High = all available indicators in high category
Low = all available indicators in low category
Medium high = 25 percent or more of available indicators in high category and no indicators in low category
Medium low = 25 percent or more of available indicators in low category and no indicators in high categroy
Medium and mixed = (a) all available indicators in medium category; (b) available indicators distributed across all three categories (high, medium, and low)

**ANNOTATIONS**
(1) No indicator available for unemployment rates for this case for this period
(2) No indicator available for GDP growth per capita for this case for this period
(3) No indicator available for CPI growth for this case for this period
(4) No indicator available for government debt relative to GDP for this case for this period

economic performance may need to be disaggregated to explore these puzzles more carefully. But on these data, the provisional conclusion seems to be that there are factors other than, or in addition to, level macroeconomic performance (either in the post–oil shock 1970s or in the 1980s) that affect the degree of emphasis placed on NPM.

## Size of Government

New Public Management has frequently been interpreted (e.g., by trade union critics) as little more than a means of slimming down big government and saving on resources in the public sector. If slimline public management is what counts in the competition among industrial (or post-industrial) states for economic advantage, we would presumably expect a convergence effect, with the least slimline countries making the most dramatic strides in shifting to NPM doctrines (because they have the most to worry about in terms of comparative advantage). Equally, countries with small-size public bureaucracy might have proportionately less to gain from putting greater stress on such doctrines.

Finding useful indicators for government size is no easier than arriving at robust measures of the nature of party political incumbency. Indeed, it is commonly observed that conventional measures of government size can conceal as much as they reveal (Peters and Heisler, 1983). But we can get a first idea by rolling up four conventional measures of government size (i.e., government employment as percent of total employment, government expenditure as percent of GDP, social security expenditure as percent of GDP, and tax revenue as percent of GDP) and again breaking out the extremes by separating those cases which are more than one standard deviation away from the mean. Table 13.4 indicates where the cases fall in such an analysis.

As can be seen in Table 13.4, only two slimline government cases in the OECD group are in the "low NPM emphasis" category, as would be expected. However, not all large government cases are in the "high NPM emphasis" group, and the medium-sized government cases spread themselves across all three groups of NPM emphasis. On this analysis, if government size plays a part in determining NPM emphasis, it is probably a subsidiary one rather than the single determinant.

## Other factors

In spite of conventional wisdom, there seem to be important cases that do not readily fit the standard explanations for why NPM developed in the 1980s. It is possible that better data (of the kind called for by Peters, McGregor and Solano in other chapters in this book) might remove these apparent anomalies in respect of "Englishness," right-wing political incumbency, economic performance, and government size. What remains to be dis-

TABLE 13.4

**NPM Emphasis and Government Size**

| | Government size | | | | |
|---|---|---|---|---|---|
| NPM emphasis | Large | Medium large | Medium | Medium small | Small |
| High | Sweden | | Canada New Zealand U.K. | Australia | |
| Medium | Denmark Netherlands | Belgium | Austria Finland France Ireland Italy Norway Portugal | U.S.A. | |
| Low | | | Germany (Fed. Rep.) Greece Spain | Switzerland | Japan Turkey |

*Source: OECD Historical Statistics 1988; figures are for 1987*[3]

cussed here is whether there are other possible explanations that might be more persuasive.

One popular explanation for the rise of NPM, which has not been discussed in the sections above because it is not easily reducible to numerical indices, is that it reflects the rise of a new sociotechnical system—"post-Fordism," postindustrialism, the "information society" (see, e.g., Taylor and Williams, 1991). However, the difficulties of using such ideas to understand variations among countries, particularly of the OECD type, are not confined to operationalizing difficulties. It might well be objected that any linkage between trends in public management and level and type of sociotechnical development might be expected to operate only at the global level, and that the explanation is, therefore, too general to explain the sort of intracountry variations considered here.

An element which at first sight seems more promising for these purposes is the baseline, or initial endowment from which different administrative systems start. We could explore this idea from a convergence perspective, examining the hypothesis that the greater the emphasis each system puts on an NPM profile at the baseline, the less movement one might expect (with implications for upward convergence, or even overtaking by the initially laggard cases), or conversely, that initial closeness to such a profile might "program" such a system to make faster strides in that direction (with implications for a widening gap in public management).

Additionally, we could explore the effect of different baselines on NPM development from more of a contingency framework. A possible hypothesis is indicated in table 13.5 below. Two basic elements shaping the context of public management are shown: first, the degree to which there is an integrated public service without significant jurisdictional breaks and with a stress on the role of the core public sector; and second, the degree to which there is a stress on collectivism as opposed to individualism in service provision (broadly, a measure of government size). Using these distinctions, we can identify four polar types: what is called for convenience the "Japanese way," where public service integration is high but collectivism is low; what is called for convenience the "Swedish way," where both integration and collectivism are high; what is called for convenience the "American way," where both integration and collectivism are low; and what is called for convenience the "German way," where collectivism is high but integration is low. (Though, in interpreting the German case, it should be noted that Germany is comparatively high on spending but not on employment, so it would rank high on collectivism only in a spending sense and would need to be counted with the American way if public service employment were the sole measure of collectivism.)

We could then suggest that in order to move significantly toward NPM, there must be both motive and opportunity for incumbent politicians to move the system sharply in that direction. Motive in this case might be expected to consist mainly in the promise or hope of resource saving from the adoption of NPM measures, and could therefore be expected to be proportionately higher in systems that are high on collectivism at the baseline than in low-collectivism systems. Opportunity might be expected to depend on the existence of some Archimedean point to influence the public sector as a whole, and could therefore be expected to be proportionately higher in systems that are high on integration at the baseline than in low-integration systems.

Such an analysis would suggest varying propensities to move toward NPM among the different types of systems. Based on these assumptions, for the polar type labeled the American way, there would be neither motive nor opportunity to make a major shift toward NPM; for the polar type labeled the Japanese way, there would be opportunity but no motive; for the polar type labeled the German way, there would be motive but no opportunity. Only in the polar type labeled the Swedish way would there be *both* motive and opportunity. Hence it might be argued that this would be the type most prone to develop NPM rapidly over a period.

Such an explanation is certainly crude, but it would fit the data presented earlier better than the four conventional explanations considered in the last sec-

TABLE 13.5

**Public Management Baseline Contexts and Propensity to Shift toward NPM:
A Tentative Hypothesis**

| | Stress on "collectivism" in service provision | |
|---|---|---|
| Stress on integration of public service | Low | High |
| High | Japanese Way<br><br>Motive for switch:  low<br>Opportunity:  high | Swedish Way<br><br>Motive for switch:  high<br>Opportunity:  high |
| Low | American Way<br><br>Motive for switch:  low<br>Opportunity:  low | German Way<br><br>Motive for switch:  high<br>Opportunity:  low |

tion, and it would help us to explain apparently "anomalous" cases such as Sweden or Japan, where political incumbency or economic performance run contrary to the expected direction. All of the high NPM emphasis cases in this analysis approximated at the baseline to the Swedish way box on table 13.5, and the same goes for some of the medium/high cases, such as France and Denmark.

## CONCLUSION

This discussion is an exploratory exercise. Its purpose is to raise questions, not to give answers. It has solved none of the methodological problems raised by Peters in chapter 2, though it fits his agenda for the development of comparative research in public administration. The conclusion is that there are puzzles worth looking at and methodological issues worth debating for cross-national analysis of public management developments. There are puzzles worth looking at because some of the stock interpretations of NPM developments in the 1980s do not fit very easily with the simple data presented here. There are methodological issues worth debating because the issues subject to debate (like most phenomena in the social sciences) are not directly observable, and if we are to move away from the data free environment, methodology needs to be refined in order to develop a new generation of cross-national research in this area.

This discussion would suggest a research agenda with the following aims:

(1) Better data

Measuring trends such as those discussed here is always likely to be a highly inexact science. But a more definitive discussion of variations in the extent of adoption of NPM doctrines among OECD countries in the 1980s would need to be built either on a systematic survey or on an intensive joint project, involving repeated meetings among different country experts using a detailed and uniform analytic frame. Until one or the other has been done, we must be content with preliminary and impressionist analysis.

(2) A dimensional approach

As was stressed earlier, NPM is no more than convenient shorthand, and the ranking of cases as involving more or less emphasis on NPM, as has been done here, is a highly aggregative process. The paper has not spelled out the way in which the cases vary within each one of the seven separate dimensions. But it is equally important to examine such variation among the seven dimensions (and others that might be identified), so that we can better identify different styles of public management change and get away from the pervasive tendency of social science to emphasize simple dichotomies that fail to capture the variety of institutional developments.

(3) A contingency framework or a diffusion model?

Developing a contingency approach implies an attempt to move away from the univariate explanations considered here and toward a more multivariate approach to explanation, that is, to relate a multidimensional picture of public management developments to a variety of possible causal factors, each of which may have more power to explain some dimensions of organization than others. Such an approach would be one obvious development from better cross-national data. The obvious drawback of a conventional contingency approach is the difficulty in capturing dynamics in a way that a convergence or diffusion model can do. The way forward may be some hybrid of a contingency approach and a diffusion/convergence approach.

*NOTES*

1. Explanation of table 13:2: The placings are indicative not exact and are intended only as a broad-brush picture.

NPM scorings are based on country reports to the OECD on Public Management (1988 and 1990), with a maximum score of 2 on each of 7 dimensions of doctrine, as described earlier, High scorers are those whose overall score is more than one standard deviation above the mean score; low scorers are those whose overall score is more than one standard deviation below the mean score. Medium scorers are the rest.

Political incumbency scorings are based on the number of years during 1990 that a country was governed by parties to the right or left of its own political spectrum (score +1 for each year a right party governed alone, −1 for each year that a left party governed alone, +0.5 for each year that a center-right coalition governed, −0.5 for each year that a center-left coalition governed, 0 for a grand or similar coalition). Countries that score high (more than one standard deviation above the mean) are taken as "right" in incumbency terms, and countries that score low (more than one standard deviation below the mean) are taken as "left" in incumbency terms. "Center" scorers are the rest.

2. Explanation of table 13:3: As with table 13.2, the placings are indicative and general.

NPM scorings are described in n. 1 above for table 13.2.

Economic performance scorings are based on OECD Historical Statistics 1974–79 and 1980–88. Four conventional series were used: average unemployment rates as percent of total labor force; average rates of growth in real GDP per capita; average growth rate in consumer price index; and average public debt levels as percentage of GDP. For each of these indices, the countries were divided into high, medium, and low scorers by the method described in n. 1, except that for the CPI index, two abnormally low-scoring cases (Turkey and Iceland) were taken out, insofar as both had scores more than twice the mean and the effect of including them would have been to put almost all countries in the medium category.

3. Explanation of table 13:4: As with tables 13.2 and 13.3, the placings are merely indicative and NPM scorings are as described for table 13.2 in n. 1 above. Government size indicators are taken from a country's overall score on four indicators of government size in 1987: government employment as percentage of total employment; government expenditure as percentage of GNP; total government social expenditure as percentage of GNP; and total government tax income as percentage of GNP. Countries that score high on at least three of the four indicators are taken as "large," and countries that score low on at least three of the four indicators are taken as "small" government countries.

## REFERENCES

Aucoin, P. 1990. "Administrative Reform in Public Management: Paradigms, Principles, Paradoxes and Pendulums." *Governance* 3: 115–37.

Castles, F. 1989. "Big Government in Weak States: The Paradox of State Size in the English-Speaking Nations of Advanced Capitalism." *Journal of Commonwealth and Comparative Politics* 27: 267–93.

Castles, F., and V. Merrill. 1989. "Towards a General Model of Public Policy Outcomes." *Journal of Theoretical Politics* 1: 177–212.

Douglas, M. 1982. *In the Active Voice.* London: Routledge.

Downs, G. W., and P. Larkey. 1986. *The Search for Government Efficiency: From Hubris to Helplessness.* Philadelphia: Temple University Press.

Dunleavy, P. 1985. "Bureaucrats, Budgets and the Growth of the State." *British Journal of Political Science* 15: 299–328.

Dunsire, A., and C. Hood. 1989. *Cutback Management in Public Bureaucracies: Popular Theories and Observed Outcomes in Whitehall.* Cambridge: Cambridge University Press.

Gorvin, I., ed. 1989. *Elections Since 1945: A Worldwide Reference Companion.* Harlow: Longman.

Hegewisch, A. 1991. "Public and Private Sector Trends in Remuneration Policies and Contract Flexibility in Europe." Paper presented at a seminar on International Comparisons of Public Sector Pay in 10 Countries: 1990 Results from the Price Waterhouse/Cranfield Survey. London, Public Finance Foundation, 5 September.

Hood, C. 1987. "Public Administration." In V. Bogdanor, ed., *The Blackwell Encyclopaedia of Political Institutions.* Oxford: Blackwell.

————. 1990a. "Public Administration: Lost an Empire, Not Yet Found a Role." In A. Leftwich, ed., *New Directions in Political Science.* Aldershot: Elgar.

————. 1990b. "Beyond the Public Bureaucracy State? Public Administration in the 1990s." Inaugural lecture, London School of Economics, 16 January 1990.

————. 1990c. "De-Sir Humphreyfying the Westminster Model of Governance: A New Style of Governance?" *Governance* 3: 205–14.

————. 1991. "A Public Management for All Seasons?" *Public Administration* 69: 3–19.

Hood, C., and A. Dunsire. 1981. *Bureaumetrics: The Quantitative Comparison of British Central Government Agencies.* Tuscaloosa: University of Alabama Press.

Hood, C., and M. W. Jackson. 1991. *Administrative Argument.* Aldershot: Dartmouth.

Hume, L. 1981. *Bentham and Bureaucracy.* Cambridge: Cambridge University Press.

Jessop, B. 1988. "Conservative Regimes and the Transition to Post-Fordism." *Essex Papers in Politics and Government* 47. Department of Government: University of Essex.

Kamenka, E. 1989. *Bureaucracy.* Oxford: Basil Blackwell.

Keating, M. 1989. "Quo Vadis: Challenges of Public Administration." Address to Royal Australian Institute of Public Administration. Perth, 12 April.

Marini, F. 1971. *Toward a New Public Administration.* Scranton, PA: Chandler.

Martin, J. 1988. *A Profession of Statecraft? Three Essays on Some Current Issues in the New Zealand Public Service.* Wellington: Victoria University Press.

Merkle, J. 1980. *Management and Ideology: The Legacy of the International Scientific Management Movement.* Berkeley: University of California Press.

Nethercote, J. 1989. "Public Service Reform: Commonwealth Experience." Paper presented to the Academy of Social Sciences of Australia, University House, Australian National University, 25 February.

OECD (Organization for Economic Cooperation and Development). 1988. *Public Management Developments.* Paris: OECD.

———. 1990. *Public Management Developments.* Paris: OECD.

———. 1992. *Public Management: OECD Country Profiles.* Paris: OECD.

Osborne, D., and T. Gaebler. 1992. *Reinventing Government.* Reading, MA: Addison-Wesley.

Ostrom, V. 1974. *The Intellectual Crisis in American Public Administration.* Rev. ed. Tuscaloosa: University of Alabama Press.

Overman, E. S. 1984. "Public Management: What's New and Different?" *Public Administration Review* 44: 275–78.

Peters, B. G., and M. Heisler. 1983. "Thinking about Public Sector Growth: Conceptual, Operational, Theoretical and Policy Considerations." In C. L. Taylor, ed., *Why Governments Grow: Measuring Public Sector Size.* Beverly Hills, CA: Sage.

Piore, M., and C. Sabel. 1984. *The Second Industrial Divide.* New York: Basic Books.

Pollitt, C. 1990. *Managerialism and the Public Services: The Anglo-American Experience.* Oxford: Basil Blackwell.

Scharpf, F. 1987. "The Political Calculus of Inflation and Unemployment in Western Europe: A Game-Theoretical Interpretation." *Journal of Public Policy* 7: 227–58.

Scott, G., P. Bushnell, and N. Sallee. 1990. "Reform of the Core Public Sector: New Zealand Experience." *Governance* 3: 138–67.

Small, A. 1909. *The Cameralists.* Chicago: Chicago University Press.

Spann, R. N. 1981. "Fashions and Fantasies in Public Administration." *Australian Journal of Public Administration* 40: 12–25.

Sturgess, G. 1989. "First Keynote Address." In B. Carey and P. Ryan, eds., *In Transition: NSW and the Corporatisation Agenda.* Sydney: Macquarie Public Sector Studies Program/Association for Management Education and Research.

Taylor, J., and H. Williams. 1991. "Public Administration and the Information Polity." *Public Administration* 69: 171–90.

Thompson, M., R. Ellis, and A. Wildavsky. 1990. *Cultural Theory.* Boulder, CO: Westview.

Von Beyme, K. 1984. "Do Parties Matter? The Impact of Parties on the Key Decisions in the Political System." *Government and Opposition* 19: 5–29.

Yeatman, A. 1987. "The Concept of Public Management and the Australian State in the 1980s." *Australian Journal of Public Administration* 46: 339–53.

# 14 THE DIFFUSION OF CIVIL SERVICE REFORM

John Halligan

Internationally, civil service reform has had one of its best decades this century. In the 1980s, there were administrative changes of great magnitude, many seemingly irreversible; reform was rediscovered internationally as viable and even effective (Aucoin, 1990; Caiden, 1991). For a number of countries, the main indicator that things were different was that the character of the reform was comprehensive as opposed to incremental.

Despite substantial variations among countries in the process, and differences in the magnitude and impact of the reforms, there were some strong similarities. This was quite apparent among Anglo-American countries, with general parallels being drawn between the United Kingdom and the United States (Pollitt, 1990), and Australia, Canada, New Zealand, Sweden, and the United Kingdom being grouped because they more explicitly adhered to precepts of what is called the New Public Management than other OECD countries (Hood, chap. 13, this volume). The emergence of a distinctive pattern of reforms in the 1980s and the resemblances among reforms in different countries raises the question of whether these developments were connected and to what extent reform transfers have been occurring. What appear to be extensive borrowings provide the opportunity for revisiting diffusion in the context of the administrative reforms of the 1980s.

Diffusion has been the subject of a large, mainly American literature (e.g., Downs, 1976; Eyestone, 1977; Rogers, 1983), which has been less concerned with international connections, despite what one observer has described as "a thriving international exchange market in political institutions" (Hill, 1976: 19). On the other hand, the substantial literature on the international transfer of institutions generally ignores the diffusion literature (e.g., Lyon and Manor, 1983; Thomas, 1987). Comparative public policy literature has also ventured into this field with its own language (e.g., policy convergence and policy transfers) and some fresh perspectives (Bennett, 1991; Wolman, 1992).

This study explores in some depth several cases of diffusion. It examines relationships between countries linked through common systems by considering the genesis of two different types of civil service reforms: a program of reform in one system, and a specific reform as it moves among several systems.[1]

The first task is to consider the borrowings engaged in by a country as it developed a comprehensive package of reforms. The reform of the Australian civil service in the 1980s provides a relevant case study. It was one of the countries associated with the new managerialism (Aucoin, 1990; Halligan and Power, 1992; Hood, 1990) where the reform process was rapid, comprehensive, sustained, and registered substantial impact. The study of comprehensive reform presents difficulties because it embraces complex agendas covering both managerial and political objectives. As others have noted (e.g., Garnett, 1980), there may be several types of explanations for administrative reform, only one of which involves diffusion. This becomes more complicated where many reforms are under consideration simultaneously.

The second task is to track a sequence of adoptions—the movement of a specific reform along a pathway involving several government systems. The reform chosen here—the creation of the Senior Executive Service—both reflects the character of recent reform programs and is integral to the functioning of civil services. Since it was introduced into the United States by the Carter administration in 1979, a Senior Executive Service has been adopted in several countries.

Two questions about the diffusion process are of particular interest. First, to what extent is the design of reforms borrowed from other countries? The question of separate development or independent invention versus diffusion has a long lineage in the social sciences. The literature on the subject questions how readily we can isolate the role of diffusion, how explicit we can be about attributing responsibility to diffusion and how definite about its extent. This paper argues that diffusion takes a range of forms. A second set of issues centers on the range of processes by which reforms are communicated and diffused. The role of communication networks is well established for diffusion generally. Some attention has been accorded to processes within federal systems; less clear is how they operate internationally.

## ANALYZING DIFFUSION

### Borrowing Reform Designs

Two strands of diffusion research are exemplified by different studies. The first strand has been preoccupied with the question of independent development versus common characteristics. Karvonen (1981: 92) reflects this position by arguing that it is necessary to demonstrate a substantial degree of similarity in policy content. The essential problem is represented in several ways but is centered on the question of the relative merits of diffusion explanations resulting from interaction and the existence of common characteristics that produce similar policies. The difficulty in distinguishing the two is made clear by Downs (1976: 30; cf. Eyestone, 1977: 441–42): if the two are "mutually reinforcing," disentangling the respective impact is problematic.

A second position is adopted by Rogers and Kim (1985; see also Rogers, 1983) who criticize four decades of diffusion research as "oversimplified" because innovations "were regarded as invariant, essentially unchanging in the process of their diffusion and adoption." They develop their position by suggesting that innovation may not remain a fixed entity during diffusion but "is frequently redefined in the process of its implementation" (Rogers and Kim, 1985: 99, 101, 103).

The extent to which diffusion plays a role varies widely. It is common practice, as Rogers recognized, to adapt a borrowed reform to a different context. We can differentiate between types of reform diffusion or consider different degrees of diffusion. A proposition which follows from this is that diffusion comes in a number of forms. Just as the Rogers conception suggests a given case is not unitary, so should conceptions of different cases not be monolithic. We should not be confined to narrow conceptions of borrowing that focus on specific and detailed cases: "Policy borrowing should. . . . be seen as encompassing a broad continuum from general concepts, to policy tools, to highly specific program design" (Wolman, 1992: 41). In addition, there is recognition that diffusion is not an isolated process but one of a set of options (Bennett, 1991: 419; Wolman, 1992: 43). Borrowing is a normal and constant element in the policymaker's range of options.

We therefore have two departures from a narrower and more static view of diffusion: a sense of the reform changing with diffusion and of the diffusion of reform taking a number of shapes.

For the purposes of this analysis, we distinguish three types. First, there is the borrowing of a broad direction or approach, where the influence centers on a general concept. Second, there is the situation where a more specific concept is taken on without regard to close correspondence of detail. Wolman (1992: 41) also recognizes that a specific idea can be borrowed but that "the specific design or structure through which this occurs in the original country may not be." Third, there is the case of an innovation being replicated in fairly precise detail.

The distinction between policy and management innovation needs clarification for both are used in the literature. It is difficult to maintain a fixed distinction between the two for they often merge or overlap (see the concern with mixed cases of technical and administrative in Gow, 1992: 435). In this context management reform is the primary focus and refers to across the system changes to a civil service in contrast to policy reform which is specific to a policy field.

## Diffusion Mechanisms

By what processes does diffusion occur? What has been termed "exoge-neously inspired change" (Hill, 1976: 18) has been previously presented in terms of three main forms: international intervention (coercive); guided change involv-ing the activity of external agents (e.g., federal support or inducements); and vol-untary borrowing (Hill, 1976: 18–19; Wickwar, 1991: 167–79). Our primary concern here is with the latter category, although the role of external agents can-not be ignored. Further, a number of diffusion mechanisms have been identified by Eyestone (1977: 441, 446), who suggests that there is "more than one possible pattern of emulation of policy innovations." Eyestone distinguishes four mecha-nisms that recognize processes both internal and external to a country.

The first centers on the interactive effects among subnational units in a fed-eral system (Eyestone, 1977; Painter, 1991). Interactive effects include those arising from being seen as performing well compared to similar systems, or from simply seeking the best practice. A performance gap between practice and desired performance may also be perceived (Painter, 1991: 144; see also Garnett, 1980; 19; and Nelson, 1985).

A number of studies have sought to explain how the process of diffusion operates within a federal system. Walker (1969: 889–90) focuses on the dynam-ics of policy-making within a federal system, arguing that innovations in one state provide guides to action in others. Reformers are able to overcome inertia by pointing to successful adoptions elsewhere. Painter identifies similar phe-nomena in Australia, arguing that fads and fashions may "sweep across the country from state to state as . . . innovation in one state provokes imitation." These phenomena are "manifestations of the 'self-exciting' consequences of having concurrent polities with overlapping jurisdictions in the one place" (Painter, 1988: 60).

A second means is the so-called "federal effect," where the federal level pro-vides an example to which the states respond. This may entail the federal level offering incentives for subnational units to adopt a policy (Eyestone, 1977; Perry and Kraemer, 1979), although the literature is equivocal on this point. Cases of federal government intervention are not central to this study, although its role in according legitimacy to a type of reform cannot be discounted.

The third, the interactive effects among countries within an international sys-tem, is of particular relevance here. Just as the well-studied states in the United States respond to various pressures to emulate, so does interaction internation-ally produce changes within specific systems. It adds an extra jurisdictional consideration to those already mentioned. One important element is networks that facilitate regular interaction at the international level. In some cases this may amount to "shared experience of learning" about a problem by an international policy community, and it may therefore better be considered policy convergence (Bennett, 1991: 224). Akin to intracountry processes, there are in practice, a number of factors operating, including diffusion. The increasing role of transnational policy communities is still a field that has not been well studied.

A fourth possibility is the impact of international organizations (this of course corresponds at the international level to federal effects). It reflects the increasing role of international organizations and transnational cooperation in the handling of policy issues. "International regimes" have a "shared and long-term commitment to a set of governing arrangements" (Bennett, 1991: 226). Supranational organizations such as the European Union and international aid organizations qualify, although neither case is relevant to this analysis. One can also include less formalized arrangements that nevertheless exert great influence on member nations: institutional pressures for harmonization lead individual nations to adopt what is deemed to be good practice. The objection might well be made that this is moving beyond conventional notions of diffusion; it will depend in practice on how the processes work.

Turning from the types of effects, we can examine how the mechanisms operate, and what it is that influences countries' decisions to use one type of reform rather than another. Three issues are relevant here. First, having identified processes operating at both the federal and international levels, the question arises as to the relationships between them, for in practice they may be closely linked. The interaction among the mechanisms therefore has to be taken into account.

Second, the patterns of diffusion have taken three main forms: hierarchical, spatial, and specialized communication channels. Previous explanations have centered on hierarchical diffusion: larger or more developed units adopt new policies earlier. There is also evidence of systems following regional leaders, leading to spatial diffusion (Collier and Messick, 1975: 1306; Walker, 1969). The third pattern is of particular interest. The role of communication networks is well established in the diffusion literature, a central principle being the development of relationships among units with similar characteristics: "the heart of the diffusion process is the modeling and imitation by potential adopters of their near-peers who have previously adopted a new idea"; decisions about whether to adopt an innovation are largely dependent upon "the communicated experience of others much like ourselves who have already adopted" (Rogers, 1983: 293).

Another way of approaching the question of patterns is to examine the propensity of countries to look outward, and their preparedness to borrow others' innovations. Some countries (e.g., Britain) have been absorbed in their own traditions and have traditionally styled themselves repositories of a distinctive form of government that exports institutions and is relatively impervious to external influences. Small nations (e.g., Australia) are more externally oriented, either because of colonially induced reactions or the natural inclination to scan automatically the experience of larger kindred systems and the broader international environment.

## COMPREHENSIVE REFORMS: THE AUSTRALIAN CASE

In examining the genesis of the comprehensive set of reforms in Australia, the discussion must be selective because of the breadth of the changes and the interest of this chapter in gauging the extent of the borrowing from other systems. Reform has been comprehensive, rapid, and systemic. The range of changes covers the gamut of possibilities: philosophy, operational style, structure, personnel, and culture (Campbell and Halligan, 1992; Halligan and Power, 1992).

There had been experimentation for a decade, laying some of the foundations for a major shift; but fundamental change only proceeded in the early 1980s. The reform program was particularly susceptible to the influence of others in the early stages of formulation and during its initial implementation. This coincides with the twilight of the Fraser coalition government and the early years of the Hawke government, in other words, the period 1982–86. During this time, priorities changed; some elements were modified, others added. Under the Hawke government, three stages in the reform program can be distinguished: the initial program for action (1983–84); redirection as fiscal austerity intensified (1986); and restructuring combined with implementation and refinement following the government's reelection for a third term in 1987, a stage which also signaled less reliance on external models.

The initial reform program proposed by the new Labor government in 1983 had three components: the roles of senior advisers and managers, resource allocation, and personnel policies (Commonwealth of Australia, 1983). The legislative basis for many changes was provided by the Public Service Reform Act of 1984. The elements given attention here are financial management, efficiency scrutinies, and central personnel management and the senior public service. But first consideration is given to the reform concept and package, for the derivation of its managerial and political elements are somewhat different.

## THE REFORM CONCEPT AND PACKAGE

### The Political Party within the Federal Nexus

The major changes within the executive branch were not the product of a single master plan in one public sector. Rather they resulted from experimentation at both state and national levels over a fifteen-year period. The Australian states are large and powerful units of government that share the same form of government with the federal level. It is therefore possible to examine administrative reform through comparative analysis of several similar units of government as they move through different developmental stages (Halligan and Power, 1991; 1992).

The reform program consisted essentially of two broad agendas, political and managerial, which in turn comprised a set of reforms. In order to accomplish change, the political executive had to secure control over the bureaucracy. This was eventually accomplished by relying on a shift from administering to managing within the bureaucracy. Taken together, the two have been termed political management (Halligan and Power, 1992).

The enhancement of the political executive proceeded through several phases during the seventies and early eighties. The product of these reforms was a set of political mechanisms for influencing and directing the public service: improved central capacity to set directions and establish priorities, greater ministerial resources, and more effective and diverse external policy advice. A range of tested political methods became available for facilitating the political control of the executive branch. However, the package remained incomplete.

A new stage emerged in the 1980s when governments embraced managerialist approaches to enforcing and maintaining control, at which point the contemporary packages won general acceptance. Although managerial ideas had been infiltrating for some time, what was strikingly different was that managerial change was now both accepted and seen in systemic and strategic terms, and it complemented political agendas.

The first system to get the package together was a Labor government elected in the state of Victoria in 1982. What was termed "the Labor approach," as developed in the two largest states, was explicitly recognized in the party document *Labor and the Quality of Government* published a month before the 1983 national elections:

> The Task Force has been closely monitoring the experience of the Cain Government in Victoria . . . [it] has been conspicuously successful to date in its administrative performance, at both Cabinet and official level, and we have learned much from that experience. We have also been in close consultation with members and advisers of the much longer established Wran Government [in New South Wales] and have learned an equally great deal from them. (Hawke and Evans, 1983: 5)

The pattern of diffusion in this case is complex. The federal nexus is of the utmost importance, and the influence of the state level experience is explicit, but there is still difficulty in disentangling the elements. What is clear is that the main mechanism by which the reforms were diffused was a political organization, the Labor Party, which was organized on a federal basis. The process was also dominated by the Labor Party because it controlled most Australian governments at the state and national levels in the 1980s and drew on the same basic principles for reform programs.[2]

The types of operational and evaluative information that were transmitted through the political party were those which served the primary objectives of Labor's political executives. Reform programs were driven by a foremost concern of Labor, political control, which had come to be regarded as both an end in itself and a means to implementing party policy. To achieve this required a redistribution of power between the bureaucracy and the politicians. Other reforms were not ignored; they either conformed with the political objectives (e.g., top-down, centrally directed budgeting and management) or were simply subservient.

## Managerialism and the International Linkage

The international influences on the overall conception are more difficult to identify than those operating within Australia. We can discern an international pattern of change from the late 1970s, centered in Anglo-American countries. There was a fundamental review and change of direction in the approach to public service management. Consequently, references appeared to new paradigms, the ideology of managerialism, and to a watershed in public management (Aucoin, 1990; Pollitt, 1990: 27; Power, 1990). Moreover, a group of countries that had shifted, if not in unison in the nineteenth century then at least in a linked sequence, were now moving again in broadly similar ways. The set of countries—Australia, Canada, New Zealand, and the United Kingdom—embarked on major reform programs during the 1980s. In so doing, they more explicitly adhered to precepts of managerialism than did almost any other country in the OECD.

Establishing the links between reform packages is tricky. The influences came through two channels: bilateral relations between countries, and international organizations. The formal networks based on the Commonwealth provided a key channel of communication among these countries. In the past, new British reforms had been studied by members of the Commonwealth. Australia was influenced by Britain, Canada, and the United States. Britain embarked on major changes under Thatcher in the early 1980s. Canada had been experimenting with management changes since the 1960s and was regarded as the most closely comparable to Australia (federal, but parliamentary, with British traditions). The U.S. reforms of the late 1970s also attracted much attention. At various points, New Zealand's experiments were acknowledged (particularly in the late 1980s, when its radical changes had a trans-Tasman impact).

The networks have had two operating features: the regular meeting of civil service elites, and staff exchanges among members of the network.[3] The most immediate communication system, a regionally based mixture of federal and international links, has been centered in Australia and New Zealand. Essentially, the network comprised Australian federal units, but neighboring countries (e.g., from Melanesia) have had representation. The best example is the Australasian

Public Service Commissioners' Conference, the annual meeting of senior officials from Australia—including the states and territories, and New Zealand.

The most coherent international network has been that based on the Commonwealth: Canada, Britain, Australia, and New Zealand (see, e.g., PSB/DoF 1984: appendix 2). The basis lay in a common language, cultural legacy, and institutions, and established connections of great strength until relatively recently. A formal example is the biennial meeting of public service commissioners. More recently the Organization for Economic Cooperation and Development (OECD) has provided the basis for an important network. Its publications (e.g., OECD, 1990), forums, and data bank (on-line from Paris) have become important sources of knowledge about managerial change in member countries.

Central agencies have maintained active relations with counterparts overseas. The Department of the Prime Minister and Cabinet (DPMC) has regularly exchanged personnel with the Canadian Privy Council Office and the former British Civil Service Department and Cabinet Office; similar arrangements also existed with New Zealand. The department also maintained links with the OECD, attending meetings and seminars as well as sending staff on temporary transfer to the institution. The Department of Finance (DoF) has regularly exchanged officers with the Canadian Treasury Board Secretariat, Her Majesty's Treasury, the International Monetary Fund, and the OECD. It also maintained regular contact with budgetary officials in the United States, the United Kingdom, New Zealand, Canada, and several European countries, discussing the general economic outlook and issues related to budgetary decision-making processes, financial management and expenditure control techniques, as well as general issues of public sector reform (see, e.g., PSB/DoF, 1984). The Public Service Board (and its successor, the Public Service Commission) monitored overseas developments in public administration, maintained regular direct relations with and sent officers to the U.K. Management and Personnel Office and Treasury, the U.S. Office of Personnel Management, the Canadian Treasury Board, and the New Zealand State Services Commission (PSB, 1980: 6–7; PSB, 1981: 42, 120; PSB, 1982: 33; PSB, 1983: 69).

A more prominent role for the OECD was also apparent in the 1980s. The OECD provided an important forum for the exchange of information between the department and its overseas counterparts. The DoF has acknowledged the many similarities between Australian and overseas reforms of budgetary process and financial management procedures. Referring to the Australian contribution to a three-year, OECD "Capacity to Budget" study, the DoF noted that "a striking feature of the Study is the commonality of the economic and budgetary problems that have confronted the participating countries, particularly over the past decade, and the similarity of approaches adopted to solving these problems" (DoF, 1986: 42). This role for the transnational organizations has received recognition in other policy fields: "the EC. . . . and OECD have provided indispensable institutional frameworks for building a common response [and] developing congruent policies" (quoted in Bennett, 1991: 226).

The extent to which a transnational policy community for managerial change was already operating in the early 1980s is difficult to determine. The OECD played a role in providing a hothouse for reformist economists on temporary transfer, who were attracted to emergent managerialism (which was to contribute to crystallizing the reform program in Australia). There was an international confluence of ideas about the role of management, but it has yet to be effectively documented. There is no doubt about the constancy, extent, and regularity of the contact between the countries under discussion, or that the OECD became a key international focal point for managerial change in some member countries.

In the case of Australia, such international links became sufficiently important to attract national attention between 1991 and 1992. This followed public reflection on the impact of economic rationalist policies that were designed to make Australia more competitive internationally. These policies were reflected in bureaucratic reforms that focused on efficiency and economy to the exclusion of other considerations. As Aucoin (1990: 134) comments, "the internationalization of public management parallels the internationalization of public and private economies." The backlash against the dominance of economic rationalism in government centered on the argument that countries that borrowed such policies reproduced the mistakes of others. Economic rationalism was seen to have been imported with pernicious consequences both for Australia generally and the higher public service specifically, and the OECD was the main vehicle (Pusey, 1991).

Linking packages of reforms is highly problematic. The packages are composites of reforms that vary from country to country. They are put together at different points, and they generally evolve over several years. Naturally, they reflect the needs of the target system as well as features common to others. To give one example, Britain eventually opted for the Next Steps approach as the centerpiece of its package, but other countries have not moved to adopt a similar scheme. As will be seen in the next section, Australia was willing to draw on both British and American reforms.

## Managerial Reforms and Specific Influences

There are three reforms to be examined here. The first was the Financial Management Improvement Program, which provided the basis for the managerialism of the 1980s. The second involves reforms to central personnel management and the introduction of a senior executive service. Both were to register an impact in the longer term. The third was a flourish without durable effects—efficiency scrutinies. A counterpart to each can be found elsewhere (table 14.1), though as the discussion will indicate, the strength of the link varies from case to case.

TABLE 14.1

**Diffusion Linkage Examined**

| Reform | Overseas | | | Australia | |
|---|---|---|---|---|---|
| | Name | Country | Date Introduced | Name | Date Introduced |
| Financial Management | FMI | U.K. | 1982 | FMIP | 1983 |
| Central Personnel Management | CSRA | U.S. | 1978 | PSRA | 1984 |
| Senior Executive Service | SES | U.S. | 1978 | SES | 1984 |
| Efficiency Scrutiny | Efficiency Scrutiny | U.K. | 1979 | Efficiency Scrutiny Unit | 1986 |

CSRA: Civil Service Reform Act
PSRA: Public Service Reform Act

*Financial management improvement program.*

Resource allocation and priorities constituted one of the three components of the government's 1983 policy statement on *Reforming the Australian Public Service.* The reforms were also described as designed to improve management capacity within government. The relationship between allocation and priorities was made explicit by defining management as "the process of setting objectives, organising resources to attain them and evaluating the results for the purposes of determining future action" (Commonwealth of Australia, 1983: 27). The two major dimensions of the Australian reforms were budgetary reform and management improvement. Great emphasis was placed on devolving responsibility, developing information systems, emphasizing effectiveness in program management, and accounting for results.

A number of the proposals were not particularly innovative: some were "solutions" awaiting a problem and government sponsorship (e.g., program budgeting), others were recommended by the Review of Commonwealth Administration's report of early 1983 (e.g., Financial Management Improvement Program [FMIP], and the Management Improvement Plan [MIP]). The government contributed an official conceptualization of management improvement as a relatively integrated and comprehensive program for action.

There were at least two sets of influences from overseas. The first occurred in the 1970s through an English-trained political scientist, Hugh Emy, who was a consultant on the topic of the public service and political control for the Royal Commission on Australian Government Administration (RCAGA, 1976a). His study pronounced that the concept of ministerial responsibility was defunct for the purposes of ensuring accountability: "a new system is to be found in institutionalising a set of measures to be called accountable management." His proposed revision to "the philosophy of government," was to provide "the conceptual framework for a new system of control." It drew on the British experience, in particular the report of the Fulton Committee of 1968, which had recommended accountable management and managerialism for the United Kingdom (RCAGA, 1976b: 15, 47–48). In neither country was the concept immediately taken up. The second and more arresting links were the parallels between the United Kingdom's Financial Management Initiative and the Australian Financial Management Improvement Program. The Financial Management Initiative [FMI] was launched in May 1982 by the treasury and endorsed by the government in September 1982. The treasury invited departments to "define a programme for the improvement of financial management" (PSB/DoF, 1984: 52; Metcalfe and Richards, 1990: chap. 9).

In January 1983, the Australian Review of Commonwealth Administration commended the fundamental principles of the FMI and recommended that a financial management improvement program be commenced as a matter of high priority. In according this such urgency, the review board appeared to be heeding the exhortations of the Department of Finance (RCA, 1983: 40, 73–74). The minister who was responsible for the public service, Mr. John Dawkins, personally examined the developments in the United Kingdom. The existence of an Australian Financial Management Improvement Program, developed by the Public Service Board and the Department of Finance, was formally acknowledged in June 1983 and endorsed by the government in December 1983 (Commonwealth of Australia, 1983: 30; PSB/DoF, 1984: v).

The contents of the FMI and FMIP were broadly the same: an emphasis on objectives and results, accountability and information, and performance measurement. In both cases, comparable central financial and personnel agencies were involved.

Despite this correspondence, participants in the process argue that it was not a direct borrowing solely from the United Kingdom. (But compare Schick, 1990: 26, who argues that "British activities. . . . strongly influenced Australian and Canadian innovations.") Australian officials were participating in a climate that favored managerial change and which was given coherence in Britain at this time. The British conception of a financial management initiative was undoubtedly important, but the details of the Australian program also drew on the longer experience of Canada, a pioneer in the field, and New Zealand (RCA, 1983; PSB/DoF, 1984: 50–53).

*Off the shelf: Efficiency scrutinies.*

The adoption of the efficiency scrutiny model from Britain represents an explicit case of diffusion that was officially acknowledged as a borrowing. In September 1986, the government announced the establishment of an Efficiency Scrutiny Unit (ESU) as the central element in a package of changes for stream-lining the public service. According to the prime minister, it was designed to stimulate improvements in administrative management procedures through "an extensive program of scrutinies of public sector operations" (Hawke, 1986: 2–3). The irony was that in the United Kingdom, the FMI was depicted as an "extension of the scrutiny programme" (Metcalfe and Richards, 1990: 178); in Australia, efficiency scrutinies were adopted after the introduction of the FMIP to respond to a particular crisis.

The concept was borrowed directly from the system of efficiency scrutinies introduced into Britain in 1979 under the guidance of Sir Derek Rayner. The approach developed in the United States, the Grace report (President's Private Sector Survey on Cost Control, 1984) on cost control, was also given considera-tion. It differed in being an external review and was ultimately deemed to be relatively less successful and was explicitly avoided.

The U.K. arrangement involved a central unit located in the prime minister's office, which assisted departments in undertaking scrutinies of selected areas of activity that offered prospects for better resource utilization. The general process adopted in Australia followed that of the United Kingdom. The similarities included the appointment of a private sector adviser, who was a senior busi-nessman, and the use of a small staff to undertake scrutinies of activities or func-tion in order to identify possible efficiencies. The scrutinies were undertaken by departments under ministers but were subject to advice from the central unit both as to the selection of subjects and the control of scrutinies.

There was explicit acknowledgment of the source of the Australian concept (ESU, 1986; Hawke, 1986; SSCFPA, 1989: 13). This was most clearly indicated by the Department of the Prime Minister and Cabinet: "the methodology [of the scrutinies] follows the basic approach of the United Kingdom Efficiency Unit established by Sir Derek Rayner. . . . The Unit acknowledges the assistance given by Sir Robin Ibbs, now head of the United Kingdom Unit" (DPMC, 1987: 35). The two guides produced for explaining and undertaking a scrutiny were simply copied from the British Efficiency Unit (e.g., compare Efficiency Unit, 1985, with ESU, 1986). The ESU was created as a small unit, headed by Mr. David Block, a Sydney merchant banker and consultant, with a departmental secretary.

There were several departures from the Rayner approach; the most important were tighter control over the process (greater ministerial responsibility and a shorter time scale for the total scrutiny and implementation process), and the provision of incentives to departments to implement the recommendations. The Australian exercise was, however, terminated after forty-four scrutinies; it lasted for less than two years of its projected three-year term. Efficiency scrutinies were shifted from the ESU to individual departments, which were subsequently reported as being inactive in this area.

There were parallels between the results in the United Kingdom and Australia. Both achieved savings, the British being more successful, though official calculations were substantially higher than the reported outcomes. Both exercises were also accused of being essentially about cost reduction although other aims were proclaimed and improving public sector practices were meant to be a by-product of this activity.

The adoption of the British efficiency scrutinies was an officially acknowledged case of borrowing. It was a quick solution to pressing economic problems in 1986, but it was also quickly discarded. It can be claimed as only a modest success.

*Central personnel reform and senior executives.*

Establishing the links between the Civil Service Reform Act (CSRA) in the United States and Australia is more challenging. The two elements of greatest interest are the changes in the central personnel agency and the higher civil service. The first produced an agency more subject to political direction. The second was designed to develop a senior executive service based on generalist managers who could be readily redeployed to different positions and could be evaluated and rewarded on the basis of performance (considered in the next section).

The Civil Service Act of 1978 inaugurated a new period of personnel management in the United States.[4] Two components found imitation in Australia almost immediately, although the link is explicit only with the Senior Executive Service.

Mounting pressure to strengthen the political executive led the New South Wales state government to initiate the first major break with past practice. The state's public service had been subject to the dictates of the most powerful central personnel agency in the country. The Public Service Board, an independent authority, had statutory powers that covered recruitment and promotions, staff levels, industrial relations, and the efficiency and economy of public service administration. In 1979, the state's Labor government moved to curb its power and to assert the paramountcy of the government. Subsequently, Public Service Boards in all states, and eventually at the federal level (1984 and 1987), lost powers, independence, and their very existence.

The functions of the board were assigned to new agencies. A most important outcome was that personnel management came under political direction, although special provision was made for merit protection (a Merit Protection

Authority) and a Public Service Commissioner retained statutory responsibility for senior appointments and personnel policy. A number of responsibilities were delegated to departments and became more directly subject to ministerial direction. The Public Service Reform Act of 1984 was the main vehicle for the Australian changes.

The evidence of an international transfer is inconclusive with regard to the package of relevant reforms. There were parallels between the reforms of central agencies in both countries. International transfer is unequivocal, however, for a central element of the CSRA, the Senior Executive Service.

## SENIOR EXECUTIVE SERVICE

The diffusion of the Senior Executive Service (SES) has been chosen for closer examination for several reasons. First, there was a distinctive concept with an associated reform design. Second, a clear sequence of adoptions can be argued to have followed the introduction of the original system. Diffusion, to adapt Eyestone (1977: 441), can be depicted as a pattern of successive adoptions of a reform. Third, the countries involved have developed from a relatively common base: the higher civil services of Australia, Canada, New Zealand, and the United States have important shared features.

The differences between the senior civil services, and in particular the major models, have been a perennial preoccupation of academics (e.g., Smith, 1984), the question of an administrative elite and the relative importance of generalists and specialists providing two foci for this work. The common experience has been an unwillingness to consider seriously an administrative class, and the high status of the specialist relative to the generalist (Subramaniam, 1977: 2). Thus, an American visitor to Australia in the early post–second world war period reported that: "Both the Australian and United States Services are based on a similar classification concept, give wide scope to the specialist, and are founded on a strong and valuable egalitarian tradition" (Scarrow, 1957: 139–40).

Subramaniam (1977: 3–4) has examined why Afro-Asian countries have systems patterned on the British model, while "old" Commonwealth countries and the United States have been reluctant to create an administrative class:

> In spite of persistent advice from academic admirers of this Class in the twenties and thirties, the U.S. federal authorities did not seriously look at the idea till the time of the Second Hoover Commission—and its late acceptance was both grudging and qualified. Australia and New Zealand set their faces more deliberately against it for decades—for reasons of equalitarianism and pragmatism and all efforts. . . . were met with stiff opposition for years from the respective Labour parties and civil service unions.

Between the late 1970s and late 1980s, all countries moved toward the development of a managerial elite.

The Senior Executive Service is credited to the United States, where the concept was first developed at the state level and then emerged as part of the federal government's Civil Service Reform Act of 1978. The sequence of change then proceeded as follows: Canada introduced the Management Category, which incorporated similar principles, in 1981. The diffusion of the SES concept to and within Australia proceeded in the 1980s, being introduced first in the state of Victoria in 1982 and nationally in 1984. Four of the five other Australian states followed in the late 1980s. New Zealand created its SES in 1988.

The focus here is on the Australian and New Zealand stages of the sequence, but the Canadian scheme needs to be acknowledged because it exercised some influence. The Canadian system was designed to replace appointment-to-position with appointment-to-level in order to create a single classification for senior management because a coherent group was lacking. Performance review and appraisal, which had been introduced in 1979, was taken a step further by the establishment of a link between the pay system and performance. Increased accountability, training, and development were also emphasized. The scheme also aimed "to minimize the barriers to flexible deployment of senior personnel, such as interposition transfer within departments. . . . The concept offers more managerial authority and flexibility to act in return for accountability for results achieved" (Dwivdei and Phidd, 1990: 141; Fisher and Gallagher, 1982). The Canadian system was developed after CSRA and shared a number of characteristics with the neighboring scheme, although the title was not adopted.

The initial schemes in Australia and New Zealand pertained to the Victorian and the Australian public services. The state government of Victoria was the first to establish an SES. The then head of the Public Service Board or central personnel agency played a key role. He was an admirer of American public administration, but he was influenced more by the Californian and Canadian systems than by the U.S. federal scheme.[5] Both the name and the essence of the U.S. concept were accordingly transferred to Australia.

A Senior Executive Service was a central component of the Australian reform program (Commonwealth of Australia, 1983). The Australian parliament's Joint Committee of Public Accounts (1982), having investigated Canada, the United States, and the United Kingdom, pronounced that the latter had nothing to offer and recommended a Senior Executive Group in 1982. The Review of Commonwealth Administration (1983) also recommended changes to improve the quality of senior managers.[6]

The new Labor government's main reform statement devoted more attention to a Senior Executive Service than to most subjects, observing that:

Recent reviews of the Public Service have recommended that special measures be taken to improve the performance of senior management. These include:

> formation of a senior executive category or group; more open competition for
> positions including from outside the Service . . .; more emphasis on the devel-
> opment of managerial skills; introduction of formal staff appraisals; greater
> mobility of senior managers in accordance with Service needs; and more flexi-
> bility for Department heads in the allocation and use of senior staff resources.
> The Government has decided upon reforms in each of these areas.
> (Commonwealth of Australia, 1983: 12–13)

The Australian public service scheme reshaped the second division into a
"unified group" called the Senior Executive Service, with mandatory membership for senior public servants.

New Zealand adopted an SES once it had become firmly established in
Australia. The radical reform program in that country largely ignored the rich
Australian experience; the treasury-dominated agenda produced changes that
were in some respects unique among countries adopting managerialism. The
interesting exception was the Senior Executive Service, a scheme that was credited to the State Service Commission (SSC), a body in regular contact with
Australian counterparts. The Commission "had been interested in the concept for
several years. . . . The trigger in this case was the SSC's concern about the possible negative implications which the abandonment of a single, unified, career
public service might have on interdepartmental co-operation and policy co-ordi-
nation" (Boston, 1991: 104). It was officially described as a "unifying force at the
most senior levels of the Public Service" (quoted in Boston, 1991: 104).

Four Australian states—Western Australia (1988), New South Wales (1989),
Queensland (1990), and Tasmania (1990)—also adopted a senior executive service. The schemes were broadly similar and were derived from the existing
ones. A senior executive service became part of the Labor model (in a decade
when they dominated Australian government) as successive new governments
included the concept, and was thereby extended around Australia. The main
differences occurred in New South Wales, where a conservative coalition government injected new elements that moved the concept closer to private sector
practice.

*Comparison of processes.*

The basis of the concept was an executive group that was to operate as a ser-
vice-wide, corporate entity, rather than as simply the sum of departmental and
agency members. Emphasis was placed on the active deployment of senior staff
across the public service. At this systemic level, the quality of public service
management was to be enhanced by greater movement of senior managers
within the service and by recruiting lateral entrants. At the departmental level,
there was to be greater opportunity for deploying senior staff. Staff development
and staff appraisal were to receive greater emphasis. Performance pay was recognized in some cases.

TABLE 14.2

**Formal Features of the Senior Executive Services in Five Systems**

| Features | United States | Victoria | Australia | New Zealand | New South Wales |
|---|---|---|---|---|---|
| Date established | 1979 | 1982 | 1984 | 1988 | 1989 |
| Open recruitment | Yes | Yes | Yes | Yes | Yes |
| Main employment basis | Career* | Career* | Career* | Contract | Contract |
| Managerial skills | Yes | Yes | Yes | Yes | Yes |
| Mobility programs | Yes | Yes | Yes | Yes | No |
| Executive development | Yes | Yes | Yes | Yes | No |
| Performance appraisal | Yes | Yes | No† | Yes | Yes |
| Performance pay | Yes | Yes | No# | Yes | No¶ |
| Service identity | Yes | Yes | Yes | Yes | No |

*Contract employment coexists with career service but is relatively unimportant in the Australian SESs
†Initially provided for but not systematically developed until the end of the 1980s
#Now policy, and finally being implemented in 1993
¶Part of original concept, but unimplemented
*Sources: adapted from Halligan, 1990; Renfrow, 1989*

The various systems can be studied according to the extent to which they conformed to the original concept and in what ways they modified it. Table 14.2 covers formal characteristics common to the systems; it does not seek to estimate the extent to which they were implemented, and acknowledges only a few of the differences among them. Table 14.2 shows that the same basic concept was accepted by each of the systems, though schemes in the late 1980s moved further from the original.

The scheme of the state of Victoria was associated with a government that was the first in Australia to introduce a new reform package (Halligan and Power, 1992). The package included a performance pay system that focused on rewarding performance. In the case of the federal public service (and two of the state systems), the major contrast with the U.S. system was the lack of a bonus package as an incentive to performance (and there was no provision, of course, for political appointments).

The other two variants, in New South Wales and New Zealand, took the SES principle further by disbanding the career service and by showing considerable deference to performance and market values. New Zealand also incorporated a form of performance pay, while New South Wales offered the highest remuneration packages in the region (Boston, 1991; Halligan, forthcoming).

### Diffusion and the SES.

We can identify several processes at work. First, there had been earlier proposals in Australia. Just as the SES did not emerge as an entirely original scheme at one critical point in time in the United States, so in Australia a Senior Executive Category had previously been recommended for the Australian public service by the Royal Commission on Australian Government Administration (RCAGA, 1976a: 249, 272). The Canadian public service's Management Category had also been closely studied. In 1982 the Public Service Board was proposing to rename the second division the Senior Executive Group, apparently combining the terms used in Canada and the United States (Cole, 1982: 9).

Second, interaction among the adoptees was important, particularly where they became intermediaries. The early experiments were studied directly and discussed at conferences. The role of intermediaries was important for those who adopted the SES later. Victoria influenced the Australian government, and both were emulated by other states during the 1980s. New Zealand followed Australia.

Third, the short-term needs of governments were important. In Australia in 1983, Labor needed a solution that recognized the pressures for change but avoided tampering excessively with traditional practice. Prior to the election of that year, the Labor Party had developed policy that favored an American-style approach to appointments and involved 5 percent of the senior public service. After attaining government power in 1983 (and under a new leader), it opted for a Senior Executive Service based on the career public servant. While the SES was highly significant as a managerial departure, the government had avoided departing from Australian conventions regarding the separation of the political and bureaucratic spheres (Halligan, 1992). Similarly, the New Zealand SES was the product of an immediate need to balance radical changes in a public service that favored autonomous agencies.

Finally, there is no doubt that the concept originated in the United States and was borrowed successively by other countries. The title was acquired from the American SES, and North American principles were followed. This is acknowledged in an Australian Senate review of the SES and elsewhere (SSCFPA, 1990:

5): "The establishment of an SES was a fashionable reform in the 1980s. The senior cadre of the United States Civil Service had been reorganised in 1978 with the title of SES and features broadly similar to those adopted in the APS in 1984." A scholar who has studied the legislation claims that "the 1978 CSRA and the 1984 Public Service Reform Act exhibit marked similarities in both goals and design" (Renfrow, 1989: 90). Similarly, one New Zealand observer notes that the creation of an SES followed "similar moves in other OECD countries," namely, the United States, Canada, and Australia (Boston, 1991: 105).

## BORROWING REFORM DESIGNS: EXTENT AND MEANS

The borrowing of reform designs from other countries has been explored by examining a range of reforms within the comprehensive program of one country as well as by looking at one sequence transferred internationally. Several types of reform transfer can be differentiated according to the nature of the borrowed element.

A distinction has been drawn here between the overall reform concept or package and specific reforms within the package. At this general level, one period of intensive reform produced a fundamental change of direction in the approach to the public service. Australia, Canada, New Zealand, and the United Kingdom embraced managerialism quickly. While there were differences between their managerialist programs, this group stood out from most other countries (see Hood, chap. 13). Similarly, there was also transfer of reform programs within Australia. A package of political and management reforms emerged in Australia in the early 1980s and was circulated through the Labor Party.

We have examined the broad direction or approach to reform through the general concept of financial management improvement. This concept was highly influential, and it satisfied both a short-term need and acquired longer-term significance as part of more extensive reform programs.

We have also considered the case of a specific concept being borrowed, and to a substantial but variable extent, the design was also largely transferred. The third type of transfer involved the borrowing of a reform in precise detail. The Efficiency Scrutiny reform was the only case where there was a wholesale adoption of another country's reform with only relatively minor modifications, but this reform was the most short-lived. There is an argument that the uncritical transplanting of a reform can be dysfunctional. While cases can be produced to both support and reject this proposition, the variability of outcomes suggests that too much borrowing can be hazardous.

Three other propositions can be offered about the borrowing process. First, the need to act expeditiously clearly forces the issue of obtaining a new reform concept. The efficiency scrutiny transfer was the product of a governmental crisis. Efficiency was rapidly propelled to the top of the agenda, and streamlining the public service acquired urgency. In pursuing the new agenda, an "off-the-shelf" solution was relied on. Second, in the making of design decisions, reformers in most cases wisely drew on several sources. They did not usually slavishly follow one model. The third proposition is that the cases, with one exception, were not clear-cut. The reforms were a product of a combination of factors. There is some agreement here between the literature on reform and that on diffusion. As Garnett (1980) has argued, different types of explanations can explain reform and offer insights. Studies of diffusion also indicate the complexity of decision-making and the difficulty of establishing single linkages.

### Role of Diffusion Mechanisms

Our primary interest has been in international mechanisms for diffusing reform, though it has been impossible to ignore the involvement of mechanisms of a different order. Diffusion may involve interaction within either a federal system or an international community. In addition, a national government or an international body may be important. It is perhaps inevitable that comprehensive reform might involve the interaction of several processes. It is worth examining the relationship between two of these processes.

Diffusion commonly results from a combination of processes. The case of the Senior Executive Service illustrated the interaction of international, federal, and regional processes: the SES was transferred to Australia from the United States (with some Canadian influence). It was then rapidly diffused from the state to the federal level and from thence to four of the other states over a seven-year period. The most closely related country in the region, New Zealand, also picked up the concept during this time.

The importance of internal diffusion in a federation relative to external processes remains unanswered. In a federal system, "once a program has gained the stamp of legitimacy, it acquires a momentum of its own" (Walker, 1969: 890); it may be subject to a "bandwagon effect. . . . as successful vote-winning stratagems are imitated by political entrepreneurs at the different levels and across the states" (Painter, 1988: 59). During a period of state resurgence in the 1970s and early 1980s, the influence of the two largest states on national agendas was apparent. The importing of concepts to Australia occurred via state governments; these changes then spread to the federal level and other states (e.g., a new type of central personnel agency and the first Senior Executive Service).

In contrast to a federal system where the combination of federal and international borrowings was important, the case of unitary New Zealand is instructive. The latter country proceeded upon a relatively idiosyncratic reform path. Although closely linked to Australia, it was immune to many of the interactive and federal effects experienced in Australia because those who controlled the reform agenda were unresponsive to positions favored within the regional network. The benefits were that it produced a fresh stance on reform (Boston et al., 1991). The cost was that New Zealand was denied the lessons of the Australian experience (Halligan and Power, 1992).

The international processes were primary in some cases. The interaction took the form of exchanges between members of a network—whether conceived of as a policy community or otherwise—and supranational organizations that operated independently of member countries. The mechanisms were primarily bureaucratic. There has been some overlap between bureaucratic mechanisms for communicating innovation at both the international level and within the federal system. The latter have consisted of professional specialists based primarily in central agencies: treasury, finance, personnel, auditing, and prime ministers' departments.

Political mechanisms have operated on a federal basis, the key element being the political party. The Labor Party, while federally organized and divided into factions spanning a left-right spectrum, has nevertheless maintained core attitudes toward the role of the public service. The models provided by early experiments were circulated through party channels. Members of Parliament played a role as party actors and as ministers responsible for the public service (e.g., Hawke, 1986; Hawke and Evans, 1983); as legislators, they have been marginal players, except as members of parliamentary committees (e.g., JCPA, 1982).

It should not be forgotten that a borrowing may also be a product of expediency driven by an immediate need. It has been argued that "diffusion patterns may record the spread of necessity rather than the emulation of virtue," leading to the "timely model" that provides a solution to a problem (Eyestone, 1977: 441, 446). A more sophisticated perspective is available by drawing on the garbage can model. Reorganizations have been depicted as garbage cans: "highly contextual combinations of people, choice opportunities, problems, and solutions" (March and Olsen, 1989: 80–81; cf. Wolman, 1992: 44). According to Kingdon (1984), solutions, problems, and politics form three processes that may or may not coincide. Adapting this argument, a reform can be borrowed to handle a major problem that has arisen, providing it accords with the politics of the day.

### Broader Exchanges

Despite the close association between managerialism and commonwealth countries, the adoption of managerial change is fairly well advanced in several European countries: as Hood (1993) indicates, Sweden falls into the same high category, while Denmark, France, and the Netherlands are not far behind (although the extent to which practice corresponds to rhetoric still needs to be clarified). The imperatives of reform in the 1990s and the wider circulation of experiences of recent reform experiments suggest that convergence of reform programs is likely to continue among this broader group.

There are clearly broad parallels between the experiences reported here and those found by others who have examined either policy or management innovations. There are cases of reform transfer that cross existing boundaries between different linguistic and administrative traditions. One example is the institutional transfer of the ombudsman from Denmark to New Zealand, where similarities between the sociopolitical environment of Scandinavia and New Zealand were argued to be important in institutionalizing the office in the latter country. But note that New Zealand provided the pivot for further diffusion to countries with a common language and traditions. As the first non-Scandinavian country to adopt the institution of the ombudsman, New Zealand, rather than Denmark or Sweden, became the "primary model" which influenced the early Anglo-Saxon forms (Hill, 1976: 9–10, 71–72, 344).[7] Such translations may become unnecessary with management convergence taking place among OECD countries in the 1990s.

An interesting case worthy of closer examination is that of performance pay because it suggests a broader pattern of international diffusion than that for the SES. There were early experiments in France, Japan, and Canada that did not clearly have immediate imitators. The acceptance of the practice by the United States in 1979 was rather more influential. There was a series of adoptions in the mid-1980s: Spain (1984), Sweden (1985), and the United Kingdom (1985), and more in the late 1980s/early 1990s: New Zealand (1988), Denmark (1989), Ireland (1990), and Australia (1992). A majority of OECD countries were reported as either implementing or testing performance pay (U.S. GAO, 1990: 3; OECD, 1993: 15 and passim).

## CONCLUSIONS

This study has examined different types of diffusion. It has argued that diffusion may operate at several levels, the form varying according to whether a general concept is transferred through to quite detailed cases. To focus only on the latter is to ignore the rich linkages and influences which occur. However, studying the more general attracts the problem of differentiating the extent and form of the borrowing. The use of different types of reform borrowing as a means of recording the extent of diffusion has been found to be helpful.

In the Australian context, early borrowings were important for giving the reform program a kick-start and then for giving emphasis to redirection. Looking at the pattern of change overall for the last decade, it is possible to discern a shift from borrowing to innovating as Australia has moved from being more an importer of ideas to a country that has become at least a source of interest and study (and occasionally an exporter) of management innovations: the overall package, specific experiments, and refinements to reforms have attracted international interest. Although Australia is believed by many of the key players within its public service to be at the forefront of reform internationally, they continue to scrutinize and absorb the overseas experience.

With internationalization, both the extent and range of contacts among countries have increased; countries have become more receptive and more used to scanning and drawing on others' experience. Reform transfer is a normal part of the process of change. As Wolman (1992: 43) argues, "policy transfer is not an isolated endeavour, but an integral part of the policy process [and] best understood in Kingdon's terms as part of a variety of alternatives competing in the 'policy' stream of the process." With these points in mind, suggestions can be made for future research.

### Focus of Research

There is a case for according greater attention to the increasing international linkages. Clearer distinctions need to be made between federal and international dimensions, for they are not usually combined within one study. The relationship between the two could also be explored through the contribution of the gatekeeper's role, which introduces and translates international experience into countries with well-established subnational governments.

### Concepts for Empirical Research

There is a need for further clarification of concepts used in comparative research on management reform. The distinction between management innovation and policy innovation—the former system-wide, the latter specific to a policy field—is one starting point. It should also be possible to delineate different types of borrowings with greater precision than has been attempted here. The categories proposed by Ingraham in chapter 14 could be helpful here: budgetary and financial, structural, procedural or technical, and relational reforms (cf. also Gow's "subjective" choice in his 1992 study of intrafederal diffusion: financial, legal, equality, economic and managerial, and government-sovereignty). With some refinement as distinctive types of reforms, these categories could be used as a basis for comparisons.

### Types of Cross-national Research

There are several types of cross-national research that need to be undertaken in order to advance understanding of diffusion processes. Consideration needs to be given to moving beyond the bicountry comparisons that have been highly favored. This should involve tracking of distinctive reforms across several countries: performance pay is one obvious candidate. Multifaceted reform programs or multiple reforms deserve more attention.

It may be becoming more difficult to isolate and track diffusion in management innovation because of the range of countries experimenting with similar techniques and approaches. The study of diffusion across administrative traditions remains, however, a potentially fruitful if challenging area. The OECD is stimulating wider international scrutiny of management innovation and providing some of the data by which this might be done (OECD, 1990; 1992). The scope for studying cross-national transfers has yet to be really tested, and even if the field is becoming more complicated, this changing character is itself worthy of attention.

*NOTES*

1. Ian Beckett of the Centre for Research in Public Sector Management assisted with much of the literature analysis, and he and Penelope St. Clair made perceptive comments on earlier drafts. Comments from a number of scholars and senior public servants have helped in the development of this paper, including those by Hal Colebatch, Ron Cullen, Del Dunn, Malcolm Holmes, Allan Jarman, Keith Linard, John Power, Spencer Zifcak, and the editors of this volume.

2. One factor in the communication of ideas was the role played by party activists and reformers such as Dr. Peter Wilenski, a former bureaucrat whose subsequent career flourished under Labor governments at state and national levels. He was the most significant of the advisers referred to by Hawke and Evans, and he conducted a major inquiry into the public service of the largest state, New South Wales (1976–82), and published on reform (Wilenski, 1986; Halligan and Power, 1992).

3. The role of international consulting firms in circulating management principles and practices is another important field, which has only recently become the subject of study in Australia.

4. The suggestion has been made that there were Australian echos of the U.S. Pendleton Act, because 1883 produced the first significant central personnel management legislation (Halligan, 1992).

5. In addition to introducing the SES to Victoria, Dr. Ron Cullen pursued decentralization on the basis of the U.S. experience, recruiting an American consultant to review the state's central agencies (Cullen, 1982; 1986). Victoria also established a Department of Management and Budget at this time.

6. In May 1982, an officer of the Public Service Board, Brendan Preiss, visited the United Kingdom, Canada, and the United States in order to "examine developments in matters of [then] current interest to the Board, particularly in relation to the management and conditions of staff at senior executive levels" (PSB, 1982: 92).

7. Compare also the Next Steps scheme for executive agencies in the United Kingdom which has been described as an attempt to "implement an Anglicised version of the Swedish decentralised model of government" (Fudge and Gustafsson, 1989: 33).

## REFERENCES

Aucoin, P. 1990. "Administrative Reform in Public Management: Paradigms, Principles, Paradoxes and Pendulums." *Governance* 3, no. 2: 115–37.

Bennett, C. J. 1991. Review article: "What is Policy Convergence and What Causes it?" *British Journal of Political Science* 21: 215–33.

Boston, J. 1991. "Chief Executives and the Senior Executive Service." In Boston et al., 1991.

Boston, J., J. Martin, J. Pallot, and P. Walsh, eds. 1991. *Reshaping the State: New Zealand's Bureaucratic Revolution.* Auckland: Oxford University Press.

Caiden, G. E. 1991. *Administrative Reform Comes of Age.* Berlin: Walter de Gruyter.

Campbell, C., and J. Halligan. 1992. *Leadership in an Age of Constraint.* Pittsburgh: University of Pittsburgh Press.

Cole, R. W. 1982. "Options for Development of the Executive Service." Address to the Australian Institute of Public Administration (ACT Group). Canberra, 23 June.

Collier, D., and R. E. Messick. 1975. "Prerequisites versus Diffusion: Testing Alternative Explanations of Social Security Adoption." *American Political Science Review* 69, no. 4: 1299–1315.

Commonwealth of Australia. 1983. *Reforming the Australian Public Service: A Statement of the Government's Intentions.* Canberra: Australian Government Publishing Service.

Cullen, R. B. 1982. "Public Sector Management in Victoria." Paper presented at the national conference of the American Society for Public Administration. Honolulu, 22 March.

Cullen, R. B. 1986. "The Victorian Senior Executive Service: A Performance Based Approach to the Management of Senior Managers." *Australian Journal of Public Administration* 45, no. 1 (March): 60–73.

DoF (Department of Finance). 1986. *Annual Report 1985–86.* Canberra: Australian Government Publishing Service.

DPMC (Department of the Prime Minister and Cabinet). 1987. *Annual Report 1986–87.* Canberra: Australian Government Publishing Service.

Downs, G. W. 1976. *Bureaucracy, Innovation, and Public Policy.* Lexington, MA: Lexington Books.

Dwivedi, O. P., and R. W. Phidd. 1990. "Political Management in Canada." Pages 115–47 in O. P. Dwivedi and K. M. Henderson, eds., *Public Administration in World Perspective.* Ames: Iowa State University Press.

ESU (Efficiency Scrutiny Unit). 1986. *Scrutinies: A Guide for Ministers and Managers.* Canberra, December.

———. 1987. "Report on Proposed Successor Arrangements to the Public Service Board." Canberra, July.

Efficiency Unit. 1985. *Managing Scrutinies: A Guide for Ministers and Managers.* London: Her Majesty's Stationery Office.

Eyestone, R. 1977. "Confusion, Diffusion and Innovation." *American Political Science Review* 71, no. 2: 441–47.

Fisher, N. W. F., and T. Gallagher. 1982. "Recent Developments in Executive Service Overseas: Canada, USA, and UK." In JCPA (Joint Committee of Public Accounts).

Francisco, R. A. 1985. "Large-scale Policy Innovation in East and West European Agriculture." In R. L. Merritt and A. J. Merritt, eds., *Innovation in the Public Sector.* Beverly Hills, CA: Sage.

Fudge, C., and L. Gustafsson. 1989. "Administrative Reform and Public Management in Sweden and the United Kingdom." *Public Money and Management* (Summer): 29–33.

Garnett, J. L. 1980. *Reorganizing State Government: The Executive Branch Boulder, CO:* Westview Press.

Gow, J. I. 1992. "Diffusion of Administrative Innovations in Canadian Public Administrations." *Administration and Society* 23, no. 4: 430–54.

Halligan. J. 1990. *Development of the Senior Executive Service.* Submission to Senate Standing Committee on Finance and Public Administration.

———. 1992. "A Comparative Analysis: The Senior Executive Service in Australia." In P. W. Ingraham and D. H. Rosenbloom, eds., *Reform and Change in Public Bureaucracies: The Impact of the Civil Service Reform Act of 1978.* Pittsburgh: University of Pittsburgh Press.

———. Forthcoming. "Senior Executive Pay Policies in the Australian Public Service in Comparative Perspective." *Public Administration Quarterly.*

Halligan, J., and J. Power. 1991. "A Framework for the Analysis of Recent Changes in Australian Executive Branches." In A. Farazmand, ed., *Handbook of Comparative and Development Public Administration.* New York: Marcel Dekker.

————. 1992. *Political Management in the 1990s.* Melbourne: Oxford University Press.

Hawke, R. J. 1986. "Statement to Parliament by the Prime Minister on Public Service Reforms." 25 September.

Hawke, B., and G. Evans. 1983. *Labor and Quality of Government.* Policy presented. Canberra, February.

Hill, L. B. 1976. *The Model Ombudsman: Institutionalizing New Zealand's Democratic Experiment.* Princeton: Princeton University Press.

Hood, C. 1990. "De-Sir Humphreyfying the Westminster Model of Governance: A New Style of Governance?" *Governance* 3, no. 2: 205–14.

JCPA (Joint Committee of Public Accounts), Parliament of the Commonwealth of Australia. 1982. *The Selection and Development of Senior Managers in the Commonwealth Public Service: Report 202.* Canberra: Australian Government Publishing Service.

Karvonen, L. 1981. "Semi-Domestic Politics: Policy Diffusion from Sweden to Finland." *Cooperation and Conflict* 16, no. 2: 91–107.

Kingdon, J. W. 1984. *Agendas, Alternatives, and Public Policies.* Boston: Little, Brown & Company.

Lyon, P., and J. Manor. 1983. *Transfer and Transformation: Political Institutions in the New Commonwealth: Essays in Honour of W. H. Morris-Jones.* Leicester: Leicester University Press.

March, J. G., and J. P. Olsen. 1989. *Rediscovering Institutions: The Organizational Basis of Politics.* New York: Free Press.

Metcalfe, L., and S. Richards. 1990. *Improving Public Management.* London: Sage.

Nelson, H. 1985. "Policy Innovation in the Australian States." *Politics* 20, no. 2 (November): 77–87.

OECD (Organization for Economic Cooperation and Development), Public Management Committee. 1990. *Public Management Development: Survey—1990.* Paris: OECD.

————. 1992. *Private Pay for Public Work: Peformance-Related Pay for Public Sector Managers.* Paris: OECD.

Painter, M. 1988. "Australian Federalism and the Policy Process: Politics with Extra Vitamins." *Politics* 23, no. 2 (November): 57–66.

————. 1991. "Policy Diversity and Policy Learning in a Federation: The Case of Australian State Betting Laws." *Publius: The Journal of Federalism* 21 (Winter): 143–57.

Perry, J. L., and K. L. Kraemer. 1979. *Technological Innovation in American Local Governments: The Case of Computing.* New York: Pergamon Press.

Pollitt, C. 1990. *Managerialism and the Public Services: The Anglo-American Experience.* Oxford: Basil Blackwell.

Power, J., ed. 1990. *Public Administration in Australia: A Watershed.* Sydney: Hale and Iremonger.

President's Private Sector Survey on Cost Control (Chairman: J. P. Grace). 1984. *War on Waste.* New York: Macmillan.

PSB (Public Service Board). 1980–83. *Annual Reports.* Canberra: Australian Government Publishing Service.

PSB/DoF (Public Service Board and Department of Finance). 1984. *Financial Management Improvement Program: Diagnostic Study.* Canberra: Australian Government Publishing Service.

Pusey, M. 1991. *Economic Rationalism in Canberra: A Nation Building State Changes Its Mind.* Melbourne: Cambridge University Press.

RCA (Review of Commonwealth Administration [Chairman: J. B. Reid]). 1983. *Report.* Canberra: Australian Government Publishing Service.

RCAGA (Royal Commission on Australian Government Administration [Chairman: H. C. Coombs]). 1976a. *Report.* Canberra: Australian Government Publishing Service.

————. 1976b. *Appendixes to Report: Volume One.* Canberra: Australian Government Publishing Service.

Renfrow, P. 1989. "Corporate Management and the Senior Executive Service: An American and Australian Comparison." Pages 89–102 in G. Davis, P. Weller, and C. Lewis, eds., *Corporate Management in Australian Government.* Melbourne: Macmillan.

Rogers, E. M. 1983. *Diffusion of Innovations.* 3rd ed. New York: Free Press.

Rogers, E. M., and J.-Im Kim. 1985. "Diffusion of Innovations in Public Organizations." In R. L. Merritt and A. J. Merritt, eds., *Innovation in the Public Sector.* Beverly Hills, CA: Sage.

Scarrow, H. A. 1957. *The Higher Public Service of the Commonwealth of Australia.* Durham, NC: Duke University Press.

Schick, A. 1990. "Budgeting for Results: Recent Developments in Five Industrialized Countries." *Public Administration Review* (January/February): 26–34.

SSCFPA (Senate Standing Committee on Finance and Public Administration), Parliament of the Commonwealth of Australia. 1989. *Review of the Efficiency Scrutiny Program.* Canberra: Australian Government Publishing Service.

————. 1990. *Development of the Senior Executive Service.* Canberra: Australian Government Publishing Service.

Smith, B. L. R., ed. 1984. *The Higher Civil Service in Europe and Canada: Lessons for the United States.* Washington, DC: Brookings Institution.

Subramaniam, V. 1977. *Transplanted Indo-British Administration.* New Delhi: Ashish.

Thomas, R. 1987. "The Experience of Other Countries." In R. A. Chapman and M. Hunt, eds., *Open Government: A Study of the Prospects of Open Government within the Limitations of the British Political System.* London: Croom Helm.

U.S. GAO (General Accounting Office). 1990. *Pay for Performance: State and International Public Sector Pay-for-Performance Systems.* Washington, DC.

Walker, J. L. 1969. "The Diffusions of Innovations among the American States." *American Political Science Review* 63, no. 3: 880–99.

Wettenhall, R. 1988. "Local Governments as Innovators." *Australian Journal of Public Administration* 47, no. 4: 351–74.

Wickwar, H. 1991. *Power and Service: A Cross-National Analysis of Public Administration.* New York: Greenwood Press.

Wilenski, P. 1986. *Public Power and Public Administration.* Sydney: Hale and Iremonger.

Wolman, H. 1992. "Understanding Cross National Policy Transfers: The Case of Britain and the US." *Governance* 5, no. 1 (January): 27–45.

# 15 CONCLUSION: ASSESSMENT OF PROGRESS AND A RESEARCH AGENDA

Hans A. G. M. Bekke, James L. Perry, and Theo A. J. Toonen

The contributions to this book offer a variety of perspectives for comparative research on civil service systems. In this concluding chapter, we will frame the contributions around themes we initiated in the introductory chapter. We will begin by reviewing what the contributors have said about one central theme, that is, the institutional analysis of civil service systems. In the introductory chapter we argued that an institutional perspective is a productive way to frame comparative research on civil service systems; we will review this argument in light of the evidence provided by the contributors.

We will then examine several generalizations drawn from the theoretical and empirical arguments of the contributors in order to highlight broad areas of agreement among the contributors. These generalizations capture issues central to the institutional perspective, among them the processes of institutionalization—origination, persistence, change, and reform of civil service systems.

We will conclude with a discussion of two aspects of an agenda for future research. The first involves a general strategy for studying civil service systems; the second is a sketch of specific research issues suggested by the contributions to this volume.

## THE INSTITUTIONAL CONTENT OF CIVIL SERVICE SYSTEMS

We have defined civil service systems as "mediating institutions that mobilize human resources in the service of the affairs of the state in a given territory." By "institutions" we mean that civil service systems create rules and authority relationships that structure behavior and tend to persist over time (Krasner, 1988; Kiser and Ostrom, 1982; Powell and DiMaggio, 1991). In order to extend the conceptual perspective with which we began, it will be helpful to review how the contributors have elaborated the institutional content of civil service systems.

The history of civil service systems highlights how rules have evolved to define institutional structures. Raadschelders and Rutgers have identified five phases in the evolution of civil service systems. Social, economic, and political forces were largely responsible for the evolutionary changes they documented. For example, from the late 1700s until the mid-1800s, rapid industrialization, colonization by European powers, and the growth of constitutional government necessitated administrative mechanisms responsible to civil society rather than to the personal whims of a monarch. These forces produced demands for structures to facilitate an evolving rule of law. The result was the development of a civil service nested in new constitutional, collective choice, and operational rules. As Raadschelders and Rutgers note, the constitutional state and separation of powers gave rise to operational rules specifying formal ranks, conditions of employment, and pensions. These operational rules were well suited to facilitating civil sovereignty. Although Raadschelders and Rutgers do not fully specify the dynamic mechanisms that guided the phases of civil service evolution, they do provide compelling evidence that shifts in personnel policies, that is, operational rules, are typically preceded by major environmental changes involving constitutions and collective choice mechanisms.

Wise identifies a way of looking systematically at the operational rules governing civil service systems using the internal labor market construct. Internal labor markets represent the "rules pertaining to job definition or classification, deployment, job security and membership, and reward structures and wage rules." Wise notes that one irony associated with internal labor markets is that very little research has focused on public organizations despite the uniqueness of the rule configurations of civil service systems.

The internal labor market construct focuses attention on administrative practices as systems that "determine the way human resources are used and rewarded." Much of the attention devoted to personnel practices tends to be piecemeal, looking at specific personnel policies and their implications. The internal labor market construct unifies the assessment of operating rules, both formal and informal, around their effects on utilization and incentives. It also calls attention to internal variations across different types of work and different organizations. This contrasts with traditional bureaucratic theory that emphasizes the invariant quality of the rules underpinning bureaucracy. To the extent that particular rules covary and follow predictable patterns, they also serve as a parsimonious device for linking practices internal to civil service systems to the wider environment.

Wise concludes that the rules governing internal labor markets have political and social consequences. She writes: "Opportunities for upward mobility and access to elite positions in government are important indicators of the level of democracy and social equity in a system." Her argument echoes the observation of Raadschelders and Rutgers that civil service rules have often evolved to accommodate social status, which has led to increasing differentiation and stratification within civil services. Judging from the contributions by Raadschelders and Rutgers as well as Wise, causality appears to be bidirectional. Operating rules influence the distribution of rewards which, in turn, affect collective choice processes. At the same time, collective choice mechanisms constrain civil service operations.

Van der Meer and Roborgh, Hojnacki, and Hill and Gillespie direct their attention primarily to how the collective choice and constitutional levels bound and constrain civil service operations. The concept of representativeness is linked by van der Meer and Roborgh to concerns about the civil service's responsiveness and legitimacy within the broader society. In many countries civil servants play a crucial role in collective action because of their influence in policy-making processes. This, in turn, produces efforts to control and channel the influence of civil servants using norm-filtering and modifying mechanisms such as selection and socialization.

An important conclusion of van der Meer and Roborgh's review is that what passes for representativeness and what is socially acceptable is highly variable from society to society. Because representativeness is relational, reflecting the alignment of civil service with its social and political environment, functional patterns of active and passive representation will be highly variable. Their observation coincides with Peters's general argument about action meaning, that is, that the "same" things are perceived and interpreted differently by civil servants, politicians, and citizens in countries with different social settings, constitutions, and collective choice mechanisms. With respect to the specific issue of representativeness, van der Meer and Roborgh assert: "When assessing representativeness in one political, administrative, and societal setting, one must therefore use criteria appropriate to that situation." Thus, normative models of representation will vary widely.

The variations in normative models are indicated by the range of rules that are used to assure appropriate levels of passive and active representation. Some countries that place high premiums on nondiscrimination, such as the United States, are characterized by highly articulated legal and procedural mechanisms for facilitating a mirror image relationship between internal and external labor markets. The objective of the rule structure in other countries, such as Malaysia, is to promote regime values that favor particular groups in the population, thus, according to van der Meer and Roborgh producing personal discrimination.

Hojnacki's focus is on the broad political system rather than on representation, but he reaches a conclusion very similar to that of van der Meer and Roborgh: "Most societies have, at least formally, established principles that guide the involvement of civil servants in the policy-making process." Laws regulating political involvement of civil servants (for example, the recently reformed Hatch Act provisions in the United States) are clearly formal. Hojnacki reveals that many rules are informal as well. For instance, implicit rules embedded in tradition constrain and direct political activity by civil servants.

Hill and Gillespie extend the control perspective to other social mechanisms, specifically, public participation and grievance procedures. Public participation and grievance procedures represent two formal collective choice mechanisms that influence the behavior of civil servants in somewhat different ways. Participation is typically an a priori control on the behavior of civil servants. It affects factors such as who is involved in decision-making, procedures for reaching a decision, and the criteria considered. Grievance procedures are post hoc influences on collective choices. Citizen grievance procedures govern the application of administrative law to "the 'sovereign's servants,' who from time to time—normally without criminal intent—misinterpret, misunderstand, or over-amplify their powers."

It is apparent that the contributors identified many rules that are consequential for understanding variations in civil service systems and ought to be part of a comparative research agenda. They also suggest ways for managing the scope of the agenda. Heady's analysis of civil service configurations suggests that three sets of rules, involving the relation to the political regime, focus for personnel management, and qualifications requirements,, are central for defining the overall character of the system. Morgan and Wise also present clarifying schemes for thinking about civil service in developing countries and for conceptualizing internal labor markets. We will return later to a consideration of the application of these frameworks in our discussion of the research agenda.

## GENERALIZATIONS

The preceding discussion of institutional *content* has focused on rules as a property of civil service systems. We turn our attention now to institutionalization—the *processes* by which civil service systems come into being, persist, and change (Tolbert and Zucker, 1983). Unlike rules, which are static attributes, processes connote dynamics associated with civil service systems.

This section synthesizes some general statements about the institutionalization of civil service systems from the evidence provided by the contributors. We have, as Peters suggested, searched for "comparative statements," as a principal route to theory construction. We begin with a global proposition about the origin of civil service systems:

> *Proposition 1.* The origin of national civil service systems is dependent on nation-state development.

As Raadschelders and Rutgers note in chapter 4: "The origin of civil services is closely related to nation-state development in general." Some differentiation of roles is implicit in our definition of civil service as a "mediating institution" in the service of the "state" in a given "territory." Thus, it is reasonable to expect that the origin of national civil service systems would be linked to nation-state development.

The historical evidence presented by Raadschelders and Rutgers makes a compelling case for the proposition. They show how, beginning with the role of civil servants as personal servants to the monarch, civil service systems gradually became institutionalized as systems for state service, and how personal characteristics of the single servant developed into a professionalized socioeconomic group.

The link between nation-state development and civil service systems is reinforced by Morgan. His theoretical perspective about civil service systems is informed by the context of developing countries, which contrasts with developed countries. He indicates how civil service systems in developing countries can develop from instruments in "inchoate" states into systems in institutionalized nation-states.

The contributions also shed light on another feature of the institutionalization of civil service systems—their persistence over time. This suggests a second proposition:

> *Proposition 2.* Civil service systems tend to persist because they are overdetermined, perpetuated by the operational, collective choice, and constitutional systems in which they are nested.

Several general arguments help to explain the persistence of civil service systems. The first is the "nesting" of civil service systems. We noted in proposition 1 that national civil service systems originate as a product of nation-state development. The fact that civil service systems are outgrowths of external determinants suggests that they are not simply artifacts of their designers that can be remolded at will. Civil service systems are instead natural outgrowths of their context, in some respects organic parts of their surroundings.

Not only can civil service systems be understood as an organic part of context, they are overdetermined, that is, caused and reinforced by a variety of external influences. Among these factors are constitutional and collective choice processes. For example, van der Meer and Roborgh emphasize that the representativeness of civil service is pivotal to the persistence of civil service systems in democratic societies. The legitimacy of civil service as an instrument of government hinges on its perceived representativeness. If the civil service is perceived as legitimate, then it can perform effectively in the collective choice roles allocated to it. Deviation of the civil service system from representation norms is likely to engender conflict. Depending on a particular society's capacity to manage conflict, the consequences of lack of representativeness may vary from public debate to political upheaval and civil war.

Although a civil service system's operational rules represent its most concrete and particular features, they too contribute to perpetuating civil service systems. One way is by their influence on the cognitions of actors. The rules may serve to sensitize some actors, particularly members of the civil service, to what they value, that is, their vested interests (Selznick, 1949). In doing so, the operating rules become an object that may be simultaneously valued and protected. The operating rules may also acquire a taken-for-granted quality (Meyer and Rowan, 1977; Tolbert and Zucker, 1983), thereby limiting initiatives for change and alternatives that might surface for active consideration. When operational rules acquire this taken-for-granted status, they are no longer objects of conscious attention because they attain an independent status as social reality defining the "way things are" (Scott, 1987).

Another way in which operating rules serve to perpetuate civil service systems is that they are technical solutions to perceived problems. As technical solutions, operating rules may become the objects of conscious scrutiny. Even when they are critically scrutinized, however, they are likely to persist unless a plausible technical alternative exists. The lack of an alternative technical solution can be a powerful basis for keeping an existing operating system. The history of position classification in the U.S. federal civil service is an example of an operating system persisting because of a lack of an alternative technical solution (National Academy of Public Administration, 1991).

Although the forces for persistence of civil service systems are substantial, a discussion of persistence inherently raises questions about its antithesis, change. This brings us to a third proposition:

> *Proposition 3.* Lack of congruence between civil service systems and their constitutional environments produces the strongest forces for change; lesser pressures for change are produced by lack of congruence at the collective choice and operational levels.

This proposition emphasizes the dynamics underlying change. Change is used here to refer to a global phenomenon, distinct from the narrower concept of planned change, commonly called reform in public administration and civil service literature. Although reform is a dynamic that is central to research about civil service systems, most change in social systems is unplanned (March, 1981). Civil service transformations resulting from adaptations to work force growth or cultural change are more common than planned change. Change is also a product of sequential attention to conflicting values within political systems (Kaufman, 1956; March and Olsen, 1989).

Proposition 3 envisions change as likely to vary along a continuum represented by two polar forms (Miller and Mintzberg, 1984). At one extreme is incremental change, gradual and piecemeal progression of small modifications or adjustments in the civil service system. As the institutional perspective implies generally and proposition 2 asserts explicitly, civil service systems are elements of order, so processes of change typically appear as long-term processes of evolution and transformation along gradual lines. At the opposite pole is quantum change, reflecting a rapid and radical shift in the system.

The change dynamic the proposition posits is grounded in the concept of congruence introduced by McGregor and Solano in chapter 3. They use the concepts to refer to two meanings of fit, between the organization and its environment and among internal system components. The proposition suggests that poor fit in either area is a stimulus for change. But the proposition asserts that mismatches between a civil service system and its constitutional environment are the more powerful of the two stimuli for change.

The proposition helps to explain the recent universality of changes in civil service systems as documented by Ingraham and Hood. Recent changes in civil service systems have been preceded by powerful realignments in international economic systems and political regimes. These changes have altered the constitutional environment, in some cases informally and in others formally, precipitating enormous pressures for civil service change.

Environmental mismatches are the probable source of quantum changes in civil service systems, but the proposition does not specify mechanisms, timing, probability, or other details about the process of change. Civil service changes will often lag by years behind the changes that trigger them. This is consistent with proposition 2, which maintains that civil service systems persist because they are overdetermined. The recent experiences in Eastern Europe provide an illustration of the loose coupling between fundamental environmental change and civil service change. They also illustrate how operational rules can be perpetuated in the absence of alternative technical solutions (Rice, 1992).

Another explanation for the loose coupling between environmental elements and civil service are the expectations a particular society establishes for the relationship between the two. Roborgh and van der Meer's concepts of mirror image versus equal opportunity representation is a good illustration of how social expectations or rules influence the tightness of the coupling. Mirror image rules impose a direct correspondence, a tight coupling, between environmental elements and civil service characteristics. Equal opportunity representation requires a looser correspondence.

Morgan compares the evolution of civil service systems in developing countries. Here some elements of the March and Olsen (1989) definition of transformation by radical shock can be identified. Changes over time from the colonial configuration to the independent status of the new central state, or the centrifugal tendencies of the patrimonial or prebendal state often involve processes of radical change and shock. As Morgan indicates, the public service in many developing countries is in fundamental crisis, as is the state itself.

A fourth generalization, involving the diffusion of civil service reforms, can also be inferred from the contributions:

*Proposition 4.* Diffusion processes will limit the variety of civil service reforms; the probability of successful reform will be constrained by incongruence between new and existing structures and difficulties of displacing existing structures.

As Halligan emphasizes, the amount of borrowing that transpires across national systems, and the mechanisms by which diffusion occurs are difficult to identify definitively. However, it is obvious from the clustering of reforms into a small number of configurations, as discussed by Ingraham, Hood, and Halligan, that the variety of reforms is far less than the variety of nation-states seeking to make planned changes.

Although this argument is grounded in details about the recent history of reforms, Raadschelders and Rutgers advance similar evidence in their review of the evolution of civil service systems. One of the first manifestations of diffusion affecting civil service design was the nobility taking its cues from the Catholic church during the Middle Ages.

The success of civil service reforms can be partially explained by the diffusion processes that accompany them. Some civil service reforms are local innovations, strictly products of the systems in which they developed. Other reforms are to varying degrees creations of exogenous systems, driven by the diffusion mechanisms outlined by Halligan. Extrapolating from Morgan's analysis of civil service systems in developing countries, we anticipate that, all other factors being equal, indigenous systems are more likely to take hold than exogenous systems. The assessment of probable success is, in actuality, much more complex because some diffusion processes incorporate a high degree of reinvention in which the reform is adapted to local circumstances. Diffusion processes that do not incorporate an assessment of context-reform fit increase the prospects for failure. Furthermore, the force field influencing the success of civil service reform is a product not only of context-reform fit but also of the prospects for displacing existing structures. Thus, reforms are more likely to succeed if a strong case is made for reform and adequate pressures, as suggested in proposition 3, have developed to displace existing structures.

Although the diffusion effect constrains the variety of reforms, the contributors provide evidence that the diffusion effect is not universal. Hood finds that the new public management reforms spread among "family groups" of countries, some of which (for example, Australia, the United Kingdom, and New Zealand) decentralized personnel management to line departments away from central personnel agencies, and other (for example, Japan) that strengthened central control.

To summarize, these four propositions represent agreement among the contributors about processes by which civil service systems come into being, persist, and change. We have developed the generalizations to reflect broad areas of agreement among the contributors and to stimulate theory construction. The creation of more fully developed comparative theories of civil service systems must await further empirical and theoretical developments. It is to the future research agenda that we now turn.

## AN AGENDA FOR FURTHER RESEARCH

Although we initiated our collective inquiry by recognizing the limits of knowledge about civil service systems, the contributions to this volume provide a rich and varied foundation on which to build. The general argument that civil service systems may be studied comparatively as institutions whose rules and contexts are highly variable has been made persuasively. Despite the variability in context and institutional rules, key processes surrounding these institutions— formation, persistence, change, and reform—appear to be similar.

The discussion in this concluding section proceeds in two stages. First, we will look at the implications of the contributions for research strategies. The focus is on a single question: What general strategy for comparative research about civil service systems is likely to result in new, useful knowledge? Second, we will look at specific research issues whose investigation is likely to enlighten us about civil service systems.

### General Research Strategies

The contributors collectively acknowledge that comparative empirical research on civil service systems requires methodological pluralism. A variety of methods are represented in this volume, among them history (Raadschelders and Rutgers), survey research (Rainey), and the case survey (Hood). Peters provides a compelling argument for methodological pluralism in his discussion of how scholars penetrate the meanings of actions within different social systems. Each contribution to this volume has emphasized the embeddedness of civil service systems within broader administrative, political, and social systems. Because of this embeddedness, close observations of behavior within context rather than survey analyses would be an appropriate research strategy. Thus, Peters argues that methods for effective research on civil service systems should draw more from anthropology than from conventional social science.

Peters's strategy is embraced by van der Meer and Roborgh in their discussion of representativeness. They contend that the comparative study of different meanings of representativeness will provide better understanding of unique characteristics of civil service systems. Fixing the focus of research about representativeness on its meanings rather than on quantifiable artifacts, as has frequently been the case (Meier, 1993), should illuminate variations across systems. If variations in representativeness were studied in conjunction with civil service rules and the attributes of the systems within which they are embedded, then progress might also be made in understanding cross-level effects. The meanings of representativeness might be found to vary according to civil service rules, attributes of broader systems, or interactions between the levels. Although this strategy cannot conclusively untangle the causes for particular meanings, it reflects the merits of an anthropological strategy.

There has been at least one note of dissent from the generally favorable view toward close observation of behavior within context or what we have called the anthropological strategy. Hill and Gillespie have expressed skepticism about informal mechanisms of social control lending themselves to effective study on a comparative basis. They have emphasized instead the need to investigate formal structures. Their objection to using informal structures as the basis for comparative research hinges, however, on concerns about focus and boundedness. Given the typically broad definitions of social control used by sociologists (Janowitz, 1975; Zald, 1978), Hill and Gillespie argue that comparative research on informal mechanisms is likely to result in incongruent snapshots that raise questions about the comparability of the phenomena investigated.

The problem of action meaning discussed by Peters and others limits the utility of traditional survey research and quantitative analyses. Another, perhaps more significant constraint on these methodologies involves a practical consideration: the capacity to successfully obtain data that are comparable across systems. McGregor and Solano's analysis indicates that the list of data requirements is long while the availability of comparable data is limited.

Although survey-based or quantitative research may have limited applicability for comparative research, there are roles for collection of basic data and rigorous quantitative research. One illustration is provided by Rainey. His proposals for public opinion research represent a middle ground between positivist and anthropological approaches—quantification of subjective judgments. The research he proposes would contribute to answering questions about relationships between general political attitudes and perceptions of civil service and the public's ability to discriminate about the performance of different institutions. Rainey's research program would also facilitate an investigation of public perceptions of the state, a variable central to Morgan's analysis of civil service in developing countries.

The type of civil service "systematics" implied by Heady's and Morgan's configurations certainly would benefit from a well-constructed, cross-national data base, containing elements identified by McGregor and Solano. Such a data base might contain, at a minimum, a combination of nominal and categorical data about political regime, social groups, civil service structural arrangements, and rules. This basic data set might be supplemented by elements such as a description of the backgrounds of civil servants, methods of recruitment, education, and training, and attributes of external and internal labor markets.

Given the difficulties of obtaining extensive, high quality, commensurable data across systems, the inclination of many of the contributors for research built on typologies and ideal types is reassuring. Heady points to the difference between conceptual and empirical typologies, the former being deductive and theoretical in character, the latter inductive and inferred from data. Conceptual configurations can help us to make correct decisions in data collection by giving us heuristic tools. Peters asserts that ideal types can help us to have "a standard against which real world systems can be compared. Even if the 'model' itself is rather ethnocentric . . . the comparison is meaningful."

In many instances, the authors have eschewed precise conceptual and operational definitions for constructs such as politicization and representativeness. We believe this strategy is appropriate because it avoids premature closure about matters that might be better addressed after exploratory empirical research. The near unanimity no doubt reflects the contributors' experience with what Peters calls false "scientism" as a route to knowledge development.

To summarize, the consensus for a general research strategy appears to favor methodological pluralism, with a general bias toward qualitative approaches. The primary reasons underlying the bias are the difficulties of quantification, the need to penetrate the action meanings of a situation, and the immaturity of this arena of comparative research.

### Research Themes

The contributors have suggested a variety of research themes geared to their individual subject matters and cross-cutting issues. The concluding discussion focuses on cross-cutting issues that we believe have strategic implications for comparative civil service research. We are interested specifically in four issues: (1) empirical configurations; (2) the "institutionness" of civil service systems; (3) public opinion about civil service systems; and (4) the efficacy of strategies for planned change.

*Empirical configurations of civil service systems.*

One strategic area for empirical research involves the configurations presented by Heady and Morgan. Studying configurations encourages synthesis rather than analysis, which is precisely the reason it was developed (Miller and Mintzberg, 1984). Far too much comparative research on civil service systems has focused on the myriad operational rules within civil service systems. The advantage of configuration research is that it is attentive simultaneously to patterns of variation at the operational, collective choice, and constitutional levels of analysis, and that key variables are amenable to categorical measurement.

Several types of studies might be conducted. A starting point would be a confirmatory analysis of the configurations developed by Heady. As he has suggested, a test of the adequacy of his conceptual effort is whether it can be replicated. A more ambitious effort would be to eschew a priori categories completely and develop dimensions and configurations empirically. Heady has emphasized that his categories and variables are appropriate, but not the only ones nor necessarily the best ones available. Thus, there is a role and a need for this research.

Another course would be to develop more complete descriptions of the configuration dimensions. For instance, Wise's internal labor market variables could be clustered to provide a small set of types of internal labor markets that could be used either in lieu of or in addition to the qualifications requirements dimension she proposes. Kanter's (1989) distinctions between bureaucratic, professional, and entrepreneurial career forms represents a prototype for this clustering of internal labor market elements.

*Institutionalization.*

Another research issue involves the point at which civil service systems become institutionalized. How can we tell when civil service systems take on a quasi-permanent, stable existence? What differentiates civil service systems that are institutionalized from those that are not? This line of inquiry might be characterized as research about "institutionness."

To differentiate the extent of institutionalization, researchers might turn to measuring various defining properties, much as scholars have sought to define organizational creation or organizational indicia (Katz and Gartner, 1988; Kaufman, 1991). What are the indicia that might be used to measure institutionalization of civil service systems? Four seem to be relevant: boundaries, exchange, routinization, and connectedness.

Our definition of civil service systems suggests that they are mediating institutions in the service of the state. This implies that civil service systems are bounded from the state and other social institutions. Morgan's discussion of patrimonial systems reflects the status of civil service, satisfying the lower limits of the boundary condition. In patrimonial systems, civil service is negligible because of the blurring of boundaries between traditional social systems and the civil service.

In general, how the boundaries are drawn between state, civil society, and civil service provides important insights into the institutional character of civil service systems. An extension of the boundary issue involves transactions across boundaries, that is, exchange. Transactions between the state and civil service are essential to the identity of civil service. What are the characteristics of the structure of social organizations and groups oriented toward government? What are the relations between civil service and such organizations and groups? Here such things as public management roles of civil service, the general image of the civil service held by the public, representativeness of civil servants, social control and politicization of the roles of civil servants are of central interest.

Institutionalization is also contingent on the extent to which the operational and collective choice aspects of the civil service system have become standard practice. For instance, if civil service operating rules are purely ad hoc, then the system falls short of being what we term institutionalized. In contrast, if exchanges at the operational (e.g., recruitment and pay) and collective choice (e.g., representativeness) levels are routinized, then the civil service system is institutionalized. Routinization does not imply that civil service has become a taken-for-granted entity. However, it does suggest that it has achieved sufficient stability to reach the threshold for institutionalization.

A final attribute that might be used to define and measure institutionalization is connectedness, the extent to which a particular set of rules is common or variable across a governmental system. Connectedness addresses an issue we raised in the introductory chapter, that is, the systemic character of civil service.

Institutionalization research has practical utility with respect to reform. Reformers seeking to facilitate planned change are confronted with the need to de-institutionalize existing practices and institutionalize new practices. Understanding processes of institutionalization and de-institutionalization might be enormously useful for planned change efforts.

*Public opinion.*

Among the most extensively specified of the individual research themes is Rainey's research program on public opinion toward civil service. Although we noted above a general bias of the contributors against quantification, we have also argued that methodological pluralism is an important principle in a general research strategy for studying civil service systems. Public opinion research would complement anthropological and other predominantly qualitative strategies. Previous public opinion research has had a salutary effect in other comparative arenas for both framing and stimulating research. Representative examples are Almond and Verba's (1963) classic study of civic culture, and Aberbach, Putnam, and Rockman's (1981) semistructured, open-ended interviews of bureaucrats and politicians in seven countries.

The framework proposed by Rainey has the potential for shedding light on issues raised in many of the other contributions. For example, the measurement of Morgan's prostate/antistate dimension requires something similar to Rainey's opinion survey. Public opinion research could also pay dividends with respect to comparative analysis of action meaning, the influence of social attitudes, and the effects of different representational and political structures.

*Efficacy of strategies for reform.*

One issue of tremendous practical importance is the efficacy of reform. Can civil service systems be designed and administered to serve the purposes of the state? As both we and the contributors have frequently noted, states in Africa, Eastern Europe, and other regions of the world are struggling to build new democratic governments. A central part of their struggle involves the reliability and accountability of new civil service structures. Can the study of civil service systems contribute anything to facilitating constitutional and collective choice transitions, or should we assume either that the process is undecipherable or that it is unmanageable?

We believe social science research can help to identify and narrow the choices available to state builders for designing and transforming civil service systems. Where shall we begin? In our discussion of proposition 3, we argued that change under most circumstances is likely to be incremental, that is, a gradual and piecemeal progression of small modifications or adjustments in the civil service system. Civil service systems are elements of order, so processes of change typically appear as long-term processes of evolution and transformation along gradual lines. If this scenario is accurate most of the time, then the management of change involves identifying internal and external leverage points that facilitate transformation and speed transition. Although past patterns of change may not be repeated in the future, a strategy for acquiring better knowledge about transformation would be to chart the progression of change and its consequences in a small number of countries.

## REFERENCES

Aberbach, J. D., R. D. Putnam, and B. A. Rockman. 1981. *Bureaucrats and Politicians in Western Democracies.* Cambridge: Harvard University Press.

Almond, G. A., and S. Verba. 1963. *The Civic Culture.* Princeton: Princeton University Press.

Janowitz, M. 1975. "Sociological Theory and Social Control." *American Journal of Sociology* 81 (July): 82–108.

Kanter, R. M. 1989. "Careers and the Wealth of Nations: A Macro-perspective on the Structure and Implications of Career Forms." Pages 506–21 in Michael B. Arthur, Douglas T. Hall, and Barbara S. Lawrence, eds., *Handbook of Career Theory.* Cambridge: Cambridge University Press.

Katz, J., and W. B. Gartner. 1988. "Properties of Emerging Organizations." *Academy of Management Review* 13 (July): 429–41.

Kaufman, H. 1956. "Emerging Conflicts in the Doctrine of American Public Administration." *American Political Science Review* 50: 1057–73.

————. 1991. *Time, Chance, and Organizations.* 2nd ed. Chatham, NJ: Chatham House.

Kiser, L. L., and E. Ostrom. 1982. "The Three Worlds of Action: A Metatheoretical Synthesis of Institutional Approaches." Pages 179–222 in E. Ostrom, ed., *Strategies of Political Inquiry.* Beverly Hills, CA: Sage.

Krasner, S. D. 1988. "Sovereignty: An Institutional Perspective." *Comparative Political Studies* 21, no. 1: 66–94.

March, J. G. 1981. "Footnotes to Organizational Change." *Administrative Science Quarterly* 26: 563–77.

March, J. G., and J. P. Olsen. 1984. "The New Institutionalism: Organizational Factors in Political Life." *American Political Science Review* 78 (September): 734–49.

———. 1989. *Rediscovering Institutions: The Organizational Basis of Politics.* New York: Free Press.

Meier, Kenneth J. 1993. "Representative Bureaucracy: A Theoretical and Empirical Exposition." *Research in Public Administration* 2: 1–35.

Meyer, J. W., and B. Rowan. 1977. "Institutional Organizations: Formal Structure as Myth and Ceremony." *American Journal of Sociology* 83: 340–63.

Miller, D., and H. Mintzberg. 1984. "The Case for Configuration." Pages 10–30 in Danny Miller and Peter H. Friesen, *Organizations: A Quantum View.* Englewood Cliffs, NJ: Prentice Hall.

National Academy of Public Administration. 1991. *Modernizing Federal Classification: An Opportunity for Excellence.* Washington, DC: NAPA.

Powell, W. W., and P. DiMaggio, eds. 1991. *The New Institutionalism in Organizational Analysis.* Chicago: University of Chicago Press.

Rice, E. M. 1992. "Public Administration in Post-Socialist Eastern Europe." *Public Administration Review* 52 (March/April): 116–24.

Scott, W. R. 1987. "The Adolescence of Institutional Theory." *Administrative Science Quarterly* 32 (December): 493–511.

Selznick, P. 1949. *TVA and the Grass Roots.* Berkeley: University of California Press.

Tolbert, P. S., and L. G. Zucker. 1983. "Institutional Sources of Change in the Formal Structure of Organizations: The Diffusion of Civil Service Reform, 1880–1935." *Administrative Science Quarterly* 28: 22–39.

Zald, M. 1978. "On the Social Control of Industries." *Social Forces* 57 (September): 79–102.

# CONTRIBUTORS

**Hans A. G. M. Bekke** is Professor of Public Administration at the University of Leiden. He was a member of the 1981 National Committee for Administrative Reform in the Netherlands and is a member of the Dutch Society for Management Consultancy. His publications include *Isolation of Public Administration* and *The Reliable Bureaucracy.*

**Desi Gillespie** is currently working in the National Health Service in Great Britain. He previously served as a policy adviser in local government and as an elected member of the Bedfordshire County Council; he taught part-time at the universities of Durham, Newcastle, and Northumbria.

**John Halligan** is Director for the Centre for Research in Public Sector Management, University of Canberra. He is co-author of *Political Management in the 1990s* and *Political Leadership in an Age of Constraint.* He has also edited several books on public administration and has authored numerous articles in the field. He serves as review editor for the *Australian Journal of Public Administration* and is a member of the editorial boards of *Australian Journal of Public Administration* and *Governance.*

**Ferrel Heady** is Professor Emeritus of Public Administration and Political Science at the University of New Mexico, where he also served as Academic Vice President and President. His publications include *Public Administration: A Comparative Perspective.* He is a past president of the American Society for Public Administration, a member of the National Academy of Public Administration, and recipient of the Fred W. Riggs Award from the Section on International and Comparative Administration of ASPA and the Dwight Waldo Award from ASPA for career contributions to the field. In 1992 he was a Fulbright Senior Lecturer in Colombia.

**Michael Hill** is Professor of Social Policy at the University of Newcastle upon Tyne, England. He was a civil servant in social security administration and subsequently held academic posts at the universities of Reading, Oxford, and Bristol. He is the author of several books, including *The Policy Process in the Modern Capitalist State* (with Christopher Ham), *Policy Process: A Reader,* and *Understanding Social Policy.*

**William P. Hojnacki** is Assistant Dean and Program Director at the School of Public and Environmental Affairs, Indiana University, South Bend. He has served on the governing boards of the Indiana Academy of Social Science and the Indiana Political Science Association, was the president of the St. Joseph Valley Chapter of the American Society of Public Administration and the World Affairs Council of Michiana. He is editor of *Politics and Public in Indiana: Prospects for Change in State and Local Government.*

**Christopher Hood** is Professor of Public Administration and Public Policy at the London School of Economics. He has taught public administration and public policy for over twenty years at five universities on three continents. He has published extensively on the analysis of public bureaucracy, the study of policy instruments, and contested ideas in public administration. He recently published *Explaining Economic Policy Reversals.*

**Patricia W. Ingraham** is Professor of Public Administration at the Maxwell School of Citizenship and Public Affairs, Syracuse University. She received the ASPA/NASPAA Distinguished Research Award in 1994. She is author of numerous articles dealing with civil service reform, public management, and the relationship between the president and the career civil service. She is author of *The Foundation of Merit: Public Service in American Democracy,* and co-editor of five books, among them *Legislating Bureaucratic Change: The Civil Service Reform Act of 1978* and *New Paradigms for Government: Issues for the Changing Public Service.* She serves on the Board of Editors of *Policy Studies Journal,* the *American Review of Public Administration,* the *Journal of Public Administration Research and Theory,* and the *Public Manager.*

**Eugene B. McGregor Jr.** is Professor of Public and Environmental Affairs at Indiana University, Bloomington. He is co-author of *Policy Choices and Public Action* and author of *Strategic Management of Human Knowledge, Skills, and Abilities: Workforce Decision Making in the Post-Industrial Era.* His research interests include the role of information technology in public sector organization design and management, and the connection between education and development.

**E. Philip Morgan,** a veteran faculty member in the School of Public and Environ-mental Affairs at Indiana University, Bloomington, has a special interest in public sector management. His research and consulting have focused on public organizational per-formance and institutional development in developing countries, especially in Africa, where these subjects are closely related to developmental assistance. He is a former director of Indiana University's International Development Institute. Most recently, Morgan has been a co-principal investigator of a multidimensional World Bank study on Indigenous Institutions and Management Practices in Africa. He is the editor of *The Administration of Change in Africa: Essays in the Theory and Practice of Development Administration in Africa.*

**James L. Perry** is Professor in the School of Public and Environmental Affairs, Indiana University, Bloomington. In 1992 he was a National Association of Schools of Public Affairs and Administration (NASPAA) Fellow, serving as special assistant to the Assistant Secretary for Personnel Administration, Department of Health and Human Services. He is author of *Technological Innovation in American Local Government, Labor-Management Relations and Public Agency Effectiveness,* and *Public Management: Public and Private Perspectives.* His articles have appeared in such journals as the *Academy of Management Journal, Academy of Management Review, Administrative Science Quarterly, American Political Science Review,* and *Public Administration Review.* He is also editor of the *Handbook of Public Administration,* sponsored by the American Society for Public Administration. Perry's many awards include the Charles H. Levine Memorial Award for Excellence in Public Administration, awarded jointly by ASPA and NASPAA.

**B. Guy Peters** is Maurice Falk Professor of American Government and Chair of the Department of Political Science at the University of Pittsburgh. He has held Fulbright Fellowships at the University of Strathclyde (Scotland) and at the Hochschule St. Gallen (Switzerland), a Hailsworth Fellowship at the University of Manchester, and has been a Fellow at the Canadian Centre for Management Development. His publications include

*The Politics of Bureaucracy; The Politics of Taxation: A Comparative Perspective; Comparing Public Bureaucracies; American Public Policy; European Politics Reconsidered; Policy Dynamics;* and *The Pathology of Public Policy.* He is past editor of *Governance* and current editor of the *International Library of Comparative Public Policy.*

**Jos C. N. Raadschelders** is Associate Professor of Public Administration at the University of Leiden. He has published widely on the institutional development of western nations, on Dutch as well as on comparative administrative history, and is currently preparing a handbook of administrative history. He is Director of International Programs of the Leiden Public Affairs department.

**Hal G. Rainey** is Professor of Political Science at the University of Georgia. His research concentrates on management and organization in the public sector, with an emphasis on leadership, incentives, organizational change and organizational performance, and comparisons of the public and private sectors. His book, *Understanding and Managing Public Organizations,* won the Best Book Award of the Public and Nonprofit Sector Division of the Academy of Management in 1992. He has served as Chair of the Public and Nonprofit Sector Division of the Academy of Management, and is Chairperson of the Public Administration Section of the American Political Science Association.

**Renk L. J. Roborgh** is Associate Professor of Public Administration at the University of Leiden. He is editor of *Dutch Government Departments* and co-author, with Frits M. van der Meer, of *Civil Servants in the Netherlands.*

**Mark R. Rutgers** is Associate Professor, Department of Public Administration, Leiden University. He has published several articles on the historical, epistemological, and philosophical foundations of the study of public administration.

**Paul Solano** is a political economist and Associate Professor in the College of Urban Affairs and Public Policy at the University of Delaware. As a member of the M.P.A. program, he specializes in public finance and financial management, benefit-cost analysis, municipal bonds, and public budgeting. He has worked as a budget analyst/planner for county government and as program evaluation analyst for the Agency for International Development, and he has served as a financial consultant to state and local governments. He has published articles in the *National Tax Journal, Public Finance, Journal of Regional Science,* and was a contributor to the ICMA's *Management Policies in Local Government Finance* and *Comparative Public Management.*

**Theo A. J. Toonen** is Professor of Comparative Government and Public Administration and Head of the Department of Public Administration of Leiden University. He has served on the Editorial Board of *Public Administration Review* and serves in an editorial capacity with *Administration and Society* and the *European Yearbook of Comparative Government and Public Administration.* His publications and research deal with the constitutional theory of the unitary state, comparative intergovernmental relations, local government in international perspective, and comparative and transformational processes in central and eastern Europe.

**Frits M. van der Meer** is currently working at the Department of Public Administration at Leiden University. He is co-author of *Civil Servants in the Netherlands,* and has written on central and local government organization and reform, most specifically on the changes in civil service in The Netherlands.

**Lois Recascino Wise** is Associate Professor in the School of Public and Environmental Affairs at Indiana University. Her research and teaching interests center on the broad area of employment policies and practices with a special focus on the public sector. She has served as a consultant to public and private sector organizations in the United States and Europe. She is author of *Labor Market Policies and Employment Patterns in the United States*. Her work has also been published in *Public Administration Review, Public Administration Quarterly, The British Journal of Industrial Relations, The International Labor Review, The Public Productivity and Management Review, The Review of Public Personnel Administration, Public Personnel Management, Knowledge in Society, Forskning om utbildning*, and *Scandinavian Studies*.

# INDEX

Aberbach, Joel D., 4-5, 330; on civil service data, 43; on comparative public administration, 17-18, 248; on policy roles, 51, 218; on political appointees, 14; on politicization, 137-40, 143-44, 153; on representativeness, 46
Abueva, J. V., 24
Accountability, 21, 50-51, 55, 146
Action meaning, 22
Adamolekun, L., 229
Administrative studies, 13-14. *See also* Comparative public administration
Affirmative action. *See* Representativeness of civil servants
Affirmative Action Plan (Canada), 88
African civil service systems: educational requirements, 107; institutionalization levels, 233; mobility in, 113; and patrimonialism, 230; and politicization, 157; reform, 239, 247, 258; responsiveness, 146
Agranoff, R., 31
Albrow, M., 70, 77, 83
Allison, G. T., 26
Almond, G. A., 15, 137-38, 142, 144-46, 330
Althusius, 75
Amburger, E., 69, 80, 83
Archivization, origins of, 79
Argyriades, Demetrios, 54
Arnold, P., 143, 154, 254
Arnstein, S. R., 16
Astley, W. G., 25
Aucoin, P., 252, 258, 288-89, 295, 297
Australian civil service: executive control of, 293-94; and federalism, 294; international links, 295-307; and New Public Management, 288; as policy receptive, 224; reform, 54, 251, 253, 254, 260, 289, 293-307
Austrian civil service, 224, 275

Barker, E., 75, 76, 240
Barrington, T. J., 168, 171
Beck, Paul A., 181, 184-86
Bekke, Hans A. G. M., 181, 190, 192, 193
Belgian civil service, 224

Bemelmans-Videc, M. L., 87
Benda, P. M., 149
Bendix, R., 86, 188
Bendor, J., 16
Bennett, C. J., 288, 292
Berger, M., 20, 30
Berman, H. J., 71-73
Best, J., 25
Birch, A. H., 87
Blais, A., 23
Bödeker, H. E., 69
Bodiguel, J., 103, 113
Boone, Catherine, 231
Boston, J., 304, 306-307, 309
Bozeman, B., 26
Van Braam, A., 71
Braibanti, R., 24
Bräuchli, M. W., 146, 157
Brazilian civil service, 146, 225; reform, 54; socioeconomic context, 215
Brim, Orville C., 128
British civil service: agentry, 50; and the British legal system, 150; citizen participation, 177; and the constitutional system, 147-48; criticism of, 87; divided management, 216; education, 84; influence on Australia, 295-301; mobility in, 48, 113; neutrality, 86-87, 121, 143; and New Public Management, 288; Next Steps initiative, 28, 54, 255, 297; part-time/temporary workers, 108; patronage, 84, 145; pay-for-performance system, 260; pension fund, 81; as policy receptive, 222, 224; politicization control, 144, 152-54; professionalism in, 218; public opinion of, 183, 187-89; reform, 54-55, 77-78, 247, 250-51, 254-55, 259-61, 295; socioeconomic context, 214; system of ranks, 80; wage structure, 114
Brockhaus, R. H., 111
Brunei civil service, 211; as ruler trustworthy, 222
Buitendam, A., 103
Bureaucracy. *See* Civil service systems
Burger, P. L., 148